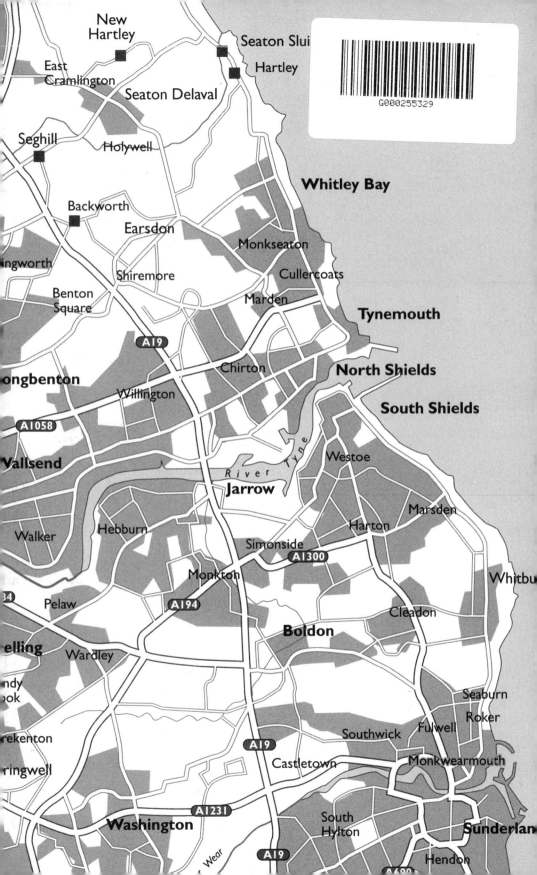

TYNESIDE

For John Leathley

TYNESIDE

A History of Newcastle and Gateshead from Earliest Times

Alistair Moffat and George Rosie

MAINSTREAM
PUBLISHING
EDINBURGH AND LONDON

First published in Great Britain in 2005 by
MAINSTREAM PUBLISHING COMPANY (EDINBURGH) LTD
7 Albany Street
Edinburgh EH1 3UG

ISBN 1 84596 013 0

Typeset in Caslon, Copperplate Gothic and Frutiger

Printed and bound in Great Britain by
Clays Ltd, St Ives plc

ACKNOWLEDGEMENTS

Writers often write what they would like to read. For a television project (which has yet to happen), I looked in vain for a single-volume history of Tyneside from earliest times to the present day. None exists. There are several very good modern histories and much of a specialist nature, but nothing for the general reader interested in the complete and continuous story of the communities who have lived on the banks of the Tyne since a time out of mind. It is a sparkling, sweeping, immense and intricately detailed tale, and I quickly realised that if I was to write it, I would need help, a great deal of help. By a stroke of outrageous good luck, the distinguished journalist and historian George Rosie allowed himself to be persuaded to write the second half of this book. I want to record how tremendously enjoyable the collaboration was and how much I appreciated frequent opportunities to moan and complain with a fellow scribbler about the same project. It was different from the usual exchange, where one has to wait for the other to finish whining before embarking on a separate rant. For this book, we did it all in perfect harmony, and it was grand.

I would like to thank my stalwart proofreaders, Walter Elliot and Barbara Milligan, for their patience and also to remember the constant kindness of our agent, David Godwin. Bill Campbell and Pete MacKenzie of Mainstream have taken a substantial chance on this book and I hope we will not disappoint them. Newcastle City Library has been very helpful, as have all the authors whose excellent work supplied many insights. For those who wish to read more widely, there is a bibliography listing much good scholarship.

This book is dedicated to John Leathley, a true son of the Tyne. His everyday kindness, humour and warmth are all salted, made special and enriched by a life spent on the banks of the great river. I hope he enjoys the story.

Alistair Moffat

* * *

Information about a subject as varied and ancient as Tyneside lies with sources too numerous to list in detail. But I would like to express my gratitude to information officers, archivists, librarians, politicians and individuals all along both banks of the River Tyne, and to the endlessly helpful staffs of the Mitchell Library in Glasgow and the National Library of Scotland in Edinburgh.

George Rosie

CONTENTS

FOREWORD

No one who has been there can fail to feel the body warmth of the most pungent regional identity in Britain. In the bustle and racket of the centre of Newcastle and on the quaysides of Gateshead and the River Towns, people chatter, acknowledge each other, behave like a community, talk readily to strangers, show none of the deadpan, dystopian anonymity of other conurbations, especially London. And they are proud. Not strutting or precious or ridiculously overblown, but cheerfully proud of the canny place they live in, a warm, coal-lit corner against the snell blast of an east wind blowing off the North Sea.

The story of Tyneside supplies good reason for the pungency of that pride. It is an epic story, an immense tale ranging from the very beginnings of human society in Britain to the everyday dramas of the present age.

This telling will begin as early as any and every sort of record allows, starting with the pioneers who came to live in the North-east after the end of the last ice age. Because of the sparseness of information about prehistory, the story of Tyneside will start out wide, taking in almost all of what is now Northumberland and some of Durham, scouring the ground for traces of how lives were lived 10,000 years ago. But the focus suddenly sharpens in the second century AD with the building of the Emperor's bridge, the Pons Aelius, not far from where the Swing Bridge now spans the river. The Romans left written records, names, lists and opinions (not flattering), and some of them have come down to us.

Once the geographical scope of this story settles, Tyneside moves into the centre of the narrative and stays there. And by 'Tyneside', we will mean the riverside conurbation which comprises Blaydon, Newburn, Newcastle, Whickham, Gateshead, Wallsend, Jarrow, South Shields, North Shields and Tynemouth. Of course the story will sometimes stray further afield, perhaps to Ponteland, certainly to Whitley Bay.

Distributed throughout the text are boxed items of information which seemed to add to the narrative without being an integral part of it. They are intended as expanded footnotes which can be skipped, read later or visited during a reading of the main text.

Tyneside is a unique, magical, infuriating and dynamic place, and what follows is its story, the tale of the remarkable people who made it.

1

AFTER THE ICE

10,000 BC–AD 43

Ten thousand years ago, the world was changing. For many millennia, nothing, no people and no animals, had lived on Tyneside. What was to become the river and its banks had long lain under the frozen grip of the last ice age. Incessant hurricanes raged around the flanks of the ice domes, cold mountains of snow and sleet packed hard into blocks sometimes more than half a mile thick. No memory of the ice has come down to us, no stories, no account or legend from the frozen centuries to animate its endless white horizons. But the ice shaped the landscape of the North-east and the landscape remembers it.

Ten thousand years ago, the cold was retreating across the face of the land, the edges of the icefields moving further and further northwards each summer. Glaciers began to rumble down from the slopes of the vast domes, scraping along like geological sandpaper, boulders and debris locked inside them, scouring out the river valleys of the North and South Tyne, breaking open the Hexham Gap, bulldozing the landscape into its modern shape. At Whitley Bay, geologists have detected the shadow of an ancient river valley which predated the ice age. It was filled in with sediment shoved downhill by the groaning and cracking glaciers. Meltwater roared in torrents, mapping out new watercourses, pushing the river systems eastwards. And the North Sea slowly came into being, its level rising and falling as the ice melted and its crushing weight was lifted off the land.

Scientists are uncertain about the origins of ice ages. In the comparatively brief interval of the last 1.6 million years, there have been seven, occurring about every 100,000 years. The current warm period will probably end with another ice age, perhaps sooner rather than later. The most plausible causes of widespread glaciation in the northern hemisphere relate to the orbit of the Earth around the Sun. When the ice began to melt 10,000 years ago, it appears that the tilt of the Earth altered slightly, and its solar orbit became less elliptical and more circular, warming more of the surface of our planet. And these fluctuations could be dangerously eccentric. Like a child's spinning top slowing down, the orbit of the Earth could sometimes lurch wildly out of kilter. Something of this sort seems to have happened around 9400 BC. After temperatures had warmed close to modern norms by 10,000 BC, the weather suddenly began to worsen. Within only a few generations, summers shortened, storms blew and the cold crept back over the land. What historians call 'the Cold Snap' had begun. The ice domes formed again over Drumalban, the range of high mountains north of Loch Lomond, and glaciers once again filled the corries of the Southern Uplands around Broad Law. The Cold Snap ended pioneer activity in the North-east, wiping out almost all traces of human habitation, probably chasing communities down as far as the vales of Pickering and York in the lee of the Cleveland Hills and the North York Moors.

Evidence of the earliest datable prehistoric people in the North has been found at Seamer Carr and Star Carr near Scarborough. Some time around 9000 BC, a summer hunting camp was pitched near a lake (now long disappeared). Archaeologists have found harpoons made from antler tines, the remains of some stone tools and arrowheads. A brilliant analysis of the soil has shown that the hunters regularly burned the reed beds around the lake at Star Carr, perhaps to drive out game, perhaps to get better access to their boats, perhaps to encourage the growth of green shoots to bring grazing deer within range of their bows and spears. It is impossible to know for sure. There are hints that the burning may also have been part of a ritual of some forgotten sort. These early peoples were more than skilled hunters. Their lives knew mystery and ceremony. Near the site of the camp, archaeologists uncovered deer masks, spreads of antlers with holes drilled in the bases to allow thongs to be passed through. The antler tines appear to have been planed down to make them lighter. It seems that the deer masks were worn by shamans or priests, perhaps in a ritual dance, a ceremony to celebrate the spirit of the animal they hunted, just as the American Plains Indians of the nineteenth century danced to celebrate the buffalo. Much corrupted over many centuries and certainly reduced in its elemental drama, the Horn Dance of Abbots Bromley in Staffordshire sounds an ancient echo of the rituals at Star Carr. Six men each balance a set of deer antlers on their shoulders and while they engage in a stately fight, a young boy shoots imaginary arrows at them. The ceremony began life as an affirmation of hunting rights granted to the villagers in the nearby Needwood Forest, and it may be that the hunters at Star Carr were asserting something similar 11,000 years ago.

As temperatures improved steadily in the decades after the Cold Snap, communities began to move northwards again, perhaps prompted by stories surviving from the warmer period only a few centuries before. The hunting bands of Star Carr and Seamer Carr may have ventured north of the Cleveland Hills, but it is highly unlikely that they walked. Even though the ancient coastline extended further east than it does now, the sea still offered the easiest and fastest means of travel. It seems highly likely that the hunters of the Vale of Pickering used deer hides and hazel rods to make their boats, what we call coracles or curraghs. Because all of the construction materials are organic and perishable, no remains have been found to confirm this.

SKIN BOATS

Providing that enough good quality hide is to hand, the skin boats known as curraghs and coracles can be assembled quickly. The curragh is the bigger sort, has a more canoe-like shape and is better suited to sea voyages. Coracles resemble large baskets and are usually paddled by a single individual in lakes and rivers. They are still made in south-western Ireland. The most effective way to propel a coracle forward looks odd. Kneeling down in the front of the boat so that it tips slightly, an experienced coracle-man uses a wooden paddle in a side-to-side motion as if clearing the water out of the path of his vessel. Curraghs and coracles are both made from a frame of greenwood poles (hazel – a magic wood – is thought best) lashed together in such a way as to maintain a natural tension. This keeps the hide stretched and watertight. Once the skin had been attached to the frame, pine resin or fat was used to caulk the joins and keep out as much water as possible. These were very light craft, which could be easily taken apart and reassembled at need. And their use enabled long journeys, far longer than we might imagine was usual for the prehistoric peoples of the North-east.

When the permafrost of the Cold Snap melted and the tundra gave way to summer vegetation, herds of flight animals such as deer, reindeer and wild horses moved north in search of fresh and open grazing. Ever sensitive to the migrations of their food source, hunter-gatherers would not have been far behind the herds, ready to make expeditions into a new landscape north of their sheltering hills. It may be that, like modern bands of hunter-gatherers, they tracked, trapped and camped right up to the edge of the retreating ice sheets. And each summer, returning groups would have noticed new movement as more of the snowfields melted. These courageous and enterprising pioneers who first came into what is now the north-east of England began slowly to understand that the world was indeed changing.

Coasting northwards on summer expeditions, the pioneers used river-mouths to penetrate the interior. Wide and inviting, they were understood as highways, as well as good sources of fish, fowl and other prey. At the mouth of the Tees beyond Redcar, an expedition from Seamer Carr or Star Carr might have recognised familiar territory. The place names have the same derivation. In all, the 'car' element means marsh, and 'Redcar' specifically refers to a reed marsh. The outfall of the Wear at Sunderland also offered an invitation to explore a hinterland of marsh, and the meandering Tyne probably made its way to the sea through a similar landscape. These rivers, and the Tyne in particular, all look different now. In the past, they were broader, their tidal reaches exposing wide areas of mudflats and fringed by thick vegetation well into the nineteenth century. Industry, the needs of river transport and the advance of the cities to their banks have forced the arterial rivers of the North-east into narrower channels, making them seem more like barriers than waterways and removing almost completely their ancient value as a food source.

CORIOLIS

The currents which swirl around the North Sea are created by the Coriolis effect. Named for Gustave Gaspard de Coriolis, the early-nineteenth-century French scientist who first explained it, the effect is simple yet remarkably important to the flow of the world's history. Because the Earth rotates on its own axis, the winds blowing in the northern hemisphere move in a clockwise direction, and those in the southern hemisphere go anti-clockwise. The prevailing winds in turn affect the sea currents, and as a consequence of the Coriolis effect, the Gulf Stream moves north-eastwards to warm Britain and Ireland. In the North Sea, the currents also tend to move clockwise. And that fact has determined much population movement and the direction of trade and ideas. With their sails billowing with north-easterlies and carried by the coastal currents, Dutch traders worked the European coastline, crossed the southern North Sea and moved north to the north-east of England and on to Scotland.

Most cities are built on their own rubbish. Trapped and hidden under the concrete and the cobbles, Tyneside's prehistory will probably remain for ever unknown, its delicate traces effaced. Occasional demolition offers momentary opportunities for keyhole archaeology, but such is the ground disturbance made over the centuries by the restless movement of cities and towns that usually the earliest remains robust enough to come to light are Roman. But for the prehistory of the banks of the Tyne, analogy and example are close at hand.

Perhaps pushed on by people who had settled at the mouths of the Tyne, the Blyth and the Aln, a band of pioneers saw the shores of a bay now known as Howick Haven and decided to make it their own. They were most likely a family group, a band bound together by blood and marriage and, to modern minds, very youthful in appearance. Later evidence from prehistoric burials suggests that most men did not live much beyond their late 20s and that the average life expectancy for women was reduced to around the early 20s by frequent fatalities caused by complications in childbirth. Those who did survive longer could expect their bones to be quickly thickened by arthritis through constant hard labour.

ANKLE BONES AND FOOT BONES

In the course of several excavations, the Tomb of the Eagles on the Orkney island of South Ronaldsay has been found to contain vital statistics. Over the seven centuries between 3150 BC and 2400 BC at least 300 people were interred there and enough bits of their skeletons survived to allow some fascinating general conclusions about what prehistoric people looked like. Men averaged 5 ft 7 in. in height and women 5 ft 3½ in., not so very different from the nineteenth-century population average in Britain. There was another striking connection. Many of the people from the Tomb of the Eagles had had heavily muscled calves and ankles, and some had the beginnings of an articulation for a third bone on the ends of their thumbs and big toes. Modern analogy makes it absolutely clear what these people had been doing. The physiology of twentieth-century St Kildans and the people of certain of the Orkney

Islands was very similar to that of their prehistorical ancestors. Separated by millennia, both communities worked the sea cliffs near their homes, collecting eggs in the spring and catching the young, as yet flightless, birds in the late summer. To keep a grip on the slippery cliffs, they needed to flex their lower legs a great deal and use their hands and feet to hang on. The Howick people will have done exactly the same thing on the cliffs on either side of their small estuary. Some aspects of life were, until recently, unchanged over an immense span of time.

When the first hunting band landed at Howick Haven, they would have seen a pristine landscape. Trees grew right down to the salty margins of the beach, and for those scouts who climbed up through their branches, all that could be made out was an unbroken green canopy, a temperate wildwood stretching far inland, covering everything, even the Cheviot Hills to the distant west. Willow scrub, birches and hazels first colonised the warming tundra and were growing in abundance by the eighth millennium BC when the pioneers paddled into the bay. Oaks and elms were well established by 6500 BC and the improving climate encouraged broad-leaved trees to thrive at much higher altitudes than they do now. Every hill in what is now Northumberland was carpeted in green and the effect was jungle-like. Beneath the summer canopy, it must have been heavily shaded and more humid than we might imagine, a dark, mysterious, even threatening, place. There were no paths other than those made by animals, and thick undergrowth covered the rotting deadwood and leafy debris. As late as 1538, fewer than 500 years ago, the antiquarian John Leland remembered the ancient wildwood when he complained that 'the great wood of Cheviot' was 'spoyled now and crokyd old trees and scrubs remayne'.

As the cold receded, herds of flight animals followed the grassland plains as they replaced the tundra. Reindeer and wild horses needed the uninterrupted views of the wide plains to see any approaching predator before it was too late, and for them, the dense woods were a hostile, dangerous environment. Both species became extinct in Britain as they ran out of safe grassland. But in the forest, others thrived. Wild boar rooted and browsed amongst the trees, while the giant wild cattle known as aurochs grazed in clearings and on riverbanks or reached up for tender young leaves and other greenery. With a hornspread of four feet, they were huge beasts, and at Chillingham Park, not far from Howick Haven, a herd of their descendants survives. No longer crashing through the wildwood in search of pasture or being pursued by bands of hunters (and much smaller than their ancestors), the aurochs are now protected but still very dangerous. Cows with calves are completely unapproachable, and because of their unpredictable temperament, the wild cattle cannot be treated by vets in any way. Their DNA has been sampled and tested against other breeds. It appears to be entirely unique in western Europe, and it looks as though the 40-strong herd at Chillingham is indeed a survival from the wildwood which covered Northumberland 10,000 years ago.

Elk were almost as large as aurochs, and along with their distant cousins the red and roe deer, they too browsed in the forest. By the streams and rivers in the valley bottoms, beavers felled trees to make their dams and otters silently slipped into the shady pools to fish. Because so few human beings hunted in the wildwood, it is likely that many species of animals were more curious than afraid of groups of bipeds, and tempted to investigate rather than flee – at least before it was too late. Other predators competed with the hunter-gatherer-fishers. Bears lived their solitary lives amongst the trees and packs of wolves roamed in the upland areas. Lynx hunted alongside smaller carnivores such as stoats and weasels.

It would be misleading, however, to focus too closely on the hunted and the hunters. The band who landed at Howick Haven also gathered a wild harvest in the woods and on the seashore, and it was the traces of this which formed one of the most telling pieces in the archaeological jigsaw. Like many important discoveries, this one came about through a mixture of chance and acute observation.

Walkers on the cliffs above Howick Haven noticed a scatter of small flints – sharp pieces of worked stone – some still embedded in the sandy margins of the path. They immediately notified a local archaeologist and a dig was quickly organised on the fragile site. The area had never been ploughed and hopes were high for the discovery of a hunter-gatherer-fisher campsite. What eventually came out of the ground was something sensational, a far more profound and revolutionary find than any historian or archaeologist could have imagined. Hazelnut shells, one of the remains of the hunters' wild harvest, were turned up and since they grow in only one season, they allowed some very precise carbon dating. It seems that the pioneers guided their boats into Howick Haven at a much earlier date than had been previously believed, appearing around 7800 BC. And even more surprisingly, instead of pitching camp or constructing the flimsy shelters thought to be characteristic of these prehistoric peoples, they built a large, robust and permanent house. Post holes big enough to take thick tree-trunks were excavated and traces of a conical thatched roof were uncovered. Great technical skill, efficient stone tools, forward planning and determination were needed to make the roundhouse. And more than that surprising level of advancement, the discovery of the Howick house exploded the notion that the early hunter-gatherer bands were transients who flitted wraith-like through the shaded woods, barely rustling the fallen leaves as they passed. The Howick band had come there to stay, a community of settlers. Archaeologists have shown that the house lasted for around one hundred years, the span of four or five generations. It housed at least six people comfortably and was rebuilt several times, always in exactly the same footprint. And the Howick house cannot have been unique in Northumberland. Others surely had the same knowledge, the same tools and as much expertise. Perhaps the landscape was patterned with these large houses, most of them now obliterated by modern cultivation or younger settlements built over the top of them.

EAST BARNS

Archaeologists have recently discovered another house very like that at Howick. Near Dunbar in East Lothian, at the farm of East Barns and close to the sea, an oval shape was identified in an otherwise unremarkable field. Perhaps even older than the Howick house, the East Barns structure was held up by thirty sturdy posts and could comfortably accommodate seven or eight people around a central hearth. Now that these ancient settlements are beginning to be uncovered in numbers, surely more will come to light and our perception of the lives of the hunter-gatherer-fishers will alter radically.

Much flows from the dig on the Northumberland coast. When the builders marked out the circle for the house around 7800 BC, they would doubtless have surveyed the surrounding area. It was certainly suitable, able to sustain a community or a large family band. Fresh water could be drawn from a handy burn near by, and the seaside location supplied a year-round source of food in the shape of shellfish and what might be caught offshore. The reedbeds of the inland marshes offered further bounty, and the hunters would have observed the seasonal migration patterns of wetland birds and been waiting for them with traps and nets. In the summer and autumn, the woods produced their crops of berries, nuts and roots as well as game birds, eggs and other animals. Howick was a good place to live, and to settle.

It is this last implication of the permanent house which is most surprising. Its construction must have entailed ideas of ownership of some kind, or at least the assertion of rights over a substantial area of land. And this was likely very extensive. A hunter-gatherer-fisher band with the acumen to build the house at Howick (and possibly others which have subsided off the sand cliff) would have had the ability to control access to a wide territory to support itself. Coastal expeditions probably ranged down to the estuaries of the Aln and Coquet, up to the Farne Islands to kill seals and on to the singular crags of Bamburgh and Lindisfarne. The lack of navigable rivers near the roundhouse may have inhibited much penetration of the interior.

There are wisps of ritual swirling around the bay at Howick, a sense of a spiritual life amongst the hunter-gatherer-fisher band. Although the ground in the vicinity of the house was suitable, not much different from the original site, the inhabitants always opted to renew the timber posts and supports which held up their thatched roof rather than take the easier option of rebuilding. Maintaining the house exactly where it was seems to have been of central importance. More striking and more vivid was the discovery of the remains of sticks of red and yellow ochre. A mixture of clay and iron oxide, one of ochre's main uses in the prehistoric period was as a colouring agent (it is also an antiseptic, a good insect repellent and a sunblock). With these pencils of red and yellow, it seems likely that the band at Howick painted their bodies and faces, almost certainly as a part of some unknowable religious ceremony. There is later evidence that ochre was used to paint the pale features of the dead and to decorate their graves. But no traces of early hunter-gatherer-fisher burials have been found around the bay.

The gaze of the Howick hunters may have been mostly to seaward. Now, all that can be seen east of the shallow bay is the grey horizon of the North Sea, but 9,000 years ago, the view was quite different.

The North Sea did not exist. At least not in the form we see it now. Across a wide estuary fed by the rivers Ouse, Trent and Tyne, the band of hunters could see land, a far horizon of sandy beaches fringed by tall pine trees. Sharp eyes could also have made out flocks of geese rising in formation over the wetlands, and a clear, westering sun might have lit a range of low hills beyond the coastal plains. This shimmering land in the east was a land the Howick hunters almost certainly knew; they would have heard its stories and understood something of the lives of its people – because it was very likely the place they themselves had come from.

Known to prehistorians as Doggerland, a huge area of dry land existed between the Danish and German coasts and what is now England. The Dogger Hills were its northern bulwark against a much smaller North Sea, and they were flanked on either side by the long estuaries of the Greater Elbe and the Greater Ouse. In the south, the English Channel reached only as far as the southern Kentish coast, and the river systems of the Thames and Rhine drained into it. Britain was geographically and culturally linked to the European continent for at least 4,000 years after the end of the last ice age. There is strong evidence to suggest that the huge expanse of land now submerged under the North Sea became free of ice much earlier than the higher landmass which bordered it. Hunter-gatherer-fisher populations moved into Doggerland long before the first pioneers ventured into the frozen north of Britain – and when temperatures did rise over the higher landmass, it is likely that those living in the eastern lowlands were the first to observe the improving weather and the first to take advantage of it. Perhaps they organised summer hunting parties in pursuit of reindeer and other herd animals which followed the seasonal grazing on the post-glacial tundra plains. What this means is something as simple as it is intriguing: the ancestors of the early peoples of the North-east, and therefore the ancestors of most of the modern population, probably originated in Doggerland, the drowned subcontinent almost entirely lost to history.

The ice made Doggerland. When the massive weight of the ice dome centred on southern Sweden was at its greatest extent, it pushed the land under it down at least 2,500 ft lower than it is now. This caused a straightforward and fascinating reaction. To the south of the ice dome, beyond the jagged edges of the glaciers, the unfrozen land now under the North Sea rose up in a forebulge. The remains of the forebulge can still be seen in the Dogger Bank, a shallow fishing ground ('dogger' is the Dutch word for a trawler) off the Yorkshire coast. In the distant past, it was a range of hills surrounded by flatlands. As the ice melted after the Cold Snap, sea levels rose and Doggerland began slowly to sink. It was finally completely drowned some time around 4000 BC, and its existence passed out of all memory.

NORTH SEA TILT

Doggerland is still sinking, even though it long ago disappeared beneath the waves. In fact, most of the southern North Sea basin is gradually sinking, while the coastlines to the north are bouncing up in a very long-delayed reaction to the end of the last ice age. When the great weight of the ice domes was lifted off what is now Sweden, the land rose dramatically. In Britain, it is still bouncing back. Dunbar in East Lothian got 20 in. higher in the nineteenth century. In the south, the opposite trend has had disastrous results. In 1953, devastating floods engulfed Canvey Island in the lower reaches of the Thames. And since the great St Elizabeth's Day Flood of 1421, when more than 100,000 people drowned, the Dutch have fought an increasingly difficult battle against the rising tides.

Prehistorians knew that Britain had been connected to Europe by a land-bridge but had always described it as just that – a means of passing dryshod from east to west. Until a freakish find in 1931, no one had suspected the existence of a vast subcontinent, a destination in itself rather than a mere bridge.

When Captain Pilgrim Lockwood took the wheel of the SS *Colinda* and guided it out of Lowestoft harbour on a spring evening in 1931, he was intent only on fishing, a good catch of herring. Lockwood could have had no idea that his nets would bring up something which would radically change how we understand our ancient past. The captain set a course for the Leman and Ower banks. Lying about 25 miles north-east of the Norfolk coast, they were a reliable fishing ground where shoals often fed. When the *Colinda*'s crew first shot their net into the shallow waters and began to drag it over the banks, it was dark. But there was enough moonlight for Captain Lockwood to notice something strange when his crew wound the net in and spilled the silvery catch on deck. It was a large clod of peat, something with no business being at the bottom of the sea. Perplexed, the captain went to fetch a shovel, and when he broke open the clod, he was amazed to pick up a beautifully worked white bone harpoon point.

When archaeologists examined the find, they concluded the obvious, despite everything. Trapped inside the lump of peat, the harpoon was not something lost overboard by a seaborne hunter paddling between two ancient shorelines. It had been dropped on what was once dry land by someone who was hunting there – 25 miles off the coast of Norfolk, 250 ft down, on the Leman and Ower banks. And the peat? A botanist from Cambridge University, Dr Harry

Godwin, analysed it for pollen traces. He declared himself astonished by the results and made several trips out to the banks to have more peat dredged up. There was no doubt: the hunter who had dropped the harpoon point had been stalking his prey in oak woodlands. Much later, in 1989, a bit of the harpoon (it had been carved from deer antler) was radiocarbon dated to 11000 BC, more than 2,000 years earlier than the bands who had hunted at Star Carr in North Yorkshire. The traces indicated that long before similar activity had occurred in what is now the north of Britain, hunting had been going on in Doggerland. It was – literally – an epoch-making discovery.

Since the voyage of the *Colinda*, more finds have come to the surface of the North Sea. A piece of aurochs bone with a hole drilled in it to allow a wooden haft to be attached to form a pick or an axe was retrieved from the seabed at Brown Bank, off the Suffolk coast. Bits of flint and a drilled stone were found in the northern North Sea, off the Shetland Islands, in what was probably the farthest extent of Doggerland. More recently, divers off the Northumberland coast, at Tynemouth, have come across the remains of two hunter-gatherer-fisher settlements, complete with flint debris. What this shows is a coastline extending in places a long way to the east, much further than was previously understood. Similar flints which hint at very early activity on what is now the seabed have been picked up on the Farne Islands and Lindisfarne.

Analyses of these and other finds suggest strongly that life in Doggerland was good. By the time the hunting band settled at Howick Haven, their neighbours across the wide estuary of the Greater Ouse lived on the edges of a productive woodland. In addition to oak, there grew stands of birch, willow, lime and hazel – the last providing an important winter staple in the shape of its nutritious nuts. Herds of wild horses galloped across the wide plains of Doggerland, while the mighty aurochs browsed the quiet woodland glades. Boar snuffled after roots, elk, roe and red deer grazed, and otters and beavers fished. But it was the coast and the shores of the great estuaries which offered year-round sustenance and probably supported many bands, perhaps living in clusters of houses like the one built at Howick. Seals could have been hunted with harpoons in the winter and shellfish gathered at low tide. In the spring, duck and other birds' eggs made good eating, and both swans and geese could be trapped in the reedbeds. Later in the year, young and unfledged birds were no doubt taken, and in the summer and autumn, the wild harvest of fruits, roots and nuts was ripe. And when Doggerland's animals were in peak condition in the early winter, their glossy pelts would have made the warmest clothing. Fish were extremely important to the seasonal existence of hunter bands; the migration of shoals around the Doggerland coastline and the yearly journey of the salmon upriver would have been well understood.

Hunters are observant. Their ability to notice change is as important as rapid reflexes, and when Doggerland began to sink, its people will have watched it happen and wondered. As the sea approached closer and closer, and tides found new marks, many bands will have sought the higher ground. Within the knowledge of several generations, the great estuaries will have widened and lengthened, their waters growing brackish and less productive. But nothing could have prepared the communities for what happened some time around 5800 BC.

Far to the north, in the freezing darkness of the Norway Deeps, 2,000 ft below the surface of the North Sea, the bottom feeders sensed an unknowable danger. Above them, sharks, rays and wolf-fish instinctively swam upwards as the seabed began to quiver and rocks tumbled through the wrack. Dust darkened the water even more as small marine creatures panicked and scattered. And then the undersea world disintegrated. Some time around the year 5840 BC, seismic movement in the Earth's crust caused millions of cubic tons of rock, gravel and sand to slip into the Norway Deeps. The momentary gap sucked in vast quantities of sea water and set in train a devastating chain of events. Around the coasts of what are now Norway, Sweden, Denmark, Germany and Britain, the sea retreated rapidly, revealing great tracts of the seabed. At first, there must have been astonishment. Perhaps the world was ending, perhaps the gods were angry. Then seabirds suddenly shrieked and took to the air. A distant rumble was heard, and before anyone had the presence of mind to run for their lives, a gigantic, 25-ft-high wave roared onto the shore. Travelling at an incredible 300 miles an hour, the tsunami crashed over coastal communities, raining down boulders, debris and sand far inland.

No one saw this undersea earthquake, and evidence for it was only discovered by accident when archaeologists exposed a mysterious layer of white deep-sea sand on a recent dig in Inverness in the north of Scotland. Excavated between numbers 13 and 21 Castle Street (while a new development of shops and flats waited), the stratum of sand had been deposited in such a way as to allow a precise dating and reading of its presence. It could only have arrived in Inverness on what used to be called a tidal wave. Matching deposits have since been found down the North Sea coastline. It is difficult to be sure that the tsunami from the Norway Deeps saw the end of Doggerland; some prehistorians date the final inundation much later, to around 4000 BC. But its effect must have been utterly devastating.

SEASLIDES

At least a dozen big rivers empty millions of tons of silt into the North Sea every year. The Tyne, Wear and Tees used regularly to be dredged so that shipping could continue to make its way at least part way upstream. Considering how much silt is carried by the rivers of the east and how long they have been flowing, why has the North Sea not filled up? The reason is that the Earth's crust absorbs the silt, sometimes with catastrophic results like the tsunami of 5840 BC. In what are known as subduction trenches, one tectonic plate carrying silt is pushed under another and down towards the Earth's mantle. The ocean floor is in constant motion because of the action of a massive range of undersea mountains in the middle of the Atlantic. Down the middle of the ocean there runs a huge seam, a continuous range of mighty peaks (some of them crowned by islands, such as the Azores or Ascension Island) which extends around Africa, into the Indian Ocean, skirting southern Australia and ending at the west coast of the USA.

It is 45,000 miles long and arguably the most spectacular geographical feature on our planet.

But in the middle of the Atlantic section of the range, there is another, even more extraordinary, feature. A wide rift valley, measuring 50 to 65 ft across, lies between parallel ranges. It measures 12,000 miles in length and is constantly in motion. Core samples have confirmed that in the rift valley the Earth's crust is extremely thin and very new. What appears to be happening is that magma is forcing its way up through the valley and forming new margins of crust. This is then pushed out sideways so that, in very short periods of geological time, the floor of the North Atlantic is edging towards the European and American landmasses.

The edges of the disaster of 5840 BC are hard to find down the North Sea coast of Britain, but it is likely that the tsunami will have spent its energy ploughing through the trees of the wildwood, snapping them like matchsticks, before it reached its furthest extent. Where there was no river-mouth to funnel its huge power into the interior of Northumberland, the wave and those that followed it would not have reached beyond the bottoms of the low hills which border the coastal plain. But news would have travelled fast. Perhaps the hunting band who built the shelter amongst the rocks of Goatscrag, in the hills east of Milfield, saw what happened below them. They almost certainly heard the booming roar of the incoming tsunami racing towards the seashore. Perhaps instinct took over and they ran for cover in their shelter. Perhaps they anxiously scanned the skies for more signs of the wrath of the gods. And when news came of the utter devastation only a few miles away, they will have offered thanks at least for their deliverance.

There is no doubt that the prehistoric peoples of Britain believed in gods of some kind or, at any rate, forces external to their lives which might shape them. What exactly they believed is unknowable, and the meagre, gossamer traces which these men and women left behind them only serve to underscore our profound ignorance and to focus our sense of them on more practical themes. At the rock shelter at Goatscrag, archaeologists found flint tools made by the inhabitants and they are representative of the toolkit needed by a hunting band. Small flakes of flint of razor sharpness, called microliths, were hafted to wooden shafts and used as spears or harpoons. Barbed and tanged in an A-shape, arrowheads show that archery was part of the repertoire of skills, although, being made from perishable wood and strung with gut, bows have been very hard to find. One made from yew was pulled well-preserved out of a peat bog at Rotten Bottom in the Tweedsmuir Hills in 1990, and it is a beautifully crafted object. Burins for piercing hides and scrapers for removing the subcutaneous fat from them have been picked up by fieldwalkers in many parts of Northumberland, and axeheads are also often retrieved.

The hunting band at Goatscrag are known to have been skilled with the flint axe because archaeologists have found slots and post sockets around the overhanging cliff. In what appears to have been part of an annual cycle, hunting expeditions (probably made up only of men) set out from a base camp similar to the house at Howick and built a summer shelter in a place where game was accessible. When they arrived at Goatscrag in the spring, the men either retrieved posts hidden away in the autumn of the previous season or cut new ones with their axes to make the frame of a lean-to structure. They then wedged it into slots and post holes around the overhang. When bracken and branches had been cut and woven into the frame and probably weighted down, the shelter was weathertight.

FLINTS

Little naturally occurring flint is found in the North-east. The beach is usually the handiest source and prehistoric hunter-gatherer-fishers probably picked up much of what they needed when nodules were washed up on the seashore. Some could also be found amongst the gravel on river-beds. Where flint was unavailable, chert could be taken out of local glacial deposits. This black, grey, green or brown stone is very hard and could be split predictably and reworked to make the smaller type of tool. Early communities consumed a great deal of flint and chert, and prehistoric factories existed to supply the demand. The most famous is the huge complex at Grimes Graves in Norfolk, where 800 shafts were sunk. Merchants probably supplied Tyneside by sea. Nearer but less easily accessible were the great axe factories of Langdale in the Lake District. Flint was knapped, that is flaked by striking a nodule in a skilled, controlled fashion. Blades broke off and were hafted onto wooden shafts to make spears, knives or axes. Other pieces made good scrapers or burins for boring holes. Flint can be razor sharp and is very durable.

The purpose behind the summer expeditions was straightforward: to hunt and gather in areas away from base and thereby allow both the fauna and flora of that area to recover. While they exploited new sources of food, it is unlikely that the band at Goatscrag stayed there continuously until the autumn. When kills were made, they probably cooked the meat and made frequent trips back to base before it spoiled. Base was likely somewhere on the Milfield Plain. Another summer camp has been found at Corby's Crags in the hills west of Alnwick. Given the wide range of territory needed to support a community of hunter-gatherer-fishers, it is not impossible that the shelter at Corby's Crags was an outpost of a successor settlement at Howick Haven. It lies 15 miles to the east. Around 5840 BC, when the tsunami hit, the summer expedition would have had nowhere to go home to.

Despite disasters, the life of hunter-gatherers must often have been good. Extracted from boggy, anaerobic ground, pollen cores tell us that there were long periods, lasting centuries, when the climate was benign, with longer summers and less severe winters. Between successful hunting trips and after the late summer harvest of nuts, roots, fruits and berries, bands will have had time to sit and talk, gossip, argue, wonder, tease and flirt. For the reality is that these people were not the grunting, subhuman savages of popular myth, dressed in ragged animal skins, scurrying from cave to cave, clubs in hands. Their brains were as large as ours, and all of the studies of the bones of early populations show that they looked like us, although smaller in stature. And while they lived much shorter lives and no doubt suffered much pain in the absence of antibiotics or dentistry, they will have experienced many of the joys and sadnesses familiar to twenty-first-century men and women.

But in many other ways, they were utterly unlike us. Because of the lack of evidence, it is impossible to do more than guess at how our early ancestors saw the world, what their spiritual life was like. The sole certainty is that it was very different from ours. Tantalising hints exist. On the walls of the rock shelter at Goatscrag, hunters have carved the outlines of four animals which look very much like deer. Three are shown strung out in a line, with the fourth some way above them, perhaps intended to look as though it is on higher ground. Goatscrag commands a view of a narrow defile leading down to the Milfield Plain. It may be that the carvings are documentary rather than symbolic, depicting a group of hinds and their stag moving down to lower-lying grazing. Such a defile would have been very obviously suitable for an ambush, allowing flight in only two directions. And like the community at Star Carr in North Yorkshire, the band at Goatscrag probably saw the red deer as central to their lives, capable of supplying all sorts of bounty, and worthy of commemoration and perhaps celebration on the walls of their shelter.

Making these pictures may have been important in another, more indirect, way. At Altamira, near Santander in Spain, and in south-west France at Lascaux, cave paintings of dazzling beauty have been found. It seems that the act of creating these vivid images was itself very important. At Lascaux and Altamira, many are to be found in inaccessible places while others are over-paintings covering earlier images. Perhaps there was a sense in which these painters, and the carvers at Goatscrag (it is possible that the deer were coloured with ochre – red for red deer?), captured the likeness of the animal as a prelude to capturing its body. Perhaps.

WE ARE WHO WE WERE

In 2001, Professor Bryan Sykes published a book which revolutionised how we ought to consider our prehistory. *The Seven Daughters of Eve* showed that 80 per cent of us in Britain are the direct descendants of the pioneer bands of hunter-gatherers who repopulated the North when the last ice age ended. Through analysing sequences of mitochondrial DNA (only passed on by mothers) and comparing it to DNA extracted from prehistoric skeletons, Sykes disposed of the myth of the British as a mongrel race made up from many genetic components over our long history. It turns out that we are not an amalgam of Anglo-Saxons, Vikings and Normans. Instead, we have been forced to recognise that the prehistoric peoples whose courage, enterprise and ingenuity converted a trackless wilderness into a productive home are in fact our ancestors. Perhaps that will at last draw us away from the easy and misleading stereotype of grunting cavemen whose primitive lives had little to do with our own.

Around 4000 BC, a series of new ideas arrived in Britain, having completed a long westward journey from what is now Iraq. Known as the Fertile Crescent, the land between the rivers Euphrates and Tigris had seen the birth of the greatest revolution in human history, a change so profound that it is impossible to overstate its impact. In the eighth millennium BC, farming began. Communities added food production to their skills in food gathering. Stock-rearing may have come first, as herds of cattle, sheep, goats and pigs were brought together, controlled (pastoral dogs or tamed wolves also come onto the archaeological record at the same time – and the paw bones of two were found at Howick), moved around different pastures, milked, clipped, and killed for meat or skinned for hides. In the Fertile Crescent, stocksmen also developed the notions of planting from seed kept back from the previous harvest, of extending natural beds of wild grasses and root vegetables, of fencing animals to keep them away from crops and of harvesting at the end of the growing season.

These ideas travelled west in spurts along two arterial routes. In the fifth millennium BC, over a period of six or seven centuries, farmers working in the lower Danube Valley passed on techniques, seeds and breeding animals to their neighbours to the north-west. Perhaps surplus population moved, perhaps it was a simple exchange of ideas, perhaps one community simply copied another. Following the geography of central Europe, these revolutionary principles funnelled up the great river before breaking through into the northern plains. By 4000 BC, stock-rearing and the cultivation of crops had begun in what is now the Netherlands. Doggerland had probably drowned by that time, but contact with the new island of Britain was not noticeably inhibited. Remembering that for all but the last 150 years of our history, the sea has provided a faster means of travel than any on land, we should not be surprised to discover spectacular evidence of the arrival of farming in Britain very soon after it had reached the Dutch coast.

On the south bank of the River Dee, not far from Aberdeen, in the middle of an otherwise unremarkable cornfield near a place called Balbridie, the remains of a huge timber hall have been discovered. Spotted from the air, it was at first thought to be a northern version of the great Anglo-Saxon halls celebrated in *Beowulf* and elsewhere. It was certainly big enough, at 85 ft in length and 43 ft wide, with its massive uprights able to support a roof pitch more than 30 ft high. And there was an interior space so large that it could easily accommodate 40 or 50 people. Perhaps it was a royal or aristocratic feasting hall where mead was drunk and epic tales of battle recounted. But when carbon dating produced its first results, the excavators were astounded to discover that Balbridie was nearly 5,000 years older than the Anglo-Saxon period. The great hall had been raised some time around 3900 BC. Comparisons with similar structures found in northern Germany have convinced historians that the hall was built by recent immigrants with particular engineering skills who sailed across the North Sea with new ideas on how to produce food. In other words, early farmers. Three other halls have been found in Scotland: one near Balbridie at Crathes, another at Claish Farm on Tayside and a third at

Whitmuirhaugh Farm near Kelso, only two miles from the Northumberland border.

It looks as though these early farmers favoured the fertile banks of navigable rivers, perhaps settling temporarily near the river-mouths before moving into the interior to build their halls. Archaeological discovery is by nature a chancy business, but now that experts know what they are looking for and what they might be looking at, it may well be that more timber halls will be identified in Northumberland, perhaps along the banks of the Tyne, Aln or Coquet.

Farming arrived in Britain by another, longer route, mostly by hops along the sea coasts. Finds of related items of archaeology chart its voyage westwards through the Mediterranean, past the Straits of Gibraltar and up the Atlantic seaboard to Britain. The traces of this ancient journey can be seen in a modern cultural unity. From Galicia in Spain to the Outer Hebrides in Scotland and at several points between, Celtic languages are still spoken, just. And while these languages are by no means mutually intelligible, they do retain close affinities. Intriguingly, both Ireland and Scotland promoted origin legends (in the medieval period in particular) which spoke of the arrival of new people after long journeys from Spain and the Mediterranean.

Hard scientific evidence exists to support these half-forgotten wisps of myth-history. Professor Bryan Sykes' brilliant analysis of our mitochondrial DNA shows that 20 per cent of Britons can trace a direct ancestry back to people who once farmed in the Fertile Crescent. And it also demonstrates that these people arrived in the centuries around 4000 BC, long after the repopulation of Britain by hunter-gatherers at the end of the last ice age. Sykes has recently revealed more fascinating corroboration. In sampling large groups of modern Britons, he and his team have noticed an east–west split. Either side of a line drawn, very approximately, from Inverness to Southampton, the modern population divides broadly into two slightly different sub-groups. Geography has undoubtedly influenced this difference, with communication to the north and south being generally much easier for each group than moving between east and west. Because the Irish Sea and the scatter of islands off Scotland have made for straightforward navigation by pilotage (that is, by using seamarks such as mountains or headlands), rapid and regular contact took place for millennia. It was a simpler business for a Cornishman to sail to North Wales than to travel overland to, say, Devizes or Salisbury. The same was true of the calmer waters of the North Sea. It turns out that Tynesiders have genetically more in common with south-eastern Scots than with Cumbrians.

A HUM

Most people would characterise the sound of the North Sea as that of crashing breakers washing over sand, or the roll of waves as they are whipped up by the wind. But scientists have discovered another noise. In common with all the oceans and seas of the Earth, the North Sea is humming. Inaudible to the human ear, a steady note is emitted which, in musical terms, researchers have placed at about 16 octaves below middle C – not something even dogs can prick up their ears at. This consistent hum is thought to be made by storms and the way in which their tremendous energy is transformed into deep oceanic waves rumbling over the Earth's crust.

Archaeology notes a hesitation in the adoption of farming in north-eastern Europe. In what might have been a long inheritance from the comfortable communities of Doggerland, it seems that many preferred to continue with a life of hunting and gathering. Herding, planting and harvesting was tried for a time and then abandoned in several places. Or perhaps certain bands simply preferred a wandering existence. Crops and domesticated animals tie a community to one place at the best time of the year, the summer.

At Low Hauxley near Amble, a prehistoric shell midden has been found. In essence, this was a pile of rubbish deposited by hunter-gatherer-fishers collecting mussels, limpets, oysters, clams and other seaside fauna. Very similar (and much larger) middens have been identified in the Hebrides, as it seems that their creation was not so much a matter of tidiness as a deliberate and meaningful act. The mounds of shells proclaimed the ownership of rights to a particular and productive stretch of coastline. No investigation of the midden at Low Hauxley has yet revealed a date but it may well be that more shells were added after the first introduction of farming into Northumberland. The practical reality is that few sensible people gave up hunting and gathering entirely (many modern country people still go hunting – for food such as rabbits, hares, salmon, trout, pheasants and whatever else might be edible, and legal).

In the transitional period of adoption and abandonment, the prehistoric community who lived at Seaton Carew near Hartlepool appear to have retained a canny, well-organised interest in sea fishing. Part of a fish weir (known as a yair in the Tweed Basin) has been found there and dated to 3700 BC. The mouth of the Tees is more obviously tidal than either the Tyne or the Wear, exposing wide expanses of sandbank when the sea retreats. Fish weirs were simple arrangements of wicker plaited into gappy fences wide enough to allow water to pass through without washing them away and narrow enough to prevent the escape of big fish. Across the estuaries of tidal rivers, fish could swim over the top of a submerged wicker weir as they made their way upriver but could easily be trapped at low tide as they returned seawards.

Fencing of a similar sort but made for a completely different purpose has been discovered at Bolam Lake, a few miles north of Ponteland. Or rather its absence has been detected. Perishable organic materials like wood rarely survive (the weir at Seaton Carew was preserved in the anaerobic conditions of a peat bog), but the post holes which held it up often do. Excavators reasoned that the depth of the holes found at Bolam Lake could not have supported the load-bearing posts needed for a building and that they must have been used for a hurdle fence, a temporary stock fence which could be moved at need. Around the same time as the fishermen of Seaton Carew splashed out at low tide to see if their traps had done their work, stocksmen at Bolam were anxious to pen their animals for any number of good reasons.

Archaeologists believe that this band of early farmers were mobile, staying at Bolam Lake only for the summer. Perhaps the hurdle pens kept animals off ripening cereal and vegetable patches until harvest. In the autumn, the herdsmen are thought to have moved their beasts down to lower-lying winter pasture, perhaps meadows by the Tyne.

The increasingly widespread adoption of farming had important social effects. Once groups like those at Bolam Lake stopped migrating and settled on one piece of ground, they naturally wanted to assert rights over it, if not outright ownership. The population was rising and land may have become a matter of contention or competition at this time. In any case, groups often needed to take decisive action – perhaps in defence of their rights or in choosing to abandon them – and that clearly implies a decision-making process carried out by some on behalf of others. Which in its turn suggests the development of hierarchies and the idea of leadership in farming kindreds. Much later, by about 2000 BC, this sort of leadership certainly existed and had evolved into something hereditary, power passing down only through one part of a kindred. At Howick Haven, children's remains have been detected in specially made small cists (stone-lined graves), while at Turf Knowe in the Breamish Valley, the remains of no fewer than 22 children have been uncovered. Burials of this sort were only accorded to an elite, and those for children clearly imply the operation of inherited privilege – special treatment for aristocratic early deaths.

All manner of other changes followed the take-up of a settled farming life. Pottery became the preferred sort of container because it was versatile in size and thickness, and also durable if carefully handled. It is not that the hunter-gatherers could not make pots – they were familiar with the properties of clay and knew how it hardened when fired – but rather that pottery was too heavy and fragile to be carried around. Tough leather buckets, wooden bowls and bark containers did the job just as well, were lighter and did not shatter when dropped. But there was one important difference. Pots could be used for the cooking of hot food. Coupled with the new diet of cereals, roots, milk and domesticated meat, the use of large, tough and well-fired pots led to new methods of processing food and the invention of soup or 'potage'. A staple of farming households until the twentieth century, potage, made in a pot bubbling with softening grains and pulses, bones, vegetables and whatever else was handy and nourishing, would have sat on the edge of every cooking fire, no doubt being constantly emptied and replenished.

Everyday revolutions like those at the hearthside are impossible to chart or date. The spectacular consequences of the adoption of farming catch the eye and the imagination more readily, and Northumberland is rich in monuments raised by these early communities. In the shape of cereals and pulses (which dried and preserved well), farming could produce surpluses in good years, and that allowed the diversion of labour and planning into activities which had nothing to do with food production and were almost certainly directed by a governing elite of some kind.

North of the Coquet, the soil is a sandy, fertile loam, much easier to work and more productive than the heavy clays around Tyneside. And that simple geological fact has had a profound impact on the balance of Northumberland's history. In the millennia when everything depended on farming, a much larger and wealthier population lived in the northern districts. That is why the early history of the North-east seems to cluster in that area, concentrating around places like Bamburgh, Lindisfarne and Alnwick. Now that the population distribution is reversed, it is easily forgotten that kings ruled at what is now the small village of Bamburgh. Before the fires of the industrial revolution roared into life, the wealth of Northumberland lay above the Coquet and in the other river valleys to the north.

That is why one of the greatest concentrations of prehistoric monuments is to be found near the tiny hamlet of Milfield. It was once a tremendously impressive ritual landscape, but very little of it is now visible to the naked or casual eye. Because the Milfield Plain is fertile farmland with a favourable microclimate in the Cheviot rain-shadow, centuries of ploughing have reduced the monuments to crop-marks best seen from the air and even then not always visible. But they were spectacular. At least eight henges existed and the Coupland circle was more than 325 ft in diameter. It should be pointed out that although 'henge' derives from Stonehenge, most henges in Britain did not look much like the tremendous structure of standing stones and lintels in Wiltshire. A circular ditch and bank, usually cut with two entrances opposite each other, is the simple definition of a henge.

What exactly went on inside these circles is impossible to know. No texts exist and the few substantial archaeological remains do not offer many clues. Most of the Milfield henges are not huge – the average diameter is about 80 ft – and not many finds have come out of the ground in and around them. But the shape, construction and clustering of these monuments do allow some general observations. They were built by communities whose members could afford to take time off from food production and were fed from a surplus while doing the work. This strongly suggests a controlling authority directing matters – size, location, ceremonies of dedication accompanying the work and so on. Henges were used for some unknowable ceremonial purpose. To farming communities, the changing of the seasons and the vicissitudes of the weather will have been of central importance, and all of these circles were open to the sky. It may be that the farmers and their priests or priest-kings believed that there existed sky gods able to bring fine weather for harvest and rain for growing shoots – or thunderstorms to pound and wash all away. Perhaps the henges were holy places where they could communicate with their gods; most temples in most cultures are used for variants on that purpose.

There also seems to have been a close association with the dead, the ancestors and perhaps an afterlife. Ancestors were certainly venerated by the early peoples. Special arrangements were made for their burials, and ceremonies not unlike wakes were held around their graves at the time of interment. The ownership of rights to land depended on history, on the demonstrable fact that ancestors had long ago established these rights and were often planted in tombs on their land. Few burials have been found inside henges, but the connection may be more symbolic than physical. The arrangement of the ditch and its bank offers a teasing clue. The basic purpose of expending great labour in digging out (with antler picks and wicker baskets) a V-shaped ditch and piling the upcast beside it was to demarcate a sacred area, a place apart from the world. When early farmers dug ditches and banks as boundaries or for defensive purposes, they marked out the ditch on the outside and formed the bank on the inside. This arrangement was obviously intended to present a barrier to repel attack. But at the Milfield henges (and many others) this plan is reversed. Near the modern village, the Milfield North henge has been reconstructed according to the layout of the ancient crop-mark nearby. The ditch is on the inside and the bank on the outside. Why?

Perhaps henges were indeed seen as defensive by the community who built them, as a defence against whatever lived inside the circle. Perhaps they were symbolic prisons to hold back the power of malignant ancestors or savage gods. And in places where the old gods were close, a cluster of henges was needed to pen them in. Too readily we lay the template of a Christian god of love and forgiveness on beliefs held throughout a long past, which were almost certainly entirely different. It is equally possible that the prehistoric gods were gods of spite and fury, or of unpredictable capriciousness, whose evil had to be contained inside a magic circle.

DOGON AMAZING

What took place inside the henges on the Milfield Plain is now unknowable, but many scholars have argued convincingly for an astrological dimension to the ceremonies. In upstanding stone circles, alignments of particular stones with stars, planets and events in the astral year can be demonstrated, and there seems little doubt that prehistoric priests studied the night sky and understood how it changed through the seasons of the year. A modern African tribe has shown how extraordinarily sophisticated this knowledge might have been. When two French anthropologists interviewed priests from the Dogon tribe of the Western Sahara in 1931, they listened to an amazing tale. An integral part of the traditional beliefs of the Dogon was based on detailed knowledge of Sirius, the star which sparkles 8.6 light years from the Earth. More remarkably, the priests spoke of a companion star which moved in a 50-year elliptical orbit around Sirius. And, even more remarkably, they knew it was white, very heavy and very small. So small that it is invisible to the naked eye, was first seen through a telescope in 1862 and not photographed until 1970. And yet the Dogon's knowledge of the movements of the star we know as Sirius B predated all that research – and by some distance. They could point to objects at least 400 years old on which the orbit of Sirius B had been carved. The priests also had knowledge of all the planets in the solar system and names for the four major moons of Jupiter and the rings of Saturn. How? How was it possible for a West African tribe without any of the technology needed to acquire all of this modern astronomical data to know this? Their explanation only serves to deepen the mystery and raise a sceptical eyebrow. Beings called the Nommos, part fish, part human, arrived in boats to impart this knowledge, they said. Similar myths appear in ancient Egyptian and Mesopotamian culture, but whatever its origin, the astronomy of the Dogon was correct, absolutely correct.

Most henges were not built in stone like those at Stonehenge and Avebury and on Orkney. Wooden posts, probably carved and painted, were set up on sites which had been carefully chosen. Often they lay near routeways or in places with a long history of sanctity. And often they stood on spectacular sites, visible on the skyline for many miles. At Tynemouth, there is a suspected henge almost obliterated by housing. But 5,000 years ago, it would have seemed a magical, powerful place to boatmen entering the estuary after a day's fishing, or to people approaching the rising ground of the headland from landward.

Few standing stones survive in Northumberland. On the northern borders, there is a beautiful stone circle near the village of Duddo. It is marooned in the midst of cultivation, but with a surprising view to the west to another great prehistoric monument, the sacred precinct on Eildon Hill North, near Melrose. Over 50 centuries, the stones have been chiselled by the wind into remarkable fluted shapes, but on one are unmistakable marks of human handiwork. It is an example of a mysterious and ancient artform in which Northumberland is peculiarly rich.

Known as cup-and-ring marks, these abstract patterns are found in many places. First patiently pecked onto natural rocks, these cup shapes, spirals, whorls and trailing, tendril-like lines continue to baffle historians. Dating from after 4000 BC, when farming and farmers arrived in the north, most of the earliest are found on rocky outcrops, often in high places. There is a beautiful sequence on Dod Law, above the Milfield Plain, and another at Roughting Linn, near Wooler. There is a whisper of decoration in these carvings on what our ancestors might have seen as the bones of the earth. Similar patterns are used in other cultures as body decoration, and perhaps cup-and-ring marks were seen as tattoos on the body of the earth. Their incised nature suggests that they may have been coloured, perhaps with red or yellow ochre. Many occur near sacred sites and another interpreter holds that they were like wayside Christian crosses, announcing that a place separate from the temporal world was being approached and that an attitude of humility or reverence or wariness should be adopted. Later cup-and-ring marks are cut into vertical surfaces (like the stone at Duddo) and could only have been coloured with difficulty and temporarily, but these marks were made for 2,000 years, from the fourth to the second millennium BC, and by the end of their currency, their use might have become symbolic rather than practical.

The distribution of cup-and-ring marks may hold some significance. They do not occur south of the Peak District but do extend north to Argyll. And there is also a scatter of examples down the Atlantic seaboard of Europe, as far as Galicia in northern Spain. The cup-and-ring marks follow in the wake of the early farmers who made their way to Britain by sea. So do such pockets of Celtic languages as remain in western Europe. Galician, Breton, Cornish, Welsh, and Irish and Scottish Gaelic are all spoken by communities whose lives are spent along the ocean shore. Before the Romans swept across what is now Italy, France and Spain, other ancient Celtic languages were used. Lepontic was spoken on the fertile plains either side of the Alps, dialects of Gaulish were found all over France (philologists believe that Breton is a descendant) and Celtiberian was the common speech of Spain. It is tempting to associate the arrival of farming on the Atlantic seaboard with the gradual adoption of a new language to describe it. As innovative ideas are passed on, they tend to move with jargon attached, and as farming began to outweigh hunting and gathering, that jargon may have come to replace or update an earlier way of describing the world.

Certainly Celtic languages deal with the natural world, the weather, colour, domestic animals and cultivation with a precision and lexical tightness which would test the perceptional muscles of a monoglot English-speaker. The moods of the sea, for example, attract a dictionary of complex and exact description which is either untranslatable or produces clumsy and unsatisfactory compounds. *Sluaisreadh* in Scottish Gaelic (pronounced slewashrigh) is a near-perfect piece of onomatopoeia for the action of the tide washing in and out over the sands of a beach. *Torunn* means the particular thump of a breaker as it hits wet sand.

A Celtic language was certainly current throughout Britain in the first millennium BC and probably long before. From Caithness to Cornwall, an ancestor of what became the Welsh language was spoken, no doubt in a wide variety of dialects. Rivers are generally thought to have the oldest names of all geographical features and the Aln is a good example. Cognate with Allan, Ellen and other names, 'Aln' probably originally meant 'rocky river'. 'Tyne' is a very ancient word and like several of the 'T' rivers of the east (Thames, Trent, Tees, Tweed, Tay, Dee and Don), it appears to derive from an Indo-European root meaning simply 'to flow' or, even more simply, 'the river'. Tees has more detail – it means 'the boiling, surging river'. Blyth, Coquet, Derwent and even Northumberland contain Celtic elements ('humber' meant something like 'well-river'). The language of Old Welsh lasted a long time, well into the historic period. When Anglian invaders began to take over in the sixth century AD and rename what they had come to own in the North-east, some of the new place names they conferred recognised the persistence of a bilingual population. The first elements in Walworth, Wallington and Whalton all refer to a surviving community of Welsh-speakers. Ironically, 'wealhas' is the Anglo-Saxon word for foreigner, and it came in time to be a description of a native.

ASTERIX THE GAULISH

Despite its extinction under 400 years of Roman rule, Gaulish, the ancient Celtic language of France, has survived in half a dozen very rare inscriptions. These are bilingual, with Latin alongside the Gaulish text, and they have allowed philologists to reconstruct the language. Many similarities with its cousin languages in Britain were found. 'Mother' was *matir* in Gaulish and it is obviously cognate with *mathair* in Scottish Gaelic. DNA scientists became involved and they were able to reinforce the notion that Celtic languages related to Gaulish did indeed arrive in Britain in the fourth millennium BC, at the same time as groups of pioneer farmers and ideas about farming. Judging by the linguistic evidence, it seems likely that Gaulish was also closely related to the Indo-European languages spoken in the Middle East where farming originated.

Three thousand years before those names were attached by the Anglian invaders, a new and magical technology arrived in the North-east. Shiny, hard and fearsomely sharp objects began to be made by men with dazzling, transformative skills. The first metalworkers may have been itinerants who arrived at centres of power in Northumberland to make bespoke items for an elite who could afford to reward them. And the earliest smiths may even have come to Northumberland directly across the North Sea from Europe.

In 2002, a Bronze-Age burial site was discovered at Amesbury, near Stonehenge. When archaeologists opened it, they came upon the richest array of grave goods any of them had ever seen. In addition to five fine Beaker pots, there were three copper knives, two full sets of archery kit, fifteen flint arrowheads, two gold hair clasps – in all, more than a hundred artefacts. But perhaps one of the most surprising was also the least precious. A square piece of greenish stone was immediately recognised as a cushion stone, used by smiths as a last when working with gold, copper or bronze. The recipient of this lavish burial was, it seems, an early blacksmith, a man whose magical skills were prized, even worshipped, in the last centuries of the third millennium BC.

But there were more surprises waiting in the grave at Amesbury. When the chemical make-up of the teeth of the smith (who became known as the Amesbury Archer) was analysed, archaeologists realised that he had not been born and raised in Britain. More, the tests showed that he originated in the northern ranges of the Alps, in what is now Switzerland. All sorts of possibilities came into focus. Were the new metalworking skills physically brought to Britain? Did they arrive in the hands and brains of a tiny number of craftsmen? Was there a secret society, a closed shop of smiths who guarded their valued knowledge? Next to the Amesbury Archer, another grave was found and it too was richly endowed, with identical gold hair clasps found next to the male skeleton. DNA tests demonstrated that the two men were close relatives, perhaps father and son, but that the younger man had certainly been born and raised in Britain. He too was a smith and it looks as though their magical, secret skills had been handed down within a family.

The earliest bronze objects found in Northumberland date to 2500 BC, around two centuries before the Archer and his son died. A short dagger with rivets in the thicker end to haft it to a wooden grip has been found at Barrasford and several socketed axes discovered around Wallington. Amongst the great variety of bronze objects made in the North-east after 2000 BC, axes were perhaps the most important. There is evidence that prehistoric Northumberland was heavily wooded, but pollen core samples show that tree felling and woodland clearance began to gather pace in the latter half of the second millennium BC. The increasing availability and quality of bronze axes was obviously central to this development. Finely sharpened, even edges also advanced carpentry skills, allowing larger and more complex buildings to be raised.

The population of prehistoric Northumberland was rising and there is evidence that in the second millennium BC, pressure was increasing on the fertile lowlands like the Milfield Plain and the lower reaches of the Coquet and Aln valleys. By 1500 BC communities were moving up to cultivate the higher ground. The weather was generally better than it is now, with longer growing seasons, and cereals could be ripened at much higher altitudes. These upland farmers began to build homesteads in a style which would persist for at least 2,000 years. Because their settlements have never been disturbed by modern (or medieval) ploughing, many of the sites have survived and can be recognised in outline. Known as roundhouses, these timber-framed hill farms are dotted all over the Cheviots and the Northumberland uplands. Excavators have been able to reconstruct them. Some had stone footings, but most roundhouses were raised as conical structures of heavy wooden beams which were then covered with thatch. With no windows, one door (usually it faced east to catch the morning sun) and a central hearth, these would be snug houses for those who lived high in the windy valleys of the Cheviots. They were built all over Britain and the basic style endured for a long time. Under the Roman fort at South Shields, its excavators found the outlines of roundhouses and also traces of small fields which grew wheat and barley.

By 1500 BC, the old ritual landscapes of the North appear to have been abandoned. No one any longer walked in procession to the henges of the Milfield Plain and the mysterious rites celebrated at the Duddo stones passed out of use and understanding. Society seems to have grown more hierarchical, perhaps under the tightening control of a warrior aristocracy. Blacksmiths were hammering new sorts of weapons into shape; rapiers, dirks, beautifully wrought spearheads and palstaves (an axe-headed spear) have all been found in Northumberland. Personal ornaments such as armlets, fasteners, and cloak and tunic pins were also being turned out – the accessories of an elite. But perhaps the most fearsome weapon to be produced was something which could never have been made from stone, bone or wood. Swords began to be used. Razor-sharpened, their long blades were intended for slashing rather than stabbing. Horses and metal horse gear begin to come onto the archaeological record at this time and it may well be that the new swords were designed for use on horseback, like sabres. By the time Roman commentators saw the Celtic cavalry of the North in action, around AD 70, that was certainly how they fought.

In 1159 BC, the world of bronze-age Northumberland changed all in a moment. With a roar heard hundreds of miles away, the Icelandic volcano, Hekla, blew itself apart in an immense eruption. Rocketing into the atmosphere at more than 700 miles an hour, a huge plume of debris spewed out of the mountain. Extremely hot, but cooling as it climbed high into the sky, the ash cloud quickly became more and more buoyant until it was picked up by the prevailing stratospheric winds. These drove the black cloud eastwards, accelerating towards the coast of Britain. When it reached the landmass, and particularly in mountainous areas, a dense black rain fell, a deadly mixture of condensing water vapour, volcanic ash and sulphuric acid. Those watching must have believed that the gods were angry.

And more divine rage was to come – in only a very short time. As the black cloud screened out the sun and made day into darkest night, another roar was heard. Racing across the ocean at more than 150 miles an hour, a gigantic wave, a tsunami, smashed into the Atlantic coastline and funnelled down the North Sea littoral. Snapping trees like twigs, it reached far inland, sweeping all before it.

When the terror had at last subsided, when the terrible vengeance of the gods was spent, those few who had watched it must have believed that the world had ended. As they stumbled like shadows from their villages and farmhouses, blinking and shivering in the half-dark of a volcanic winter, they might have gone up to the ancient sacred places to pray. But the fluted grey stones of the circle at Duddo were covered in black ash. The old henge at Tynemouth had been spattered with sea wrack ripped off its holdfasts and the precinct cluttered with debris thrown onto the shore by the force of the tsunami. The gods were not in these places; they had gone and their people were alone in the bleak, cold landscape of disaster.

And it was bleak. The eruption of Hekla was a cataclysm for the peoples of northern Britain. It sent millions of tons of sulphuric acid into the troposphere where it was chemically changed into a fatal aerosol which screened out most sunlight for a long time, perhaps several years. Mean temperatures dropped drastically and rainfall increased. An analysis of tree-ring formation in ancient Irish oaks shows 18 very poor growing seasons in the years immediately after 1159 BC. Over several sites in north Northumberland, an abrupt break in cultivation took place. No carbon dates for the settlements at Linhope Burn or Stanhope Rigg in the Cheviots or Houseledge in Glendale have been recorded after 1100 BC.

In the immediate aftermath of the eruption, the dark volcanic winter, the cold and the months of rain made cultivation impossible. When such stores of food as had survived were exhausted, widespread famine must have gripped the land. Only a hazy, watery sun sometimes shone on the beach-harbours and the village gardens. There was little warmth in it and such shoots as could be nursed out of the ground refused to ripen, blackening and rotting instead as the incessant rain fell. Fields were abandoned and when soaking vegetation died back in the winter, peat began to blanket the land. It had long existed in upland areas, but after 1159 BC, its formation accelerated rapidly. All over the north, the grassland and the homely geometry of arable plots became sodden bogland, eventually overtaking and covering field walls and tree stumps. Peat was the waterlogged deposit of a disaster. Only heather and bracken would grow on it.

CATACLYSM

The eruption of Hekla seems a distant catastrophe, but anyone who believed something of its kind to be inconceivable nowadays would have been stunned by the staggering elemental power of the Boxing Day tsunami of 2004. Earlier that year, in *The Guardian* of 10 August, a disturbing story appeared which may herald a disaster of even greater proportions – and much closer to home. The director of the Benfield Hazard Research Centre at University College London, Bill McGuire, warned that an enormous chunk of rock, approximately the size of the Isle of Man, is likely to break off an Atlantic volcano and crash into the ocean. Cumbre Vieja on La Palma in the Canary Islands has been growing increasingly active. In 1949, it erupted and a huge part of its western flank slid down 15 ft into the ocean and then stopped. Or so it was thought. Bill McGuire is convinced that the massive piece of rock is still moving, albeit very slowly. Even a minor tremor could loosen it sufficiently to send the whole mass plunging into the Atlantic. If that happened, it would unleash a tsunami of horrific power. Computer modelling has predicted a wave between 75 and 150 ft high travelling at an astonishing 560 miles per hour. In less than 10 or 11 hours, it could cross the Atlantic and smash into the Caribbean archipelago and the coast of the eastern United States and Canada. Harbours like New York are reckoned to be particularly vulnerable, their mouths and estuaries likely to funnel the huge tsunami far inland. Manhattan would suffer tremendous damage and loss of life.

Despite their plausibility (and urgency), Bill McGuire's findings on La Palma have caused barely a ripple with either world governments or environmental agencies. They have simply continued to ignore his predictions. The power of the mighty Atlantic has been forgotten, consigned to the history books as the preserve of archaeologists. But when the roar of the tsunami is heard, it will be too late to run. Perhaps the dreadful events and the huge death toll in the Indian Ocean on Boxing Day 2004 in the wake of the undersea earthquake off the Indonesian island of Sumatra will change attitudes and force governments to take McGuire's warnings more seriously.

Historians now believe that the effects of Hekla's eruption were indeed epoch-making, with as much as half of the surviving population of Britain perishing of hunger and disease within months of the disaster, sending Bronze Age society spiralling into a violent decline.

As the cool, damp but temperate Atlantic climate became established, those few who remained in the upland areas turned increasingly to pastoralism. Grass is hardy, dependable and, providing enough rain falls, able to colonise areas of poor soil. Uniquely, it thrives on being cropped, growing from the bottom of its shoots rather than the top. Flocks and herds roamed the Cheviot and Pennine moorlands after 1159 BC, moving between winter and summer pasture, and communities began to learn how to use their milk, meat, wool and hides as staples. Cattle in particular became a measure of wealth. As agriculture declined, the archaeological record shows a sharp decline in the production of tools, axes in particular. Weapons were preferred: dirks, spearheads, longswords. It is difficult to avoid the impression of dark times descending over the North-east after 1159 BC – the sufferings of a fearful society and the rise of fearsomely armed warlords.

Perhaps the most spectacular evidence in Northumberland for the power of the warlords is the huge fort on Yeavering Bell. A rounded, impressive hill dominating the eastern ranges of the Cheviots, not far from Milfield, the Bell is worth the long climb. Around its oval summit are the remains of a mighty stone rampart. It had two entrances and enclosed one hundred and twenty-five roundhouses, enough accommodation for a thousand people. But it was almost certainly not a fort, at least not in a practical, military sense. The perimeter was far too long to be effectively defended, there was no source of water and virtually everything needed to withstand a siege or sustained attack had to be brought up the steep and winding track. It is much more likely that Yeavering Bell was a symbolic fort, built to underline status, a place where power was exercised and the sky gods were worshipped. In accordance with a calendar which evolved into the ancient cycle of the Celtic quarter days of Beltane, Lughnasa, Samhuinn and Imbolc, a thousand people or more probably climbed the winding track to pray, celebrate, pay their taxes and listen to the law being laid down. Eildon Hill North is clearly visible from the Bell through a nick in the intervening hills and it was used in much the same manner. Yeavering Bell had been a sacred place for a long time. The henge at Milfield North was aligned to face it and archaeologists believe that it had some arcane spiritual significance.

The warlords who spent much of the year on the hill appear to have believed that their gods required regular sacrifice, and they often threw away extremely valuable possessions to placate them. After the eruption of Hekla in 1159 BC, there arose a widespread practice of placing metal objects in watery places. It may be that the worsening weather convinced people that bogs, lakes, rivers and streams were the deposits of the wrath of the gods and that these places would best receive sacrifice. At Ewart Park near Wooler, two exquisitely made swords were thrust straight into the boggy ground and left there with no intent to recover. They were an offering to the gods. Similar swords have been found at Newcastle and Glanton. Often, hoards of weapons and other metal objects – axes, shields, dirks, spearheads – have been recovered from wet places. There is an echo of this cultural habit in a famous story. When Sir Bedivere took Excalibur from the dead hand of King Arthur and threw it in the lake, he was only doing what many warlords of the first millennium BC had done.

By c.750 BC, iron had replaced bronze in the forges of the smiths, and since it was a commonly available metal, many more implements could be produced. Agriculture seems to have recovered, and farmers once again ventured into the hills to cultivate and pasture their herds and flocks. This is also a period when it is possible to discern some basic political structures and even attach some names. When the Romans arrived in the North after the invasion of AD 43, their commentators produced histories of their campaigns and maps to guide their generals. They noted down Latinised versions of Celtic tribal names and recorded some of the gods worshipped along what became the line of Hadrian's Wall. Now, these names were not coined the day before the legions tramped northwards; they have a pedigree stretching back to the first millennium BC. And while it is extremely difficult to judge just how far back, some assumptions are possible about the general pattern they describe.

By far the largest tribe in the North were the Brigantes. They were a federation of smaller groups based in and around the Pennines. Variously interpreted as meaning 'the people of the uplands' or 'those who worship Briga', their name is hard to parse. The great toponymic scholar, W.J. Watson, believed that it derived from the Old Welsh word *bryeint* which means 'honour'. 'Brigantes' may simply mean 'the honoured people'. Their federation included the Carvetii, or the deer people, from Carlisle and the Ladenses further south, the tribe who gave their name to Leeds. Others, whose names are obscure, were strung out along the Hexham Gap and the Tyne Valley: the Lopocares and the Tectoverdi. The first element of the name of the tribe who seem to have controlled the lower Tyne, the Corionototae, is found in the place name Corbridge and it may mean 'the host'.

In north Northumberland, the fertile plain between the Cheviots and the sea was part of the territory of the Votadini, a federation whose power extended to the Tweed Valley, the Lothians and as far west as Stirling. Their number may have included the kings who sat on the summit of Yeavering Bell. Their name too is obscure and probably means something unhelpful like 'the followers of Fothad', perhaps a divine ancestor. But what is clear is the existence of an ancient division, that between the hillmen and plainsmen, between shepherds and ploughmen, between wildness and cultivation. When the Romans arrived to play local rivalries one against another, they exploited that division (and almost certainly a pre-existing enmity) by making enemies of the Brigantes and allies of the Votadini.

The gods of the early Celtic tribes of the North peep through the Roman records. Cocidius and Belatucadros were warrior gods worshipped in the Brigantian confederacy, and Coventina a goddess who received offerings thrown into water. At Carrawburgh on Hadrian's Wall, Coventina's Well contained 14,000 metal objects. Antenociticus, a god whose worship we know of only through one dedication at Benwell in Newcastle, is a complete mystery, there being no clue as to his nature.

However sparse the evidence, however anonymous its peoples seem to us now, however obscure their names, we should not make the mistake of asssuming that the real history of Tyneside only began when the Romans arrived and wrote things down about what they found. Eight thousand years of history, much of it admittedly very shadowy, had passed before emperors, senators and centurions took an interest in the north of what they called Britannia. The peoples they met were part of a highly developed Celtic society whose way of seeing the world survived the alien Roman invasion and contributed much to the modern character of the place.

2

THE EMPEROR'S BRIDGE

43–410

No one who saw it would ever forget the day the Empire came. Watchers on the headlands at Tynemouth saw so many sails in the south that they could not number them. Hugging the coastline, the whole British Fleet was making its way northwards. And inside the screen of warships, scores of troop transports moved in convoy towards the mouth of the Tyne. Amongst the triremes, the sharp-eyed could make out a huge ship sailing near the head of the fleet. Its pennants fluttered in the summer breeze and at the stern were planted the standard of the Legio VI Victrix (the Sixth Legion) and the imperial eagle of the Emperor himself. Shaded by a canopy, attended by the ship's captain and Platorius Nepos, his new governor of Britannia, Hadrian sat and surveyed the northernmost coastline of his Empire.

As the leading triremes trimmed their sails and slowed, a small boat carried river pilots out from the fort at South Shields. The imperial flagship glided ahead and was rowed into the estuary, keeping to the rocky northern bank, avoiding the sandbanks to the south as instructed. When the river pilot had positioned himself in the prow of the Emperor's trireme, the captain gave orders for the drum to pound its steady rhythm below decks. Three ranks of oarsmen pulled hard in sequence and the huge ship sliced through the water, making way like a sea monster with its red ramming beak and painted shark's eyes. The pilot leaned over the prow looking for sandbars, shallows and rocks, and occasionally roared instructions aft to the steersman to adjust his course as they rowed up the winding, narrowing channel of the Tyne.

Most of the fleet dropped anchor in the mouth of the river, their cargoes of men and supplies to be taken off by lighters. Meanwhile, the imperial trireme and those carrying the general staff and the praetorian bodyguard made their stately way upriver, almost certainly to a wooden quay built out into the Tyne near where the Swing Bridge now stands. When Hadrian disembarked, the place now known as Newcastle immediately became the capital of Europe. Wherever the imperial court found itself, there was the centre of power for the whole Roman Empire, from Persia to North Africa, from the shores of the Black Sea up the rivers Danube and Rhine to the North Sea and the mouth of the Tyne. The day the Empire came – it is a spectacular opening to the recorded history of Newcastle and of Tyneside.

Two years before the imperial trireme heaved to at the quayside, large detachments of Roman troops landed at the same place. They came from the legions stationed in what is now Belgium and the Netherlands. Perhaps it had been a rough crossing, long and enervating for the soldiers. Junius Dubitatus might have made that excuse when he dropped his shield in the Tyne while disembarking. No doubt his centurion said it was the same for everyone as he beat the soldier and promised to dock his pay for such carelessness. The metal boss, the umbo, of Dubitatus' shield was dredged up almost 2,000 years later. Also recovered from the mirk of the river-bed, in the nineteenth century, was a coin, a sestertius from the reign of Hadrian. The obverse shows a trireme with the Emperor seated under a canopy in the stern, flanked by an imperial and a legionary standard, both crowned by eagles. Perhaps it was struck at Newcastle to mark the events which must have astonished all who saw them. And there is no doubt that these things were seen, witnessed. Even in the Empire's furthest flung outposts, imperial politics involved show, an impressive demonstration of military and naval power intended to overawe and to discourage dissent.

BIG NOSE AND THE HAIRY MAN

Romans had lots of names and emperors more than most. Ordinary men generally had three, what were known as a praenomen, a nomen and a cognomen. The first was chosen from about a hundred possibilities, although only a dozen were common. This could be Gaius, Marcus or Publius, as in the case of Publius Aelius Hadrianus. This was the name men were addressed by. No one ever said 'Hail Caesar' since he was Gaius Julius Caesar and would have been called 'Gaius'. The second name, the nomen, was the family name or surname. Hadrian's was Aelius and the bridge at Newcastle, the Pons Aelius, was to commemorate his family. The cognomen – for example, Hadrianus or Caesar – was used to refer to people when they were not present. The Romans had an endearing habit of occasionally incorporating nicknames. 'Caesar' originally meant 'hairy', even though Julius was bald; an entertaining thought, when the later adaptation of the name as 'Kaiser' or 'Tsar' is remembered. Hairy Bill, Hairy Nicholas. Cicero's name comes from the Latin word for a chickpea and probably referred to a nose with a cleft at its point. Tacitus meant 'the quiet man', Vespasian was waspish and Publius Ovidius Naso, the poet, had a big nose.

The remains of the first Roman quay on the banks of the Tyne have never been found. And nor are they likely to be. So much building has taken place, so many strata of occupation laid down that a wooden pier reaching out into the course of the river will almost certainly have been lost for ever. But what does remain evident is the geographical reason for the building of a quay and hence the reason for the establishment of Newcastle itself. The river narrows slightly where the Swing Bridge spans it (it is noticeably broader upstream at Dunston) and on the northern bank there is a steep slope leading up from it to a small plateau of flattish ground. To the north and east, the course of a lost stream, now followed by the streetline of the Side, ran at the foot of a steep bank, supplying more natural defences. It seemed to Roman surveyors a good site for a quay and a commanding place for a temporary military camp, the traces of which have all been obliterated. What was certainly created in 122 when Hadrian arrived was an impregnable security cordon around the Emperor and his court, probably a large camp with outlying defences on all sides, including the riverside, and a screen of cavalry patrols beyond that.

When the Sixth Legion disembarked with their Emperor, they set about improving road communications immediately. A bridge was thrown across the Tyne. At first almost certainly built out of wood and resting on piles driven down into the mud and silt of the river-bed, it was named the Pons Aelius. This first name for Newcastle/Gateshead remembers the presence of the Emperor, his full name being Publius Aelius Hadrianus. The Sixth Legion set up two altars on the new bridge so that they could make thanksgiving sacrifices after their voyage across the North Sea. Roman soldiers were traditionally unenthusiastic sailors. One altar was dedicated to the god Oceanus because he controlled the tidal waters of the sea, while the other was raised to Neptune, who was seen as a river god. Legionaries often set up altars after successful campaigns or journeys, and because they were carved in stone, many of these dedications have survived. The altars to Oceanus and Neptune were housed in a shrine built into the bridge's structure. Perhaps the priests attending Hadrian made sacrifice there on behalf of the Emperor.

Suitably sanctified, the Emperor's bridge was more than a convenience for travellers; it was a strategic linchpin for the great enterprise at hand, the reason the Empire had come north. After the extensive conquests of his predecessor, the Emperor Trajan, Hadrian reversed imperial policy. Since the defeat of Hannibal and Carthage at the close of the third century BC, Rome had steadily expanded its empire. In fact, its armies appeared to be invincible and the politicians behind them had difficulty in catching up with their extraordinary success. Hadrian realised that blindly pursuing perpetual conquest was not sustainable, that one day Rome would overextend itself, perhaps fatally. A limit was to be set. What could not be held should be given up, decreed the Emperor. The success of imperial generals in northern Britannia in the 40 years before Hadrian's arrival was to be set aside. Cerialis' and Agricola's conquests in Scotland were to be abandoned and an obvious, permanent, daunting and prestigious frontier drawn along the north bank of the Tyne, through the Hexham Gap, following the Irthing to Carlisle and down the Solway coast. It became known to history as Hadrian's Wall.

It was an enormous undertaking, calling on the resources not only of the whole province of Britannia but also of parts of north-western Roman Europe. For every man who worked on actually building the Wall itself, there were nine others engaged in quarrying, transport and supply. So that this massive operation could begin, a bridge across the Tyne at Newcastle/Gateshead was essential. From the moment the last beams were fitted into place, carts carrying stone, lime, tools and wood rumbled across to the north bank.

Archaeologists have yet to find any trace of the Pons Aelius in the Tyne. The anaerobic conditions of the river-bed may well have preserved the original timbers – Roman beams have been pulled out of the Thames – but so far nothing has come to light. On one of the walls of St Nicholas Cathedral a piece of old brown wood is mounted, and to the side is a plaque claiming it as a piece of the original Roman bridge. Perhaps it is.

Reasonable analogy offers some sense of what the bridge and its successors looked like. Further upstream, at Chesters and Willowford where the Wall crossed water, the original wooden bridges were swept away by flooding, and it seems likely that the same spate, carrying an even greater volume, pressed against the Pons Aelius and shattered it. At Chesters, a stone replacement was built. It had a parapet on either side of the roadway and decorative pillars were added as a flourish of imperial grandeur. At one end of the bridge, the remains of a substantial gatehouse were found. It is very likely that the Pons Aelius, a much larger and more important structure, was rebuilt in stone and also carried decorative features to remind those crossing of the might of the Empire. The existence of a gatehouse on the Gateshead bank to control movement across the bridge can scarcely be doubted.

WINE ON THE TYNE

Bulk cargoes were much more easily transported by sea, and many wine amphorae must have entered the mouth of the Tyne as ship's ballast for the thirsty Wall garrison. Archaeologists have found plenty of evidence of wine consumption at all the big forts. But it did not come from the south of France or the Chianti Hills in Tuscany. Most travelled only a few miles. The warmer climate of the period of the Roman occupation allowed vineyards to flourish as far north as the south bank of the Humber, and there is hard evidence for the commercial production of wine in the Roman period around Lincoln. As the planet warms up again, one beneficial effect might be that these northern boundaries extend even further. Grapes are currently being grown around Harrogate in Yorkshire, and it is said that the gentle slopes of the Tyne Valley around Hexham and Corbridge might see rows of vines planted. Tyne wine might be more profitable than other more traditional sorts of cultivation. Professor Richard Selly of Imperial College London reckons that viticulture could even become a feature of the Scottish economy, with prime growing areas in the Borders. The Côte d'Écosse? Possibly.

The Emperor's bridge may in fact have been even more substantial in its wooden form. The Wall running between the fort at its north end and Wallsend seems to have been an afterthought, and the terminus first set at what became Newcastle. Hadrian's military planners may have initially believed the Tyne itself to be a sufficiently substantial barrier beyond the bridge, easily patrolled by boat and on foot along the bank.

One of the characteristic features of the construction of Hadrian's

Wall along most of its length was the way in which the area immediately to the south was treated. This was cleared of all forms of habitation, trees and undergrowth so that the garrison could easily see any approach coming from that direction. In a real sense, they looked both north and south. While the stone-built run of the Wall itself has disappeared completely in many places, especially at its eastern end, the deep ditch dug into the cleared area, known as the *vallum*, can still be made out in many places. But there was no vallum dug in the area of modern Newcastle or along the Wall's run to Wallsend. It seems that its course was so close to the Tyne that the planners felt no artificial ditch was necessary and they simply instructed soldiers to clear the area between the Wall and the river. This omission has interesting implications. Every Roman camp needed to be supplied, and around many of them on Hadrian's Wall, small civilian settlements grew up. Known as *vici*, these housed tradesmen, retailers, inns and women. Because the cleared area behind the Wall as it ran through Newcastle could not be built on, and because a tightly controlled crossing probably existed in the shape of the gatehouse on the Emperor's bridge, it seems more than likely that the first small step to urbanisation on Tyneside was made not at Newcastle but at what is now Gateshead. Some historians also believe that the earliest fort at the bridge stood on the southern bank. However all that may be, when many of the huge garrison on the Tyne had time off, business of all sorts in Gateshead would have been brisk.

The arrival of more than 15,000 soldiers had a dramatic effect on the local economy. Legionary quartermasters requisitioned – and paid for (so that a regular supply could be maintained) – all sorts of provisions and equipment, and producers of food, drink, leather, textiles, draught-animals and many other items available in the North-east would have organised themselves to take advantage. Some supplies were no doubt taken in lieu of taxes.

Roman military planners had paved the way well before substantial numbers of soldiers arrived on the Tyne. From AD 43, when a full-scale invasion of Britain was begun, diplomats made contact of some kind with all of the powerful tribal courts in Britain. Treaties were cheaper than wars, and when the Emperor Claudius rode in triumph into Colchester to complete the first phase of the invasion, he received the submission of 11 British kings. One of them is very likely to have been the king of the Votadini, the tribe who occupied north Northumberland. Evidence of sustained and strong kingship in the eastern coastlands had appeared 300 years before. Archaeologists have uncovered traces of a mass migration of farmers into the eastern ranges of the Cheviots at that time. Probably because of population pressure in the river basins, cultivation at higher altitudes was undertaken in the Bowmont Valley, the College Valley and the upper reaches of the Cocquet and Breamish at approximately the same time, around 250 BC. This suggests the exertion of a powerful and well-organised central authority whose writ ran from East Lothian to Northumberland, perhaps reaching as far south as the Tyne. And the name itself, the Votadini, or 'the followers of Fothad', implies a tradition of focused leadership.

It may be that the Votadini headed a federation of eastern sub-kings, perhaps including the leader of the Corionototae of the lower Tyne. In any event, there seems little doubt that Roman diplomats came to some sort of accommodation with the Northumbrian tribes. The contrasting arrangement of coastal defences at either end of Hadrian's Wall is eloquent on this point. Because the Solway tribes and those in Ireland were known to be hostile, the Wall did not end at Carlisle but continued down the Cumbrian shore as a string of towers, mile-fortlets and larger forts. It ran on for fully 26 miles. The most southerly fort was built at Ravenglass, a site covering 6.5 acres, room for 1,000 men. Flotillas of warships were probably based at Maryport, Moresby and Ravenglass itself. The defences were expensive, extensive and designed to deal with the threat from Galloway in particular, a vigorous people known as the Novantes. Their naval capacity must have been considerable to merit such a response from Roman strategists.

At the other end of the Wall, on the Northumberland, Durham and Yorkshire coasts, no such defences were thought necessary. Aside from those at Wallsend and South Shields, there were no coastal forts; there was no string of towers and mile-fortlets, nothing. This must be the deposit of successful diplomacy. The Votadini, the Corionototae and others had agreed terms of some kind with Rome and were no doubt well rewarded. Much later, in the fourth century, a huge hoard of Roman silver was buried on Traprain Law in East Lothian, a Votadinian centre. It probably represented payment or tribute, the profits of a long tradition of bowing to the inevitable and accepting the presence of a mighty empire and its garrisons. Perhaps their kings, the descendents of Fothad, watched the Emperor's trireme glide up the Tyne in 122.

There were also sound political reasons for siding with Rome. The adage 'divide and conquer' was adopted and modified by the Italian political theorist Niccolo Machiavelli, but he borrowed it from Roman historians. Originally *divide et impera*, or 'divide and rule', it formed the basis of the Romans' diplomatic strategy in Britain. When the invasion of 43 was being planned, Claudius's generals knew that the patchwork of tribes in what is now England were divided and they skilfully exploited their differences. Fighting some and making allies of others, the invaders kept their military activity to a minimum, avoiding the loss of precious highly trained legionaries wherever possible.

MEDICS

Known as *medici*, legionary doctors went to war along with the Roman army. Their assistants, called *capsarii* after the bandage case they carried, administered first aid on the battlefield and probably tried to staunch bleeding long enough to allow treatment. Many wounds were punctures, and the medici developed alarming-looking instruments for extracting barbed arrowheads. They resembled hooks, and there was of course no anaesthetic. What we know of the Celtic materia medica, the sort of treatment available on the opposing side, indicates that it was remarkably sophisticated. Preserved in the medical texts of the Beaton family, hereditary doctors to Scottish kings until Charles I, the treatments for wounds included many herbal remedies, poultices applied with bandages to coagulate blood, and so on. The therapies were often effective and have now

> regained respectability and are used in complementary
> medicine.

This approach had worked well in the creation of the Empire. One of Europe's classic cultural faultlines is that which divides hill peoples from plainsmen, shepherds from ploughmen and largely rural settlement from urban. When the legionaries landed in Britain, their generals found that it was no different, and in southern Scotland, for example, the Selgovae of the Southern Uplands turned out to be the enemies of the Votadini of the Tweed Basin and the coastal flatlands. Much later, the remnants of this sort of rift could still be detected in the different languages people spoke in the uplands and lowlands. The ancient speech community of Old Welsh may have survived in Northumberland well into the medieval period; in the western hill country, Celtic personal names were being given to children as late as the 12th and 13th centuries. A Gillemichael (Michael's boy) was living at Longframlington, a Wesescop (the Bishop's lad – evidently the consequence of a liberal interpretation of priestly celibacy) was in upper Tynedale and a Gillefani (Vani's boy) at Hethpool. Existing Old Welsh place names also show a decided bias towards the western uplands, whereas Old English dominates the more fertile coastal areas. That basic cultural difference was well understood by the Romans.

In the North, they made an ally of Cartimandua, queen of the Brigantes. Noted by the historian Tacitus as the most populous of the British tribes, the Brigantes were a federation which straddled the Pennines. They were granted a tribal capital at Isurium Brigantium, now Aldbrough, north-west of York on the edge of the Dales. This may have been Cartimandua's principal residence.

It suited Roman strategy to maintain a client queen in the north. They firmly believed that in the south of England they had conquered and secured the only bit of Britain worth having. The rest was too mountainous, too poor, and too difficult and expensive to garrison. So when in 69 Cartimandua's consort, Venutius, objected strongly to her handing over the rebel British king Caratacus, and he himself rose in rebellion, the Romans reluctantly marched their legions north. At

Stanwick hill fort, near Scotch Corner, the Brigantian warbands were overwhelmed and the systematic subjugation of their territory began.

CELTIC WOMEN

The Romans found it difficult to accept that Celtic women could be held in high esteem, even to the extent of becoming queens. Cartimandua (interestingly, her name means 'Sleek Pony', perhaps a reference to fertility) ruled the largest tribe in Britain, the Brigantes, and the famous Boudicca reigned over the Iceni of East Anglia. The Romans made a tremendous miscalculation with the latter. When Boudicca's husband, Prasutagus, died, she assumed that she would rule in his stead. The Romans assumed that they would absorb the territory of the Iceni directly into the Empire. When Boudicca objected, they were first bewildered and then did something very ill-advised. To teach her a lesson about the proper place of women and disgrace her publicly, Boudicca was dragged in front of an assembly of her people, stripped, tied to a stake and whipped. Centurions raped her daughters. The result was incendiary. The Iceni and other tribes rose in rebellion, burned Colchester and London, and slaughtered thousands.

Roads and the ability to move soldiers quickly and safely from one flashpoint to another had been central to Roman military thinking for centuries. And when a limit was set on their new gains in the North, it was marked by a road. The Latin origin of limit is *limes*, meaning 'path'. Later called the Stanegate ('the Stone Road'), it ran from what is now Carlisle to Corbridge and possibly on to the southern banks of the lower Tyne, linking a series of forts of varying size. Its other prime purpose was to act as a military fire-break. Running along the upper Tyne, through the Hexham Gap to the valleys of the Irthing and the Eden, it divided the territory of the Brigantian confederacy into two parts. When Venutius fought the legions at Stanwick hill fort, Roman commentators noted that he had help from outside. This almost certainly meant the northern kingdoms of the Selgovae in the Southern Uplands and the Novantes in Galloway. These allies used the hidden trackways of the hills to move their warbands around. But the Stanegate was intensively patrolled and that made it difficult for these peoples to unite with the Brigantes – a concrete example of divide et impera.

One of the largest and most impressive forts on the great stone road was built around 85 and known to its garrison as Vindolanda. Near Chesterholm, between Haltwhistle and Hexham, it has been extensively – and brilliantly – excavated by the Birley family. In 1973, Robin Birley came across what the British Museum believes to be the greatest archaeological find ever made in Britain. Not a glittering and sumptuous hoard of treasure or a magnificent burial, but a series of small, wafer-thin wooden tablets. Pulled out of the soggy ground which had preserved them, they were quickly recognised by Birley as letters written to and by the soldiers and scribes stationed at Vindolanda. Without a handy supply of papyrus and since vellum (calfskin) was too scarce and expensive, the scribes made use of very thin wafers of local wood. They wrote in ink on one side, then scored the letter down the centre, folded it in half, put the address on the blank side and handed it to the military postal service. Once a letter had been read, replied to or acted on, it was chucked away as rubbish – for Robin Birley to find 2,000 years later. Nothing like them had ever come to light before, nor has it since.

PORRIDGE

A blocked drain leading from a latrine may not be the most attractive of historical records, but it can be very instructive. At the Bearsden fort in Glasgow, on the line of the Antonine Wall (begun in 139), the 2,000-year-old remains of what Roman soldiers ate have been found. They were fond of porridge made with wheat (this may have more resembled polenta) or oats and they went out gathering wild raspberries, bilberries, brambles and hazelnuts to give

---

it flavour. Clearly it was good roughage. Although predominantly vegetarian, the military diet did contain pork, beef and mutton, as well as the occasional bit of venison. Hunting and gathering still went on and no doubt forage parties left the Tyneside forts often. The Wall garrison spent the vast majority of its time not fighting and the vital business of supply will have seen many summer and autumn expeditions to find the best bramble bushes and hazel trees.

Dating from 90 onwards, more than 400 Vindolanda letters have been identified and made legible with the careful use of chemicals. They deal with all sorts of business: lists of clothing and equipment, requests for supplies, invitations to dinner, complaints, applications for leave and much else. The major reason the letters are considered so precious, however, is that they allow us to hear voices. Their voices echoing over two millennia, we can listen to the Roman garrison of the North talking, we can understand something of their attitudes and, through their eyes, gather some sense of what native society was like.

The soldiers based at Vindolanda were Batavians, recent recruits to the Roman army from what is now Holland and Belgium. Before the letters came to light, it may have been thought that since the occupiers originally came from the same sort of tribal society as existed in Britain, they might have had some residual sympathy for the newly colonised north-easterners, perhaps even speaking a Celtic cousin language. Not a bit of it. They had become, it seems, more Roman than the noblest Roman. Here is a dinner invitation from an aristocratic Batavian lady:

> Claudia Severa to her Lepidina greetings. On the third day before the Ides of September, sister, for the day of the celebration of my birthday, I give you a warm invitation to make sure that you come to us, to make the day more enjoyable for me by your arrival . . . Give my greetings to your Cerialis. My Aelius and my little son send him their greetings.

I shall expect you, sister. Farewell, sister, my dearest soul, as I hope to prosper, and hail. To Sulpicia Lepidina, [wife] of Cerialis, from Severa.

The atmosphere behind this formal but warm and human letter is redolent of what life was like in a similar, more modern, circumstance – the British Raj in India: lonely, upper-class women posted with their husbands to one of the more distant parts of the Empire, anxious to see each other, solicitous about their families. There is perhaps also a sense of maintaining civilised standards in trying circumstances.

Other letters contain everyday comments which resonate now. One correspondent complains bitterly about the terrible stormy weather while advising someone not to travel while the roads are so bad. So much for Roman engineering.

Attitudes to the native peoples are clear in this extract: 'The Britons are unprotected by armour. There are very many cavalry. The cavalry do not use swords nor do the wretched Britons mount in order to throw javelins.' This is the earliest confirmation, by outsiders, of the Celtic habit of fighting on horseback in the North (one of the reasons for the widespread wearing of trousers by native warriors). But it is the use of '*Brittunculi*' – 'wretched Britons' – which stands out. Occupying soldiers have always referred to the natives as wogs, and the use of '*Brittunculi*' belongs to that tradition – somewhat watered down by being written down in this case. The commander at Vindolanda and his officers and troops will have looked on north-easterners in a similar way: as a bunch of simple, illiterate, unsophisticated and sometimes sly wogs. There is nothing surprising in this, although it does invite the passing observation of how inappropriate it would be to begin a history of Tyneside with the doings of the Romans.

NEWSFLASHES

The postal service of the Roman Empire was very efficient. At its peak, urgent messages could travel from Rome to Newcastle or South Shields in as little as 10 or 11 days. If something epoch-changing happened, such as the death of an emperor, a system of smoke and fire signals could transmit a simple message from Italy to Tyneside in a matter of hours. For routine business, imperial post travelled in light carriages which averaged about 50 miles a day. That meant news from Rome reached Hadrian's Wall in about 30 days.

Nevertheless, historians are often easily seduced by a culture which wrote things down, which kept records and which appeared to act in a rational, predictable and orderly fashion. The Romans were a literate people and much has survived which can be read and made into an intelligible pattern. But they were exceptional. Almost all other European cultures of this period, including the Celtic kingdoms of north Britain, were non-literate. Their societies depended on memory and custom. These habits of mind can be evanescent, not frozen in time like an inscription, a poem or a shopping list. And because little of the texture of their way of life has come down to us for this reason, the native peoples tend to fade into a grey background for the technicolor pomp and grandeur of emperors and legions. As a bright Mediterranean light shines on their purple togas, eagle standards, red cloaks and polished body armour, and as Roman armies clattered and jangled along the straight stone roads, we are apt to be dazzled and forget those who were watching, those whose land was taken from them. They were our ancestors, people whose genes inhabit our bodies and who are the proper subject of this history. The province of Britannia was vivid, fascinating – and transient. The Romans came, saw, conquered, made a tremendous mess and ultimately went.

But they are interesting, and Roman records often have something to say about the natives of the North-east, the wretched Britons, the wogs. In the precious Vindolanda letters, the first recorded personal names of local people can be found.

BOARD AT WALLSEND

Roman bathhouses like the one at Wallsend were for socialising as well as washing. Men drank wine and ate snacks. At South Shields and Benwell, the remains of both oysters and mussels have been found. Off-duty soldiers also played board games and dice, no doubt for money and with side-bets from onlookers. A favourite was *'ludus latrunculorum'*, or 'robber-soldiers', a battle game like chess. At Wallsend fort a board and a set of counters were found, and it seems that pieces were moved according to throws of the dice. All the pieces moved in straight lines, like the rook in chess, and could be captured if their advance or retreat were cut off.

In the period after AD 100, the size of the frontier garrison on Hadrian's Wall began to grow, until it reached 15,350 by the end of the century. The need for a large force of colonising soldiers implies a large population, but beyond that generalisation, only a broad estimate can be produced. However, it is certain that the rapid introduction of such a huge new group will have greatly stimulated the Tyneside economy. Taking into account suppliers, specialist merchants, craftsmen, wives, families and others, a modest figure of at the very least 30,000 new people needed to be fed and supplied with all manner of goods. The Vindolanda tablets mention a merchant called Metto, and in all likelihood he was a north-easterner, perhaps the first to have his name mentioned in the written historical record. Metto sold parts for wheeled vehicles, and he sent the fort a consignment of hubs, axles, spokes and seats. Given the well-attested native expertise in making wagons and chariots, these parts could have been manufactured in any number of locations, but it appears that the vehicles were assembled at Vindolanda. At the end of the list, Metto notes that he has also sent six goatskins, and this probably confirms him as a merchant rather than a producer of cart parts negotiating on behalf of this business alone. What is also clear is that he troubled to write decent Latin, something doubtless essential to commerce with the Roman army. The vici which grew up around forts would also have been predominantly Latin-speaking, and those who came to live and work in them would need more than a few words to transact their business. The massive presence of the army ensured a similarly deep penetration of the Latin language into the Tyneside culture of the time.

Mention is made of two other men who might have been local entrepreneurs: Gavo supplied cloth and provisions, while Atrectus was a brewer making *cervesa*, which translates as Celtic beer. It should be noted that the calorific content of beer was well known at this time and its chief value was as a food rather than an intoxicating drink. Although it was that too. Perhaps Atrectus deserves more than a passing mention since he was the first north-easterner to be noted in the historical record as a brewer. He began a long and honourable tradition of beer-making and beer-drinking on Tyneside.

WAR-GODS

At Wallsend, fort archaeologists found a portable lead shrine to the Roman god Mercury. There was probably a temple to him near by. It was a surprising find since, as messenger of the gods and protector of traders (who travelled often), Mercury was not a warlike deity. Most other dedications along Hadrian's Wall are to Mars or Celtic equivalents, or merged versions of the two. Belatucadros means 'the Fair Killer' in Old Welsh and Bewcastle fort was also known as Fanum Cocidii, 'the shrine of Cocidius'. Both were Celtic war-gods. This sort of bias is hardly surprising in a military zone, but the close affinities with local gods suggest the later involvement of native warriors in the service of the Empire. At Benwell, the shrine to Antenociticus suggests something else. The tiny one-roomed temple may have stood on the site of a sacred grove of trees or a gentle hill above the Tyne, somewhere already thought holy. Three high-ranking officers dedicated altars to Antenociticus, a horned god. Two were prefects and the third a centurion. Their names were not Celtic and they may have simply adopted a local god.

Towards the end of his reign (he died in 117), Hadrian's predecessor, Trajan, pulled back the northern frontier of Britannia to the Stanegate line. He was anxious to campaign in the more valuable eastern provinces of the Empire. There is some evidence that the garrisons of the North were depleted to supply reinforcements in Europe and Asia. Military intelligence cannot have been the sole prerogative of the Romans, and it is highly likely that Brigantian kings and their counsellors were well aware of the shifts in imperial policy. In any event, probably in the spring of 115, royal messengers rode north over the hill trails and slipped unseen across the Stanegate to make contact with the courts of the Selgovan and Novantan kings in southern Scotland. Unnoticed by Roman patrols, warbands mustered, exploding out of the eastern Pennines to fall upon and destroy the great legionary fortress at York. Tradition holds that the Brigantian alliance annihilated the IX Hispana legion and inflicted enduring dishonour by capturing their eagle standards. The Roman historian Fronto wrote of heavy losses of troops in Britain at this time and mourned the destruction of York and the Ninth Legion as a disaster. Another commentator complained the Britons could not be kept under Roman control. Forty years, two generations after the invasion of the North and the building of the Stanegate, Rome was still hated in the hill country, and the independence of the Brigantes and their federation unquenched.

A radical solution was required. And when the Emperor Hadrian sailed up the Tyne in 122, he was determined to supply it. His reasoning for a new course of action was discovered by stonemasons in 1783 while they were doing restoration work on the ancient church of St Paul in Jarrow. The men came across two huge pieces of beautifully carved Roman stonework which had been reused in the construction of the old church. They carried two parts of an inscription which summarised the Emperor's purpose in building the great Wall:

> Son of all deified emperors, the Emperor Caesar Trajan Hadrian Augustus, after the necessity of keeping the empire within its limits had been laid on him by divine command . . .

once the barbarians had been scattered and the province of Britannia recovered, added a frontier between either shore of Ocean for 80 miles. The army of the province built the wall under the direction of Aulus Platorius Nepos, Pro-Praetorian Legate of Augustus.

Despite the formal attribution of the task to his governor, there seems little doubt that Hadrian himself, with divine help, directed the building of the Wall, certainly in its early stages. It was to be Hadrian's Wall in every sense. Having been posted as a very young military tribune to the frontiers on the Rhine, Danube and Euphrates, he understood something of frontier defence. And he clearly fancied himself as an architect – he was the originator of many grand projects. During a long reign, Hadrian had an enormous villa built for himself near Rome, many new cities bore his name and his grand mausoleum is now called the Castel Sant'Angelo and was the stronghold of the popes in times of trouble. The bridge across the Tiber which led to it was also called the Pons Aelius. When Trajan's architect, Apollodorus, cast doubts on the new Emperor's architectural skills, he was immediately banished and then executed.

HORSE MASTERS

From Persia to Wallsend, Roman forts were built to very similar plans. But they often had different sorts of garrisons. For greater mobility and as a means of countering the 'very many cavalry' of the native warbands, some forts on Hadrian's Wall had units of cavalry stationed in them. A question which has troubled archaeologists about these is a simple one: where did they keep the horses? The answer came to light at Wallsend. Into rooms only 3.5 m square, Roman cavalry troopers squeezed three ponies. Even allowing for their smaller size – they were not the great snorting black beasts which carry the Household Cavalry along The Mall – it seems a very restricted space. The large soakaway pits for urine and droppings in each stable provided the clue. No matter how much porridge soldiers ate, the pits could only have been for animals. But in these tiny stables, the smell each morning must have been eye-watering.

Despite the high cost of his opinions, Apollodorus may have had a point. The early stages of the construction of Hadrian's Wall are littered with expensive mistakes. Its width had to be altered part way along its length, the cost spiralled and the estimate of the number and position of forts needed was changed more than once. And the whole enterprise was conceived on a grand scale, intended to leave an indelible impression of Hadrian's power on all who saw it. But something cheaper and less elaborate might have had a similar effect. There is evidence that the face of the ramparts was rendered in white plaster, not finished with the grey and reddish stone we see now. The visual effect of that – an immense white ribbon running for 80 miles across the waist of Britain – must have been extraordinary. A symbol of the mastery of the Empire over the land and its people.

But perhaps the most impressive memorial to the might of the Emperor has been lost – except for a fascinating remnant. The two fragmentary inscriptions recovered from St Paul's Jarrow came from a huge panel, the whole thing measuring 6 ft wide and 8 ft high. This in turn strongly suggests a massive base or pedestal for an enormous statue. Emperors often caused effigies of themselves to be raised, and size mattered. It would be entirely in keeping with Hadrian's architectural interests and his personality to mark his construction of his Wall by having such a sculpture carved. The scattering of the barbarians two years before also needed to be memorialised for all to see and remember. The probable location of the massive effigy was spectacular. When the Wall was extended from Newcastle to Wallsend, the rampart or branch wall turned south and appears to have extended into the channel of the Tyne. At its end, near the middle of the river, the huge statue of the Emperor was probably erected to face and overawe all who sailed upstream. Not quite the Statue of Liberty, but monumental nevertheless. At Richborough, on the Channel coast of

Kent, the remains of a gigantic triumphal arch erected by the Emperor Domitian have been found. It was intended to announce the power of Rome to those entering the province of Britannia in the south, and it may be that the huge statue of Hadrian in the Tyne served a similar symbolic purpose. The architect-emperor may have found that symmetry, to say nothing of trumping a predecessor, irresistible.

The impact of Hadrian's Wall was also very practical. According to the conventional historical wisdom, it was never designed as a fighting platform facing north towards the usual source of trouble, its wall-walk being too narrow to allow one soldier to pass behind another. This would have meant a garrison only one man deep. If it faced a sustained attack, fatal gaps would have quickly appeared. Also, there were no projecting towers to enable enfilading fire along the length of the Wall at a point where an assault was concentrating. Or indeed any positions where artillery could be mounted. Until recently, archaeologists believed that the Wall was certainly a barrier, but one intended only to observe and control movement, and, like the Stanegate, to act as a fire-break. Roman armies much preferred to fight on open ground, and when attacks began, an important function of the Wall and its demilitarised zone was to funnel troops quickly to a trouble spot.

All of these sensible interpretations appear to be logical and to form part of an overall understanding of how the Wall operated. But recent excavations at Byker and Throckley have thrown into doubt the notion that the Wall was not primarily defensive. In the winter of 2000–2001, archaeologists set to work in advance of the construction of a new square in front of Byker Public Library. They quickly uncovered the masonry footings of Hadrian's Wall, as expected, but in doing that, they came across something else, something entirely unexpected. In the area immediately north of the Wall, they discovered 49 shallow pits. Comparisons with similar pits found in France confirmed that they held the Roman equivalent of barbed wire. Each contained two forked branches cut from trees, sharpened and tied together. There were three rows of pits in front of the Wall and the entanglement of branches would have slowed down any attackers just as they came within range of missiles – javelins, arrows and slingshots. Later excavations at

Throckley, seven miles to the west of Byker, on the outskirts of Newcastle, revealed a row of pits dug along more than half a mile's length of the Wall. These also contained the sharpened branches known to the Romans as *cippi*. Archaeologists believe that these northern defences were laid down at the same time as the Wall was built and that they may well have extended all the way to its western terminus, a distance of 73 miles and 250,000 pits.

What these discoveries mean is obvious. The Romans certainly saw the Wall as a north-facing line of defence – as well as a fire-break and the other frontier functions. The labour of all that digging and the cutting and placing of all those branches was immense, a huge logistical exercise in itself. It is no mere detail, but a reflection of one of the central functions of the Wall. Trouble came out of the north and the Romans were determined to deal with it.

When modern reconstructions of stretches of the Wall have been undertaken, workers have not found the building work to be too onerous. Rather, it was the ditch digging which slowed the pace, especially in the clay soils of Tyneside. In wet weather it was like slippery putty and in dry like concrete. When the Wall passed through the area of modern Newcastle, the work gangs would doubtless have been grateful for the decision to use the course of the Tyne as the vallum instead of digging into the difficult clay.

When the Emperor arrived at Newcastle in 122, the ramparts of the temporary camp to house the court and its Praetorian bodyguard will have been thrown up quickly no matter what the difficulty. But all trace of these has vanished beneath the modern city. Around 150, a stone-walled fort was built on the site above the Pons Aelius and careful archaeology has discovered parts of it. It stood on the promontory known as the Castle Garth, at the north end of the Swing Bridge, the area occupied by the Castle Keep and the Black Gate.

It is difficult to read the site of the Roman fort now. In the 1840s, a viaduct to carry the Newcastle to Edinburgh railway was built directly through the Castle Garth, separating the Keep from the Black Gate, no doubt sweeping away a great deal of archaeology. Recent excavations have discovered a small fort laid out in an unusual plan.

Traces of walling and ditching enclose fragments of granaries, the headquarters building, the commander's house and a building which had underfloor heating. The fort's precise relationship to Hadrian's Wall is unclear. The Wall did, however, run very close by.

Other forts were built on Tyneside in the same period. The earliest may have been at Washingwells in Whickham. As yet unexcavated, the site lies in open ground just to the north of Watergate Country Park. It may have been an eastern extension of the Stanegate system and those soldiers stationed there engaged in patrolling the southern bank of the Tyne. Washingwells is a commanding location, a vantage point for monitoring native movement and anticipating trouble.

An ancient road runs to the south-east of the fort. Called the *Wrekendike* in Old English (it may mean 'the Outlaw Road'), it ran straight to the fort at South Shields which guarded the mouth of the Tyne. Since traces of turf ramparts have been detected under the stonework laid down in 158, it is very likely that an earlier fort stood at South Shields, another extension of the Stanegate system. The oldest datable buildings went up in 125, but they are not military, being part of the *vicus*, the civilian settlement which grew up outside the walls. A substantial garrison of 480 infantry soldiers and 120 cavalry troopers occupied the fort after the stonework went up in 158, and they would have needed the services of many tradesmen, innkeepers and other extramural establishments.

Four miles upstream, on the opposite bank of the Tyne, the fort at Wallsend was built as the eastern terminus of Hadrian's Wall. The decision to extend the Wall on from Newcastle appears to have been made two or three years after construction first got under way. Another expensive alteration. What took place at Wallsend was summary, even brutal. Archaeologists have found under the Roman fort the criss-cross marks of the ard, an early wooden plough. It seems that Roman surveyors chose an area of freshly tilled farmland, cleared the native people and their crops off it, and filled in the furrows so that building work could begin on a flat platform. This sort of ruthless incident was doubtless repeated many times along the length of Hadrian's Wall. Between the fort at Wallsend and the Tyne lay the vicus, and nineteenth-century discoveries suggest that a bathhouse stood near where the Ship in the Hole pub stands today. There was almost certainly a quay out into the river in what is now Swan Hunter's shipyard.

In the Roman period, Wallsend was known as Segedunum. Deriving from Old Welsh, and not Latin, it means something like 'the Strong Fort'. It may not be the original name; it is difficult to imagine Hadrian or his governors using a barbarian name for such an important place, probably the location of a statue of the Emperor. Segedunum is taken from a late-fourth-century military list known as the Notitia Dignitatum, and since the make-up of the Roman army was almost certainly native by that time, it may be a late name used by men who spoke Old Welsh and had only enough Latin for government use.

At the end of the second century, during the reign of the unstable Emperor Commodus, there was more trouble in northern Britain. Here is the historian Dio Cassius:

> [Commodus's] greatest war was in Britain. The tribes in the island crossed the Wall which separated them from the Roman legions, did a great deal of damage, and cut down a general and his troops; so Commodus in alarm sent Ulpius Marcellus against them. Marcellus inflicted a major defeat on the barbarians.

But it was not enough. The sustained pressure from the northern kings was so great that an embattled governor of Britannia was forced to buy peace by bribery in 197. And in 207, more warbands rode south in search of plunder. The Emperor Septimius Severus was exasperated and a full-scale expedition to Britain was set in train. In order to subdue Scotland and the Caledonian confederacy, the British Fleet was to be used for both supply and troop transportation. At the fort at South Shields, imperial baggage seals have been found, suggesting that Severus was based there. Between 205 and 210, the nature of the fort changed as it was converted into a huge supply depot. Barracks were demolished and replaced with granaries, the intention being to move corn by sea to feed the imperial army as it marched deeper into Scotland.

TOMB WITH A VIEW

The Roman habit was to dig burials outside the boundaries of settlements, usually along the line of a road, where they could be seen and easily visited. There is clear evidence of this practice outside the fort at High Rochester near Otterburn. At South Shields, an exotic and touching tombstone has been found. It was erected by Barates, a merchant from Palmyra in Syria, to his wife, Regina. Elaborate, with an effigy carved in high relief and seated inside an architectural frame, it is impressive and surprising. Regina came from the tribe of the Catuvellauni, who were based around St Albans, and she had been Barates' slave. Below the Latin inscription is a line in Aramaic mourning her passing in her husband's native language. He must have loved her very much.

Severus was successful in subduing the Caledonians but he died at York in 211 before he could consolidate. Believing Scotland to be too difficult to hold and probably not worth the expense anyway, his son and heir, Caracalla, withdrew the frontier back to Hadrian's Wall, where it stayed for two centuries.

After the upheaval of the Severan campaigns, Tyneside enjoyed a century of relative tranquillity. But peace does not make news, and records for the third and early fourth century are sparse. Sometime around 300, the fort at South Shields was remodelled (almost certainly after a fire caused by hostile action), with granaries in the northern half and barracks in the southern. So that goods could be transferred from big ships anchored at the mouth of the Tyne and safely moved upriver, a new garrison of bargemen arrived after the rebuilding. Perhaps the river was silting up, or perhaps the bargemen were used to supply as far upstream as Corbridge. The new garrison came from the River Tigris, which flows through what is now Iraq, and their presence changed the old name of the fort. It became known as Arbeia, or 'the place of the Arabs'. They are the first recorded keelmen in Tyneside's history.

DRAGON FLAGS

There is some evidence that, to counter the Brigantian cavalry, the Romans brought in specialist troops from across the Empire. At Ribchester in Lancashire, the Emperor Marcus Aurelius settled a large number of Sarmatian veterans after a revolt in the Pennines in 180. These were an exotic import. The Sarmatians came from the area of the Black Sea and it is possible that as many as 5,500 were posted to Britain with their cavalry ponies. Such a large number must have influenced equine bloodstock in the north, but they also brought another, intriguing import. When the Sarmatian cavalry charged, they carried a dragon flag. Mounted on a pole, a dragon's head (usually with a reed in its mouth so that it hissed) had a long windsock of red fabric which flowed behind as the ponies galloped. A fearsome sight and sound, it was adopted by late Roman cavalry in Britain and became the very earliest of the British national flags, the Red Dragon of Wales.

In the third and fourth centuries, the Roman army was changing. The Tigris bargemen may have been one of the last units to be brought into Roman Britain from another part of the Empire. The Notitia Dignitatum notes the formal names of detachments of troops such as the Fourth Cohort of Lingonians at Wallsend, but although they came originally from eastern France, it is very likely that they had been recruiting locally for some time. By the end of the fourth century, the Lingonians, the Tigris bargemen and the Spanish cavalry based at Benwell were probably no more than traditional labels applied to units of native soldiers. The rules of recruitment had long been relaxed to allow marriage and soldiers were also offered the inducement of Roman citizenship.

At Wallsend, archaeologists have found hard evidence of these developments. Barracks designed to house platoons of soldiers were altered to make chalets which could each accommodate a small family. The fort may have come to resemble a village rather than a military facility. Along Hadrian's Wall, mile-castles appear to have been adapted in a similar way, providing a small house and acting as a focus for a farm. These troops were still soldiers, though, in receipt of army pay and under the command of the Dux Britanniarum, the Duke of the British Provinces, the supreme military leader of the North. It is likely that he too was a native.

In the third and fourth centuries, Rome organised and reorganised the province until it was split into four administrative areas. And by 395, when the Notitia Dignitatum was compiled, the Duke was joined by a more junior officer, the Count of the British Provinces. He commanded a mobile field army of about 6,000. By previous imperial standards, this was a small force, but it was still larger than any which marched in Britain in the following centuries. William the Conqueror's invading army of 1066 was the first to be of equivalent size. The Duke's other lieutenant recognised a mounting threat to Britannia. The Count of the Saxon Shore oversaw a string of watchtowers and strongholds down the North Sea coast, from Huntcliffe on Teesside to Kent and beyond.

SHIELDS AND ARMOUR

In the summer of 2004, archaeologists made a remarkable find. In what is believed to have been a junior officer's room in a barracks block in the fort at South Shields, a suit of Roman chain-mail armour was found. The first ever to come to light in Britain, it was forged from more than 30,000 iron rings and is one of only seven discovered in Europe. The suit was dated to about 300. It was a very expensive item of war gear and its presence inside a fire-damaged building makes it certain that its owner could not get it out, or was killed before he could. This in turn implies hostile action at South Shields at a time when it is thought the Wall zone was peaceful. Were the Brigantes still active – or the Picts? It

> may well have been the latter, since one Roman historian
> called them 'transmarini', or 'sea-raiders'.

Since the posting of the Batavians to Vindolanda in the first century, Germanic warriors from across the North Sea were seen on Tyneside as units in the Roman army, but as the Empire in the west grew ever weaker and more prey to barbarian incursion, these men became more like mercenaries than regular soldiers. At first, they seem to have been used to contain the warbands of the remarkable peoples of northern and eastern Scotland known as the Picts. Writing only three centuries later, the great historian Bede of Jarrow called them 'the Scourge of Britain'. In 343, they attacked and burned the outpost forts of Bewcastle and Risingham (where the Rede flows into the North Tyne). Intent on plunder, the Pictish warbands usually raided for a season, returned home at the end of the summer with as much as could be carried on their ponies and then went into their fields to bring in the harvest. They were not interested in Roman-style conquest of territory and saw Britannia as a source of valuables rather than valuable in itself.

Despite the historical impression of bands of highly mobile hooligans, the Picts were not merely unsophisticated destroyers. There was method too. In the early summer of 367, what Roman historians called 'the Barbarian Conspiracy' burst over Britain. It was the result of sustained and well-organised diplomacy and planning; the Picts, the Scots of Argyll and northern Ireland, and the Franks from across the North Sea all combined in a simultaneous assault on the province. The Saxon shore forts and the field army were overrun and the Duke of the British Provinces was killed. He had a German name, Fullofaudes, and was probably the leader of a band of mercenaries in imperial service.

COEL THE OLD

One of the last dukes of the British Provinces was probably a man called Coel Hen. In Old Welsh, it means 'Coel the Old', and in a historical quirk, his name has survived in a nursery rhyme. Old King Cole was named as the founder of several northern native dynasties in the post-Roman period,

but how merry he was and whether or not he liked fiddle
music is lost to us.

The Barbarian Conspiracy was more than a huge raid; it threatened
the stability of the entire province. Two years after the first attacks, an
experienced and tough soldier arrived to restore order. After declaring
an amnesty for deserters and rounding up some of the raiders, Count
Theodosius advanced north to Hadrian's Wall. It was important to
reorganise the garrison and strengthen defences but he soon saw that a
more radical approach was needed. Using the same method the
Romans had employed to deter the Berber tribes bordering the North
African provinces, Theodosius began to set up a network of buffer
kingdoms north of the Wall.

The surviving kinglists of the Novantes, the southern Votadini and
the peoples who formed the ancient kingdom of Strathclyde contain a
smattering of fascinating names. Celticised and shortened into Annwn
Donadd was a man called Antonius Donatus of the Novantes; in
Strathclyde, Cluim was Clemens and his successor Cinhil or
Quintilius; and the first three kings of the southern Votadini were
Tacit, Patern and Aetern, or Tacitus, Paternus and Aeternus. Who
were these men? In North Africa, the imperial administration had set
Roman prefects over the Berber tribesmen and it is very likely that
Theodosius did something similar north of the Wall. Paternus had a
nickname attached. It was Pesrut, Old Welsh for 'the Man with the
Red Cloak', surely a serving Roman officer or the holder of Roman
rank.

HADRIAN, REIVERS AND JACOBITES

Housesteads Fort was occupied by an unlikely garrison. In
the seventeenth century, a clan of moss-troopers, the
successors of the Border Reivers, built houses on Roman
foundations (and with Roman masonry, probably giving the
fort its modern name) and corralled their ponies inside the
perimeter walls. They were Armstrongs and their warlike
disposition and lawlessness discouraged historical enquiry;

the antiquarian William Camden chose not to visit Housesteads in 1599 'for fear of the rank robbers there'.

In the eighteenth century, General Wade destroyed much of the Wall in and around Newcastle when he had a military road built west out of the city. After the Jacobite Rebellion of 1745–6, it was thought, just as it was by the Romans 17 centuries before, that communications needed to improve. Perhaps as much as 30 miles of the Wall was demolished for roadstone.

Theodosius' strategy worked. There was peace in the area of the Wall and Britain appeared better protected. And it was worth protecting. A rich province at the end of the fourth century, it may have boasted a population of around 3.5 million. Using modern percentage proportions, that would give Tyneside a late-Roman-period population of about 70,000. With few large settlements and the only possible town at Corbridge, this meant a dense rural population in areas where the land would support it. There is every reason to believe that Tyneside flourished in the decades of the late fourth and early fifth centuries as a Romanised area. Scholars have shown that Carlisle maintained itself as a small, self-governing city well into the fifth century and its Roman water supply survived at least to the seventh. And this despite its close proximity to the Wall and the trouble that lay beyond it.

By the early years of the fifth century, the Roman Empire in the west was beginning to disintegrate. Large-scale and repeated barbarian incursions caused widespread disruption, and by 410, the hard-pressed Emperor Honorius had written to the cities of Britain advising them to look to their own defences. The Empire could no longer help. This moment is often seen as the end of Roman Britain, a historical turning point, but for the people living along the Wall and on Tyneside, very little would have changed. Army pay, erratic at the best of times, stopped, but the soldiers and their families at Wallsend, South Shields, Newcastle and Benwell probably carried on much as before.

The memory of the Empire would remain powerful for many

centuries to come, but its most enduring legacy, something which gave rise to remarkable events and remarkable people on Tyneside, had arrived unnoticed and unseen. Christianity almost certainly first came to Britain in the private beliefs of Roman soldiers, and after Constantine's edict made it the official imperial religion in 312, it spread amongst the Wall garrison over a long period. The Word of God was to transform Tyneside and make the place famous across Europe in the centuries to come.

3

A WORLD HISTORY
OF JARROW

410–1066

In a draughty stone church, newly built at Jarrow on the southern bank of the Tyne, a small boy faced the altar and sang the responses to a simple mass. His piping voice answered the bass tones of an old priest who presided over the sacraments. It was some time after the year 683, and after the plague had raged through the monastery leaving only two who knew how to sing an antiphonic mass. The small boy was to grow into a truly great scholar, perhaps England's greatest historian, certainly an intellectual of towering significance. Bede, or Baeda, was probably born in the area of modern Newcastle, in the territory of the twin monasteries of St Peter and St Paul at Wearmouth and Jarrow, and he lived there until the age of seven, when his parents sent him away to take holy orders. He is surely Newcastle's pre-eminent son. The old monk who celebrated the sung mass was Ceolfrith, abbot of the twin monasteries, and Bede's teacher and inspiration.

When he was 59 and nearing the end of a remarkable life, Bede finished what was the first history of the English people. It has remained in manuscript and then in print for 1,300 years. Meticulously researched, beautifully and sympathetically written, *The Ecclesiastical*

History of the English People supplies the only reliable source for the story of Britain after the end of Britannia. But it was by no means Bede's only achievement, or indeed his principal work. Before all else, he was a biblical commentator, compiling exegeses on passages from both the Old and New Testaments. Also part of a prodigious output were a *Life of St Cuthbert*, a treatise *On the Reckoning of Time*, which established the BC/AD system of dating (and showed how to count from 0 to 9,999 using 10 fingers) and biographies of all the abbots of Jarrow and Wearmouth up to 730. It was an extraordinary feat of scholarship, particularly since Bede never left the twin monasteries in all his long life. He could see the world from the banks of the Tyne and create a picture of places, people and events without ever having travelled outside his native North-east. Almost everything was gleaned from the monastic library of, at most, a few hundred books. Within the frame of a Christian cosmology, scholars believed until recently – as late as the Renaissance – that it was possible to know everything. There was a finite sum of human knowledge and if a library was sufficiently extensive, it could be comprehended by one mind. But Bede was not content only to research by reading, and in his thoroughness and sheer curiosity, he reached out beyond the cloister to informants, travellers from distant parts who visited Jarrow and Wearmouth; he wrote letters requesting material and picked up casual bits of information from brother monks who had either gone on pilgrimage or who originated from beyond Tyneside and Wearside. Modern students of Bede can spot an occasional passage inserted late into the text of his great history, almost certainly because it came in the form of a letter or a conversation.

AD/BC

Because he was the first genuinely scrupulous and generally accurate historian in British history, Bede took great trouble over the dates in his *Ecclesiastical History of the English People*. To make the sequence of events as clear as possible, he adopted the AD system. It was invented by Dionysius Exiguus (died AD 550), who worked out AD 1 as the year in which Christ was both conceived and born. There is no evidence that he was correct and some that he got it wrong. According to the gospel writers, Christ may have been born in the last year of the reign of Herod the Great, that is, 4 BC, or in the year of the first Roman census of Judaea, which was AD 6–7. Bede wrote *De temporum ratione*, or *On the Reckoning of Time*, in 725 not only to establish the AD system but also to work out a table of dates for Easter up to 1063, and to sort out a chronology of world history to the reign of his contemporary, Leo the Isaurian, Emperor of Rome in the East at Constantinople. Roman methods of dating affected chronological thinking at that time and a popular alternative to AD dating was AUC; it stands for *ab urbe condita*, 'from the founding of the city', that is, the founding of Rome in the eighth century BC. Regnal years (counting from the year of a king's accession) were also used widely, and in Spain and Portugal a system of reckoning dates from the Roman invasions of 39 BC persisted until the fourteenth century. Although AD was a concept created by someone else, it was Bede's adoption of it which led to its use in Europe and its ultimate ratification in 1049 by Pope Leo IX.

There is one glaring, and surprising, omission from *The Ecclesiastical History of the English People*: it is just that, and not much more. Bede concentrates almost exclusively on the story of the English settlers who came across the North Sea to Britain in the period following the fall of Britannia. For someone so palpably consumed by curiosity about the world, he has very little to say about native Celtic society and very little indeed to say about Tyneside and the north-east of England before the creation of the powerful kingdom of Northumbria.

Instead, archaeology, analogy and meagre snippets from very late transcriptions of Old Welsh poetry and tradition have to be deployed to supply an unsteady footing for the story of the North after Rome. When the imperial administration withdrew, however nominally, many who worked and lived around the eastern terminal of Hadrian's Wall probably believed the situation to be temporary. That was politics. Barbarians had invaded the European Empire before, had been contained, bought off and absorbed, and imperial control had been re-established. The wealthy province of Britannia had existed for 400 years, after all. No one knew for certain that the legions had gone and would never return.

Meanwhile, the forts continued on Tyneside. Archaeologists have uncovered a complex series of ditches which were dug outside the west gate at South Shields some time after the Roman withdrawal. And the west gate itself was rebuilt in timber and the fort occupied well on into the fifth century. It is highly likely that Wallsend, Newcastle and Benwell were also occupied, at least in part. These impressive stone structures had been seats of power for centuries, and whoever stepped into the post-Roman political vacuum will have needed little prompting to create the impression of continuity and use the forts as conspicuous strongholds, well connected by paved and serviceable roads. In any case, there is evidence of later occupation, in the sixth and seventh centuries, at Wallsend, Newcastle and Benwell. With their stout stone walls and roofed buildings, the old forts would have been at the very least welcome places of refuge in times of emergency. At South Shields, there is a tradition that the fort was occupied by native kings long after the Empire passed into history. The sixteenth-century antiquarian John Leland wrote that it was called Caer Urfe, 'the Fort of Urfe', probably a Celtic personal name.

CLEANSING MUCK

If the suspicion that some of the early churches on Tyneside were founded inside the walls of the old Roman forts turns out to be confirmed by archaeologists, it should surprise no one who has studied prehistoric society. Ideas of enclosure, of sacred precincts, had been embedded in native culture for millennia. It is a simple but powerful notion. There existed demarcated areas – inside ditches and banks, stone or wooden circles or stockades – where the gods were thought to be closer. A *sanctum sanctorum*, a holy of holies. Roman walls such as those at Newcastle's fort (where a later Anglo-Saxon cemetery was found) made clear divisions between outside and inside, and may have been attractive to priests for that reason – particularly if there had been an altar or church established there before the end of Britannia. Later foundations such as Lindisfarne, Jarrow and Wearmouth were surrounded by a ditch and bank, the *vallum monasterium*. At Iona, Scottish kings continued to be buried in a graveyard inside the vallum long after the power of Columba's church had declined, because it was believed that the holy ground walked by the saint would cleanse away their earthly sins. Partly for this practical (as they saw it) reason, Northumbrian kings retired to monasteries towards the close of their reigns. This was a persistent belief and in the Middle Ages wealthy noblemen often gave rich gifts to abbeys on condition that they were admitted as novice monks at the end of their lives, ensuring burial inside the sacred precinct. The process of taking these vows was described as *ad succurundum* – in a hurry.

The Welsh genealogies and much of the surviving poetry of the post-Roman period were written down long after the events they describe, and they need to be treated with care. But some do whisper at what may have happened in the North-east after 410. Coel Hen, perhaps the last Duke of the British Provinces to be appointed by Rome, may have retained considerable power in the North. The kinglists place him as the founder of no fewer than eight native dynasties in Celtic Britain. In some heavily corrupted texts, his wife is named as Stradwawl, which translates as 'Wall-road', and his daughter was Gwawl, or 'The Wall'. This sounds very much like a confusion of areas of command with members of a family. If Coel controlled the military zone around the Wall and tracts of territory on either side, as the traditions insist, then his great power did not outlive him. His dominion either side of the Pennines disintegrated after his death. Two names loom out of the mists swirling around the genealogies, both associated with the post-Roman power politics of the North-east, both anxious to maintain the memory of the Empire. Cunedda (pronounced 'Kunetha') was said to be Coel's son-in-law, and his name has a curious historical survival in the Christian name of Kenneth. It means 'Good Leader' and must have been used as a title like 'General'. Cunedda did a remarkable thing. When Irish invaders sailed to North Wales to colonise the Lleyn Peninsula, he mounted an expedition of more than 1,000 cavalry warriors. Clattering down the Roman roads, this mighty warband not only succeeded in expelling the Irish but also decided to settle in North Wales. The name Gwynedd derives from Cunedda.

WALL-NAMED

Hadrian's Wall must have dominated the landscape of Dark Ages Tyneside. Bede wrote that it was 8 ft wide and 12 ft high, a very considerable barrier which must have restricted local movement for many centuries. Stone-robbers did their work, not least at Tynemouth and Jarrow, where the monastic builders made good use of dressed Roman stone. The number of place names associated with the Wall bear witness to its looming presence. In addition to Wallsend, there is Walker, Wall, Walbottle, Walltown and Walwick. Others are more heavily disguised, like Benwell, which derives from the Anglian 'bionnan-walle', meaning 'the settlement inside the Wall' (an interesting distinction), or Dissington, the first element of which probably comes from the ditch, or vallum, which runs beside Hadrian's Wall.

This was the only time invading barbarians were permanently removed from what remained of the western Empire. But more than that, it demonstrates political strength and continuity. Although firmly in a Celtic context, Cunedda's expedition to Wales shows the native rulers of Britain taking on the mantle of Empire, attempting to preserve a polity created by the Romans – even if only for a historical moment. And it also shows that fighting men could be spared from the North-east. Confidence must have been high – or competition amongst native warriors intense.

The bards sang of another warlike son of Coel Hen. Unlike Cunedda, Germanianus took a Roman title. Like the Emperor Claudius, who styled himself Britannicus after the invasion of 43, this man's name remembered a successful campaign against warriors from across the North Sea. These Germans may have been a rebellious band of mercenaries who had been employed at the Saxon Shore forts of Yorkshire (there is some archaeological evidence to support this). Or perhaps they represented something altogether more serious. When the Kentish leader known as the Vortigern (meaning 'Great Lord' in Old Welsh) brought over Saxons under the command of Hengist and Hrosa, he began a process which, according to Bede, led to wholesale colonisation. Hengist advised the Vortigern to send two sealords, Octha and Ebissa, to 'the lands of the north, next to the Wall'. It was almost certainly not his land to give, but, in any event, the sealords coasted up to Tyneside 'with 40 keels', and it may have been Germanianus who dealt with them.

These sons and descendants of Coel Hen fought for more than the ghost of the Empire. By 550, and almost certainly much earlier, they had become soldiers of Christ. Old Welsh praise poems recount the glory and the triumphs of *Y Bedydd*, 'the Baptised', in their wars against the despised heathens, *Y Gynt* (a term deriving from the biblical 'gentile'). The Baptised British saw their religion as part of Roman-ness, of *Romanitas*, and as an enduring link with the immense prestige of the imperial past. Holy Mother Church was attractive to powerful elites on all sorts of levels. It represented literacy and Latinity, and was led by a bishop in the Holy City. Y Gynt were the heathen Germanic rabble, the damned, and they deserved nothing more than a speedy dispatch to the torments of the fire below.

THE FAT HOUND

Only once in *The Ecclesiastical History of the English People* does Bede's sober and precise tone turn into a rant. When he mentions the heretic Pelagius, the old monk really lets fly. Most of the Church Fathers were agin the teachings of this British priest and St Jerome sneers that he was 'a fat hound weighed down by Scotch porridge'. Since his name is a Latin calque of 'Morgan', it may well be that Pelagius was from Strathclyde or Rheged and his lifetime (c. 360 to c. 420) coincided with those of three other eminent evangelists from the west – St Patrick, St Ninian and, later, St Kentigern (or Mungo). By the end of the sixth century, all of the native British kingdoms of the west were Christian. A series of inscribed memorial stones found in Galloway and elsewhere are concrete witness to an organised Church. Although Pelagius passed his career in the Mediterranean, it may be that he sprang from a strong religious tradition in the west which Bede found uncomfortably close to home.

Coel Hen, Cunedda and Germanianus were Celts as well as Christians, and it is striking how quickly the province of Britannia broke down into native kingdoms and reverted to the sort of political structures last seen in the centuries before the Roman invasion. There was even a fashion for ancient Celtic personal names. These kings led small warbands, not legions. They received tribute rather than taxes, and the reach of their power fluctuated, sometimes wildly, between dazzling victory and total oblivion. In the songs the bards sang of their exploits, the atmosphere seems self-consciously heroic, much more like Homer's warriors below the walls of Troy than Caesar's in Gaul or Anthony's in Egypt. Boastful, manly, often drunken, devoted totally to the martial art and the fruits of plunder, the warbands of post-Roman Britain appeared to lead a simple, if brutal, life. In return for loyalty until death, Celtic kings gave their men a river of gifts of gold, jewellery, horses, weapons, anything portable. Land was something to be controlled, its bounty extracted and feasted upon, but it seems very rarely to have been something a warrior thought of owning.

PAGAN TEMPLE

At Yeavering, the only example of a pagan temple built by the Anglo-Saxons has been discovered. Not surprisingly, it has little to say about the early religion of these peoples, those known as Y Gynt. A nearby pit full of ox skulls and bones suggests ritual feasting, perhaps sacrifice. But the most obvious survival of their gods is to be found in our days of the week. Woden gave us 'Wednesday', and he appears to have been the paramount deity. The Vikings knew him as Odin and the Germans as Wotan. Thunor, the sky god of lightning (and of course thunder), left us 'Thursday'; Friga, a goddess of love and fertility, is in 'Friday'; and Tiw, a war-god, in 'Tuesday'.

And yet it was certainly a highly organised landscape in the Northeast, almost completely rural in character. With the disappearance of coinage and its immense convenience as a means of exchange, towns could not easily hold markets and feed large populations, and they slowly shrivelled into villages or were deserted. Carlisle in the west, however, seems to have survived in some form until well into the seventh century. But the only possible substantial centre of population in the east, at Corbridge, seems to have withered quickly. Roofs collapsed and the rain, frost, snow and stone-robbers did the rest.

Meanwhile, in the countryside, farms began to be organised into estates. Remnants of what was known as the *maenor* structure are preserved in southern Scotland and northern England. In fact, the name itself survives in the Manor Valley, near Peebles, in what later became part of Northumbria.

And it was a remarkable survival. This ancient Celtic system of landholding was described in a tenth-century codex of laws set down in the reign of the powerful Welsh king Hywel Dda. The date may be late, but Hywel's clerks were collecting and writing down traditional codes of conduct and methods of rural organisation which were old, having been held in memory for many centuries, probably reaching back beyond the coming of the Romans and into the first millennium

BC. These likely extended in various forms all over Britain, and were definitely in use in the less Romanised North-east.

In essence, the maenor system meant an estate of thirteen upland farms (in Hywel Dda's Laws, most of the Welsh farms were upland, but estates in more productive, lowland areas comprised only seven farms) controlled from a single centre, and by the fifth and sixth centuries a church had usually been established in the same place. The people who lived in the maenors were part of a pyramidal society, with a king and his aristocratic warband at its pinnacle. In the Welsh codex, these were the *bonheddwyr*, the well-born men. Below was a deep stratum of farmers and their families who were bonded in some way to the land they cultivated or the pastures they grazed their beasts over. These *taeogion* were not slaves but not free either. True slaves, the *caethion*, were probably not numerous; the Domesday Book of 1086 enumerates only 10 per cent of the population of England as slaves.

Each maenor produced a food-rent called *gwestfa* which was rendered to a *maer*. This man lived at the principal farm on the estate, the *maerdref*, and, after taking his share, he passed on the food-rent to the king and his warband. 'Maer' was a borrowing from the Latin '*maior*' for 'better man', and it lives on in a different form of local government as 'mayor'. *Cylch* was the specific render made to the royal warband, what the Celts called the *teulu*, a term which also meant family. In the fifth and sixth centuries, the most important officer in the royal household was the *penteulu*, the chief of the warband, and he rigorously enforced the payment of cylch. As the beating heart of royal authority, the warband and its welfare were paramount.

The maenors of the North-east continued well into the historic period. But their names and shapes had consolidated into shires. Preserved as seventh-century gifts to the Church (first to Lindisfarne, then Durham), Norhamshire and Islandshire covered much of the north of the modern county. Bedlingtonshire lay between Morpeth and the sea, and Hexhamshire surrounded the town which gave it its name. Each maenor/shire church came to be seen as a *matrix ecclesia*, a mother church which oversaw other, lesser establishments. A scrap of ancient terminology was still used in the medieval period in the lists of rents owed to the cathedral at Durham. A cow owed to the priests of the great church was described as a '*vacca de metreth*', the last word being an adaptation of the Old Welsh for 'tribute'. Also attached to each shire was a moor, an area of common grazing, a place where peat, turf, bracken and wood could be cut by farmers, no doubt in some sort of organised manner. Shiremoor to the north of Tynemouth suggests the long-gone ghost of an old shire and the profusion of 'wicks' in Northumberland is also related. 'Wick' signified an outlying farm; Brunswick means the farm by the burn and Fenwick the farm by the marshland.

Less immediately obvious is the historic role of the Town Moor at Newcastle. It has been used for grazing since a time out of mind and coal was dug there as early as the thirteenth century. But is it a remnant of an ancient Newcastleshire? According to Bede, who was generally precise in his use of language, Peada, the son of King Penda of Mercia (a temporary overlord of Northumbria in the mid-seventh century), was baptised at 'a famous royal estate' which lay 12 miles inland from the eastern sea. It was known as Ad Murum, literally 'at the Wall'. Bede knew Tyneside intimately and it may well be that he was describing the name and location of his birthplace, what became Newcastle, the centre of an old maenor/shire. Was the Roman fort above the Tyne still occupied, and had it developed outlying farms and a moor to supply those who lived behind its walls? Did the bridge still stand? There was certainly a later Anglian cemetery inside or near the precincts of the fort, and it may be that it was associated with a church built there to serve the famous royal estate. The tradition of Monkchester as another early name for the site supports the notion of a church. In fact, it may be that the old forts were seen as sacred precincts. Perhaps they had chapels or Christian altars in them during the late Roman period, or soon after 410.

These fragments and suppositions are characteristic of the history of Britain between 400 and 600. There are very few sources of any sort to rely on, and the question of continuity at the Roman fort at the Pons Aelius can only be that – a question. But Ad Murum is more than Bede Latinising a local name. It may overlie an original Celtic version and perhaps Coel Hen's Gwawl was the first name for Newcastle. On the opposite bank of the Tyne, Gateshead has been a model of toponymic consistency. When Bede notes the monastery of Ad Caput Caprae, it translates directly into English as Goatshead, or Gateshead. The monastery certainly existed in 653 under the rule of Abbot Utta, but its exact location is buried under the modern town.

Further north, Celtic names were also changing. Towards the end of the sixth century, Din Guauroy became Bebbanburh, now Bamburgh. It is surely the most impressive site for a fortress in all Britain. The restored castle which now stands on the great rock that gazes out to sea is much larger than any fortification of the sixth century or earlier, but even a small stockade will have dominated the area. Whoever held Bamburgh held much of north Northumberland. And Bede wrote that in 547 Ida began to reign and from him all the kings of Northumbria were descended. It is likely that Ida held Bamburgh and that his arrival at the rock ignited half a century of war.

The native kings of Northumberland knew their domain as Bernicia, or, more properly, Berneich, a Celtic name meaning 'Land of the Mountain Passes'. It probably derived from the geography around the kings' principal inland centre. These kings were often at Yeavering, near Wooler, and their halls and cattle pens stood in the narrow valley of the River Glen, where a pass leads through the Cheviots to the Tweed Basin. Ida may originally have been in their employ, a mercenary whose naval expertise was useful in denying the plunder raids of the Picts from the north, or other Germanic bands from across the North Sea or from further down the English coast. However that may be, Ida was asserting independent authority by 547 and he sustained it for 12 years until his death. By 590, Aethelric claimed to hold Bernicia, and his reputation was sufficient to draw the attention of the last great native king of the north.

Urien is nowhere mentioned by Bede. And yet his warband controlled a huge tract of territory. Known as Rheged, his kingdom ran from Dunragit (Dun-Rheged) near Stranraer, around the Solway coast to the old Roman city at Carlisle and then south as far as Rochdale (known as Reced-ham in the early Middle Ages) in Lancashire. Some time around 590, the bards sang, Urien made war on Bernicia, forming a coalition of Celtic kings and mounting an expedition to challenge the upstart and ambitious Anglian lords of the eastern coasts. The baptised would drive the heathens into the sea. And at first they succeeded. Bamburgh fell and the stockade was garrisoned by Fiachna, an Ulster king and close ally of Urien. The Anglian warband were bottled up on Lindisfarne, and, rather than risk more warriors in a ferocious battle against desperate enemies, the coalition pitched camp near the mouth of the River Lowe. Urien would wait and starve out the heathens, forcing them into their ships and away. But at the moment of victory, the native alliance exploded in blood. Urien was murdered in his tent 'out of jealousy' by Morgant, a Gododdin prince ('Gododdin' was a more modern version of 'Votadini') who may have ruled on the Tweed. The allies scattered, the Anglian warband escaped and history began to turn decisively in another direction.

Aethelric and his son Aethelfrith consolidated their hold on Bernicia and Anglian ambitions blazed undimmed. Exasperated by their presumption, the Gododdin kings in Edinburgh Castle determined to succeed where mighty Urien had failed. Their campaign against the Angles is recorded in a remarkable epic poem composed by the bard Taliesin. And it is a tale of disaster. Led by Yrfai (pronounced 'Urvai'), Lord of Edinburgh, the Celtic coalition met the heathens in battle at Catterick in north Yorkshire in the year 600. Their army was slaughtered, almost to the last man. Never again would native kings mount such a serious challenge to the incoming Anglian and Saxon settlers. Catterick was the pivotal moment in the war for Britain.

The battle was also a good illustration of how battle lines are blurred, of how complex the apparently simple divide between Celt and Anglo-Saxon, native and incomer could be. The general of the Celtic army was almost certainly an Angle. The genealogists gave him a giveaway patronymic: he was Yrfai map Golistan. And Golistan is an Old Welsh version of a common Anglian name, Wulfstan. More than that, the bard noted that 'It was usual for Golistan's son – though his father was no sovereign lord – that what he said was heeded.' It may well be that Wulfstan was not an aristocrat and had sought employment as a mercenary in the royal warband at Edinburgh.

His son probably fought against Celtic warriors at Catterick. It is significant that when the descendants of Ida asserted control over the kingdom of Bernicia, they did not change the Celtic name, and nor did those who took over Deira (derived from the Celtic Deur) in Yorkshire. Perhaps that was because these old names were more recognisable and commanded loyalty from a large Celtic contingent in the Anglian warband. When Aethelfrith's prowess began to win him more plunder and more revenue from neighbouring kingdoms, his band would have expanded. And the warriors gave him a nickname, as soldiers often do for their general. He was called Am Fleisaur, well translated as 'The Artful Dodger' – a collection of talents worth having in war.

But most tellingly, it is an Old Welsh nickname bestowed by Old-Welsh-speaking native admirers. All of this points to the early kingdom of Northumbria being a fusion between Celts and Angles, dismissing the absolute distinctions historians normally make and modifying the notion of the first flowering of a specifically English culture trumpeted by Bede and most historians since. Archaeologists might well support this altered view. Compared with England south of the Humber, there are very few Anglo-Saxon cemeteries in Durham and Northumberland. It looks as though a native kingdom had fallen into the power of a dynamic but numerically tiny Anglian military elite. They gradually changed the dominant language and place names, but their English veneer was initially wafer-thin over a thoroughly Celtic society. This cultural fusion, highly unusual in Dark Ages Britain, was to give birth to an extraordinary flowering of literature, sculpture, art and learning in the seventh and eighth centuries. The swords and spears of Aethelfrith, the Artful Dodger, were ultimately to enable the dawning of a golden age and make Northumbria the centre of political power in Britain.

FORTNIGHTS

To an American, the term 'fortnight' means nothing. Which is not surprising, since the word is a relic of ancient timekeeping and simply meant '14 nights'. Although they had names for them, the Anglo-Saxons did not count days but reckoned in nights. The old term 'sennight' for a week has withered into disuse, but fortnight is still with us.

Addinston Farm in upper Lauderdale used to be a busier and better-known place than it is now. To the north-west of the farm lie the contours of a hill fort, its ditches probably dug some time in the first millennium BC, and to the west the line of the great Roman road known as Dere Street snakes up to Soutra Hill before dropping down into the Lothians and the shores of the Forth. Travellers, merchants, messengers and armies had tramped up the old straight road for centuries and perhaps rested near Addinston before the long climb up to the Lammermuirs. Another ancient track joined Dere Street near by, at what is now Carfraemill, coming from Berwickshire and the coastal districts of north Northumberland. And it was along this highway that Aedan MacGabrain, king of the Argyll Scots, led his warband in the summer of 603. They had been plundering in the Tweed Basin and were laden with valuables, driving stolen cattle in front of them.

Each time the Gaelic warband breasted a rise in the track, Aedan's captains will have wheeled their ponies to look south and search the horizon – for Aethelfrith, king of Bernicia, had ambitions to rule on the Tweed, and he and his warriors were riding in furious pursuit of the Argyll raiders and their northern allies. The Artful Dodger caught them at Addinston, and, according to Bede, it was a hard fight. Aethelfrith's brother, Theodbald, was killed 'and all his following', but Aedan's loss was even greater, and the remnants of his raiding party limped over the Lammermuirs to find refuge in Lothian.

Called 'Degsastan' by Bede, the battle was more significant than it sounds. It established Aethelfrith's lordship over an immense area. His men collected tribute and attracted warriors from the Tweed Basin, all of modern Northumberland and much of Durham and Yorkshire. The Humber was a defining southern frontier, as well as supplying the emerging kingdom and its people with the name Northanhymbre. It simply meant 'those who live north of the Humber'. This was a handy geographical – rather than ethnic – label which covered all those who feared and respected Aethelfrith's warband. The Humber was difficult to cross, being 8 miles wide at its mouth, and even 35 miles inland it was never less than a mile from bank to bank. Marshland fringed the great estuary and diverted landward journeys well to the west and the higher, drier ground. The Northumbrians' southern neighbours were also defined by the estuary. They lived below the Marches, that is the borders, and the equivalent term in Old English, 'Mierce', became Mercia.

These were not frontiers in a modern sense. What separated the different English and native kingdoms of the seventh and eighth centuries was not so much a border (although these were attempted, particularly by the Mercians when Offa caused his dyke to be raised) as a measure of the reach of a powerful king and his warband. Aethelfrith campaigned effectively from Lauderdale to Chester and North Wales, his men using their tough little ponies to move quickly and far in the summer battle season. Victory meant the right to exact tribute from the land formerly controlled by the defeated, and the attendant prestige inflated the ranks of a royal warband with those who were ambitious for glory and plunder. In this way, success bred success.

Like almost all the Northumbrian kings of the seventh century, Aethelfrith died in battle and, like many, he was not immediately succeeded by his son. On the banks of the River Idle, a tributary of the Trent, the Artful Dodger's army was annihilated by an alliance of Raedwald, King of East Anglia, and Edwin, a prince from the royal house of Deira. This was a kingdom based south of the Tees and north of the Humber. In 604, Aethelfrith had gained control and expelled Edwin, who had taken refuge in the west, in what remained of the native kingdom of Rheged after the death of Urien and his son, Owain. That exile was to prove important to Northumbria's history.

After victory on the River Idle, Edwin combined the kingdoms of

Deira and Bernicia, and Aethelfrith's sons fled to the protection of the Argyll kings. Puffed with English pride, Bede reported that Edwin was the first Northumbrian king to convert to Christianity. After much discussion, he was baptised at York in 627 in the church of St Peter the Apostle, which the king had hastily built of timber during the time of his instruction and preparation for baptism. But the reason for Edwin's hesitation had nothing to with diffidence or the proper consideration of his immortal soul. It was all about politics. While in exile in Rheged, Edwin had already been baptised, but not in the Roman tradition. According to a fragment from a lost North British chronicle, a Celtic bishop under the sway of Columba's Iona had brought the young prince into the Church. This was Rhun, son of Urien, and probably Bishop of Carlisle. Bede, naturally, suppressed what must have been common knowledge, as the Roman bishop and missionary Paulinus, sent by the Pope, officiated in the timber church at York and baptised the king according to the Roman rites. And Edwin went along with it all. After the defeat of Aethelfrith, he had claimed the semi-imperial title of Bretwalda, or 'Britain-ruler', which involved asserting hegemony over all the other Anglo-Saxon kings on the island. And when Edwin went in royal progress from one estate to another, it was a grand affair, at least when anyone was watching. Led by a man carrying a *tufa*, a winged orb of the sort popular in Roman ceremonial, his warband had morphed into the *comitatus*, his tribute-gatherers into *praefecti*. Edwin and his successors had imperial pretensions, and Christianity, controlled from Rome, fitted in well with their self-image. More importantly, Paulinus and his priests will have promised victory in battle under the cross of Christ. Oswald, Edwin's saintly successor, had a cross erected at a battle known as Heavenfield, near Hexham. And it worked. The enemy was scattered.

When Paulinus came north on his mission of conversion, it turned out to be a wholesale business. In the wake of the king's baptism, the aristocracy and many other, lesser people were brought into the Church. At Yeavering, near Wooler, where Edwin had inherited the royal centre of the Celtic kings of Bernicia, Paulinus dunked thousands of converts in the River Glen for weeks. His efforts elsewhere are even recalled by a place name between Milfield and Cornhill, Pallinsburn.

BEOWULF

Far from being the dusty bane of any English student's academic life, the famous Anglo-Saxon epic is a sparkling, vivid tale. Seamus Heaney's recent translation entered the bestseller lists and carried off literary prizes. Like many great stories, *The Lord of the Rings* included, it deals with the slaying of monsters. Beowulf begins as a youthful hero who frees King Hrothgar from the terror of Grendel and his evil mother. Probably composed in the seventh or eighth century, the poem has an atmosphere which is absolutely authentic. Loyal warriors feast in firelit halls, talking of glory and the riches of plunder. Like almost all early poetry, it was recited from memory, embellished and constantly changed long before it was ever written down. Some scholars believe that the duel between Beowulf and Grendel was first fought in the imagination of a bard in the royal hall at Yeavering.

Meanwhile, Aethelfrith's sons also converted, while in exile in the west, coming under the powerful influence of Iona. The North British chronicler wrote that Oswy married into the royal house of Rheged. His bride had a lyrical name, but a brief life. Rieinmellt means 'Queen of Lightning'. It was said that she was very beautiful and that she died tragically young, her grief-stricken husband probably endowing the great church at Hoddom in Dumfriesshire in Rieinmellt's memory. Oswy and his older brother, Oswald, no doubt waited upon events in Northumbria, listening to intelligence reports, anxious for an opportunity. It came in 633 at Hatfield Chase, near Doncaster. Edwin was killed in a battle against Cadwallon of Gwynedd and Penda of Mercia. The victorious warbands ravaged Northumbria, until Oswald was able to establish himself and restore order.

Amongst the new king's first and most significant acts was to send to Iona for priests. Oswald wanted to establish the Church in his kingdom and Aidan came to set up a community of monks on Lindisfarne (in Old Welsh, Metcaud, 'the Island of Tides'). It is an atmospheric place, where land, sea and sky seem to be one, where spirituality whispers at each windswept corner. Celtic monks loved places like Lindisfarne. Peace, solitude and undisturbed prayer waited for those with the faith and resilience needed for the contemplative life. Early monks much admired the Middle Eastern hermits called the Desert Fathers. In the sandy wastes of Sinai and the lands east of the River Jordan, these men fled the temporal world and the persecution of the towns, and devoted themselves entirely to worship. The Irish word *diseart*, used to describe remote monasteries where the sea stood for the Middle Eastern sand, is scarcely even a translation. That was the prime attraction of Lindisfarne: its isolation. Other Northumbrian monasteries, such as Coquet Island, could also have been called diseartan. The word 'monk' itself means 'solitary'.

Heathen kings still ruled over Mercia, and in 642 the pious Oswald was defeated by Penda at Oswestry. The Northumbrian king's body was dragged from the bloody ruck of the slain; an axeman decapitated it and cut off the hands. As a horrific trophy, Penda had Oswald's head and hands impaled on stakes, which were driven into the ground of the battlefield. Oswy took Oswald's place and, 13 years later, his revenge, when Penda was killed on the banks of the Winwaed, near the Humber. Like both his predecessors, Oswy took the title of Bretwalda, or 'Britain-ruler'. And it was meaningful. With the death of Penda, the Northumbrian warband controlled a British dominion greater than any English king who came after them. Not until the Union of the Crowns in 1603 would any British sovereign rule over wider bounds. The golden age of Northumbria in the seventh and eighth centuries was the only sustained period in England's history when political power did not concentrate in the richer and more fertile south. Such was the achievement of the three Bretwaldas of the North.

We can catch a glimpse of how power politics played along the banks of the Tyne during this period. In the early part of his reign, Oswy shared his overlordship with Oswin, king of Deira. His family occupied the old Roman fort at South Shields, and there is a persistent tradition that he was born within its walls. It may well be that the fort formed the focal point of a lost royal shire and that the Deirans stayed there each year as their retinue moved around consuming the food-rents owed to them. The rapid movements and long-distance campaigning of seventh-century armies certainly suggests continued use of paved Roman roads.

The exiles of Edwin, Oswald and Oswy in the Celtic west set up a faultline which much disrupted the Northumbrian Church, and incidentally coloured some of the normally scrupulous Bede's reporting. Aidan's Lindisfarne looked to Iona, whereas churchmen like Paulinus owed allegiance to Canterbury and Rome. Matters came to their crisis in 664 at Whitby when Oswy called together leading churchmen to resolve a dispute about the dating of Easter, Christianity's most important festival. Iona's churches used a different method of calculation from Rome, and this affected all the other dates in the liturgical calendar. It was also a question of the weight as well as the precision of the numbers. Early Christians believed that at Easter the battle between God and Satan was fiercest fought and all the faithful had to pray for victory at the same time. Different dates divided Christian soldiers.

EOSTRE

Easter is a mystery to most people, and no longer only a religious mystery. The question 'When is Easter this year?' sends them scurrying to a diary to discover the date. Unlike Christmas, it is a famously movable feast. The Anglican Book of Common Prayer contains the formula. Easter Day is the first Sunday after the first full moon on or after 21 March. It is an old-fashioned way of reckoning time, and that sentence probably needs to be read twice by many. Even more complication sets in when the formula has to be adapted to deal with clashes. If the first full moon following 21 March is on a Sunday, then Easter Day falls on the Sunday after that. This was agreed on to avoid clashing with the traditional date of the Jewish Passover. In most Mediterranean languages, the word for Easter is a derivation of the Hebrew word *Pesach* for Passover: *Pâques* in French, *Pascua* in Spanish and even *Pasg* in Welsh. Bede understood that the name of the pagan goddess of springtime, Eostre, had been adapted into the English word Easter, but he saw no irony in that.

Oswy ruled in favour of Rome – it was politically expedient to do so – and the nature of the Northumbrian Church changed quickly. Fewer than ten years after Whitby, Benedict Biscop, a member of the royal household, founded the monastery at Wearmouth, sending for masons from France who could build 'in the Roman manner'. What Bede meant by this was a church not of timber but of stone and mortar. The foundation was not spontaneous; it had been growing as an idea in Benedict's mind for many years. In 653, he went on pilgrimage to visit the tombs of the apostles in Rome. The city was second only to Jerusalem in sanctity, the place where Peter had been crucified and where his successors as bishops of Rome ruled over western Christendom. It was also the scene of the Apostle Paul's martyrdom.

After the synod at Whitby, Benedict went again to Europe, and this time took monastic vows at the monastery of St Honorat on the Îles de Lérins off the Mediterranean coast of France, near Cannes. The brothers had recently adopted the new Benedictine rule, formulated by an Italian abbot. Biscop took his name from it. After scouring the continent for books, paintings, sculpture, relics and vestments for his church, he returned and building work began on an estate near the mouth of the Wear given by Oswy's successor, Ecgfrith. In 681, the king gave more land on Tyneside and the twin monastery at Jarrow was founded. Having visited and prayed at the tombs and relics of St Peter and St Paul in Rome, Benedict dedicated the twin monastery to these great saints.

Benedict Biscop created an extraordinary environment of sanctity and learning in his two communities. To furnish glittering interiors, full of colour and richness, as a testament to God's power and glory, the monasteries were filled with treasures of all sorts. Stained-glass windows of great beauty were installed, painted stone and wooden sculptures carved, metalwork and jewellery produced and, perhaps most lavish of all, illuminated manuscripts made. It is doubtful if Tyneside has seen a flowering of artistry of such variety and quality since those days.

The Lindisfarne Gospels is the most famous of the Northumbrian illuminated manuscripts and, astonishingly, it was almost certainly the work of one copyist. Eadfrith, Bishop of Lindisfarne, did all of the scribal work and probably much of the painting. It is a remarkable achievement, but by no means unique. At Jarrow, three single-volume bibles were made, and one has survived at the monastery at Monte Amiata, about 90 miles north of Rome. The Codex Amiatinus is simply magnificent. A massive object, needing two people to lift it, the Bible was intended as a gift to the Pope from the abbot of the twin monasteries.

LINDISFARNE LETTERS

Christianity is a religion of the book, and no book yet made in Britain better exemplifies this than the Lindisfarne Gospels. It is a stunningly beautiful object. But it was never intended to be read in the way that you are reading this. So-called silent reading was probably only ever done by scholars such as Bede. The Lindisfarne Gospels were read from, aloud to a congregation, and the book itself was seen as an icon, the embodiment of the sacred story of Jesus and all his acts. The Gospels are also a window on the culture of early-eighth-century Northumbria. No expense was too great: more than 500 calfskins were used to make the book (incidentally, it is the shape of the available writing space on a calf's carcass which has determined the folded, rectangular shape of all books made since) and the colours used to illuminate it came from many faraway places. The name given to a vivid blue, ultramarine, points to an origin beyond the sea. Lapis lazuli was imported from

Afghanistan, a bright red called kermes was extracted from insects caught in southern Europe and a dark blue known as indigo came from the eastern Mediterranean. Far from being cut off, out on the edge of the world, Northumbrian monks were in frequent touch with merchants able to supply all manner of exotica.

No doubt the Codex Amiatinus formed part of a diplomatic package designed to ingratiate the Northumbrian Church with Rome. Momentum was gathering to promote a remarkable priest to sainthood. Cuthbert was raised in the hill country to the north of the Tweed, the son of a wealthy Anglian family and, while little more than a boy, he took monastic vows at the community of Old Melrose in 651. It had been established by Aidan a few years before. Eventually, Cuthbert moved to Lindisfarne where, with reluctance, he accepted the office of bishop in 685. His preference was for the hermetic, solitary life of prayer and contemplation, and, sensing his approaching death, Cuthbert resigned his bishopric and withdrew to the windy rocks of the Farne Islands. After his death in 687, a cult developed almost immediately, and he was soon regarded as a saint, the greatest native saint of England.

Cuthbert was also a politician, and in 685 he was in Carlisle with the Queen of Northumbria while her husband was away campaigning in the north against the Picts. Northumbrian power had quietly extended over the old native kingdom of Rheged and the royal official, or reeve, who showed visitors around the old Roman city was clearly well established and also knowledgeable. Waga pointed out the complete circuit of walls and a working fountain. But as the tour progressed, Cuthbert became increasingly uneasy, filling with foreboding about the king's war in Pictland, predicting disastrous consequences and advising the Queen to return to the palace at Bamburgh immediately. The old bishop was right to be anxious. At Dunnichen, near Forfar, the Pictish army utterly destroyed the Northumbrians, killing Ecgfrith and most of the royal warband.

TAWDRY AUDREY

St Cuthbert took a surprising view of marriage. Bede and others reported that he persuaded King Ecgfrith's wife, Aethelthryth, to preserve her virginity. What her husband thought of this is not recorded. To no one's surprise, Aethelthryth withdrew from her marriage and became a nun at Coldingham on the Berwickshire coast. Tradition smoothed her name into Audrey. Later, she founded the convent at Ely, and after her death and canonisation, a fair was held each year in her name. But over time, the quality of the trinkets on sale declined so dramatically that St Audrey became a word in the English dictionary – tawdry.

Dunnichen stopped Northumbrian expansion in its tracks, confining it to Lothian and the lands south of the Forth. Consolidation followed, and, under the rule of a remarkable king, royal ambitions turned in a radically different direction. Illegitimate and only a half-brother to Ecgfrith, Aldfrith must have displayed considerable adroitness to manoeuvre himself onto the throne of Northumbria. But once secure, he relegated political acumen to second place, a long way behind intellectual delight. One of Northumbria's greatest scholars turned out to be not a monk or a bishop, but a king. Raised and educated in Ireland (and with an Irish name: 'Altfrith macOssa, Fland Fina la Gaelhelv enaidh, or Aldfrith son of Oswy, called Fland Fina by the Gaels, and a learned man'), the new king was fascinated by the life of the mind, corresponded with scholars and endowed libraries. Bede hailed him as '*vir doctissimus*', or 'a most learned man'. Aldhelm, Abbot of Malmesbury and Bishop of Sherbourne in the southern kingdom of Wessex, was in frequent contact. He sent the new king a playful treatise on how the sounds of the natural world might be rendered in Latin. Did bees 'bombiz' or 'ambiz', did asses either 'onk' or 'rude', and when wine is poured, does it make the sound 'bilibit'? For his part, Aldfrith responded with riddles, some of them ingenious:

My colour ever changes as I flee,
And leave behind me heaven and earth; no home
Have I upon the earth, not in the skies.
No mortal fears an exile hard as mine,
Yet I with soaking drops make green the world.

The answer is 'a cloud'. The king composed about 100 riddles and many are beautifully written.

SUNTIME

England's earliest complete church is also home to England's earliest surviving sundial. The seventh-century Anglo-Saxon church at Escomb in County Durham was largely built with recycled Roman stone, probably from the nearby fort at Binchester, and it may be even earlier than Benedict Biscop's Roman settlement at Wearmouth. This was Bede's mother church and the home of a large community of monks. The churchyard at Escomb is circular and has sloping walls in the Celtic manner. This suggests a date earlier than the Synod of Whitby. The Saxon sundial set in the wall is capped by sculptures of snakes and has three marks incised in it to indicate the times of services for the monks.

The arts flourished in all directions during Aldfrith's reign. Sometimes he was extravagant, giving a small estate to Jarrow monastery in exchange for a book, *On Cosmography*. He also welcomed Abbot Adomnan of Iona, a great scholar, who brought with him a gift of his book about Palestine, *On the Holy Places*, something which no doubt pleased the king immensely.

TYNE AND TIDE

Bede believed that the earth was a ball or globe. In the cosmology class at Jarrow, he pointed out that this was the only possible explanation for the variations in the seasons between the northern and southern hemispheres, and the radical changes in the stars seen in the night sky at different times of year. He may also have observed that the moon is round and that during eclipses the curved shadow of the earth appears on its face for a short time. The tidal cycle also interested Bede. On the mudflats of Jarrow Slake, he saw a large area revealed and covered each day. The moon caused this, according to Bede, as it 'dragged the sea' back and forth. More than 130 manuscripts of his writings on cosmology survive, and Bede's beliefs about the roundness of the earth and tidal motion must have been widely known. It is unlikely, therefore, that Christopher Columbus thought that his ships would sail off the edge of the world.

After Aldfrith's death in 705, the chroniclers noted few events of great moment, apart from some desultory warfare against the Picts conducted by an *ealdorman*, or earl. But unreported work of great magnificence was being done in many parts of the kingdom; fragments of beautiful sculpture survive at Jedburgh and magnificent decorated crosses at Bewcastle and at Ruthwell, near Dumfries. Much damaged by the Protestant iconoclasts of the seventeenth century, the Ruthwell Cross has been reassembled and erected in the parish church. As well as intricate carving, it carries a Northumbrian poem inscribed in runes and Latin letters. Called 'The Dream of the Rood', it tells the story of the Crucifixion through the cross itself:

Almighty God stripped himself.
When he willed to mount the gallows,
Courageous before all men,
[I dared not] bow . . .
I [lifted up] a powerful king –
The Lord of Heaven I dared not tilt.
Men insulted both of us together;
I was drenched with blood poured from the man's side.

Mid-eighth-century Northumbria appears to have been peaceable, uneventful. Or perhaps it simply lacked a historian of the calibre of Bede. He died at Jarrow in 735, and the kings who reigned after that date were very different from the blood-spattered warriors of the seventh century. After eight years on the throne, Ceolwulf resigned and entered the monastery at Lindisfarne, where he lived as a monk for a further 27 years. Eadbert succeeded in 738 and 20 years later also resigned, taking his monastic vows at York.

READING THE RUNES

At Wearmouth, a very early Christian memorial stone has a rune row carved on it. Tidfirth is the name of the deceased and it is carved in an example of the script also known as futhark. Because it was much easier to cut straight lines with a metal blade, whether a chisel or a knife, runic script has no curves like Roman letters. The Anglo-Saxon version has 33 characters, and, like its northern European counterparts, it had more than a utilitarian function. Runes were magical. Often, the rune characters were carved on small bones and scattered on the ground or a cloth so that a priest could use them for divination. This is the origin of the phrase 'reading the runes'. And murmurs of ancient magic may whisper around the use of runes to inscribe 'The Dream of the Rood' on the Ruthwell Cross despite the fact that Latin, using the Roman alphabet, was the language of the Church.

Perhaps this was the drowsy high summer of Northumbrian civilisation, perhaps it was the calm before a 50-year storm of civil war. After Eadbert's resignation, his son, Oswulf, was 'killed by his household', probably members of his warband. In 759, an aristocrat known as Aethelwold Moll seized power and three years later fought a bloody battle in the Tweed Valley, at the foot of the Eildon Hills near Melrose, against Oswin, a legitimate claimant. Three years after that, Aethelwold Moll was deposed in favour of Alchred, whose credentials sounded doubtful even to a contemporary chronicler. He wrote that the new king was 'sprung, as some say, from the stock of King Ida'. Alchred in turn 'was deprived of the society of the royal household and nobles by the counsel of all his people'. And so it went on. Kings were removed and replaced regularly until Eardwulf managed to establish himself in 796.

While the Northumbrian nobility had been squabbling amongst themselves, an epoch-changing cataclysm had burst over the kingdom. In 793, the Vikings loomed out of the mists of history. The defenceless and wealthy monastery at Lindisfarne was the first place in Britain to be attacked. It was savage. A chronicler wrote that:

> Pagans came to Britain from the north with a flotilla of ships, like stinging hornets. Like fierce wolves they overran the country on all sides, plundering, tearing, killing, not only beasts, the sheep and oxen, but even priests and deacons, companies of monks and nuns. They came to the church of Lindisfarne and laid all waste with fearful plundering, they trampled upon the holy places with unhallowed feet, dug up the altar and carried off all the treasures of the holy church. They killed some of the brethren and took some away with them in chains. They drove out many of them naked and loaded with insults, and some of them they drowned in the sea.

There is a palpable sense of shock, even at a distance of 12 centuries. And it was the bloody beginning of a long agony. The following summer, in 794, Viking ships sailed into the mouth of the Tyne and rasped their keels up on the mudflats below Bede's monastery at Jarrow. No doubt information had been extracted from the screaming monks at Lindisfarne about Benedict Biscop's treasure-laden church only just down the coast. But this time, the raid did not go uncontested. Showing the hindsight of a Christian chronicler, Symeon of Durham, in his twelfth-century *History of the Church of Durham*, related the earth-shattering rape of Lindisfarne to the events which followed at Jarrow:

Yet this was not unavenged; for God speedily judged them for the injuries they had inflicted upon Saint Cuthbert.

In the following year, when they were plundering the port of King Ecgfrith, that is, Jarrow, and the monastery which is situated at the mouth of the River Don, their leader was put to a cruel death; and shortly afterwards their ships were shattered and destroyed by a furious tempest; some of themselves were drowned in the sea, while such of them as succeeded in reaching the land alive speedily perished by the swords of the inhabitants.

Clearly, a native warband had arrived to protect the community of monks at Jarrow, although if the twin monasteries did house as many as 600 men (as was noted by contemporaries) then it is not inconceivable that some may have been lay brothers able to wield a weapon and defend themselves. Or if Jarrow did indeed lie close to a royal shire at Ad Murum, or Newcastle, then a frantic message may have been dispatched when the sails of the Viking ships were first seen on the horizon.

WHY VIKINGS?

What prompted the Viking raids and the substantial migrations which followed? Overpopulation and pressure on severely restricted areas of arable land may supply a partial answer. On the shores of the Norwegian fjords, those small farms able to sustain a family were often endlessly divided amongst inheriting sons. Under the Scandinavian *odal* custom whereby each male child of a landholder was entitled to a portion on his father's death, only a handful of generations needed to pass before unviability was reached. Another reason for the Viking raids was technology. The longships, the 'dragon ships', made raiding possible as they developed into fast, seagoing vessels with a draught sufficiently shallow to make way up many rivers. The dragon ships could deliver raiders so quickly as to surprise most of their targets. And then, of course, there was a simple sense of adventure, perhaps one of the most compelling motives.

However spirited a resistance Jarrow offered to this havoc of pagan men, it was not to be enough. The arrival of the Viking longships steered the story of Tyneside in another direction. By the early tenth century, there would be no more kings of Northumbria, no more mighty Britain-rulers and none who could turn a riddle or read Latin. When Aldwine of Winchcombe and his companions came north from their abbey at Evesham in 1072, Tyneside had been a monastic desert for many generations. Here is Symeon of Durham again:

> The monastery of the blessed apostle Paul, which had been erected at Jarrow by its former Abbot Benedict, the unroofed walls of which were alone standing . . . exhibited scarce any vestige of their ancient dignity.
>
> The monastery of the blessed apostle Peter, in Wearmouth, which had formerly been a noble and august fabric, as it is described by Beda, who had resided in it from his infancy; but at the period of which we are speaking, its original state could scarce be traced, in consequence of the ruinous condition of the buildings.

Historians have recently begun to attempt a rehabilitation of the Vikings, emphasising their roles as traders, daring seafarers, saga composers, even patrons of the arts. And, to be sure, they could be all that. But to the Northumbrians of the ninth century, they were an elemental, ferocious force of nature, unequalled in their pagan disregard for God's churches, his priests and his people, and unequalled in their blood-spattered cruelty. To the people of Britain, the Vikings were truly terrifying. One incident underscores their reputation.

By 867, the Vikings had begun to settle in England, and two of their kings established themselves in the old Roman town of York, which became Jorvik. Civil war was simmering in Northumbria but the leaders of the rival factions, Osbert and Aella, patched up their differences and launched a joint attack against the invaders. It failed completely. Exulting in a signal victory, Ivar, one of the Viking kings, decided that a sacrifice in gratitude to Odin was needed. His men dragged into his presence the captured Aella and tied him face-first to a stake. His shirt was ripped off and a sealord 'carved the blood-eagle on the back of Aella'. With an axe, his ribs were hacked away from his spine and wrenched outwards like the wings of an eagle, and then his lungs were pulled out and draped over his shoulders. When the same appalling ritual was carried out on King Edmund of East Anglia, he remained alive throughout, and, to stop the screaming, Ivar had to order his head to be cut off. And these were not isolated incidents. Many reports of Viking atrocities have survived.

Alcuin was horrified at the rape of Lindisfarne, and his righteous anger booms across the centuries. Born in Northumbria and ordained and educated in York, he was the greatest English scholar since Bede. Much more worldly and immensely powerful, Alcuin had become principal advisor to Charlemagne, the great king of the Franks who had forged a new version of the Roman Empire in the West and fought off the incursions of the Moors from Spain and the south. At the imperial court at Aachen, the Northumbrian monk stood at the centre of European power politics, and with Charlemagne's chancery at his disposal and his authority behind him, he fired off stinging letters about the state of affairs in Northumbria: 'Scarcely anyone can now be found from the ancient stock of kings, and the more uncertain their origin, the more they lack valour.'

There was no doubt in Alcuin's mind that the corrupt, endlessly feuding Northumbrian aristocracy had brought the terrible raids of the Vikings down on themselves:

> Can it not be expected that from the north there will come upon our nation retribution of blood, which can be seen to have started with this attack which has lately befallen the house of God?
>
> Consider the dress, the way of wearing the hair, the luxurious

habits of the princes and people. Look at your trimming of beard and hair, in which you have wished to resemble the pagans. Are you not menaced by terror of those whose fashion you wished to follow? What also of the immoderate use of clothing beyond the needs of human nature, beyond the custom of our predecessors? . . .

Behold, judgement has begun, with great terror, at the house of God, in which rest such lights of the whole of Britain. What should be expected for other places, when the divine judgement has not spared this holy place?

The other place turned out to be Tynemouth. In 800, divine judgement brought a Viking attack on the monastery on the north bank of the river-mouth, and the countryside around was also devastated. Raiding had become an appalling fact of life, and no amount of railing from Alcuin would help the monks and nuns when the sails of a Viking fleet were seen rounding the headland. At least the attacks tended to come only in the summer. The short days and storms of winter kept the longships in their home fjords, and besides, the men who came to be called 'the Sons of Death' had crops to plant and harvest. Historical sources for the first half of the ninth century whisper that raiding became sporadic in the east as the Vikings made inroads in the Hebrides and Ireland. Feuding and civil war abated, and the Northumbrian royal succession settled.

ALCUIN

It is difficult to overstate the influence of this Northumbrian cleric and impossible not to admire his scholarship and political nous. Charlemagne was certainly impressed enough to invite Alcuin to his court in 781. More than 300 of his letters have come down to us, a tiny fraction of his output, and they show him involved in matters of state (defining the relative roles of kings and bishops), in religious affairs (his version of the Latin Bible became standard) and in fundamental cultural changes (he introduced punctuation and pioneered a clearer script called 'Carolingian minuscule'). Perhaps Alcuin's most important role was as personal tutor and confidant to Charlemagne. When the King of the Franks visited Rome in 800, he was crowned Emperor by the Pope on Christmas Day, the first to rule in the west since Romulus Augustus was deposed in 476. Alcuin almost certainly brokered the political deal behind the ceremonial. But perhaps more surprising, and revealing, was the formation of the Palatine Academy. Courtiers took nicknames (Alcuin was the Roman poet Horace, and Charlemagne the biblical King David) and played literary games. It all sounds a touched forced, self-conscious, even twee, but Alcuin wanted Charlemagne's court to be 'an Athens even more beautiful than the ancient one, since it was ennobled by the teaching of Christ'.

In the late eighth and early ninth centuries, coins began to be minted again in England. Kings and bishops employed moneyers to produce *stycas*, a low denomination made from brass. This suggests a vigorous money economy involving producers of food and merchants, and the re-establishment of substantial and regular markets. As the ninth century wore on, stycas became gradually debased, the tin content dwindling to leave an almost wholly copper coinage.

This economic downturn happened as Northumbrian kings lost control of the Solway and its coastal territories around 850. The Old Welsh-speaking Strathclyde kings displaced them and evidence of the spread of the cult of their much-loved St Kentigern (or Mungo) marched alongside political takeover. At its greatest extent, Strathclyde stretched from the head of Loch Lomond to the southern Lake District. Northumbria shrank into a kingdom of the east-coast lowlands. Soon it was to shrink even more.

Ivar, the Viking who ordered the blood-eagling of kings, arrived in East Anglia with his brother, Halfdan, in 865. They had plundered the prehistoric tombs along the River Boyne in Ireland and established themselves as masters of the profitable and expanding slaving port of

Dublin. But ambition burned in the brothers, and they mustered a huge force numbering several thousand Vikings and perhaps two hundred longships. This was the 'Great Army'. Ivar and Halfdan decided to leave Ireland, sail around southern Britain and overwinter in East Anglia. In 866, some Vikings took horse and moved north overland while others coasted the fleet up to the Humber. York was the target, the principal residence of the kings of Deira and Northumbria, the ancient legionary fortress where Constantine had declared himself emperor in 306. The fleet rowed up the Ouse and the land army clattered up the Roman road which approached the city from the south-west. The Great Army must have seemed unstoppable. Aelle and Osbert made their ill-fated alliance and were lured into the legionary fortress, trapped and cut to pieces. It was the beginning of a slow end for Northumbria.

In 874, Halfdan marched part of the Great Army north from York to link up with the fleet at the mouth of the Tyne. The monks, nuns and churches of Jarrow, Wearmouth and Tynemouth were defenceless after the disaster in the old fortress at York and were utterly destroyed. Archaeologists believe that the twin monasteries were burned and only the walls left standing. But plunder was not Halfdan's prime purpose. Here is the entry for the year 876 in the Anglo-Saxon Chronicle: 'And in this year Halfdan apportioned the lands of the Northumbrians, and from that time they [the Danes] continued ploughing and tilling them.'

This is unequivocal – but also surprising. One of the most reliable indices of the settlement of Vikings is to be found in an analysis of place names. Deira, or most of modern Yorkshire, is speckled with towns, villages and farms incorporating Scandinavian elements such as 'by' (farm or village), 'thwaite' (meadow) or 'thorpe' (outlying settlement). But names like these are very rare on Tyneside. Two of the few certain Scandinavian place names occur near the centre of modern Newcastle and also next to each other. Byker is from '*by-kiarr*', and it means 'the village marsh', while Walker has a similar root. It is from '*wall-kiarr*' and means 'the marsh next to the wall', Hadrian's Wall. These sound like appendages, outlying places attached to a central location – village marsh obviously implies a village, and perhaps Byker and Walker are the ghost of a larger estate, perhaps the 'famous royal estate' which Bede called Ad Murum and which stood on the site of the Roman fort at Newcastle. But this supposition fails to explain much. It may be that Newcastle bore a lost Scandinavian name. One or two other Viking names exist on Tyneside. Nafferton derives from a Norse personal name, Naufari. Dingbell Hill is more interesting, referring to a *thing-vellir*, an assembly field – a relic of Viking government.

However, the apportioning of the lands on Tyneside by Halfdan and the clear statement that they were ploughed and tilled might have been expected to produce more, at least a scatter of 'thorpes' and 'thwaites'. Perhaps the takeover failed in the face of local opposition. Perhaps the heavy clay soils on the banks of the Tyne were too difficult to cultivate and the Vikings abandoned the land. There is an interesting tradition that Halfdan's men raised a stockade on the high ground at Tynemouth and that a local habit of giving Scandinavian personal names persisted into the Middle Ages. But compared with the effects of the intensive Viking settlement of Yorkshire and Teesside, these glimmers of a presence on Tyneside are little more than that.

The arrival of Halfdan's army did galvanise the Lindisfarne monks. In 875, they took the momentous, doubtless emotional, decision to uproot the shrine of St Cuthbert, its relics and accumulated treasure and his miraculously uncorrupted remains, and remove them to a place of safety. The monks drove their carts and their precious cargo overland to their church at Norham on the Tweed, an inland site so far untouched by Viking attacks. It was the beginning of a long journey for Cuthbert, and it was a heartbreaking wrench to remove England's most revered saint from his beloved Lindisfarne. But by 863, Norham was no longer considered secure and the saint was taken down to Chester-le-Street, where he stayed for almost a century before travelling the short distance to his final resting place at Durham. Perhaps the church at Norham lay too close to the ambitions of the Gaelic-speaking kings of Alba (what would become Scotland). Cuthbert's close identification with Norhamshire and Islandshire had an early and defining political effect. The land gifted to the saint's community of monks (including the estates around Chester-le-Street and Durham) became known as Haliwerfolcland, or 'The Land of the Holy Man's People'. Just as the kings of Alba were pressing on Lothian and the Tweed Valley, the area immediately to the south of the river acquired a very distinct identity. In time, St Cuthbert's Land would become synonymous with England.

TYNE TIME

The monks at Jarrow had a profound influence on all our lives. Along with the other early monastic foundations all over Europe, they taught Christian society how to organise its use of time. Before the seventh century, daily life had been governed by the seasons and the weather. Winter days were short – and even shorter if the day was overcast. But the Jarrow monks saw time differently, and no matter if it was night or day, dark or sunny, warm or cold, they gathered at particular times to pray or hold services. The bells which rang the canonical hours were a striking innovation, probably the only mechanical noise to be heard regularly on Tyneside for many centuries. The monks also divided the day into alternating periods of work and leisure. And following the first chapters of Genesis, they sorted the year into seven-day weeks with six for work and one for rest. This caused problems during harvest-time, and Charlemagne had to persuade the Church to relax its rules against working on Sundays.

Northumbria was being squeezed not only by the Viking kings of York and the kings of Alba but also by the expansionist policies of Alfred the Great of Wessex and his successors, Edward and Athelstan. In the drive to achieve a unified England, Wessex would tolerate no other kings, and the Northumbrians were forced to reduce their status to an earldom. But the York/Dublin Vikings continued to be a potent threat. Ragnall, the grandson of Ivar the blood-eagler, led his Irish warband to

Corbridge in 914. They were met by an alliance of Constantine, King of Alba, and Ealdred, Earl of Bernicia. After a hard fight, Ragnall's men held the field and the allies retreated, badly beaten. But they appear to have held on to their territory. Four years later, a large Viking fleet mustered at Waterford on the Irish coast, and, rounding southern England, sailed to the mouth of the Tyne. Constantine and Ealdred were waiting. A second battle was fought on the riverbank and again the Vikings won a victory. This time, Ragnall claimed the lands between Tyne and Tees and divided it between his followers, according to contemporaries, and he went on to take York, claiming its kingship.

A chronicler also noted that the Viking army had Northumbrian noblemen in its ranks, good fighters, *'robusti bellatores'*. Elstan, called a *'comes'*, or count, his brother, Esbrid, and presumably their followers, were allied to Ragnall and their presence in his warband hints at a political pattern on Tyneside. Perhaps, in return for overall control of the area, the Viking kings of York allowed their Northumbrian puppets to rule locally and render tribute. That would explain the apparent lack of settlement on the Tyne and the retention of Anglian place names.

The Wessex kings continued to wax ever more powerful, and in 919 Edward the Elder had the most widely landed kings in Britain submit to him. At Bakewell in the Pennines, Constantine of Scotland, Ragnall of York and Ealdred of Bamburgh, and all the Northumbrians, English, Danish, Northmen and others, recognised Edward as their overlord. This was important for Northumbria. Ealdred had the Scots pressing in the north, Strathclyde in the west and Viking York in the south, and he needed the protection of the most potent king in England. The formula of submission is interesting. In addition to the by now thoroughly Anglicised native Celts, ancient Northumbria also included English, Danish and Northmen – the English most likely centred on Tyneside and modern Northumberland.

By 945, the Tweed Basin had been lost to the kings of Scotland. It was sweet revenge for the defeat at Degsastan 340 years before, but also a sad cultural disconnection. While south-eastern Scots retained the English language (Gaelic became the language of the court and therefore of power, while Latin remained the medium for learning and the Church) and many habits of life, the ancient religious foundations at Jedburgh and Melrose slowly began to lose their links with Lindisfarne and the cult of Cuthbert. Coldingham remained in the possession of Durham until 1377, when Robert II of Scotland replaced their monks with Benedictines from Dunfermline Abbey.

By 1018, the process of political absorption was complete. Malcolm II's Highland warriors charged into the shield wall of Earl Uhtred of Bamburgh's spearmen at Carham and swept them away. The battle took place on the banks of the Tweed, near where the modern England–Scotland border runs, and it was a heavy and decisive defeat for the Northumbrians. Symeon of Durham wrote that 'all the people who dwelt between Tees and Tweed were well-nigh exterminated'. For the English-speaking farmers who watched the armies pass and who stood on the ridges above the river to watch the slaughter, it must have been a disconcerting spectacle. Malcolm II's Highlanders, roaring their war cries, inciting one another to the Celtic warrior's rage-fit, were undoubtedly an alien sound and sight compared with Uhtred's spearmen. The farmers of the Tweed Valley had seen themselves as Northumbrians, the children of Cuthbert, and the process of rendering food-rents and other services to the new Scots overlords, however few in number, began long centuries of division along the line of the great river. The Tweed became a frontier and the areas on either side frontier zones, with all the misery that brings. It is possible to claim that, until the Union of the Crowns in 1603, the most consistently important political fact about Tyneside was Scotland.

Part of the reason for Uhtred's defeat at Carham in 1018 was his lack of support from the King of England. Cnut, the Viking prince who had succeeded the Wessex kings and briefly drawn together an empire around the coasts of the North Sea, was distracted elsewhere in his vast dominion and could send no troops to help the Northumbrian earl. It may have been a deliberate tactic, since it seems that Cnut had Uhtred murdered soon after the defeat. He was replaced by Eric, a Viking who had governed Norway for the king. After 1023, no more was heard of Eric and Siward became Earl of Northumbria. In Shakespeare's *Macbeth*, he was to find lasting literary fame as an ally of

Malcolm, son of the murdered Duncan. Showing considerable wisdom (interestingly, Siward is portrayed as a wise old warrior in 'the Scottish play') and political nous, he married Uhtred's granddaughter and named his son Waltheof, after Uhtred's father. The line of native Northumbrian earls did not quite run out.

But political mayhem followed Siward's death in 1055. Edward the Confessor rejected the claims of Waltheof and installed Tostig as Earl, the brother of the future Harold II. This immediately converted the earldom into a means of supporting larger ambitions. Instead of opposing Malcolm II of Scotland when he began raiding in Tyneside, Tostig bought him off with a treaty; and in 1061, when the Scots invaded again, he made even more concessions. A second treaty recognised Malcolm's claim to Cumbria (through Strathclyde) and thereby supplied the raiders with a handy base for operations. To pay for his plans, Tostig raised taxes and extracted cash from the administration of justice. Northumbrians rebelled, the Earl was expelled and a series of domino-like historical consequences followed.

In 1066, Tostig allied himself with King Harald Hardrada of Norway, landed in the north of England and moved against York. Diverted from policing the imminent Norman invasion in the south, Harold II hurried north to deal with the incursion. At Stamford Bridge, near Tadcaster, Tostig and Hardrada were killed and their army scattered. Eleven days later, an exhausted Harold died at the Battle of Hastings.

4

THE RIVER DRAGON

1066–1513

Gongu Hrolf was a giant, so big that no pony could carry him. His name translates as 'Hrolf the Walker', because that is what his size forced him to do. While the rest of his Viking warband clopped along on hardy little ponies, this huge man strode beside them, and walked towards a singular destiny.

Some time in the 880s, Gongu Hrolf sailed out of the Norwegian fjords, and he was almost certainly amongst the Viking army which laid siege to Paris in 885. The city resisted but the Vikings did not retreat, settling in the valley of the lower Seine, in what would eventually become Normandy – Normandia, or 'the Land of the Norsemen'. How all of this came about is very instructive, and it forms the first few steps on a path which led directly to the building of a new castle on the north bank of the Tyne.

The empire of Charlemagne, so ably administered by Alcuin and others, was breaking up at the end of the ninth century, partly as a result of pressure from warriors like Gongu Hrolf. The great imperial domain had been divided into three, and eventually four, parts, to be shared amongst Charlemagne's heirs. Austrasia in the east compassed western Germany; Lotharingia in the middle stretched from the

Netherlands down to northern Italy; and Neustria ultimately became modern France. As Viking attacks intensified, the great-grandson of Charlemagne, Charles the Simple of Neustria, became increasingly embattled and the imperial county structure began to disintegrate. In its place, a system of protective relationships grew up. At its most basic, it worked like this: a powerful and widely landed man, often retaining the title, if not the reality, of count, relinquished his direct control of a given piece of land in return for an oath-sworn promise of military service from a warrior who became his 'vassal'. The count or lord offered his vassal protection and in turn the vassal supplied rental income of various sorts. But principally, he was bound to muster an agreed number of warriors when called upon. This simple network of dependent relationships was pioneered in western and northern France, and it developed into what became known to generations of schoolboys as the feudal system.

But it was not enough to contain the ambitions of Gongu Hrolf. Even though the Viking army had failed to take Paris in 885, its continued presence on the Channel coastlands and the Seine valley made a settled peace impossible in northern Neustria. Charles the Simple's treasury was empty and his feudal army weak. Radical action was required. Some time around 911, the king summoned Gongu Hrolf to meet at the monastery of St-Clair-sur-Epte, near Paris. If the man the French called Rollon le Piéton would agree to become a vassal of Charles and also convert to Christianity, then he would be given the grand title of Duke of Normandy. Rollon, or Hrolf, agreed, and more than 5,000 Viking warriors were baptised. With the zeal of political converts, the new rulers of north-west France adopted feudalism wholesale and made it work brilliantly – nowhere more so than in England 150 years later.

After the victory at Hastings in 1066, Hrolf's illegitimate descendant Duke William the Bastard became King William the Conqueror, and he determined to convert his new possession into a model feudal state. Within a generation, the knights who had defeated Harold II's housecarls at Hastings had entirely replaced the native aristocracy and were busy creating a supporting web of military relationships with their tenants. Rebellions were crushed with ruthless efficiency, and a French-speaking elite began to administer justice and be appointed to the hierarchy of the English Church. It was a complete takeover, and Anglo-Saxon England was submerged beneath a sea of Norman energy.

KISSING ON THE LIPS

When a vassal swore allegiance to a lord, two gestures formed central parts of this ritual which was so important to feudal society. After the formal words were spoken, a lord took his vassal's hands and then kissed him on the lips – a surprising image for a pair of hairy Norman knights. Also known as the kiss of peace, this kiss of homage eventually developed into the loving kiss. But a remnant of this entertaining medieval practice could be seen until recently when the leaders of the old Communist regimes of eastern Europe met, usually at airports. Heavily overcoated, Homburg-hatted, these beetle-browed old autocrats would grip each other by the shoulders and plant a smacker right on the lips. Tough love.

The Conqueror, though, could not conquer Northumbria. History records persistent rebellion, an unmistakable refusal to accept Norman rule on Tyneside and to the north. William sent six men, natives and Normans, to assume the title of earl and attempt to bring the old earldom under control, and all of them failed. This political problem was of course compounded by the clear ambition of the Scottish kings to take every advantage of the instability in England and overrun the North, incorporating Northumbria into their kingdom. Today, the border may have been fixed on the Tweed and the Cheviots for almost 1,000 years, but in the 1060s and '70s, no such tradition existed. It was far from unthinkable that the reach of Scots kings should extend to the Tyne or the Tees, or even North Yorkshire. At some point in the recent past, they had ruled over all of these regions.

By 1072, William had deposed the uncooperative native Earl

Cospatric of Northumbria who had promptly sought asylum at the court of Malcolm III of Scotland. A powerful expeditionary force was gathered, and companies of Norman knights clattered up the old Roman roads to confront the Scots. Like most other invading armies, William's was supported by a fleet coasting north with supplies. Prudently, Malcolm opted for negotiation. Assurances, promises and hostages were given. But it meant little. In 1080, Malcolm sanctioned more invasions of Northumbria, and William quickly retaliated by sending his eldest son, Robert Curthose (a nickname conferred on him by his father which meant 'short boots'), on another expedition. It was not successful, and the border with Scotland had to be withdrawn to the line of the Tyne. In order to defend the lowest bridgehead on the river and force an invading army of Scots westwards to the fording point at Corbridge, Robert ordered the construction of a new castle on the site of the old Roman fort of Pons Aelius.

The name has of course stuck, but its use does beg an interesting question. What about the old castle? It had been nearly 1,000 years since Hadrian stepped ashore at the same place and had a fort built. Was that the old castle? It seems unlikely. Robert had the new castle made out of earth and wood rather than adapting Roman stonework – which had probably been robbed centuries before. Perhaps there had been a much more recent castle on the site, built to control movement over the bridge? Was it a fortress built to protect the 'famous royal estate' of Ad Murum mentioned by Bede? Perhaps the pre-existence of that old castle and its predecessors implies the continuance of the Roman bridge over all those centuries. Repaired, sometimes washed away, but nevertheless in use for almost a millennium? It is impossible to be sure, but Curthose's castle was noted as 'new' by the twelfth-century chronicler Symeon of Durham, who was usually precise in his language and certainly local enough to have known the history of the site.

The New Castle notwithstanding, instability continued in the North. A Frenchman, Walcher of Lorraine, had been appointed as Bishop of Durham in 1072 and when Waltheof, a native Earl of Northumbria, was executed for treason, the King decided to combine the two roles. Walcher became the first Earl-Bishop, an office which now appears on road signs announcing 'The Land of the Prince-Bishops'. The exaggeration is only slight. Because the bishopric of Durham extended up to and beyond Berwick-upon-Tweed, King William saw it as a frontier bulwark against the Scots and he empowered the Earl-Bishop to act independently – like a prince – when threats arose. Durham became a County Palatine, meaning that Walcher could behave as a sovereign, without prior reference to the King. Perhaps the word order led to the unique usage 'County Durham' instead of 'Durhamshire' or 'Durham County'. It is unique in England. Enduring for centuries, this unusual status proved to be the only effective political counterweight to the burgeoning local importance of the town of Newcastle.

DOMESDAY

Not long after it was compiled between Christmas 1085 and 1088, it became the Domesday Book – the Book of the Last Judgement. The name reflects the awe and wonder in which this great enterprise was held. Domesday was a systematic and highly detailed survey of all of England's counties south of the Tees and Ribble. The exclusion of Northumberland and Tyneside fairly reflects the uncertain politics of the area. William the Conqueror wanted to know two things from Domesday: how much his new kingdom was worth in taxable revenue and who owned what. But it was the blunt fact that it was all written down which proved to be as influential as any of the content. Custom and practice began to yield to facts committed to paper – even though these can be falsified or wrong – and gave rise to the modern preference for sworn, written statements over hearsay.

But the early earl-bishops failed to bargain on the strength of anti-Norman instincts in Northumbria. Walcher's officers murdered a native nobleman called Liulf Lumley, who appears to have aroused jealousies by becoming the Earl-Bishop's close confidant. On 13 May 1080, a meeting was arranged at Gateshead (the first recorded act in the town's history, incidentally). Walcher must have been surprised to be confronted by a large mob, angry at the murder of Liulf and demanding summary justice. Chants of 'Slay the Bishop!' began, and Walcher fled into the chapel of the Hospital of St Edmund, built to accommodate pilgrims on the road to the shrine of St Cuthbert at Durham. Incensed at this, the Gateshead mob set fire to the church, and when he was flushed out, they fell upon Walcher and butchered him. What happened next suggests that the riot developed into a rebellion of some military ambition and organisation. The Gateshead men marched south to Durham and laid a four-day siege to the castle, even though it was near-impregnable on the river peninsula of the Wear. The assault failed, but the point is that the mob clearly believed that they could take the power base of the earl-bishops.

The site of Robert Curthose's New Castle was almost as commanding as Durham, and no doubt the murder of Walcher and the abortive siege encouraged him and his men to get on with the building work in the late summer of 1080. The ruthlessness of the railway architects of the nineteenth century in driving a viaduct straight through the New Castle has made it difficult to appreciate how well situated it and the Pons Aelius fort were. Medieval labour gangs worked with mattocks, shovels and baskets, and their foremen would have been sorry to be dealing with heavy clay soil but glad to see steep inclines on three sides, where the ground falls away to the Tyne in the south and the now invisible Lort Burn (which once ran down the Side) in the east and north. This meant much less ditch-digging than usual. Curthose planted a motte-and-bailey castle, the sort of structure familiar in Normandy which had begun to pattern England and parts of Scotland after 1066. It was an all-purpose design able to provide a good defensive position anywhere, even on flat ground. The motte was a mound of earth on top of which a wooden stockade was hammered in. In later years, this focal point would usually be built of stone and became known as the keep, the last redoubt. It was always the most strongly fortified and defended place. Attached to the motte was a bailey, or stockaded enclosure, where people and animals could be ingathered and protected. All around the outer wall, defensive ditching was laid out, usually with only one gate crossing it. At the New Castle, the work gangs had only one set of ditches to dig, on the western edge of the site.

As did the Roman military architects, Curthose's men created a fortress roughly triangular in shape, an arrangement not unlike the much more complete medieval castles at Norham and Dunstanburgh. Historians often say that nothing now remains of the original Norman structure, but it is not true. Under the second arch (counting from the west) of the railway viaduct, archaeologists have come across the foundations of a small rectangular stone building erected soon after 1080. The stone looks to be Roman, reused by Curthose's labourers.

What visitors now see at Newcastle Castle dates from the late twelfth century. The stone keep was designed by a Frenchman, Mauricius Caementarius, or Maurice the Mason, and it rose between 1168 and 1178, costing £1,444. It has immensely thick walls, 18 ft in places, and is approximately square, with a single room on each of three storeys. Much smaller rooms have occasionally been formed in the width of the walls. Bits of the North Gate have also survived from Maurice's rebuilding. The other impressive fragment, the Black Gate, was added between 1247 and 1250. Its homely roof, chimneys and mullioned windows date from the seventeenth century, when it became a private house.

The Normans invested enormously in castles. As a small occupying force – there were only about 400 Normans on Tyneside and in Northumberland in the twelfth century – they depended on a network of strongpoints from which they could control the countryside and to which they could safely retreat if the huge majority of natives ever combined against them, as at Gateshead in 1080. Strategic positioning had to be precise, and the effect of Curthose's New Castle was not only to command the lowest bridge over the Tyne but also to plug the eastern end of the Hexham Gap. When his brother, William Rufus, became King of England in 1087, Carlisle Castle was built (also on the site of a Roman fort) and this inhibited invading Scots armies from attacking Tyneside from the west.

If a bridge over the Tyne stood in 1080 – and the construction of the castle seems to suggest that it did – it may well have been a wooden superstructure carried across by Roman piers. By 1175, the wood had been replaced by stone, and, as with the old London Bridge or the surviving Ponte Vecchio in Florence, it had houses built on it. The northern half was owned and maintained by the growing town of Newcastle and the southern by the earl-bishops of Durham. Apparently, there were more houses on the Durham half. In 1248, the bridge was damaged by fire, but not until 1771, when serious flooding swept part of it away, did it need replacing entirely. The new bridge of 1775 was eventually supplanted by the Swing Bridge in 1868–76 to allow upriver navigation for high-masted ships; but under the roadway at the north end, the sharp-eyed can still make out an arch of the medieval bridge.

William the Conqueror died in 1087 fighting his own son, Robert Curthose, and the King of France. Robert was impatient to inherit the Duchy of Normandy, and, although disappointed that England had gone to his brother, William Rufus, he and his contemporaries saw the duchy as the more valuable property. But after a time, the new Duke determined to remove his brother from the throne and have all that his father had enjoyed. Robert's support centred in the North. The new Earl of Northumbria was Robert Mowbray, and the successor of Walcher was Bishop William of Durham. Both plotted on Curthose's behalf.

William Rufus moved quickly, besieging Durham Castle and driving the bishop into exile in France. Robert Mowbray survived behind the walls of Bamburgh Castle but was eventually captured in 1095. It turned out to be a seminal moment in the history of Tyneside. After 30 years of rebellion and turbulence in Northumbria, the Norman kings took the area into their personal domain and began to divide it up amongst their followers. But most importantly, a decision was taken to develop Newcastle as a trading centre.

> ## GAY NORMANS
>
> Sodomy was violently condemned by the Church in the twelfth century, partly because it was so common in monasteries, where relationships between men could be otherwise divisive. Homosexuality was also the object of especial disapproval in the Old Testament, being regarded as a sexual deviation, a sin against nature. Many gay men were burned by the Inquisition, but, as usual, the upper classes enjoyed much more tolerance. King William Rufus was certainly gay, as was Edward II. His favourite, Pierre Gaveston, was murdered in 1312, and the King himself cruelly dispatched in 1327 by having a red-hot poker shoved up his rectum.

Kings needed cash, and successful trading towns could supply it. Between 1100 and 1135, Henry I of England promulgated the Laws of Newcastle, a very early codification of commercial privileges granted to the town and its merchants. In order to regulate and extract tax from trade, it was necessary in the Middle Ages to concentrate it in a few focal points of import and export. With its excellent bridgehead position on the Tyne, a navigable river with long hinterlands to both north and south, Newcastle was well placed. And after Earl Robert Mowbray's removal in 1095, direct royal control meant direct royal action. A king's bailiff was appointed and for farmers and herdsmen, all roads began to lead to Newcastle. There had been an Anglo-Saxon burgh at nearby Newburn, but it was rejected as a likely site and after 1201 no more is heard of it.

Central to medieval trade were regular markets, and these developed to the north-west of the parish church of St Nicholas. It is generally accepted that the church was consecrated in 1091, perhaps by St Osmund, another earl-bishop, this time of Dorset and Salisbury. Initially built out of wood on stone footings, St Nicholas stood hard by the stockade of Curthose's New Castle, and by 1122 its priests were made subject to the Prior of Carlisle – not Durham, as might have been more convenient. The ravine of the Lort Burn prevented

Newcastle's markets being set up to the east of the church, and what became the Bigg Market ('bigg' is an Old English word for barley) and the Groat Market ('groat' meant 'oats') stretched away to the north-west. It appears that, when the castle and church were built, there was no pre-existing settlement in the immediate area. Around St Andrews Church stood the shadowy Anglo-Saxon settlement of Monkchester, and there was another small village at Pandon in the east. Eventually, the Bigg Market and the Groat Market became part of a long lane connecting early Newcastle with Monkchester and its ancient church. The deep gulleys of the Lort and Pandon burns made expansion to the east slower and more difficult.

PAGAN, URBAN, POLITE

In the thirteenth century, many small to medium-sized towns like Newcastle were created and quickly flourished. And, unlike during the period of the Roman Empire, when Rome itself was really the only major urban centre in western Europe, many large towns grew up. Palermo and Barcelona had around 50,000 inhabitants; London, Ghent and Genoa 60,000; Bologna and Milan closer to 75,000; Florence and Venice around 100,000; and largest of all was Paris, which had a population of 200,000. Language began to reflect the division between country and town dwellers. The word 'peasant' or *paysan* is cognate to 'pagan', while the adjectives 'urbane' and 'polite' derive from the Latin and Greek words for a town, *urbs* and *polis*.

Towns are often built on top of their own history, and almost all of medieval Newcastle has been covered by the modern city. But some sense of what the early streets and houses looked like can be gleaned from analogy and archaeology. As at other twelfth-century town sites controlled by a royal bailiff, it seems that expansion was planned. Carlisle was divided into English, Irish, Flemish and Norman quarters, and streets were laid out on the decayed Roman grid plan. At Newcastle, it was the lie of the land which governed development. The

Bigg and Groat markets were roughly metalled streets covered with gravel and small stones, and also fouled by a good deal of rubbish (this problem grew to such an extent that the castle's ditches were eventually used as tips). Houses lined the streets but behind each there was usually a back yard of sorts. This was reached by alleyways which ran down the side of each plot. Most twelfth-century town houses were one storey high, 27 to 30 ft long by 12 to 15 ft wide, with the gable end fronting onto the street. These buildings were neither robust nor durable. To create the walls, stakes were driven into the ground and withies woven between them like basketwork, in the same way that hurdle fences are still constructed now. Mud, clay, straw or even dung was plastered on and allowed to dry so that the walls gained some solidity. Sometimes turf or peat was banked against them. And sometimes a ditch was dug along the projected line of posts and filled with loose stones before being topped with a crust of puddle clay. The idea was to mitigate rising damp. This rudimentary method of construction restricted the height of the walls to no more than 5 ft. Roofs were usually thatched and supported by a ridge pole slung between two uprights at either gable. Reached by the alleyway, doorways were set in one of the long walls and the doors themselves made out of wooden planking. In the centre of a beaten clay, sand or gravel floor (covered with bracken, heather or straw, and often mixed with meadowsweet to keep the smell manageable) sat the focus of the house, the down-hearth. This was a stone hearth on which an open fire burned to provide heat, light and a means of cooking.

SANTA CLAUS

As every child (and adult) should know, the name Santa Claus is a fragmented rendition of St Nicholas, the saint to whom Newcastle's cathedral is dedicated. Now understood to have been a purely legendary figure, there are nevertheless many stories associated with him. Having become a priest, Nicholas gave away his great wealth to the poor, and when he heard of a nobleman who had lost his fortune, he showed equal generosity. The saint threw bags of gold through the nobleman's windows at night-time. One of the most famous legends concerns Nicholas's discovery of three corpses of little children killed by a wicked innkeeper. By a miracle, of course, the saint brought them back to life and in consequence became the patron saint of little children. His dedication at Newcastle is surprising, though, particularly in view of the growing cult of the Virgin Mary and the popularity of St Cuthbert. The reason was both political and cultural. Norman expansionism had not only conquered England but also created the remarkable kingdom of Sicily and southern Italy. In 1071, the relics of St Nicholas were brought to Bari and a church built to house them. It was not his charity towards children which commended the saint to the Normans but the fact that he was the protector of travellers and sailors. That fitted in well with their plans for Newcastle.

The construction of early medieval town houses, with wall stakes in direct contact with the earth and therefore progressively rotting, did not allow a life longer than about 20 years. But this mattered less than it might have because many towns regularly suffered devastating fires, and a primary cause of these must have been sparks from the down-hearth floating up to a thatched roof on a windy day.

Drains found in the back yards of twelfth-century medieval towns show where animals were kept overnight, a milking cow and hens, for example, and these highlight a recurrent difficulty – the preservation of a clean water supply. Water was often supplied by cisterns and wells which were not only in danger of being contaminated by animal faeces but also by the sewage of the householders, who sometimes dug cesspits in restricted plots which were too close to a water supply. Typhoid and a host of other water-borne diseases raged through populations packed together in the streets of medieval Newcastle and the lack of reliably clean water always inhibited the growth of towns, particularly when they expanded quickly. The widespread brewing of ale was partly a method of avoiding a doubtful water supply. In a quirky but significant footnote from another historical period, the eighteenth-century fashion for drinking tea helped to break the Malthusian cycle and allowed the great northern cities of the Industrial Revolution – Manchester, Leeds, Newcastle and the others – to grow rapidly without the outbreak of decimating disease. Not only was water boiled before being drunk, but tea itself had long been considered a tonic drink in the Far East, with mild antibiotic properties.

PILGRIMS

Partly because his apparently genuinely pious life was so well recorded by Bede, St Cuthbert became the most revered and best-loved saint of the North. When work began on Durham Cathedral in 1093, a shrine of great magnificence was planned for his relics. Pilgrims flocked to pray beside his tomb, many touching it as they implored God's grace. This was the point of relics and shrines, to bring the faithful closer to God through the intercession of a saint. Durham grew rich on Cuthbert's bones and became the wealthiest see in England, the earl-bishops the most powerful magnates in the North. In 1540, the agents of Henry VIII broke into the cathedral and tore the gilded shrine to pieces, ransacking the cupboards of relics and removing the Lindisfarne Gospels to London (where, shamefully, they remain). The body of the saint was hurriedly reburied in the precinct. In 1827, a group of antiquaries tentatively dug into the secret grave. Miraculously, they found treasures: Cuthbert's gorgeous pectoral cross of gold and garnets, an ivory comb, a travelling altar encased in silver and a medieval copy of St John's Gospel. Pilgrims can now see something of the ancient splendour of the shrine, and Pilgrim Street in Newcastle remembers the route once taken by those who came from the north to cross the Tyne Bridge and be near the beloved saint at Durham.

At Newcastle, royal protectionism encouraged enthusiastic mercantile protectionism. Henry I's Laws laid the careful foundations of a trading monopoly:

> No merchant unless he be a burgess may buy [outside] the town either wool or leather or other merchandise, nor within the borough except [from other] burgesses . . . and no one but a burgess may buy webs [cloth] to dye, nor make nor cut them.

By 1170, the Newcastle burgesses agreed to pay the king an annual tax of £100 in return for a degree of independence and the substitution of the royal bailiff for one appointed by themselves. This was Daniel, son of Nicholas, and although the use of the title lay in the future, he is generally accepted as the first mayor of Newcastle. Municipal independence allowed the merchants to tighten their grip on trade and town government, twin aims which they pursued relentlessly. And that grip only slackened significantly in the twentieth century.

MAYORS AND MYSTERIES

Nowadays, the Lord Mayor of Newcastle holds office for a year and it is largely an honorary position. Earlier mayors often stayed in the job for several years and some returned to office quite frequently. In a complex system, mayors in medieval Newcastle were elected by members of the guilds known as the Twelve Mysteries. These were craft guilds, and the term derived from the same Latin source as 'ministry'. But in 1340–41, there was a row. An openly corrupt candidate called John Denton was sworn in and the 'lesser burgesses' retaliated by supporting an alternative, Richard de Acton. They seized the town gates, the symbol of Newcastle, and a riot ensued. The sword now carried in front of the mayoral procession has nothing to do with rival candidates; the right to bear it was a ceremonial privilege granted by King Richard II after Mayor William Bishopdale fought bravely at the Battle of Otterburn in 1388. The oar which is also carried relates to Newcastle's jurisdiction over the tidal river.

Medieval Newcastle was growing fast. Business boomed. In the later thirteenth century, buildings lined a long street between the churches of St Nicholas and St Andrew at Monkchester, connecting the Bigg and Groat markets with Newgate Street. A new parish, St John's, was created around the Westgate, and, while no population statistics yet existed, it is likely that more than 5,000 souls lived in the town. Merchants tended to build their houses and warehouses at the Sandhill, and thus the warren of 'chares' leading down to the quayside was created. 'Chare' may derive from the French word '*charge*' which means a load, cargo or pack.

This eastward development linked Newcastle with the little industrial village of Pandon. Cloth-finishing and brewing were its major occupations, and dyers, fullers (workers who used various techniques to bulk out newly woven cloth) and brewers used the waters of the Pandon Burn and a spring in Croswellgate (now Pandon Street) for their business. To regulate all of this activity, the merchants of Newcastle were granted the right to form a guild in 1216. This was an important consolidation, and it encouraged aggressive protectionism. In 1258, the guild persuaded the Earl-Bishop of Durham (surely with payment of some kind rather than out of the goodness of his Christian heart) not to develop a port at his village of South Shields. In 1290, the Prior of Tynemouth attempted to create another port at North Shields. Because of the tendency of the lower Tyne to silt up, this initiative made every sort of economic sense, and very quickly quays, bakeries, breweries and about 100 houses grew up. The merchants of Newcastle were incensed, immediately petitioning Parliament, claiming that their businesses were being dangerously undermined. And when it was explained to Edward I's exchequer clerks that royal revenue would be cut drastically – since the Prior of Tynemouth planned to retain the customs income for himself – Parliament ordered that the new port at North Shields be suppressed. And more, that the Newcastle merchants should have unfettered control of trade on the tidal river. Fishing became Tynemouth's uncontroversial business, and by 1329, there existed 14 fish quays and more than 200 fishermen's cottages.

FRIARS BLACK AND GREY

The early thirteenth century saw the foundation of two new religious orders, inspired by the exemplary lives of St Francis and St Dominic. The Black Friars, or Dominicans, and the Franciscans, or Grey Friars, were anxious to spread the gospel by preaching and pious example, and they both targeted towns like Newcastle. Because they wished to remain faithful to the early Christian ideal of poverty and true to Jesus's message, the Dominicans and Franciscans began as mendicant, or begging, orders, living only on what people gave them. But, inevitably, their success brought material reward, and by the fourteenth century, both owned substantial property and the papacy began to appoint bishops from the ranks of Europe's friars. 'Friar' derived from the French word for brother, 'frère'.

At Gateshead, the Newcastle merchants were equally robust in defence of their interests. The Earl-Bishop of Durham complained about, then was forced to prosecute, the Newcastle guild because it sent gangs of thugs to wreck his quays at Whickham and Gateshead. And by 1415, no doubt exasperated, Durham had occasion once again to move against Newcastle for the return of their section of the Tyne Bridge. Reasonably enough, the merchants pleaded that the Earl-Bishop's men had not maintained the bridge properly. In 1553, the pressure redoubled when Newcastle tried to annexe Gateshead entirely and there was a plan to raise a new bishopric based on the Church of St Nicholas. But the sponsoring king, Edward VI, inconveniently died, and Durham stayed in charge.

The Earl-Bishop also managed to confine much of Newcastle's economic activity north of the Tyne and to that part of Northumberland which lay to the south of the river, below Hexham. Hides, wool and fleeces were the staple exports, and the town became a processing centre for animals. In the Middle Ages, it was much easier and more sensible to drive cattle, sheep and goats on the hoof to the point of export. That meant animal-killing on a semi-industrial scale around Newcastle. Herdsmen and their lords hoped to derive income from several products. The hides of their animals were tanned into leather on the outskirts of the town. Since this process involved steeping hides in pits filled with noxious ingredients like dog turds and urine, no one wanted to live next door to a tannery and these were always expelled to the margins of medieval towns. It is no accident that the Skinner's Burn ran well to the west of the medieval walls. Fleshers, or butchers, then sold or salted the carcasses; horn-carvers made bone spoons, cups and ladles; and candle-makers refined the tallow. Almost nothing was wasted. By 1290, Newcastle was the leading exporter of English leather. Sheep produced fleeces which were bundled into large bales known as woolpacks, and if the animals were slaughtered, their fleeces were left on the sheepskins and sold in that form. The need to pen and pasture large numbers of animals driven down from Northumberland farms no doubt played a part in the survival of such a large Town Moor.

The stimulus for this boom in trade came from Flanders, France and northern Italy, where cloth and leather goods began to be produced in industrial quantities for re-export as well as domestic consumption. What created this demand for raw wool and hides was not new technology but the first effective deployment of merchant capital. Flemish and Italian merchants became very wealthy and powerful through taking control of supply, production and marketing. The only part of the integrated process that was beyond them was the actual rearing of sheep and cattle.

Once the raw Northumbrian wool had been cleaned in the French and Flemish depots at towns like Middleburg and St Valery, the importing merchants then distributed it to a network of outworkers. Having set up frames or looms in their cottages or sheds big enough to accommodate several people, men and women spun yarn or wove it into cloth before returning it to the entrepreneurs who controlled the trade in Flanders. The Flemings in particular were active in Newcastle, and there is a faint echo of their presence still to be heard. Foreign merchants were in the habit of establishing a base in English and Scottish wool ports, a place like a primitive embassy where their own customs and laws obtained. In Berwick-upon-Tweed, the Flemings' base was known as The Red Hall. And in a group of sixteenth-century houses still standing in the Sandhill in Newcastle, five of them are still known as The Red House, a name which may remember the site of the Flemish trading centre.

HANSA

At its peak, the Hanseatic League of trading cities had a membership of more than 200. Based on the Baltic and North Sea coastlines, it was a federation of autonomous ports with a shared interest in facilitating commerce. Rights of anchorage, storage, residence and local immunity were sought for Hanseatic merchants and they certainly found all of those at Newcastle, although the town was not a member of the League. The most important ports were Hamburg, Lübeck and Bremen, and car number plates for each city still have an 'H' in front of them for 'Hansa'. Absolutely vital to the lubrication of trade was a widely acceptable standard of payment and stable currencies. Hansa merchants were often called 'Easterlings' in England and the term 'pound sterling' derives from that nickname.

More than 85 per cent of all ships docking at the Newcastle quayside at the end of the thirteenth century belonged to Flemish or French merchants, but those who sold them the wool and leather were almost all English. This may seem obvious, but elsewhere the Europeans managed to take over even more of this lucrative trade, buying up entire wool crops direct from the producers, often large monasteries with a great deal of sheep pasture. No ship crossed the North Sea empty, and when they sailed up the Tyne, many carried all manner of exotic items: pepper, sugar, onions, cinnamon, garlic, spices, rice, metal pans and cauldrons, locks and much else. But by far the most common import was wine. Much of it no doubt went for private consumption, but the vast bulk was imported for clergymen. Wine was needed for use in the communion mass. One of the problems outgoing ships had was ballast. For their volume, wool and leather were not heavy, so an export trade in Gateshead grindstones grew up, the hard whinstone having been mined in the Gateshead Fells. Stowed in the bottom of the hold, they kept ships from being knocked down in the North Sea swells.

By the middle of the thirteenth century, Newcastle had grown sufficiently in scale and confidence to build its own walls. It is often asserted that they were raised in response to Scottish raids, but in fact there had been an unusually long period of peace, for 20 years, and in 1251, Alexander III of Scotland had married Margaret, the daughter of Henry III of England. Newcastle's walls were built to define the town, to create a clear and impressive distinction between urban and rural, inside and outside, between places where different customs and jurisdictions operated. All over medieval Europe, towns and their wealthier merchants were paying military engineers and architects substantial sums to create ramparts, towers and heavily fortified gates. Behind this, there was certainly a sound and sensible defensive purpose and a defining economic one – but the overwhelming motive was prestige. Proper towns had walls. And once Newcastle acquired the right to use seals and coats of arms, a representation of the walls became its potent symbol. The three towers on Newcastle's shield are not emblematic of the castle, as is often assumed. Each tower has a gate in it; they stand for the walls, the property and initiative of the merchants who used the seal, rather than the castle, which belonged to the King.

At 2 miles in length, never less than 7 ft thick and up to 25 ft in height, with six fortified gateways (at Sand Gate, West Gate, New Gate, Pandon Gate, Pilgrim Gate and Close Gate), the walls were not cheap. And they took a long time to complete, the advent of Edward I's war with Scotland encouraging the builders to lay the final stones in the early fourteenth century. Some impressive fragments remain. Parallel with Stowell Street in the west of the city centre there is a long run, and bits of several towers and gates are to be found elsewhere.

As a port processing animal products, Newcastle was busy; but at Berwick-upon-Tweed, business was a great deal more brisk. With the huge hinterland of sheep ranches in the Cheviots, the Lammermuirs and the upper Tweed Valley, and a network of well-organised monasteries putting wool production on a professional footing, much more trafficked through Berwick. Customs, or duty paid on goods, is a reliable indicator of throughput, and in 1286 the annual revenue at Berwick was more than £2,000, while in 1282 at Newcastle, it was £323, less than a sixth of that.

History and geology combined to change that late-thirteenth-century snapshot radically. Coal had been burned for warmth by the garrisons of Hadrian's Wall and its Tyneside forts, and no doubt long before. Until the late Middle Ages, all coal was known as sea coal, or *carbo marinus*, probably because that is where it first appeared to come from. On the North Sea beaches around Tyneside, early users, almost certainly prehistoric, gathered sea coal washed ashore after it had subsided off exposed sea-cliff seams, which had in turn been loosened by wind and waves. Nevertheless, the term applied to coal mined as far inland as the pits at Lumley or Rainton. Early coal mines are correctly called pits. Where a seam was near the surface, miners dug straight down to reach it and then excavated along it in as many directions as it ran and as far as they dared. In this way, the pit acquired a bell-shape. At most, the miners delved down to a depth of 90 ft. The coal was lifted in baskets by winding gear at the mouth of the pit, and the miners climbed in and out by a series of ladders. Collapse occurred when the base of the bell shape became too wide and the roof unstable. Flooding was another recurrent difficulty. Early mining disasters were recorded at Whickham and Thrislington, but loss of life was likely so common as rarely to merit much notice.

Cheap bulk cargos need to be easily transported to keep costs down, and the key to the expansion of Newcastle's medieval coal trade lay in the handy location of the seams. Many of them were dug near the river, and once coal had been hacked out of the bell pits, it could be loaded into panniers on the backs of packhorses or, if the roads and tracks were not impossibly rutted or waterlogged, into carts pulled by oxen. If a bell pit was located more than 3 miles from the river, as much as 60 per cent could be added to production costs. Most of Tyneside's medieval coal came from pits west of Newcastle. On the north bank of the river, rich surface seams were worked at Elswick, Denton, Benwell and Newburn, while on the south there were extensive workings at Whickham and Gateshead.

COG

Coal was carried in clinker-built cogs in the Middle Ages. These were developed from the Viking cargo ships known as knorrs, a name now found only on soup packets. Clinker building used long planks of wood overlapped, shaped and riveted into the familiar shape of a hull. The bottom planks were first attached to a keel running the whole length of the ship, making a double-ended shape. In the twelfth and thirteenth centuries, the cog design came into common use. It had a clinker-built hull but no keel. Instead, a flat bottom was formed out of heavy timbers and one end made blunt so that a new sternpost rudder could be fixed. This design allowed cogs to sit on the mud of a harbour when the tide went out and stopped them from 'keeling over'. The clinker sides of cogs were usually built up high to take more cargo, and this meant a frame was required to stiffen the structure. They had a single mast and a square sail, which was hoisted on a yard from the planked-over deck. Warships had a 'castle' built onto the hull. But the earliest recorded ship launched on the Tyne was another type, a galley. This was a rowed vessel more like a Viking ship, and the town of Newcastle paid for one to be made for Edward I in 1291.

Miners followed what they judged was the likely line of coal seams, and when one bell pit had reached a dangerous size or had begun to flood, they moved further along the line and opened up another pit.

The effect on the landscape cannot have been picturesque, and in 1256, travellers complained that night-time journeys on the road between Newcastle and Corbridge had become hazardous. People were falling into new ditches and pits.

The existence of the old Tyne Bridge and the tendency of the river to silt up meant that small boats known as keels had to be used to bring coal downriver from the western pits. When packhorses or carts arrived at the coal quays, or 'staiths', they unloaded into the keels, which were then rowed down to where tall-masted ships waited below the bridge. Some could be anchored as far down as North Shields. Because of its serpentine shape, sea captains and keelmen knew the Tyne as 'the River Dragon'. Few medieval sailors relished winter voyages, and this made the coal trade seasonal, the keelmen often coming down every spring from the valleys of north and west Northumberland, or even as far away as Scotland. By 1516, the keelmen had become respectable, consolidating themselves into a craft guild, and one of Newcastle's most impressive old buildings is the Keelmen's Hospital of 1701, which still stands in City Road.

KEEL ROW

Keelmen lived around the Newcastle street which recalls the old gate in the city walls known as the Sandgate. There is an oft-repeated tradition that they wore a particular sort of uniform: a blue jacket, a bright yellow waistcoat, bell-bottom trousers and a black silk hat tied with a ribbon. If they did, then they must have been daft. A yellow waistcoat! Five minutes loading and unloading coal from a staith would soon have rendered everything uniformly black. It all sounds like a bit of Victorian quaint. Many keelmen came from the Northumberland valleys and the Scottish Borders, and their habit of wearing a blue bonnet sounds much more plausible. Anyone who works with coal wants headgear to keep the dust out of their hair. And the famous Keel Row song has a slight Scottish lilt to it.

In the Middle Ages, coal was not used domestically, at least not outside Tyneside. Its smell was thought to be noxious, and wood was always preferred for heating and cooking. This attitude persisted, and in 1598, the writer John Stowe noted that 'the nice dames of London [would not] come into any house where sea-coales were burnt, or willingly eat of the meat which was either smoked or roasted with sea-coal'. It was industrial use which sparked the growth in mining. The first shipment of coals carried from Newcastle to London was recorded in 1305, and by 1377, the trade had reached 15,000 tons a year. Production stayed on this plateau for 150 years, despite a plentiful supply, and, while expansion was certainly inhibited by technological stagnation, there were also economic reasons. Much of the Tyneside coalfield was controlled by the Church, and priors, abbots and bishops set early limits on output. The pits at Elswick belonged to the Prior of Tynemouth, and when he leased them, it was stipulated that only 31 tons a day could be taken out. Perhaps the extent of God's Providence was not to be tested too far.

Not all of Tyneside's coal was exported. In 1990, archaeologists digging at Newcastle's Quayside came across the remains of eight medieval limekilns. It appears that coal ships brought an inward cargo of limestone as ballast in their holds, and the means of processing it stood immediately to hand at the quay. Using local coal, the stone was burned down into powdered lime, which in turn was a vital constituent of builder's mortar, or used as a fertiliser or as an ingredient in bleach. The cloth-finishers of Pandon may have been a ready market for the latter. And at South Shields, salt-panning developed, sea water being heated by coal to produce valuable sea salt.

King Henry VIII's marital problems and his consequent antipathy for the Catholic Church supplied an unexpected stimulus to the stagnating coal trade. When Henry dissolved the monasteries in the 1530s, the restrictions on output evaporated, and through the sixteenth century, the tonnage coming out of Tyneside's pits rocketed tenfold. By 1603, more than 162,000 tons a year was being shipped out; by 1608–9, it was 239,000; and 25 years later, it stood at 425,000. Newcastle coal had become famous, and indispensable to many industries.

This remarkable rise had also been driven by a group of sharp Tyneside businessmen. As with other traded items, coal could only move through the port of Newcastle if its buying and selling were handled by the town's burgesses. These had become known as Hostmen, or middlemen. The medieval monopoly granted by Henry I was still firmly in place, and it was about to pay tremendous dividends to a small group of canny merchants. Towards the end of the sixteenth century, two burgesses, Henry Anderson and William Selby, began to buy up leases in the Tyneside coalfield. Using municipal funds and acting on behalf of about 20 other burgesses, they quickly acquired a near-total monopoly on the production of coal. This became known as the Grand Lease. And the Hostmen were soon being called the 'Lords of Coal'. It was one thing to make money buying from pit-owners and selling on to consumers – but quite another to control both production and export.

In 1600, Elizabeth I ratified the Grand Lease and its stranglehold monopoly in return for payment of a tax on coal shipped down the river. The Hostmen took over town government and in the period from 1600 to 1640 only one of the twenty-five mayors of Newcastle was not a hostman. Political and economic power protected this highly lucrative position, and even aristocratic outsiders, like the Earl of Northumberland, could not break in. It was expensive and risky to develop new pits. They could flood easily, or they were less productive than hoped or too far away from water transport. And London buyers could make it very difficult for those outside the Grand Lease because they often kept suppliers waiting long periods, up to a year, for payment. Because of the scale of their business, the Hostmen could absorb all of these problems and still make fortunes for the members. Grand houses began to rise in and around Newcastle.

The Lords of Coal were not the only Tyneside merchants to become extremely wealthy. Throughout the Middle Ages, men had made money in Newcastle, mostly from the profits of the wool and leather trade. Two extended families, the Scots and the Carliols (both sound as though they were originally outsiders), dominated up to 1300, a member of one of them usually holding the office of mayor. And the idea of monopoly had not been pioneered in the North-east only by the Hostmen. In 1305, the so-called 'poor burgesses' complained to Parliament that 'by sinister collusion amongst themselves' the wealthier burgesses were excluding them from their legitimate business. There must have been a disparity of income between these two sets of merchants, but it will have seemed trivial in comparison to that between both groups and the mass of ordinary people. Medieval records are mostly silent on the lives of these people, but some generalities are possible.

In the early Middle Ages, society was overwhelmingly rural – but not isolated. The Domesday Book recorded a dense landscape of farming settlements perhaps best described as villages. These were always owned by a lord, or the King, or by the Church in the shape of a monastery or a bishop, and they were occupied by various sorts of men and their families. As over the rest of Britain, in medieval Tyneside agricultural workers were bonded in some way to the land they worked, paying rentals in kind and labour. They had no secure hold and few rights over it. There is a record of the duties owed by a small farmer in 1295. John Preston of Tynemouth farmed 36 acres belonging to the Prior. In return, he had to work for two days each week on the Prior's own land, ploughing in the winter, planting in the spring and harvesting in the autumn. But the thirteenth century saw a tremendous expansion of agriculture, with more land being brought into cultivation, even in the heavy clays of south Northumberland. And the weather was good, according to meteorological historians. Longer and warmer growing seasons sometimes allowed more than one cut of hay, and winters were less severe.

Some agricultural workers were more free than others, and the Domesday survey found that about 10 per cent of England's people were slaves. In 1256, William of Killingworth argued that he should be released from what was effectively slavery. But the courts ruled against him, and he was returned 'with all his family and goods' to his master, Galfridus of Weteslade.

THINGS

Attitudes to slaves still shock us. In antiquity, the Romans, Greeks and others based their entire economies on them and treated slaves as objects, as a commodity to buy and sell – or even kill or rape – with no regard whatever for their humanity. The medieval slave trade in England was no different, and a slave was referred to in Latin as *'res'*, or a 'thing', or as *'instrumentum vocalis'*, a 'talking tool'. But gradually, these inhumanities faded, and by approximately 1600, English men and women were no longer so regarded. Their place was being taken by black people.

When the church became important again on Tyneside, this led to better agrarian organisation. In 1074, Aldwine of Winchcombe began the revival of a once vibrant monastic culture. Although he found the church at Tynemouth to be uninhabitable, he had Jarrow rebuilt and a shrine to St Bede set up. Tynemouth was eventually reroofed and refurbished and its extensive lands were reclaimed and steadily augmented in the twelfth and thirteenth centuries.

SLAVE LANGUAGE

At least four languages were spoken on Tyneside in the Middle Ages. Latin, or 'book language', was spoken, written and sung by the Church, and it was the language of the Bible. Perhaps the version spoken by clerics sounded like Papal Latin, a close cousin to Italian. French was the language of the ruling class, the Normans, and Edward I (1272–1307) was the first English king who could speak English. For more than 200 years, his predecessors were unable to understand what 90 per cent of their subjects said. Norman French loaned about 10,000 words to English, but it was a particular dialect and it influenced our pronunciation heavily. For example, standard Parisian French says 'question' with a hard 'k', while Norman French kept the 'w' to give us 'kwestion' – also 'kwarter', 'kwit' and so on. The continued use of Celtic personal names in upper Tynedale strongly suggests that isolated hill communities still spoke a version of Old Welsh – as they certainly did in Cumbria. English was the language of the vast majority on medieval Tyneside and it was known as the vernacular. 'Verna' is Latin for a 'home-born slave', and that is how English was seen, as the language of the underclass, 'slave language'.

The land looked different 750 years ago. As elsewhere, cultivation on Tyneside was arranged in strips or rigs (measured out in ploughing time), and each tenant tilled a patchwork of these around a village. There were no fences, only drainage ditches separating the strips, and the landscape had fewer trees than it does now. Because houses and barns were made out of local stone or wood, and thatched with broom, heather or straw harvested within walking or carting distance, they would have blended in, perhaps even been difficult to make out from a distance. In wintertime, animals were brought in to the cultivated strips so that they could be fed with hay and other forage, and also muck the land to restore some of its fertility. When spring came in, the herds were driven off the strips and away to upland or other pasture. In the North-east, summer quarters for herdsmen were known as shielings, and that is the derivation of the place names of North and South Shields. On the Tyneside clay, only the free-draining land was cultivated, and many low-lying meadows would have been given over to year-round pasture.

All of the modern River Towns were tiny in the medieval period. Only Newcastle could boast any size, and at its peak of approximately 5,000 inhabitants in the thirteenth century, it would have dominated the countryside. Its weekly markets attracted suppliers from a wide catchment area, and the goods made by craftsmen in the town would have found a steady demand. Up until the last decade of the thirteenth century, Newcastle and Tyneside prospered in what historians call the climatic optimum, the balmy summer of the Middle Ages, and most lives were lived in relative peace.

In March 1286, King Alexander III of Scotland made an ill-starred night journey to visit his young and beautiful bride, Queen Yolande, at his manor of Kinghorn on the south coast of Fife. The King became detached from his escort, and his horse spooked on the path and threw him over the cliff. Next morning, his servants found Alexander's body on the beach; the last Gaelic King of Scotland was dead, and the male line of the MacMalcolm dynasty was no more. He had left no heir except a little girl, 'the Maid of Norway', and the problems of the royal succession propelled Scotland into a long and destructive period of war with England. For three centuries, much of that war was fought in the fields and meadows of Northumberland and on Tyneside.

When Edward I of England involved himself in settling the Scottish succession, he chose the unfortunate John Balliol as king. He was the son of John Balliol of Barnard Castle. In 1296, Edward's pressure proved intolerable and a Scots army invaded Northumberland. It was thrown back to Dunbar, but a year later, William Wallace was more successful, burning Hexham, Corbridge and Ryton. The new walls of Newcastle were too daunting and the Scots withdrew. But King Robert the Bruce and his lieutenants mounted at least six major raids before his death in 1329, and many more followed as the fourteenth century wore on.

The effects of decades of international conflict on agriculture were severe enough, but when long periods of extreme cold weather and successive waves of torrential rains caused several harvests to fail between 1315 and 1322, there was widespread famine in the North-east. The very young and very old died before their time, but the mortality rate would seem as nothing in the calamitous year of 1349.

THE LITTLE ICE AGE

Between 1300 and 1850, with some warmer intervals, what is now known as the Little Ice Age gripped Britain. In the early fourteenth century, cold and persistently wet summers reduced harvest yields and also had significant political effects. Torrential rain mired King Robert the Bruce's siege engines in the mud around Carlisle's town walls in 1315, and he was forced to abandon the assault. If the sun had shone and the victory at Bannockburn the year before had been consolidated, then much of the North might have passed into Scots hands and perhaps stayed there. Glacier measurement in the Alps shows dramatic surges in very cold winters in the 1590s, the 1690s and the 1810s. William Shakespeare's London held ice fairs on the Thames and a particularly severe winter decimated Napoleon's army as it retreated from Moscow in 1812.

Spreading westwards from southern Asia, the pandemic known as the Black Death struck Tyneside, probably brought in by sea. Its name came from the black blood which oozed from painful swellings in the groin, called buboes. Death was agonising but fast. After a brief and undetectable incubation, fever consumed and killed victims within 24 to 36 hours. So many died so quickly that the normal offices of the Church were suspended and across Europe many millions were thrown into mass graves. People realised that the plague was contagious because of the way in which it tore through tightly packed communities like Newcastle and was slower to reach more isolated places, sometimes bypassing them entirely. People died alone, writhing in agony, because their families were not allowed to gather around their beds, and extreme unction was almost never delivered. Funerals were abandoned and the possessions of victims were burned, especially their clothes. The Black Death paid many visits to Tyneside – five times it returned before 1400. Population suffered a catastrophic drop – in England it fell from seven million in 1348 to two million by 1400 – and there were further outbreaks of plague in the fifteenth and sixteenth centuries.

PLAGUES

Bubonic plague was the most common killer but not the only one. There were other lethal variants. Septicaemic plague poisoned the blood, and, like bubonic, it was carried by fleas hosted on black rats – also known as 'ship rats'.

Ports like Newcastle were infested by many thousands of them. Pneumonic, or pulmonary, plague affected the lungs and was particularly fast and deadly. Hardly anyone recovered, and the only way to avoid becoming infected was to flee to the country. The Italian writer Boccaccio created *The Decameron* as a direct result of the plague in Florence, where it killed more than 100,000. It told the story of a group of wealthy young people staying in the countryside to avoid 'the foul pestilence'.

The psychological impact must have been devastating, but it is difficult to gauge. Tombs of the period in St Nicholas Church and elsewhere carry a greater emphasis on the theme of *memento mori*, or 'remember that you will die', and corpses and skulls are suddenly well represented. The economic effects are easier to detect. As a consequence of such carnage, especially in towns, the cost of labour rocketed. Workers quickly realised that the simple fact of survival gave them a new bargaining power with lords and merchants. And this trend, along with continued border warfare, ensured that the fourteenth and fifteenth centuries saw only sporadic development on Tyneside. The Italian traveller Aeneas Silvius Piccolomini (later to become Pope Pius II) was not impressed. He wrote that Northumberland was 'uninhabitable, horrible, uncultivated' and was relieved to find safe lodging inside the walls of Newcastle. Houses were miserable, built only of earth or wood, and each night men sought the safety of a peel-tower in case the Scots descended. This was a landscape yet to recover from disease and warfare.

DON'T LARN GEORDIE

The English Parliament of 1332 was anxious about the decline of French-speaking in England, particularly amongst the nobility. Other commentators worried about how English could possibly replace French or Latin as a civilised language. Some believed that the northern dialects were not only entirely unsuitable but also unintelligible. Here is the chronicler Ranulph Higden writing the first recorded sneer about northern speech:

> All the language of the Northumbrians . . . is so sharp, piercing, rasping and unformed that we Southerners can rarely understand it. I believe that the reason for this is because they are near to foreigners and aliens, and also because the Kings of England have always lived far away from that country.

Well, la di da.

Newcastle did manage some advance, gaining independent status as a county with its own sheriff in 1400, and this must show an increase in confidence if nothing more. The elevation may have been the work of one of Newcastle's most illustrious mayors. Roger Thornton was wealthy, described by John Leland as 'the richest merchant that ever was dwelling in Newcastle', and he held office for periods totalling ten years between 1400 and 1425, as well as attending Westminster as an MP. The effect of county status for the town was to set it apart from Northumberland legally and in every other important way.

Great dynasties of merchants like the Thornton family controlled Newcastle in the fifteenth century, but the history of those years is little more than one of consolidation and recovery from the disasters of the fourteenth. Border warfare still flared regularly, and the looming threat of Scotland continued to inhibit Tyneside. It would take the rashness of a young Scottish king to bring this long period of uncertainty to a close. When James IV and many of his nobility were cut to pieces at Flodden Field in 1513, most in Newcastle will have been much relieved. The Scottish defeat turned out to be so profound that their kings would never again seriously contemplate the annexation of Northumberland and Tyneside. The history of Newcastle at last ceased to be dominated by the proximity of the frontier.

5

THE CITY

1513–1707

The English called it the French disease, the French called it the Neapolitan disease and the Neapolitans called it the Spanish disease. The Italians were most likely correct since it made its European landfall in 1493 at Barcelona. Syphilis was probably carried back on board the *Niña*, one of Christopher Columbus's three ships which had sailed to discover America the year before. It was to prove a deadly import.

Spreading like wildfire throughout Europe, the disease had reached Edinburgh by 1497, when the burgesses packed sufferers off to the island of Inchkeith in the Firth of Forth. Those who refused to go or hid from the town's patrols were branded. It seems highly likely that, as a port, Newcastle was infected at around the same time, but the impact of syphilis on Tyneside proved to be indirect, political and ultimately bloody. At some point in his extended amorous adventures, King Henry VIII contracted it, and its effects were probably the cause of the dynastic barrenness of the House of Tudor and all the destructive consequences that flowed from it.

When dark, doe-eyed Anne Boleyn was led up the scaffold steps in 1536, Henry's chief minister, Thomas Cromwell, put the next stage of

154

a carefully considered plan into action. In order to further the King's obsessive pursuit of a male heir and find excuses for the executions and annulled marriages which trailed in its wake, he had to neutralise the power of a hostile papacy. Parliament was persuaded to detach the Church in England from Rome. By abolishing the papal tax known as Peter's Pence, by giving the Crown complete control of appointments to the religious hierarchy and by making Henry VIII the Supreme Head of the Church of England, Cromwell laid the legal and political groundwork. Now for the bribe. In 1536, England's monasteries and nunneries were dissolved and their vast properties sold at knock-down prices to the gentry and the nobility in return for their support. By the early sixteenth century, the church owned about 20 per cent of the nation's wealth. Royal commissioners tore around the countryside, often arriving unannounced, bursting into chapter meetings and even services, subjecting abbots, priors, prioresses and mothers superior to humiliating interrogations, forcing confessions of wrongdoing out of their trembling mouths so that a veneer of legality could be applied to the wholesale despoliation. Sodomy, fornication, fiscal corruption and even treason were all trumped up as the commissioners and their thugs galloped from one ancient abbey to another. It all happened with dizzying speed, a matter of weeks and months. One commissioners' tour visited 121 monastic houses in the north of England, covering more than 1,000 miles.

THE POX

Syphilis is spread by a spiral-shaped microbe which bores through the skin of human genitals. It is therefore a sexually transmitted disease, nothing to do with toilet seats. Poor hygiene does supply the right conditions, and once the disease has taken hold, the body is covered in suppurating pustules and the hair falls out. The wildfire spread of the pox probably helped make sexual puritanism popular, brought about the replacement of kissing on the lips as the customary greeting by the handshake and encouraged the fashion for wigs.

Inside the walls of Newcastle, five religious houses had their property confiscated and their communities of brothers and sisters thrown out onto the streets. The Grey Friars, the Black Friars, the nuns of St Bartholomew, the Austin Friars and the Carmelites all saw their foundations abolished and their property sold to burgesses. The convent of the Blackfriars was leased to nine of Newcastle's craft guilds and they began to build their meeting halls in the grounds. A wealthy merchant, Robert Anderson, bought up St Bartholomew's and Greyfriars and had Newe House constructed and gardens laid out around it. It stood at the top of Pilgrim Street. Precious and sacred items were carried off by rapacious commissioners and a history built up over centuries was cast into the dust. At Tynemouth Priory and at the abbey of St Paul at Jarrow, the ancient churches were suddenly emptied of monks, the glittering legacy of Bede counting for nothing. It was a tremendous loss. The religious houses had been the backbone of education and such social welfare as there was. The poor could often depend on the charity of the brothers and sisters for a meal and perhaps some clothing. Newcastle Grammar School and others moved to fill the educational vacuum, and former monks were amongst the first masters, but the rapid removal of so many familiar institutions was not popular, particularly in the conservative North.

As a direct response to the attack on the monasteries, a widespread rising known as the Pilgrimage of Grace began to gather support in the northern counties. At first, 10,000 gathered under the banner of the Five Wounds of Christ; within weeks, the rebel army had grown to 40,000. England was still a thoroughly Catholic country, no Protestant revolution had taken place and many were appalled that a vital part of Holy Mother Church had been summarily dismantled. But it was a strangely passive, pious expression of resentment. Under their leader, Robert Aske, the pilgrims petitioned the King for the restoration of the monasteries, a return to old religious customs and the reconnection of the Church with Rome. When they heard news of the scale of the rebellion, Henry VIII and Thomas Cromwell were terrified and militarily powerless to deal with such a huge insurgency. At Doncaster, the Duke of Norfolk arrived to negotiate and meekly conceded all of the Pilgrims' demands except the restoration of monastic lands. Amazingly, the ploy worked. Pulling off their badges of the Five Wounds, ecstatic that the King had seen the light and rejected the advice of evil counsellors, the Pilgrims dispersed, happy to ride home to the warmth of their winter hearths.

SMASHING TIMES

Idols or graven (meaning 'carved') images were symbols of popishness to the reformers. In particular, they hated sculptures of the Virgin Mary, stained glass was abhorrent and wall paintings an abomination. They smashed or obliterated as many as they could. Centuries of great beauty perished. But when the monasteries were destroyed, the loss was even greater. Many thousands of precious, sometimes unique, manuscript books were destroyed or thrown out. The scientist and philosopher Dr John Dee pleaded with Queen Mary to preserve all that learning and to found a national library, but she ignored him.

The following year, Henry repudiated almost everything Norfolk had promised. Robert Aske and other ringleaders were executed and the Council of the North reformed. The latter had been in sporadic session since the reign of Richard III, but Henry used it as an instrument of oppression from its base at Darlington. As power and political and economic influence were centralised to London and the South-east by the Tudors and their ministers, the North was seen as a place apart, different, potentially hostile, in need of a specific instrument of suppression. The Council of the North had wide-ranging powers to act as a provincial police force, ever watchful for flickers of dissent.

ROMANTIC LOVE

Henry VIII's sister, Mary Tudor, was virtually ordered to make a dynastic marriage with the Archduke Charles of the Holy Roman Empire. The problem was that she had fallen in love with one Charles Brandon, secretly married him and let it be

---

known that they had consummated the match. Henry was apoplectic. Anne Boleyn watched and learned. She herself first tried to make a similar love-match and marriage. Henry Percy, the heir to the Northumberland fortune and lands, was her true love and it took all the weighty influence of Cardinal Wolsey to break it off. In an era when aristocratic marriage was a business contract, Mary and Anne both took exceptional risks – perhaps because they really were in love.

As the politics of the sixteenth century ebbed and flowed around its long walls, Newcastle grew from a town into a city. By 1547, an estimated 10,000 souls lived and worked there, and as it bustled with trade and manufacture, the city pulled the economy of Tyneside with it.

Wool still dominated, both in the countryside where it grew and in the town of Newcastle where it was sold. In 1508–9, the total value of all exports of wool was more than double that of coal exports. On several occasions – the trade and its regulation being in a constant state of flux – Newcastle was designated as a wool staple port. The only other was London, and, in effect, these two cities became for a short time the only places in England through which the export of wool could be directed. All of the other principal wool towns, such as York, Lincoln, Norwich, Bristol, Winchester, Shrewsbury and Exeter, were relegated to the status of wool collection centres. This pre-eminence delivered massive surges of trade to Newcastle, and even when the staple system was suspended or staple status moved to a European port, business remained brisk. And the corporations of merchants which monopolised it grew ever more powerful and exclusive.

In the late fifteenth and early sixteenth centuries, the wool trade was gradually changing into the cloth trade. As the crippled and contracted economies of western Europe recovered from the devastation of the Black Death (and its regular recurrences) and the vicissitudes of climate change, England began to export more cloth than raw wool. Around 1300, more than 35,000 woolsacks went to Europe, but this declined sharply to fewer than 8,000 in 1500. The mechanics of these great economic shifts affected life on Tyneside directly. As land fell out of cultivation in the aftermath of the plague (partly as a result of chronic labour shortages) and as demand for wool – as a handy cash crop – remained steady in the fifteenth century, landowners turned over more and more of their holdings to pasture and left less for cultivation. Around 1500 there were at least 8,000,000 sheep in England and 2,000,000 people. This caused hardship – and created opportunity. Inflation began to bite hard and currency values declined by a factor of 500 to 600 per cent between 1500 and 1600. Food prices and unemployment both rose steeply, but as the cloth-making industry developed, some of the slack was taken up by the need for spinners, weavers and finishers. With its long-established cloth-finishing industry at Pandon, Newcastle was already well placed to take advantage of this shift in production.

ROSES AND WARS

Tyneside was occasionally affected by the sporadic fighting between the rival factions of Lancaster and York, which took place mainly between 1455 and 1487. This period of contention for the throne was known – by Tudor propagandists – as the Wars of the Roses since the badge of the Lancastrians was a red rose and that of the Yorkists a white. Henry VII combined the two into the red-and-white Tudor rose. These were heraldic badges but they derived from an ancient iconography. For the Romans, the rose represented both love and victory. And the Christian tradition refined meaning a little further, with the red rose as a symbol of martyrdom (red for blood) and the white standing for purity. The latter was adopted by the eighteenth-century Jacobite rebels. The phrase 'sub rosa', meaning 'in confidence', has nothing to do with whispered plots for the return of the Stuarts. It comes from an early use of the flower as an emblem of silence. Roses were often carved on the ceilings of banqueting or dining rooms, and

> the clear message was that what was spoken 'sub vino'
> should not be repeated.

Another, much more radical, economic change was about to impact. The great Flemish cities of Ghent, Bruges and Antwerp had long been the predominant destinations for English wool and unfinished cloth, but, for a complex skein of reasons, this vital market suddenly began to contract in the 1520s. However, this spelt only a short term of hardship for Tyneside. The dissolution of the monasteries in 1536 released the massive coal reserves along the banks of the river from the restrictions placed on output by the religious houses. Trade leaped ahead. And at the same time, the aggressive monopoly of the Hanseatic League over routes into the Baltic was at last lifted. Fifty-two ships sailed out of Newcastle in 1537 with cargoes of cloth, leather and no doubt a ballast of Gateshead grindstones making their way across the North Sea and through the Skagerrak into the Baltic Sea. It was a natural trading ground for Newcastle merchants which had been long denied. They brought back timber, furs, salt fish, corn, amber and much else. And as in the Middle Ages, a great deal of wine flowed into the North-east through the quays of Newcastle. The town was changing, finding a role as a great trading city, part of a European network.

THE END OF FEUDALISM

Relationships between lords and tenant farmers (or peasants) were changing before the catastrophe of the Black Death. At the end of the thirteenth century, many of the great monasteries tried to introduce a money economy, commuting services and rents in kind for cash payments. The coming of the Little Ice Age and the labour shortages caused by the Black Death certainly altered the balance of feudal relationships in favour of farmers. The wool trade also had an influence, as more land was turned over to pasture and sheep-rearing. As towns like Newcastle grew and their merchant class began to operate their working capital more effectively, they too slipped out of feudal obligations, as did those who began to work in manufacturing industries. The military levy also began to depend on cash, and professional soldiers and mercenaries almost always outmatched armed farmers or shepherds even if they had managed to mass greater numbers.

A Merchant Adventurers Company was incorporated, with the Hostmen, the Lords of Coal, at its centre, and it effectively governed Tyneside. Simple technology began to develop in the coalfield. Pitmen's intuition about the run of underground seams was replaced by the use of boring rods able to bring cores to the surface. These came into general use in 1615. And at the same time a – literally – more far-reaching innovation expanded the scope of mining. At Bebside, two non-Hostmen, Huntingdon Beaumont and Peter Delaval (both speculators from London), invested large sums in opening new pits. The reason these coal-rich sites were available was an old one: they were too far from the river and the sea to make money. Transport was the key to success, and Beaumont and Delaval funded the construction of the first wagonway. It ran between Bebside and the small harbour of Blyth. About three miles long, the wagonway was a primitive, simple, but revolutionary, idea. Once the ground had been cleared and levelled (or made as level as possible), wooden rails were laid to carry coal bogies, which were in turn pulled along by heavy horses. It was a good enough solution to the problem of getting coal from the pits to the river or the sea at a reasonable price, and one which worked in most weathers. But despite this, the scheme failed, and Beaumont lost all of his money 'and rode home upon his light horse' according to one pithy commentator. But the basic idea was sound, and soon the Hostmen were investing heavily in wooden rails. Wagonways expanded the area of the Tyneside coalfield beyond the banks of the river and the volume of trade rose exponentially. And thousands more Tynesiders became miners.

In the sixteenth and early seventeenth centuries, industrial development marched alongside a rural population which was subjected to a practice which dated back to the first millennium BC and probably long before. Cattle rustling and generalised raiding plagued Northumberland. Near-constant cross-border conflict after the Battle of Flodden in 1513 had been followed by general lawlessness. Stretching over a wide area, from Dumfriesshire to the eastern terminus of the Cheviots, what became known as border reiving exasperated both southern Scotland and northern England. Galloping out of the upland valleys of Tynedale and Redesdale, family-based bands of horse-riding bandits terrorised Northumberland, as well as raiding one another and the Scots to the north. Sometimes they ventured as far as the Tyne. In the great raid of 1524, a small army of Reiver cavalry, between 500 and 700 men, rode down to south Northumberland, killing, stealing anything portable and driving off many head of cattle. The riders sometimes approached close to Newcastle, on one occasion burning and looting only eight miles from the walls.

NAGS

Far more heroic in many ways than their riders, the tough little ponies which carried the Border Reivers were remarkable. Sure-footed while traversing difficult country, often in darkness, able to carry a fully-armed man for immense distances without any loss of condition and versatile enough to double as pack animals and cavalry ponies, they were the Reivers' secret weapon. Ponies rarely stood more than 15 hands and were usually grey in colour. Contemporaries knew them as Galloway Nags, but as a breed they are now, sadly, extinct. Highland ponies are their closest cousins, so even-tempered and stolid that many riding schools favour them for the inexperienced or the timid.

Some of the larger and better-organised forays had covert government backing, and, to an extent, the Reivers knowingly allowed themselves to be used as pawns in international power politics – so long as they got their stolen cattle and settled old scores. Not surprisingly, men from up-country Northumberland enjoyed a doubtful reputation on Tyneside. In 1554, the Merchant Adventurers Company thought them unemployable, unable 'to serve in this Fellysshype of non suche as is or shall be borne or brought up in Tyndall, Ryddisdall, or any other suche lyke places'. And when the destructive days of the Reivers were coming to their close in the early seventeenth century, once-notorious surnames soon turned up in Tyneside records, particularly those of the coal trade. Perhaps they were less fussy than the merchants. Armstrongs, Robsons, Elliots, Milburns and Charltons became keelmen, pitmen and colliers. And, much later, famous industrialists and footballers.

In 1503, a princess was kissing crosses in Newcastle. On her way north to marry King James IV of Scotland, Margaret Tudor was met on the Tyne Bridge by the priests and friars of the town and asked to further sanctify their holy relics with a royal kiss. Her father, Henry VII, was anxious to cement a dynastic link with the House of Stuart and it was the first step on the road to political union between England and Scotland. On the morning of 25 July 1503, the princess knelt and prayed at mass in St Nicholas. Ten years later, her husband would be killed in battle with an English army at Flodden, and four years after that, Europe would be plunged into the convulsions of the Reformation when a monk called Martin Luther nailed a sheet of 95 theses, or arguments, to the door of the castle church of Wittenberg in southern Germany.

THE MIRACLE TOUCH

In the eleventh century, a strange tradition grew up amongst European kings which lasted well into the nineteenth century and the echoes of which can still be heard today. This was the ritual of the 'royal touch'. Ordinary people came to believe that if a king, queen, prince or princess – or anyone of the blood royal – were to touch them, it would have a magical effect, perhaps curing illness, perhaps conferring good fortune. The annual maundy ceremonies are a relic of this. It was only in 1725 that money was given by the sovereign to a group of the poor and old. Elizabeth I had doled out food and clothing, and, most importantly, she laid hands on the men and women who kneeled before her. Superstition took this belief even further in the seventeenth century. Special medallions were made bearing the king's or queen's image and worn as a pendant around the neck as a cure for scrofula, otherwise known as the king's evil.

Henry VIII hated Luther, and as a reward for his righteous hostility, the Pope awarded the King the title of Defender of the Faith. It turned out to be ironic as Henry and Thomas Cromwell defended nothing but the Crown's interest in removing England from the Church of Rome. But they did not spark a Protestant Reformation or adopt any Lutheran ideas. That task was enthusiastically taken up by Henry's successor, his only son, Edward VI, and his zealous Archbishop of Canterbury, Thomas Cranmer. No doubt to the dismay of the thousands in the North who had joined the Pilgrimage of Grace, almost all of the beloved old traditions of the Church were swept aside. Traditions like the blessing of the candles at Candlemas, the release of doves from church steeples on Whit Sunday, the creeping to the cross on Good Friday, the cult of saints and public processions in their honour, pilgrimage to shrines such as Walsingham and Durham – all of these were stopped. Inside churches, paintings of biblical scenes were obliterated by limewash, beautifully carved rood screens torn down and relics ransacked. At Durham Cathedral, a gang of thugs broke in and one threw down a Corpus Christi monstrance to the stone-flagged floor and jumped on it until it was battered unrecognisable. Stained-glass windows were smashed and all those who continued to insist on the Catholic doctrines were driven out and underground. Perhaps most dramatically, the Word of God was suddenly spoken in English. Latin disappeared overnight as translations of the Bible allowed the literate to read for themselves. And in glorious language, so familar to all in his version of the Lord's Prayer and much else, Cranmer himself created the Book of Common Prayer.

In 1550, the Scottish reformer John Knox arrived in Newcastle, having – remarkably – survived two years' brutal imprisonment as a slave on a French galley. Welcomed at St Nicholas, he was made a lecturer, a preacher who was paid a stipend. Relying on encyclopedic biblical knowledge, Knox thundered against the Pope in Rome and propounded his own Protestant beliefs. Communicants were forbidden to kneel, since there was no biblical authority for such a suspiciously popish practice, another of those vile old traditions of the medieval church. Knox's sermons at St Nicholas became extraordinarily popular, but not so much with the bulk of the population of Newcastle. Scots flocked to hear him, so many that John Dudley, Duke of Northumberland, thought that such large crowds of aliens presented a security risk. He proposed to London that the fiery preacher be removed well out of the way and made Bishop of Rochester in Kent. When a bill passed through all its parliamentary stages in 1553 to incorporate Gateshead into 'the City of Newcastle' and also carve out a separate bishopric from the see of Durham, Knox and Nicholas Ridley became front-runners to become the first bishop. The death of Edward VI in 1553 sent all of these plans into reverse. And the accession of the Catholic Queen Mary quickly persuaded Knox to flee to the Continent; Newcastle had to wait a further 329 years for a bishop and a cathedral.

THE PRAYER BOOK REBELLION

Sleepy, sunny, picturesque, Cornwall is not the first place in Britain to be associated with violent insurrection, but when the use of Cranmer's new English Prayer Book was made mandatory, the Duchy went up in flames. Thousands joined a rebel army, marched on Exeter and, in 1549, laid siege to the town. What the London government had forgotten was the existence of the Cornish language. Around 35,000 in the Duchy had no English, and, in any case, they loved the old Latin mass and its traditions. A strongly worded petition went to Edward VI, saying that the new mass was:

like a Christmas game . . . we will have our old service of Mattins, Mass, Evensong and Procession in Latin as it was before. And so we the Cornish men (whereof certain of us understand no English) utterly refuse this new English.

Cranmer had failed to realise that substantial parts of the mass – the Creed, Commandments and much else – had long been recited in Cornish. Having the whole service in English made it unintelligible to many thousands. At the village of Sampford Courtenay, on Whit Sunday the priest was forced to wear his old chasuble and conduct the mass in Latin. Afterwards, Whitsun ale and cakes were taken outside the church and a game of hurling played with a neighbouring parish, an episode which offers a strong sense of the informalities of the pre-Reformation Church. The rebellion was of course ruthlessly crushed, several parish priests hanged from their church steeples, their decaying bodies left to swing in the wind for weeks as a grim warning.

Nicholas Ridley briefly became Bishop of London but his Protestant leanings soon condemned him. Queen Mary attempted a comprehensive Counter-Reformation, reintroducing the hideous practice of burning alive those considered heretics. In three years of terror, 220 men and 60 women died agonising deaths in the flames. When Ridley's turn came on 14 February 1556, he shook with uncontrollable fear as he was dragged to his pyre in Broad Street in Oxford. His fellow martyr, Bishop Hugh Latimer of Worcester, attempted some consolation: 'Be of good comfort, Master Ridley, and play the man. We shall this day light such a candle by God's grace in England, as I trust shall never be put out.'

The childless death of Bloody Mary in 1558 ushered in a welcome period of relative stability. Her half-sister, Elizabeth, was determined to undo the excesses of the recent past; there would be no retribution, and a middle way would be found to allow all to enter the Church of England.

Tudor moderation must have seemed to contemporaries a rare phenomenon, and there can be little doubt that Elizabeth I's initial attempts to find a middle way were welcomed, particularly on Tyneside. Since the time of the Oxford academic, John Wyclif, who translated the scriptures into English in the 1380s, Newcastle had simmered with religious dissent. Known as Lollardy in the fifteenth century, the movement swirled around a general discontent with religious corruption and the Church of Rome, and focused on the central question of translating the Bible from Latin into English. It was an issue which appeared to contemporaries to threaten one of the essential mysteries of Christianity: 'This Master Wyclif translated from Latin into English – the Angle not the angel speech – and so the pearl of the Gospel is scattered abroad and trodden underfoot by swine.'

Lollardy in Newcastle and elsewhere was regularly suppressed, but in 1525, William Tyndale, a scholar with roots in Northumberland, translated the Bible from Greek into English. It was an immense labour, which led him ultimately to be burned at the stake. In 1526, Tyndale's Bible was printed in an octavo version, small enough to be portable (and easily smuggled), and 3,000 copies were printed at Worms for shipment to England. The cat was out of the bag, and in 1534, Miles Coverdale's version followed. By 1568, no fewer than seven versions of an English Bible were in circulation, all of them selling as fast as they could be printed.

BIBLE BOOM

Bibles have long been bestsellers, and the publisher William Collins made his fortune from mass-producing them in good-quality editions so that they could sell cheaply and be available to all. This last point was the key to the importance of the English translations of the Bible in the sixteenth century. Martin Luther and other reformers promoted a simple but revolutionary idea, 'the priesthood of all believers'. Individuals should no longer be dependent on the 'mumbo-jumbo' of a Latin-speaking priest to intercede with God on their behalf or interpret the scripture for them. Each man and woman was responsible for their own salvation, and to achieve that, they needed access to the Word of God – in a language they could understand.

The effects were fascinating. Bede's phrase 'book language' came to apply not to Latin but to a standardising dialect of English deriving from London and the South-east. It soon became what the literate read, although not necessarily what they said. The gulf between written and spoken English began to yawn open. And even though spoken English has continued to modify – from year to year, it seems – the major regional dialects are still directly traceable to the Anglo-Saxon period, even corresponding to those areas which coalesced into the ancient kingdoms. There is still a Kentish dialect which is descended from the Jutish kingdom of the same name, and although the name of Wessex has been lost, the gentle dialect of its people has not. And in the North-east, it is possible to claim that there is a full-blooded Northumbrian way of speaking English with a Bernician sub-division otherwise known as Geordie.

This is not to say that St Bede of Jarrow would have understood Bobby Thompson, or vice versa, unless 'the Little Waster' can speak Latin. But it does mean that they would have sounded like each other, using short vowels in words like 'path' and sentences like 'Aal larn ye.' This last is perfectly grammatical, sounding right to both Bede and Bobby, because the Anglian verb '*laeran*' meant 'to teach'. Various other words have survived virtually unchanged, such as 'deed' for 'dead', 'hoose' for 'house', 'gan' for 'going' and so on. The only awkwardness is spelling – 'deed' can mean several things when written down, but used in a Geordie context, 'deceased' is the only interpretation possible.

What surprises some is the historical universality of regional dialects. Even though literate people tended also to be wealthier than most, being middle or upper class, they wrote a standard English but did not often speak it. There is some later evidence to suggest that up until the introduction of expensive boarding schools in the nineteenth century, almost all Tynesiders spoke dialect, no matter if they had money or were just little wasters.

ENGLISHING

The publication of English Bibles, the arrival of the printing press and the invention of small, easily portable books created an enormous interest in the language. In the middle of the sixteenth century, controversy ricocheted between much-valued 'plainnesse' of expression and the introduction of 'inkhorn' terms. The latter were 'woordes of antiquitee . . . to darken the sence unto the reader', according to one critic. In contrast to this pretension, good, ordinary English words were to be preferred. The historical reality is that the ferment produced a vibrant, sinuous and beautiful language. The debate continued and when Shakespeare alluded to it in *Love's Labours Lost*, the issues were still fresh. Berowne says that he loves Rosalind but will have nothing to do with 'taffeta phrases, silken terms precise' and will be sure that 'my wooing mind shall be expressed in russet yeas and honest, kersey noes'. Despite Shakespeare's advocacy, 'kersey' has not survived. It was a kind of rough cloth.

Even though Elizabeth I was at first determined to minimise its effects, religious difference still racked English society. The North remained Catholic, except for many in Newcastle, and when Henry Howard, Duke of Norfolk, was executed in 1569 for alleged treason and undoubted Catholicism, an aristocratic rebellion known as the Rising of the Northern Earls burst into flames. Led by Thomas Percy, Earl of Northumberland, and Charles Neville, Earl of Westmorland (and Norfolk's brother-in-law), it raised the standard for conservatism and the renewal of links with Rome. Many from Durham and Northumberland were involved, but after some feckless generalship, the rebels were defeated by the Lord President of the Council of the North. Sir Thomas Radcliffe chased Percy and Neville as far as

Scotland and then turned back to dish out summary justice to their followers.

DOCTOR DEE

Elizabeth I was a highly educated woman possessed of a piercing intellect. Her relationship with Dr John Dee is illustrative. A scientist and researcher (who sometimes dabbled in dangerous ideas, some associated with magic) with a huge library of 4,000 volumes at his house at Mortlake, near London, Dee acquired an unfortunate reputation as a 'conjuror'. At Cambridge University, he built a theatrical machine for a performance of a comedy by Aristophanes. Part of it shot to the ceiling of Trinity Hall, carrying a man high in the air. Onlookers thought it magical, and not in a good way. But Dee was protected by Elizabeth I and the Earl of Leicester, who visited him in his library at Mortlake. Their interest was in science and also numerology, the study of the occult significance of numbers. Dee was also a hermetic scholar, that is, someone interested in Hermes Trismegistus, a once famous but now forgotten sage much studied in the fifteenth and sixteenth centuries. It was thought that Hermes' mystical writings were very ancient, the *'prisca theologia'*, the origin of not only Christian thought but also pagan Greek philosophy. This meant, for example, that the ideas of St Paul and Plato were not incompatible, since they both sprang from the same source. But it was all a great mistake, a radical error of dating. The work of Hermes Trismegistus actually came after the Greeks and the New Testament writers and was derived from both.

From the 1570s onwards, Tudor England began to rebuild, slowly climbing out of the long decline of the late Middle Ages and the depredations of the wars of the Reformation. On Tyneside, though, there was hesitation. Although the Scottish defeat at Flodden in 1513 had greatly reduced international tension (at least for the English), the continual irritation of the Border Reivers had sapped confidence, and the only significant economic and social development took place inside the protective walls of Newcastle. Substantial surviving houses such as the Cooperage on the Quayside and the group of five houses known collectively as the Red House all date back to the sixteenth century, and their scale does more than hint at mercantile success. In Broad Chare, leading off the Quayside, stands Trinity House. Much rebuilt but retaining original features from the 1530s, its work with lighthouses was first sanctioned by Henry VIII. He encouraged the brethren

> to build and embattle two towers, one at the entrance of the haven of the Tyne, the other on the hill adjoining, in each of which a light was to be maintained every night, for the support of which they were empowered to receive 4 d. for every foreign ship and 2 d. for every English vessel entering the Port of Tyne.

The High and Low Lights at North Shields kept many a ship off the rocks at the mouth of the river and the work of Trinity House and its dedicated brethren continues.

TRINITY HOUSE

The guild or 'Fellowship of Masters and Mariners of the ships of the town of Newcastle upon Tyne' decided in 1505 to have a chapel, a meeting hall and almshouses built. Other similar guilds existed in English ports, and Henry VIII later organised them into a network responsible for the 'relief, increase and augmentation of the shipping of this our realm of England'. Elizabeth I then commanded Trinity House to set up seamarks since so many 'steeples, woods and other marks standing upon the main shores' had disappeared. In addition to the care of lighthouses, lightships, buoys and other navigational aids, the guild also licensed river pilots for the Tyne, Thames and other major arteries. The organisation remembers the language of its medieval roots with the 'Elder Brethren', who are elected from the Merchant Navy and the Royal Navy to act as assessors in the Admiralty Division of the High Court, and the 'Younger Brethren', who do nothing except vote at elections.

On 24 March 1603, Sir Robert Carey began a journey which would consign the raids of the Border Reivers to history as fast as his horses could gallop. It would also free Tyneside and Northumberland from their special brand of terror. A kinsman of Elizabeth I and appointed by her as Warden of the English Middle March, Carey attended the old queen through her last few days, all the while keeping in touch with Holyrood Palace in Edinburgh by letter. Determined to carry the news of Elizabeth's death northwards and be the first to tell James VI of Scotland that he was also James I of England (and Great Britain and Ireland), Carey had organised a relay of posthorses to be put on constant alert for his immediate use at any time. He had travelled the north road often and could fairly claim to know it intimately. When Elizabeth died on the morning of 24 March, he was in the saddle in minutes, spurring his horse north out of London. His sister, Philadelphia, had pulled a ring from the dead queen's puffy finger and rushed to give it to Carey as a token of good faith. The ring had been a gift from James VI.

Reaching Doncaster on the first night, Robert Carey awoke early and made excellent progress to reach Berwick by nightfall. With good fortune, Edinburgh should have been possible by the following afternoon. But somewhere in Berwickshire, Carey fell from his horse and while he lay on the ground, it kicked him in the head. Spattered with mud and blood, he clattered into the inner courtyard at Holyrood on the Saturday evening only 60 hours after leaving London. Even though James VI had gone to bed, Carey was rushed in to give him the news he had been waiting for all his life. Proof was supplied when the ring taken from the dead queen's finger was shown to the new King of England.

The Union of the Crowns set an emphatic full stop to cross-border conflict of any sort. In a concerted police action, James I and VI hanged, ennobled or deported enough Reivers to stamp out their lawlessness. Business on Tyneside picked up. The salt-panning industry expanded at North and South Shields and the new business of glass-making began to flourish.

But more trouble was brewing, and the Elizabethan and early Jacobean respite from the wars of religion was soon to end. James I and VI was a strange man, bisexual, constantly seized of a perverted interest in witchcraft and torture, but nevertheless in possession of a set of sound political instincts. His son, Charles I, inherited few of these, and thoughout the 1630s, his actions and attitudes propelled all of Britain and Ireland towards what is often misnamed as the English Civil War.

THE OTHER CHURCH OF ENGLAND

It is a commonplace to observe that winners write history, but in the case of the English Reformation, it was more true than usual. England and Tyneside's Catholics were entirely written out and written off as the heretical opposition. Some accounts would have us believe that the whole nation had rejected the old beliefs overnight. But in the mid-sixteenth century, there were at least half as many Catholics in the country as there were Protestants. Hearty Henry and Good Queen Bess ruthlessly persecuted all who did not worship as they wished, and, although the worst excesses of the reign of Bloody Mary were avoided, their regimes were harsh. Posterity has been kind to the Tudor monarchs, but not all commentators have been taken in. The early-nineteenth-century journalist William Cobbett is chiefly famed for his *Rural Rides*, but he also wrote that the English Reformation was 'engendered in lust and brought forth in hypocrisy and perfidy'.

When Charles I attempted to enlarge the Union of the Crowns into religious uniformity between England and Scotland by imposing the

English prayer book and reintroducing bishops into the Kirk, Presbyterian Scotland would have none of it. Rioting broke out in Edinburgh, and at Greyfriars Kirkyard, the National Covenant of 1638 was signed by barons, lairds, townspeople and ministers. Copies were distributed for signature to other parts of Scotland. Both sides began to arm. Described by a contemporary as 'the auld wee crooked soldier', General Alexander Leslie had risen through the hard school of mercenary service in Europe. While in the armies of King Gustavus Adolphus of Sweden and his psalm-singing troopers of the Thirty Years War, Leslie had organised a signing of the National Covenant by Scots mercenaries under his command in Germany. By late 1638, war seemed to be inevitable and a contingent of battle-hardened Scots docked at Leith with the auld, wee crooked soldier on board. Immediately, Leslie put preparations in train for what became known as the First War of the Covenant in Scotland, and in England as the First Civil War.

In late May 1639, word had come that Charles I had raised an army and was marching on Berwick. Leslie led an army south to meet the King, and they occupied an impregnable position on Duns Law in Berwickshire. In addition to the core force of Scots mercenaries, the Covenanter army was stiffened by religious zeal. Regiments of ploughmen, lawyers, academics and others were drilled and driven by absolute religious conviction. They would have no bishops in the Kirk and no king would force them to break God's sacred Covenant with his chosen people of Scotland. Charles wisely chose to negotiate. The Treaty of Berwick bought him time, but his concessions over the prayer book and the episcopalian government of the Church of Scotland were a sham. The King had no intention of honouring them.

In 1640, Parliament was called to vote on a subsidy for an army to crush the Scots rebels. It refused to supply it, but the king mustered what troops he could afford under the command of Lord Conway. In Scotland, the banners unfurled once more. As they crossed the Tweed into Northumberland, each company carried a standard on which was emblazoned the Scottish arms and the motto 'For Christ's Crown and Covenant'. Conway decided to attempt to hold the line of the River

Tyne, but when Alexander Leslie's mercenaries charged at the ford at Newburn, the Royalist troopers scattered. It was a rout. The Covenanting army immediately occupied Newcastle and the more zealous entered St Nicholas Church and removed or destroyed what they considered idolatrous or papist. They had the support of the small Puritan community in the city, but some of the wealthiest merchants were Royalists. In 1640, this group was in the ascendant and had succeeded in having their leader, Sir John Marley, elected mayor. Dr Robert Jenison, a Puritan divine who seems to have led the anti-Royalist party, was forced to flee – and some distance. He took ship for Danzig on the German shore of the Baltic, well inside Protestant Europe, almost certainly a link created by the expansion of Newcastle's trade after the end of the Hansa monopoly. But once Leslie's Presbyterians had brushed aside Conway at Newburn, another Puritan, Robert Bewick, became mayor and he welcomed the Scots into the city. It was an expensive stay. For the upkeep of the army, Newcastle had to pay £200 a day, but at least the population and their property were not harmed, as was often the case. In a remarkable record of the campaign, Robert Baillie, principal of Glasgow University, wrote that the most serious misdemeanour amongst the army was the regrettable habit of swearing. In the evenings, most soldiers apparently whiled away the boredom not by drinking, whoring or baiting civilians, but by psalm-singing, prayer and reading the scriptures. Royalists in Newcastle must have found these men terrifying.

MERCENARY TACTICS

One of the solutions to border reiving was to encourage the leaders to remove the problem. In 1603, Walter Scott of Buccleuch took 2,000 Reivers to 'fight in the Belgic wars', to become mercenaries in Europe's religious and political conflicts. In the Thirty Years War, the great Swedish king Gustavus Adolphus ascribed much of his military success to the steadfastness and grit of his Scottish mercenaries. He made their leader, Alexander Leslie, a field marshal in the Swedish army.

The Scots' occupation ended in 1641, but it made the anti-Royalist faction unpopular, no doubt because of the expense. Sir Nicholas Cole had been forced to flee to King's Lynn, a staunchly Royalist town, and on his return, the burgesses elected him mayor. Newcastle seems to have vacillated between the two causes, while Northumberland and Durham were constant in their support of Charles I. Of the two Newcastle MPs who represented the city in the Long Parliament (which sat intermittently between 1640 and 1660), one became a Royalist and the other ultimately a signatory to the King's death warrant in 1649.

In 1642, London and the East Anglian ports were controlled by Parliament. Charles I's strategists realised the enormous significance of the Tyneside coalfields and Newcastle. If they could hold the city, it would act as an entry port for supplies and men, and the coal exports were now so valuable that they could help provide cash to finance the war. Despite opposition from Puritan merchants and pitmen at Tynemouth and elsewhere, the city was secured. Sir John Marley once again became mayor and the Earl of Newcastle assumed control as military governor. The scene was set. Tyneside was now to play a central role in the outcome of the Civil War.

COALS TO NEWCASTLE

The phrase 'carrying coals to Newcastle' can be a mystery even to competent learners of English. Some history is needed to aid understanding. In French, the equivalent – 'to carry water to the river' – is much clearer. In German, people say 'to carry owls to Athens', a phrase needing a lot of history to make sense (owls were the emblem bird of the goddess Athena and hence of the city), while the Russian 'to go to Tula with one's own samovar' is entirely incomprehensible.

At first, economic sanctions were applied. Parliament prevented coal ships from London and East Anglia from sailing to the Tyne. The effect was patchy. Some coal was brought out. And then diplomacy came into play. Newcastle lay deep inside the Royalist North and any Parliamentary army would have to fight its way to the Tyne. Instead, a deal was done with Scotland. The psalm-singing, battle-hardened army of the Solemn League and Covenant would attack from the north if the Parliamentarians promised that England (and Wales and Ireland) would adopt Presbyterianism. God's chosen people were ambitious for converts. In the severe winter of early 1644, the Scots marched across the frozen Tweed and immediately forced the Royalist troops to retreat, throwing down bridges as they moved south, until they finally sought refuge behind the walls of Newcastle.

There was a fierce skirmish at the fort at Shieldfield, and Mayor Marley took the ruthless decision to burn down the suburbs outside the walls at Newgate and Sandgate. The houses afforded the advancing Scots too much cover. As the defenders seemed determined, well organised and well supplied, the Scots decided to cross the Tyne and skirt around the south of the city, capturing South Shields so that they could blockade the mouth of the Tyne. But the siege eased as Alexander Leslie, now Lord Leven, diverted his army to make a decisive intervention at the battle at Marston Moor. The defeat destroyed the Royalist position in the North, but Newcastle continued to hold out. Marley had used the respite to strengthen the city walls.

The fundamental difficulty was that the walls were medieval, and, unlike the elaborate and immensely thick Elizabethan defences at Berwick-upon-Tweed, they were not designed to deal with artillery. But Marley's work gangs did what they could. The medieval ditch directly in front of the ramparts had filled up, and it was cleared and deepened. The clay upcast was plastered against the foot of the walls to help absorb cannon fire and discourage scaling. And where the masonry had been allowed to decay or had been robbed out, the gaps were filled with rubble.

Under their experienced old commander, the besieging Scots were also methodical. At Elswick and downstream at the mouth of the Ouseburn, pontoon bridges were thrown across the Tyne to prevent help and supplies arriving by boat. Batteries of cannon were trundled into place and companies of sappers set to dig mines under the walls.

These were not intended as a means of entry but rather a method of causing collapse. With its elevated position, Gateshead proved the best site for cannon. Firing across the Tyne, the batteries forced evacuation from the quayside and castle areas to beyond St Nicholas. But when the bombardment threatened the beautiful old church tower, Sir John Marley sent word to Lord Leven that he had moved his Scots prisoners of war into it. The human shield worked and the tower survived.

But Royalist Newcastle did not. Sappers and artillery broke down long stretches of the walls at the Sandgate and the Westgate, and the army of the Covenant poured in. The gallant Marley retreated to the castle but was finally forced to surrender on 22 October 1644.

With the king's defeat at Naseby in 1645, the Civil War stuttered to its close, and when Charles gave himself up to the Scots at Newark in May 1646, he was taken north to Newcastle. As he attempted to plot his way to freedom, using intermediaries and a network of secret messengers, the King was forced to attend St Nicholas each Sunday. Sermons designed for his improvement were preached as, no doubt, Charles looked disdainfully down his long aristocratic nose. There is a story, probably apocryphal and certainly apposite, that when the minister announced Psalm 52, with its first line 'Why dost thou, tyrant, boast aloud, thy wicked words to praise?', King Charles interjected. He requested that they sing Psalm 51 instead: 'Have mercy on me, Lord, I pray.' Perhaps he did.

The occupying army did not leave Newcastle until the King was taken to London in 1647. The Civil War was over, but it had stalled the Tyneside economy badly, shortages forcing up prices and doubtless enriching canny merchants. But a sustained drop in output must have caused hardship for the families of keelmen and pitmen. However, other work beckoned. Shipbuilding became important on the Tyne, and records show that in 1651 there were government contracts for 25 ships.

Surviving municipal tax records give a strong impression of seventeenth-century Newcastle's social geography. The hearth tax was a crude but accurate measure of the size of a house and the relative wealth of its owner. The distribution of the tax showed that the largest houses were to be found around the Side and on the Sandhill, and other records list many men of substance. Of the two recent Royalist mayors, Sir John Marley earned a huge £4,500 a year and Sir Nicholas Cole was also fabulously rich. The quayside buzzed with activity, and many merchants owned riverfront houses which doubled as business premises. In 1655, Newcastle commissioned Robert Trollope to build a courthouse and a customs weigh-house on the Sandhill.

After the end of the Civil War, politics was rarely allowed to interfere with business in Newcastle and the city began to grow. There were 13,400 inhabitants in 1655. Inside the circuit of the medieval walls, the open spaces were gradually filled by buildings and gardens, and, in 1690, the writer Celia Fiennes was impressed: 'It most resembles London of any place in England, its buildings lofty and large of brick mostly or stone, the streets very broad and handsome.'

When political union with Scotland was forced into consideration in the early 1700s, the motives and circumstances were mainly economic. In order to steer Scotland away from any more flirtations with Jacobitism, the English Parliament used the strong-arm tactics of the Alien Act of 1705. More than half of Scotland's trade was with England, and if at any time the Union of the Crowns was broken, then the Act ensured that economic sanctions would be enacted. When the negotiating commissioners drew up the 25 articles of union, 15 were about commercial or financial matters. One of the most enthusiastic Scottish advocates was the Earl of Roxburghe and he summed it up: 'The motives will be, trade with most, Hanover with some, ease and security with others, together with a general aversion to civil discords, intolerable poverty and the constant oppression of a bad ministry.'

KINGDOMS, PRISONERS AND ROADS

In 1707, Queen Anne attended the Houses of Parliament in person to give royal assent to the Act of Union between England and Scotland. The proceedings were both daft and businesslike. When Black Rod banged on the door of the House of Commons and commanded them to attend the Queen in the Lords, some MPs complained that the passageways were too crowded. Once the way was cleared, they all crammed in to hear the day's business. There were four pieces of legislation: the Act of Union; an act to prevent escapes from HM prisons; and two acts to allow road repairs in Bedfordshire and Herefordshire. Once each had been read out, the Clerk of Parliament shouted *'La Reyne le veult'*, or 'The Queen wills it', a surviving relic of Norman French.

For Tyneside, it was also the end of an old song. Dynastic politics, wars of religion and besieging armies would all drift into the mists of the past as merchants, industrialists, miners, factory workers and seamen rolled up their sleeves and got on with their future. The Emperor's bridge and Curthose's New Castle had become the nucleus of a town, and now it would become a city, a great commercial and industrial city whose enterprise and acumen would often dazzle the world.

GEORDIES

George Stephenson deserves enthusiastic commemoration as the inventor of the miner's safety lamp in 1815, to say nothing of the success of the *Rocket* in 1829. But the inhabitants of Tyneside are not nicknamed after him. 'Geordie' originally signified a supporter of the Hanoverian dynasty, whose first four kings were all called George. This was to distinguish them from Jacobites ('Jacobus' being Latin for 'James'), or supporters of the Stuarts. These were mostly major and minor aristocrats in the counties of Northumberland and Durham. In the 1715 rising, all of Northumberland and its small market towns declared for the Stuarts, but Newcastle closed its gates and supported the Hanoverians, and so its people became 'Geordies'.

There are plenty of examples of groups of loyalists taking their name from royal leaders or figureheads – Williamites, Elizabethans, even Carlists ('Carolus' being Latin for 'Charles') – and the term 'German Geordie' was well in currency by the early eighteenth century, long before the time of George Stephenson.

6

AFTER THE UNION

1707–1775

England has seen many strange social gatherings, but Tyneside's underground ball of 1829 must have been one of the strangest. One morning in June, 400 or so Tyneside notables were crammed into baskets and lowered more than 1,000 ft down into a pit in the Gosforth Colliery north of Newcastle. There they found an underground shaft lit with lamps and candles, tables laid with food and drink, and flunkies waiting to serve them. The Coxlodge Brass Band had been laid on to provide music for dancing on a floor that had been specially flagged for the occasion. At the end of the day, each guest was invited to hack out a lump of coal to take away as a souvenir.

This bizarre event was organised by the Reverend Ralph Henry Brandling, one of Tyneside's more unlikely coal barons, who had inherited the colliery on the death of his brother Charles. It was the Reverend Brandling's idea of celebrating the successful opening of a particularly difficult pit shaft. On the face of it, Brandling's subterranean soirée looks like sheer lunacy. A serious roof fall or a gas explosion of the kind that had already killed hundreds of Tyneside miners would have wiped out much of north-east England's polite society. More than one sensible Novocastrian grumbled about the daftness of the occasion.

But the Reverend Brandling's underground socialising might also be seen as Tyneside society's tribute to the mineral that had made them rich. Without the coal measures that lie under Northumberland and Durham, the town of Newcastle might have remained a modest frontier settlement (a bit like Berwick-upon-Tweed), and Gateshead a riverside hamlet. It was the coal measures that made them both what they are. Tyneside was geologically blessed by events that took place millions of years before anyone sailed up the River Tyne.

Which, of course, raises the question 'How did the coal get there?' The geology of the coal measures is well known. Large stretches of what is now Britain were virtual swamps, flat, low-lying lands which were incessantly battered by warm rain. This strange, alien landscape was covered with great expanses of stagnant water, thick with decaying vegetation. As it sank to the bottom, that vegetation was transformed into peat. From the fossil remains, we have some idea of what these plants were: primitive ancestors of the fern, horsehair and club moss.

Over millennia, the land subsided, the sea flooded in and millions of tons of sediment were laid down on top of the peat. As the layers piled up, they created the enormous pressure and heat which converted the peat first into lignite (brown coal) and below that into coal and rock-hard anthracite. The same slow, relentless process created all the other coalfields in Britain: South Wales, South Yorkshire, Nottinghamshire, Kent, Cumberland, Ayrshire, Fife, the Lothians, Lanarkshire. It's been argued that without the coal measures, Britain would never have led the world into the Industrial Revolution.

Roughly speaking, the Northumberland and Durham coalfield runs from the River Coquet down to the town of Hartlepool. It's around 48 miles north to south and 24 miles at its widest point. The section of it around the Tyne is bounded to the north by a fault known as the Ninety Fathom Dyke and to the south by another called the Butterknowle Fault. For the most part, it's good-quality coal, lying in a seam which is anything between 2 ft and 11 ft thick.

Tyneside was particularly lucky in that many of the coal seams had erupted through the surface of the earth and were accessible. Substantial quantities were also washed up on the beaches of Northumberland and Durham. There's good evidence that Tynesiders had been collecting and digging coal, and trading it, since the twelfth century, and probably long before. Certainly by the sixteenth century Tyneside's coal was being used to keep London warm. The Elizabethan historian William Camden described Newcastle as 'occulus, the eye of the north, the hearth that warmeth the south parts of this kingdom with fire'.

There was never any doubt about the ownership of these mineral riches. They belonged to the people who owned the land under which the coal lay. Which, of course, meant the aristocracy and gentry. According to Michael Flinn in the second volume of the official history of the British coal industry, *The History of the British Coal Industry 1700-1830*, the Duke of Northumberland, the Earl of Scarborough and families like the Lambtons, Liddells, Wortleys, Claverings and Brandlings 'drew huge incomes' from the coal trade. In that part of the coalfield lying south of the Tyne, the mineral rights belonged to the Bishop of Durham and the Dean and Chapter of Durham Cathedral.

THE PRICE OF COAL
Pit disasters in the North-east coalfield between 1707 and 1775:

1708 at Fatfield	69 dead
1743 at Bensham	80 dead
1767 at Fatfield	39 dead
1773 at Chartershaugh	23 dead

Some of the gentry coal owners took a very active part in the coal industry, while others were content to lease out their land to more enterprising folk. The result was a cat's cradle of ownership, part-ownership, leases and subleases which is often hard to disentangle. But in the early years of the eighteenth century, the Tyneside collieries were dominated by a cartel of wealthy locals who called themselves 'the Grand Alliance'. This was formed in an attempt to control the production of coal and thus keep the price steady, preferably at a high level.

It's fair to describe the Grand Alliance, signed on 27 June 1726, as a local, eighteenth-century version of OPEC. The signatories were Sidney and Edward Wortley, Thomas Ord, Sir Henry and George Liddell, William Cotesworth and George Bowes, who became the Tory MP for County Durham. According to the preamble, the purpose of the alliance was to 'enter into a friendship and partnership for the purchasing and taking of coals thereat, and to exchange benefitts and kindnesses with each other upon a lasting foundation'.

The language of the preamble may have been moderate, even kindly, but the intent was not. The Grand Allies were ruthless operators. Every time a colliery or a lease came up for sale, the Grand Allies were in the market buying. By 1750, the Grand Alliance controlled no fewer than 16 of the 27 collieries south of the Tyne. They also bought up crucial wayleaves between the collieries and the Tyne, mainly in the coal-rich area between the Team and Derwent rivers.

According to Flinn, these deals were crucial:

> Control over these wayleaves allowed the Grand Allies to force competitors either to cease mining or to spend the large sums of capital necessary to build new waggonways . . . Their near monopoly was reflected in a very sharp rise in prices in 1739. Of the nine new collieries opened on Tyneside between 1726 and 1750 the Grand Allies controlled eight.

Their rivals, of course, were furious. One investigation into the Grand Alliance was scathing. Not only did they buy or rent pits which they did not work but:

> They rent a great number of staiths or coal wharfs, of which they make no use at all, save that of debarring others from coming there. Besides all this they have got into their

possession . . . so large a share of all the lands adjoining to the river Tyne, that they have almost totally debarred all other persons from access to them, especially on the south side where the best coals are.

THE QUEEN AND THE COAL MAN

They say that the late Queen Elizabeth, the Queen Mother, looked very like her ancestor Mary Eleanor Bowes-Lyon, the Countess of Strathmore and Kinghorne. Certainly the description of Mary Eleanor seems to fit the Queen Mother: 'small and shapely, with dark brown hair, a rather large nose and a determined chin'. The Queen Mother is usually seen as the product of one of Scotland's ancient families, and so she is – on one side. But the blood-line that descended through Mary Eleanor was quite different. The Bowes family were in fact Tyneside coal owners, and enterprising ones at that.

Mary Eleanor's father was George Bowes, a County Durham landowner who had inherited (via his wife) the coal-rich Gibside estate, which he exploited to the hilt until he was one of Tyneside's biggest coal owners and a member of the powerful Grand Alliance. He was also the Tory MP for County Durham. George's first wife, Eleanor, died (at the age of 14) after a few months of marriage, and Mary was the daughter of his second, Mary Gilbert.

George Bowes died in 1760 when Mary was 12, leaving her a fortune from the coal trade. Described as pretty, lively and intelligent, as well as rich, Mary was stalked by dozens of suitors, until she fell for the handsome (if distinctly dim) John Lyon, the 9th Earl of Strathmore and Kinghorne. She married him in 1767 when she was 18 years old. The marriage was a disaster. Whatever Mary wanted, it wasn't life in a draughty old castle at Glamis, ten miles north of Dundee.

After producing two daughters and three sons (the

oldest of whom was to become the 10th Earl of Strathmore and Kinghorne), she embarked on a series of affairs, had a child by a minor poet called George Grey, then, after John Lyon died (at sea on his way to Lisbon), she married a violent young army officer called Andrew Stoney, who changed his name to Bowes in an attempt to get his hands on her money.

Following months of abuse from the brutal Stoney, she fled to lodgings in Holborn from where he had her kidnapped and then locked away in a house near Darlington. When she was rescued by locals, the authorities stepped in, and Stoney was fined and jailed for three years. Mary regained control of her estate and divorced her wretched husband on grounds of abuse and adultery.

Mary Eleanor Bowes-Lyon spent the rest of her life living quietly in London and then in Hampshire. She died in 1800 and was buried in the magnificent wedding dress in which she became the Countess of Strathmore and Kinghorne.

All of which means, of course, that thanks to Mary Eleanor Bowes-Lyon, the present Queen and her offspring have the blood of George Bowes, one of Tyneside's most hard-nosed coal owners, coursing through their veins.

Tynesiders made good use of their mineral riches. Coal is one of the best sources of heat and energy known to us. And where there is coal, there is often brine-rich water. When this is left to evaporate in the sun or heated in shallow pans, it leaves deposits of salt, yet another valuable commodity. So valuable, in fact, that people were once paid wages in salt. The word 'salary' derives from the Latin word for salt, '*salarium*' – which was how Rome occasionally paid its troops. By the beginning of the eighteenth century, there were more than 170 salt pans operating on Tyneside, most of them in North and South Shields at the mouth of the river.

The Tyneside salt industry was an intriguing one. Most of the raw material, the brine-water, came from local coal mines. The so-called salt pans in which the brine-water was cooked were long, shallow vessels, usually between 2½ and 3 ft deep, made from cast-iron boiler plate riveted together with angle irons and set up over brickwork flues.

The dimensions of the pans varied from 25 ft by 20 ft to 135 ft by 30 ft. The smaller ones were heated at 107°C to produce fine-grained salt for domestic use. The biggest of the pans were heated at 40–50°C and produced rougher 'bay' salt. In between, there was a grade known as fishery salt which, as its name suggests, was used for salting fish at sea.

It was a simple but effective chemical process. And it lasted in various parts of Britain (such as Prestonpans on the Firth of Forth) until huge seams of underground rock salt were found in places like Cheshire, Barrow-in-Furness, Droitwich and Carrickfergus, in Northern Ireland. By the end of the nineteenth century, rock salt had swamped the British market and Tyneside's salt pans had more or less ceased to exist.

Tynesiders were also quick to use their local source of energy to make glass. All the ingredients were to hand: sand from the coast (or from the ballast imported by ships); limestone from the east side of County Durham; and sodium carbonate from the salt pans. The mix – usually 75 per cent silica, 10 per cent lime and 15 per cent soda – was cooked at high temperatures (around 850°C) to melt it to a consistency at which it could be blown, or moulded. Various colours could be achieved by adding small quantities of lead (pale yellow), nickel (violet) or copper (blue).

By using the minerals under their feet and expertise imported from elsewhere in Britain and Europe (Venice, for example), Tynesiders became some of England's most skilled and prosperous glass-makers. At the beginning of the eighteenth century, there were six firms making window glass in the area, four producing bottle glass and one making flint glass, all operating along the banks of the Tyne.

But everything depended on the supply of coal. At the beginning of the century, most collieries were on the south side of the Tyne, west of Gateshead between the Team and Derwent rivers. Most were linked by wooden railways along which cartloads of coal were trundled down to staiths on the River Tyne. From there, they were sailed or rowed in shallow-bottomed keels to the coal ships ('colliers') moored in the deep water at the mouth of the river. Most of the coal shipped out of the Tyne, around 75 per cent, found its way to the kitchen hearths and grand fireplaces of London.

THE KEELS

In his biography of George Stephenson, Samuel Smiles pens a useful description of the Tyneside keels. It was written in the nineteenth century, but it applies equally to the eighteenth. In fact, Smiles contends that:

> [Keels are] of a very ancient model, perhaps the oldest extant in England; they are even said to be of the same build as those in which the Norsemen navigated the Tyne centuries ago. The keel is a tubby, grimy looking craft, rounded fore and aft with a single large, square sail which the 'keel-bullies', which the Tyne watermen are called, manage with great dexterity: the vessel being guided by the aid of the 'swape' or great oar which is used as a kind of rudder at the stern of the vessel.

Digging coal out of the ground was – as it still is – an expensive, laborious and often dangerous business. Not surprisingly, the men at the coalface, the men who hacked the mineral out of the earth, were regarded as an elite. They were the pitmen, never to be confused with mere colliers or labourers, or the men who tended the pumps or the winding gear. Mining technology saw huge advances all through the eighteenth century – except at the coalface. Which prompted Michael Flinn, in his story of the British coal industry, to remark that coal was 'brought down from the face by pick, wedge and hammer . . . human power assisted by a few, unchanging, hand tools'.

There's a particularly vivid description of the Tyneside pitman in action in *The Martyrdom of the Mine* by the miner-turned-writer E.A. Rymer. 'To see the real pitman stripped to his "buff",' he writes, 'in short breeches, low shoes and cotton skull-cap, swinging his five pound pick, while the sweat runs down his face is a sight which can never be forgotten.'

Then – as later – pitmen and their families were regarded as a breed apart. They lived in houses that were clustered around the mines, usually at some distance from the towns. They were seen as clannish, suspicious and 'not like other folk'. John Wesley regarded the Tyneside pitmen as being 'in the first rank of savage ignorance and wickedness of every kind'. Even their wives were demonised as being 'strangers to cleanliness, frugality or economy'. The fact that they had no running water with which to remove years of coal dust from skin and clothes does not seem to have been taken into account.

The pitman's trade often ran in families, handed down from father to son. Which meant that many of the men hewing coal from the face were assisted in their work by their own children, some as young as ten. The coal owners of the day had no problem with this practice. They believed in getting them young or 'they will never become colliers'. One coal owner, the Earl of Londonderry, once famously remarked that boys of 12 should be practising their trade and not wasting their time learning to read and write.

It's hardly surprising that pitmen, colliers and labourers resented the arrogance of many of the coal owners. All through the eighteenth century, trouble flared as the men who produced the coal fought to win better wages and conditions. The struggle was often violent. There were outbreaks of serious trouble in the Tyneside and Durham coalfields in 1731, 1754, 1765, 1778 and 1779. Pitmen and colliers rampaged through the collieries, smashing up the engine rooms, overturning wagons, setting fire to coal, threatening the lives of machinemen, managers and staithmen.

Time after time, they caused havoc, pulling up rails, scattering coal, panicking the pit ponies, sinking keels, threatening to flood mines or to set fire to the ships waiting at the mouth of Tyne. In 1771, the Tyneside men were reported to be 'moving from colliery to colliery to put a stop to all work, they are at present at the collieries on the Sunderland river'.

Now and again, the pitmen and colliers were joined by the keelmen, who had their own grievances and the power to blockade the river with their boats, stopping all traffic. In 1768, the keelmen and the seamen from the colliers joined forces and took to the streets of Newcastle, and, according to one contemporary witness, 'marched with flag and drum and threatened destruction wherever they came'.

Not that the coalfield workers had a monopoly on stroppiness. The quarrymen of Gateshead, who hacked out the building stone and grindstones, were also regarded as a threat to the peace of mind of their employers. 'If you do not make a publick example of some of those fellows,' one industrialist warned, 'they'll ride on your shoulders as long as you live.'

Serious though the eighteenth-century coalfield disturbances were, they were hiccups in Tyneside's coal trade. Coal production climbed year on year. From the very beginning of the century, hundreds of coal ships were ploughing up and down the east coast of England between the Tyne and the Thames.

Some were big three-masters, ship-rigged with a full set of square canvas sails. Others were smaller three-masted 'barques' or even smaller two-masted 'brigs'. They were apple-bowed and broad-sterned, and manned by modest crews of eight to a dozen men. And they were easily distinguished from other merchant ships – their canvas sails were almost always covered with black coal dust.

On the face of it, the Tyne-to-Thames coal run sounds like an easy voyage compared to, say, sailing across the Atlantic or round to Northern Russia. But it was a voyage fraught with problems. It required skilful seamanship even in harbours. At the mouth of the Tyne, at any one time, there might be more than 100 big ships crammed into the waters between the Sparrowhawk Rocks and the Herd Sand. Some would be waiting to take on coal, others would be trying to find the right tide and wind to take them out to sea. Around them swarmed dozens of keels. Manoeuvring in and out of that crush – powered only by the wind – took great skill.

Once at sea, the colliers hugged the coast, picking their way through the sandbanks, past Flamborough Head, the Wash, and Yarmouth and

Lowestoft before turning south-east into the approaches to the Thames. And, as the mouth of the Thames was (and still is) littered with sandbanks, some of which shift in heavy weather, finding a safe passage among them in fog or in a south-easterly gale could be a seaman's nightmare. Particularly as dozens of other ships would be trying to do the same thing at the same time, in both directions.

Even when the Pool of London had been safely reached, there was the problem of finding an anchorage among hundreds of other ships so that the coal could be loaded onto the Thames lighters, small sailing barges with a shallow draft, very similar to the River Tyne keels. Once the hold had been emptied, the coal dumped on the quayside and the paperwork completed, the colliers had to wait for the right wind and tide to take them out again. It required seamanship of the highest order.

There's no doubt that the men who manned the Tyneside colliers had the reputation of being among the best seamen in England. In his *Treatise upon Practical Seamanship*, William Hutchinson, one of the late eighteenth century's experts on navigation (and a former collier hand himself), claimed that the coal-ship crews were the 'most perfect in working and managing their ships in narrow, intricate, and difficult channels and in tide ways'.

According to Hutchinson, they were also the most efficient seamen afloat. 'In heaving up their anchor briskly,' he writes, 'they greatly excel other merchant ships.' He noted that the coal-ship crews could heave up an anchor with seven men in half the time it took another ship to do it with eighteen men. 'And they are equally brisk and clever in warping, or transporting a ship with ropes, and likewise in handing, reefing and steering etc.'

The efficiency of the collier crews paid off in a number of ways. As they were paid by the voyage, the more voyages they made the more they could earn. Typically they managed eight or nine return trips per year, which earned a crewman around three pounds (not a bad wage in the eighteenth century). For their part, the ship owners benefited from the brilliant seamanship because wrecks among the colliers were few. Rather than pay for often cripplingly expensive insurance, many owners carried the risks themselves. As a result, the Tyneside coal-ship owners had more money to spend than their counterparts elsewhere in Britain.

COOK'S TOUR OF DUTY

One tar who learned his trade on the Newcastle-to-London coal run was James Cook, one of the greatest seamen and maritime explorers England ever produced. The son of a farm-worker, in 1746 Cook started work on a collier owned by the Walker brothers of Whitby. For nearly eight years, he sailed up and down the coast between the Tyne and the Thames, with an occasional foray across the North Sea to the Baltic. When the ship was laid up for repairs, he studied navigation and mathematics. In 1752, he became mate of the collier *Friendship* and three years later was offered command. Cook declined and left to join the Royal Navy as an able seaman.

In later years, he would boast that he was the only man in the King's Navy who had 'gone through all the Stations belonging to a Seaman, from prentice boy in the Coal Trade to Commander in the Navy'. In the opinion of the naval historian G.J. Marcus, the great Captain Cook would never have attained his 'astonishing skill in seamanship and navigation had it not been for the thorough training he received in his early manhood in the North Sea'.

The fact that the crews of the Tyneside colliers were first-rate seamen did not go unnoticed by the Royal Navy, which all through the eighteenth century was short of hands. Naval press gangs roamed the port towns kidnapping seamen into the King's (or Queen's) service. But coal was an important, strategic resource and the press gangs were told to stay away from the crews of the coal ships, which led to seamen deserting the Royal Navy to sign on with the coal fleet. Not only was the work less dangerous but the wages were a great deal better. The Lords of the Admiralty fumed but could do nothing. Coal was central to Britain's growing industrial economy (and to the comfort of government ministers and MPs).

Not that all of Tyneside's coal went to London. There were markets for good-quality house coal in Holland, France, Germany, Norway and the Baltic countries. Some ship captains developed a triangular trade by shipping coal to Holland, then sailing in ballast to Norway (unless they could get a cargo) and returning to Newcastle with their holds and decks laden with timber. Then, as now, some ship captains took whatever cargoes they could get.

And where there was shipping, there was shipbuilding. Statistics for shipbuilding on the Tyne before the late eighteenth century are very hard to come by, but it's certain that ships had been built on the river for hundreds of years. The industry flourished in the seventeenth century, when a guild of shipwrights was formed in Newcastle. In the graveyard of what used to be All Hallow's Church, there is the tombstone of a shipbuilder called Thomas Wrangham who died in 1689 at the age of 42. According to his headstone, he had built no fewer than 45 sailing ships, probably at a yard where the Ouseburn runs into the River Tyne. In 1725, Daniel Defoe famously wrote that 'they build ships [on the Tyne] to perfection as to strength and firmness, and to bear the sea, the coal trade demanding such'.

But progress is never smooth. Events have a way of disrupting politics and politics have a way of disrupting the best-laid plans. The Union of 1707 between Scotland and England should have brought peace to Tyneside and the North-east. The threat from Scotland had been lifted. Tyneside's ancient enemies were now fellow citizens in the new United Kingdom of Great Britain and Ireland. They'd shared a monarch for more than 100 years and now they shared a parliament. To the Whig Establishment in both countries, the present looked settled and the future looked bright.

But within a very few years of the Union treaties being signed, there were rumblings of discontent from both sides of the border. The cost of King William's wars in Europe had squeezed English taxpayers. Many small landowners and merchants were suffering badly or had gone to the wall. Roman Catholics (who were fairly numerous in the north of England) suffered from low-grade harassment and official exclusion.

And James Stuart, 'the King over the Water', was intent on making a comeback to the throne from which his father had been ousted in 1688. In 1708, the Royal Navy had chased away a fleet of French warships that had tried to land the 19-year-old James on the east coast of Scotland. A few Scots Jacobites had marched up and down for a while, but to no effect, and they were soon rounded up. The second Jacobite rising (the first was in 1690) was over, but the political discontent rumbled on.

On top of which the British economy was none too healthy. The early eighteenth century was a period of recession. And when British industry took a turn for the worse, the demand for Newcastle's coal slumped. The price of coal had collapsed from around 12 shillings per chaldron (roughly 2.5 tons) to around 8 shillings. The thousands of Tyneside coal owners, colliers, hostmen, keelmen and seamen who lived by the trade began to feel the pinch. Unrest spread up along the Tyne. In 1710, there was a famous mutiny, or strike, of keelmen and shipmasters, which had to be brought to an end by troops.

By 1714, the feeling had grown in various parts of the new United Kingdom that perhaps King George I, Britain's new Hanoverian monarch, was not the man for the job. For a start, he spoke hardly a word of English and seemed more involved in the affairs of his German territories than he was in those of Britain. In short, Jacobitism was in the air, to the great alarm of Tyneside's hardline Whigs, like 'Black' William Cotesworth.

The discontent came to a head in September 1715, when the Earl of Mar raised the Jacobite standard in Scotland and kicked off the third of the Jacobite insurrections. Government troops were immediately ordered north, and into those corners of England where it was thought the virus of Jacobitism had taken hold – Cornwall, Oxford, Bristol, Bath and Lancashire. Northumberland's Jacobite sympathies were well known, and an arrest warrant was issued for the county's high Tory MP, Thomas Forster.

Forster – who was both bankrupt and discredited – thought he had nothing to lose and at the beginning of October raised the banner for 'King James VIII and III' at Greenriggs, near Hexham. He was joined by a band of 60 or so local gentrymen and their servants, most of them Roman Catholics. They accepted Forster as their leader simply because he was a Protestant from the Protestant majority. They'd have done better to elect Forster's horse. In the words of one historian, Forster was 'quite remarkably useless at everything except saving his own skin'.

The first move of 'General' Forster and his bedraggled little army was to head for Newcastle to 'declare' the town for the Stuarts. But by the time they got close, government troops had occupied the town, closed the gates and manned the walls. Forster then led his men into Scotland, where they were joined by a handful of Highlanders and turned south again, planning (or at least hoping) to enlist the Roman Catholics of Lancashire. The Jacobites swept aside a panicky local militia at Penrith and got as far as Preston, where they were surrounded by a government force. Instead of trying to break out of the ring, Forster negotiated a humiliating surrender and led his men into gaol. The Jacobite 'rebellion' in the north of England was over.

But Forster never came to trial. In April 1716, he escaped from Newgate Prison in London, having got the governor drunk. He used duplicate keys to lock up the staff and made his way out onto the crowded streets of London. Nowadays, we'd call Forster's escape an inside job. Stuart sympathisers then smuggled him out of the country and into France. Forster seems to have ended his days among the hundreds of Britons who hung around the Stuart 'court' in Paris longing for the second Restoration that was never to come.

With the Jacobite threat over (for the time being anyway), Newcastle settled down to a period of industrial growth and commercial prosperity. The coal trade was growing steadily and along with it the demand for bigger and better ships. Most of the seventeenth-century yards along the Tyne were very small, and lived and died more or less unrecorded. But as the eighteenth century progressed, bigger shipyards began to spring up along both banks of the Tyne, from South Shields up to Gateshead. They formed the nucleus of an industry that was to rival coal in its contribution to the economy of north-east England.

In 1729, Robert Wallis opened a yard under the Lawe Top at South Shields. In 1743, John and Thomas Headlam began building ships at a yard on South Shore at Gateshead. In 1756, William Rowe opened a yard at St Peter's, to the east of Newcastle. Three years later, in 1759, the brothers Francis and Thomas Hurry added to Tyneside's shipbuilding capacity with a yard at Howdon Pans, near Wallsend. These four yards were small beer by modern (or even nineteenth-century) standards, but they were substantial operations in their day.

And the building of every decent-sized ship employs a prodigious array of trades and crafts. Shipwrights, of course, but also sawyers, rope-makers, blacksmiths, toolmakers, carpenters and their suppliers. Horse-drawn transport involved carters, wheelwrights, blacksmiths, harness-makers and stable hands. Fitting out a ship called on sail-makers, glaziers, lamp-makers, brassfounders, clockmakers, instrument-makers and the experts who engraved and printed the charts and maps.

The money they earned found its way into the economy of Tyneside and, in particular, Newcastle. By the early eighteenth century, some of the treats and trappings of urban gentility were appearing on the town's streets. More and more people had money to spend on their houses and furniture, and on clothes, food, wine and amusing themselves. Shops, inns, clubs and societies began to emerge to cater for their needs.

THE IRONMASTER

One of the most remarkable industrial enterprises on eighteenth-century Tyneside was the one founded by Sir Ambrose Crawley, a Shropshire man who was at one time the Lord Mayor of London and the Tory MP for Andover. Crawley's Ironworks at Winlaton, west of Newcastle, turned out anchors, chains, pumps, cables, spades, saws and 'almost every form of which iron and steel are susceptible'. At its height, the Crawley Ironworks was the largest in Europe, employing more than 1,000 men.

Ambrose Crawley was born in 1658 in Stourbridge in Worcestershire, the son of a prosperous Quaker nail-maker. Young Ambrose set up in business at Greenwich in London, where the demand from the shipyards for nails was enormous. Some time around the year 1685, Crawley came north and set up a nail-making manufactory at Winlaton, which flourished. By 1707, Crawley had two slitting mills, two forges, four steel furnaces and a number of smithies that were turning out – among other things – nails, screws, bolts, hinges, latches, files and anchors. He distributed his products through a network of warehouses in London, Blaydon, Ware, Walsall, Wolverhampton and Stourbridge.

Crawley was an enlightened and fair-minded employer, generations ahead of his time. His firm was run by rules laid down in the Law Book of the Crawley Ironworks. All disputes, wage claims, complaints and dismissals were settled by an internal procedure known as Crawley's Court, a tribunal which was manned by both workers and management. The company's sick and disabled were looked after for life.

Not that Ambrose Crawley was any kind of radical. In fact, he was a high Tory, a sheriff of London, an alderman and a master of the prestigious Drapers' Company. When he died in 1717, the ironworks was taken over by his only son, John, who was suspected by the British government of having Jacobite sympathies.

The Tyneside shipyards built ships for owners all over England, but there was also a market for their product among local merchants. In 1730, the brothers Ralph and Robert Clarke bought an interest in a 300-ton sailing vessel. It was the modest beginning of a ship-owning dynasty that was to evolve into Britain's oldest shipping line, Stephenson Clarke. The sons of a local clergyman, both Clarke brothers were seamen themselves before they became ship owners. But it was Robert Clarke's two sons, Ralph and John, who transformed the business into a major UK enterprise.

John Clarke married one Jane Stephenson and moved to London, leaving his brother Ralph to tend things at the Newcastle end. When John Clarke died in 1792, his widow Jane (a hard-headed and able Tynesider) took his place before handing over to her eldest son Robert. When Robert Clarke died at the age of 67, his mantle fell to his younger brother, Stephenson Clarke, who gave the company his own name. Stephenson Clarke's egotism was matched by his ambition and talent. His company became one of the most successful and innovative cargo-carrying lines in Britain.

With the coal, shipbuilding, shipping, salt and glass-making industries all doing good business, and the trades which served them flourishing, the towns of eighteenth-century Tyneside began making their contribution to the intellectual and artistic life of Britain. Crucial to that was the lapsing in 1695 of the notorious Licensing Act which ruled that newspapers and periodicals could only be published under licence from the Government. Once that was removed, publishing flourished all over England.

Newcastle was at the forefront of the new boom. Throughout the century, newspapers and journals emerged to meet the needs of an increasingly literate population. In 1711, the *Newcastle Courant* was founded. That was followed in 1739 by the *Newcastle Journal*, the *Newcastle Chronicle* in 1764 and the *Newcastle Advertiser* in 1788. By the end of the century, Newcastle was home to six newspapers and ten periodicals.

And not only newspapers. The town catered for most aspects of eighteenth-century intellectual life. Book publishing, bookshops and bookbinders all flourished, along with stationery shops, subscription libraries and literary clubs. St Nicholas parish church ran its own library, containing more than 5,000 volumes. The town also had three subscription newsrooms, establishments which subscribed to the London newspapers, and some foreign ones, and charged customers to read them. By the 1770s, Newcastle was publishing more children's books than any town in England outside of London.

In 1736, the musician and composer Charles Avison began holding subscription concerts in Newcastle. Nowadays largely (and undeservedly) forgotten, Avison was regarded in his day as the finest composer in Britain. He may not have been in the same league as his great European contemporaries like Bach, Handel or Vivaldi, but he was a substantial figure in eighteenth-century Britain's musical life. Born in Newcastle in 1710, he studied with the Italian composer Geminiani in London and was the organist at St Nicholas Church from 1736 until he died in 1770, aged about 60.

Charles Avison was an interesting figure. He supplemented his £50-a-year salary by teaching. One of his pupils was William Shield, later Master of the King's Music. Avison's subscription concerts in the Groat Market Assembly Rooms were usually well attended, and he staged benefit concerts to raise money for the new infirmary. Avison's orchestra – which he ran for many years – included in its ranks some fine musicians. One of them was William Herschel, better known as an astronomer but also a musician and composer in his own right.

Avison published 50 concertos and a large number of sonatas. His 'Grand March' for the harpsichord was resurrected 100 years after his death, and he was one of the characters in Robert Browning's long poem *Parleyings with Certain People of Importance in their Day*. Avison's *Essay on Musical Expression* was a vigorous piece of musical theorising which sparked what the *Oxford Companion to Music* calls a 'lively controversy'. Charles Avison, Newcastle's own Handel, is buried in the churchyard of St Andrew's Church.

While Tyneside never produced a literary equivalent of Avison, it did have Mark Akenside. Akenside was a Newcastle butcher's son who studied theology (at Edinburgh), switched to medicine (at Leyden) and penned second-rate poetry. He's reputed to be the model for the pompous physician satirised by Smollett in *The Adventures of Peregrine Pickle*. But he was a good enough doctor to be appointed the Queen's Physician. Towards the end of his medical career, he acquired a reputation for being careless with his patients' health, swaggering round the wards wearing a full-bottomed wig with his sword at his side.

No one is likely to accuse Akenside of genius, but he was not without talent. His best-known work is a set of long, discursive poems entitled *The Pleasures of the Imagination*, which contains some highly coloured tributes to his home:

> O ye dales
> Of Tyne, and ye most ancient woodlands; where
> Oft, as the giant flood obliquely strides
> And his banks open and his lawns extend,
> Stops short the pleased traveller to view.

And much more in the same vein. It's hard to disagree with the nineteenth-century critic who observed that Akenside's 'solemn sententiousness of manner, his romantic ideas of liberty, and his unbounded admiration for the ancients exposed him occasionally to ridicule'. As for his opus *The Pleasures of the Imagination*, 'The work is an uninspired but dignified and graceful melange of reflection and illustration, reason and imagination, deism, optimism and common-place 18th century philosophising.'

A much livelier talent was the collier-turned-poet Edward Chicken. Little known outside his native Tyneside (which is a pity), Chicken's verse had a raw energy that Akenside could never match. His *Collier's Wedding* was published almost 20 years after his death:

> Dead drunk, some tumble on the floor
> And swim in what they'd drunk before
> Hiccup cries one 'reach me your hand
> The house turns round, I cannot stand'.
> So now the drunken, senseless crew
> Break pipes, spill drinks, piss, shit and spew.

There were others, although none so memorable. The scholar John Horsley's *Britannia Romana* of 1732 is the first serious attempt to explain Roman Britain. And the strange figure of Richard Dawes, headmaster of Newcastle Grammar School, whose unending rows with the school's governors almost ruined the institution, also wrote a *Miscellanea Critica* in 1745, which was much praised.

There were women too: Mary Astell, who spoke out for the rights of her sex at a time when such a thing was almost unheard of; Elizabeth Elstob, linguist, grammarian and educationist; Ann Fisher, whose guides to speaking and writing English ran into many editions; and Jane Gomeldon, who married, ran off to France dressed as a man, then returned to Tyneside after her husband died, to generate years of controversy.

But just as Tyneside was getting into its eighteenth-century stride, more trouble erupted from Scotland. In April 1745, Charles Edward Stuart, better known as Bonnie Prince Charlie, landed on the west coast of Scotland to spark yet another Jacobite insurrection. This time it looked serious. The idea of thousands of red-shanked Highlanders crashing into England was bad enough, but they trailed with them the prospect of an invasion of trained and well-equipped French troops. And as the landed gentry of Northumberland had a history of supporting the Stuarts, the burghers of Newcastle and Gateshead – most of whom were solid for King George – were distinctly jumpy.

One man who happened to be on Tyneside in the autumn of 1745 was the preacher John Wesley, the founder of Methodism. In the course of his endless criss-crossing of Britain (he often travelled more than 8,000 miles a year on horseback), Wesley was a regular visitor to Tyneside. From his journals, it's known he made at least 11 visits to Newcastle, Gateshead and the surrounding towns. There were, he thought, souls that were badly in need of saving.

In May 1742, he wrote in his journal:

> I was surprised; so much drunkenness, cursing and swearing (even from the mouths of little children) do I never remember to have seen and heard before, in so small a compass of time. Surely this place is ripe for Him who 'came not to call the righteous, but sinners to repentance.'

Wesley happened to be in Newcastle in September 1745, when news came through that the Jacobites had taken Edinburgh.

We found the generality of the inhabitants in the utmost consternation. A great concourse of people were with us in the evening, to whom I expounded the third chapter of Jonah; insisting particularly on that verse, 'Who can tell, if God will return, and repent, and turn away from his fierce anger?'

The Mayor of Newcastle, Alderman Ridley, did his best to stiffen the morale of the townsfolk. Wesley writes:

The mayor summoned all the householders of the town to meet him at the town-hall: and desired as many of them as were willing, to set their hands to a paper, importing that they would, to the hazard of their goods and lives, defend the town against the common enemy.

Wesley does not say just how many Novocastrians pledged their property and lives to King George. But he does say that 'Fear and darkness were now on every side.'

While Wesley and his followers prayed for 'an answer of peace', Alderman Ridley and his men did what they could.

The mayor ordered the townsmen to be under arms and to mount guard in their turns, over and above the guard of soldiers, a few companies of whom had been drawn into the town on the first alarm. Now, also, Pilgrim-street gate was ordered to be walled up.

No sooner had that been done than news reached Newcastle of General John Cope's defeat at Prestonpans at the hands of the Jacobites. 'Orders were now given for the doubling up of the guard, and for walling up Pandon and Sally-port gates.'

While Newcastle settled down grimly to wait the assault of the wild Jacobites (which never came), Welsey assured them, via Alderman Ridley, that they had his support.

All I can do for his Majesty, whom I honour and love, is this, I cry unto God, day by day, in public and in private, to put all his enemies to confusion; and I exhort all that hear to do the same; and, in their several situations, to exert themselves as loyal subjects; who, so long as they fear God, cannot but honour the King.

But Wesley's assurance that God was a Hanoverian didn't do much to soothe Novocastrian nerves. Frantic preparations were put in place.

The walls were mounted with cannon and all things prepared for sustaining an assault. Meantime our poor neighbours, on either hand, were busy in removing their goods. And most of the best houses in our street were left without either furniture or inhabitants. Those within the walls were busy in carrying away their money and goods; and more and more of the gentry every hour rode southward as fast as they could.

If Wesley is to be believed, most of the North-east was in a panic.

On Friday and Saturday messengers of lies terrified the poor people of the town, as if the rebels were just coming to swallow them up. Upon this the guards were increased, and abundance of country gentlemen came in, with their servants, horses and arms . . . Advice came that they [the Jacobites] were in full march southwards, so it was supposed they would reach Newcastle by Monday evening. At eight I called on a multitude of sinners in Gateshead to seek the Lord while he might be found . . . And we cried mightily to God to send his Majesty King George help from his holy place, and to spare a sinful land yet a little longer.

While Newcastle crouched behind the walls waiting for the wild and savage Jacobite host (who were, in fact, remarkably well behaved), Wesley found time to worry about the language, manners and behaviour of the King's redcoats. Wesley penned a letter to the commanding officer, which he sent via Alderman Ridley. He wrote:

> My soul has been pained day by day, even in walking the streets of Newcastle, at the senseless, shameless wickedness, the ignorant profaneness, of the poor men to whom our lives are entrusted. The continual cursing and swearing, the wanton blasphemy of the soldiers in general, must needs be a torture to the sober ear, whether of a Christian or an honest infidel.

He goes on:

> Can any that either fear God, or love their neighbour hear this without concern? Especially if they consider the interest of our country, as well as of these unhappy men themselves. For can it be expected, that God should be on their side who are daily affronting Him to His face? And if God be not on their side, how little will either their number, or courage, or strength avail?

In the end, the Jacobites came nowhere near Newcastle. They tramped down the west side of England picking up a couple of hundred English volunteers in Manchester before reaching Derby, where they decided to turn back to Scotland. The Jacobite insurgency ended on Culloden Moor, near Inverness, in April 1746, when the rebels were cut to pieces by King George's artillery. The Jacobites left a little garrison of Manchester men at Carlisle, who were quickly rounded up and tried for treason.

Alderman Ridley was asked by His Majesty's government if his town would like to stage trials of some of the Jacobite prisoners, but, to his credit, he declined. Not that he felt sorry for the Jacobites, but he suspected that the trials would involve horrors that Newcastle could do without. He was right. The trials were held in Carlisle, York and London and a ghastly business they proved to be.

It's one of the ironies of the 1745–46 insurrection that English rebels were treated more cruelly than the Scots. Disaffected

Englishmen were seen as a much greater danger to the state than rebellious Scots or Irish. The so-called Manchester Regiment (mainly untrained volunteers) had never fired a shot in anger. But no fewer than 24 of their number, including their chaplain, were tried and sentenced to death. They were drawn through the streets, hung by the neck, then, while still alive, disembowelled, beheaded and their bodies cut into pieces. The Mayor of Newcastle did well to say no to these gruesome events.

Not that the people of eighteenth-century Tyneside were particularly squeamish. Public executions brought big crowds to the gallows at the Westgate or the Town Moor to see felons go to meet their Maker. Most of these executions were hangings, although some were of soldiers, shot for desertion. These sad occasions – and many of them were plainly heart-rending – are chronicled by Barry Redfern in his book *In The Shadow of the Gallows*. What's remarkable to twenty-first-century eyes is just how many crimes were capital offences: horse-stealing, sheep-stealing, cattle-rustling, burglary, forgery and highway robbery, as well as murder and treason.

And for some wretched felons, death was not the end of their sentence. Many murderers were sentenced to the posthumous humiliation of the gibbet, having their bodies hanged in chains for months on end. And right up to the passing of the Anatomy Act of 1832, Britain's medical schools and hospitals found it almost impossible to acquire the corpses they needed to teach anatomy. The only legal source was the courts. Murderers were often sentenced not only to be hanged but also to be turned over to the medical men for dissection. To some of them, that prospect was more terrifying than being executed.

One such unfortunate was a 19-year-old Scot called Ewen Macdonald, a soldier in Guise's Highland Regiment who was hanged on the Town Moor in September 1752 for murder (he'd stabbed a man to death in the Bigg Market). After the hanging, Macdonald's strangled corpse was sent to the Barber Surgeons' Hall at Manors to be publicly anatomised. It's plain that he was not properly hanged, because after an hour on the table, and before the surgeons started cutting, the 'corpse' suddenly sat up and demanded to know what was happening. He had to be finished off with a mallet wielded by one of the surgeons and was known thereafter as 'Half-hanged Macdonald'.

This grisly tale has an intriguing footnote (which may be apocryphal). The young surgeon who malleted Macdonald to death after he'd come back to life was himself kicked to death by his own horse shortly after. For some time, the mallet he used to kill Macdonald was an exhibit at the Barber Surgeons' Hall.

But it would be wrong to give the impression that public executions in Newcastle and elsewhere on Tyneside were a common spectacle. They were not. Acquittals, reprieves and sentences commuted to transportation to the Colonies were common. Newcastle was not London, where felons were 'turned off' by the hangman almost every week. Barry Redfern has calculated that throughout the eighteenth century no more than twenty-seven men and women were hanged in Newcastle, an average of one every three or four years.

BESSIE AND JOHN

One of Newcastle's landmarks and tourist attractions is Bessie Surtees' House, which sits on the Sandhill down by the River Tyne. Now tended by English Heritage, the half-timbered house is typical of a seventeenth-century merchant's dwelling. 'A splendid example of Jacobean domestic architecture' is one writer's description. In the 1770s, it was the property of a wealthy banker named Aubone Surtees, father of 17-year-old Elizabeth, or Bessie. It was from here, in November 1772, that Bessie's admirer John Scott snatched her from under the noses of her family, bundled her into a waiting carriage and whisked her off to be married in Scotland. So far, so romantic. But eloping with Bessie Surtees was probably the only romantic thing John Scott did in his long life.

Born in Love Lane, Newcastle, in 1751, John Scott was the son of a Newcastle fitter (coal merchant). After studying law at University College, Oxford, he became a Middle

Temple barrister in 1776 and a Member of Parliament for Weobley in 1783. Able and ambitious, John Scott was an instinctive and hardline conservative. In 1788, he was knighted and in 1793 made Attorney General in William Pitt's government and charged with clamping down on radicals and subversives. Scott seems to have relished the job and in time became one of the most hated and feared men in England.

After six years of suppressing, harrying and jailing the left-wing intelligentsia, in 1799 he was made a judge (Chief Justice of the Common Pleas) and created Baron Eldon of Eldon. In 1801, he was elevated to the post of Lord Chancellor of England, which he held for the next quarter of a century, serving under five different prime ministers. In 1821, King George IV (one of his clients) created him Viscount Encombe of Encombe and Earl Eldon of Eldon. He resigned his post in 1827 in protest at Prime Minister George Canning's plan to extend the franchise to Roman Catholics.

He was also something of a snob. As he rose through the ranks of the Establishment, Eldon began to scratch around for aristocratic connections. He claimed descent from a Scottish gentry family, the Scotts of Balwearie in Fife. But there's no evidence that he was anything other than the product of hard-working Tynesiders. His grandfather William Scott went down on the record as a 'yeoman' of Sandgate, and his father was apprenticed to a coal-industry hostman until becoming one himself.

Legal historians regard John Scott, Lord Eldon, as one of the most dilatory and reactionary of lords chancellor. Conservative to the bone, he was a bitter opponent of every legal reform that came his way: the abolition of the slave trade, the system of throwing debtors into prison and reform of the House of Commons, as well as Catholic emancipation. Eldon died at his home in Middlesex in 1838.

Lady Eldon – his Bessie Surtees – preceded him to the grave in 1831. It's said he never really recovered from losing his beloved Bessie.

Newcastle's tribute to one of the city's most renowned (or notorious) citizens is Eldon Square, or what's left of it, and the huge city-centre retail complex known as the Eldon Square Shopping Centre.

The world is used to seeing Newcastle through a late-nineteenth-century prism of high smokestacks, reeking chimneys, forests of cranes and masts, and soot-blackened streets running down to the polluted River Tyne. But the eighteenth-century town was not like that. In his wanderings through Britain in 1725, Daniel Defoe described Newcastle as a 'spacious, extended, infinitely populous place'. By then, the town was the fourth biggest in England, and local architects were being commissioned by the well-heeled families of merchants and gentrymen to put up houses (in the town and in the country) that were as good as anything being built in Britain.

The best of Tyneside's architectural talent at the time was probably William Newton, a shipwright's son who emerged as an accomplished Palladian architect, and a resourceful builder and surveyor. William Newton, more than anyone, introduced Tyneside to the delights of neoclassical architecture. The best of eighteenth-century Newcastle is down to Newton: the Assembly Rooms (1774); Charlotte Square (1770); St Anne's Church (1764); Heaton Hall (1780); and a handful of country houses, some of which have long since been demolished.

Nor was Newton alone. His contemporary David Stephenson was the first Newcastle architect to study at the Royal Academy and was the man behind the stunning All Saints' Church, behind the Quayside, with its oval plan and high, elegant steeple. Stephenson was also responsible for Newcastle's first Theatre Royal, in Mosley Street, which opened in 1788 (with a comedy entitled *The Way to Keep Him*). Also operating in late-eighteenth-century Tyneside were William Stokoe and his son John. The Stokoes were responsible for Elswick Hall, completed in 1806.

In 1762, with the Jacobite menace now consigned to the past, Newcastle began dismantling the medieval walls with which the town had defended itself for hundreds of years against marauders (lawless English as well as Scots). Twelve feet high and eight feet thick, Newcastle's town walls were a formidable barrier. One sixteenth-century traveller noted that 'The strength and magnificense of the waulling of this towne far passeth all the waulles of the cities of England and most of the townes of Europe.'

By the late eighteenth century, Newcastle was fast becoming one of Britain's more spacious, handsome, better-equipped large towns. The Orphan House erected by the Methodists in Northumberland Street in 1743 was followed in 1752 by the Infirmary on Forth Banks (paid for by public subscription) and in 1760 by a lying-in hospital for poor women at Rosemary Lane near St John's churchyard. In 1766, a Custom House was opened on the Quayside. They were all handsome buildings. In 1763, street lighting was introduced when parts of the town were lit by oil lamps.

Communications with the rest of Britain were improving but were still slow. Newcastle's main coaching inn was The Cock tavern, from where stagecoaches ran north as well as south. There were three coaches a week between Tyneside and London, a journey that took three days and two nights. Even the much shorter journey to Edinburgh took two days and one night. Unless, that is, the roads were flooded or mired, in which case the journeys took much longer. And Gateshead Fell was known as a haunt of highwaymen, about whom there was nothing romantic.

The fabric of eighteenth-century Tyneside – the infrastructure, in modern parlance – suffered a heavy blow on the night of 16–17 November 1771 when the medieval bridge over the Tyne was swept away after a flood that saw the river burst its banks. The bridge was Newcastle's version of the old London Bridge or the Ponte Vecchio in Florence, a series of elegant arches on top of which sat a street lined with houses and little shops. In the centre of the bridge, there was a blue stone which marked the boundary between Newcastle and Gateshead, Northumberland and County Durham.

Within days of the disaster, a ferry service had been put in place and within months a temporary, timber-built bridge erected. Ten years later, a new, stone-built, neoclassical bridge by the Scots architect and engineer Robert Mylne was opened to traffic. It was later widened by Robert Stephenson, son of George, and survived into the late nineteenth century, until it was replaced by the hydraulically operated Swing Bridge.

The smaller Tyneside towns, like Tynemouth, North Shields, Wallsend, South Shields and Jarrow, remained little more than hamlets throughout the eighteenth century. Apart from a few country houses, they saw little of the kind of architectural splendour that graced Newcastle. As the Northumberland volume of Pevsner's *Buildings of England* says of Tynemouth, 'the settlement here was never much more than one street leading to the great Castle on Priory'. Many of them were like that – one-street towns, or little groups of houses huddled around a parish church.

All that was to change, of course, in the nineteenth century, when populations exploded in the Industrial Revolution.

7

THE ENLIGHTENMENT ON TYNESIDE

1775–1850

In the year 1774, three of Newcastle's more enterprising booksellers – Mr Slack, Mr Charnley and Mr Humble – began selling a pamphlet entitled *Chains of Slavery*. At ten shillings and sixpence, it was an expensive item for the time. It purported to be:

> A work in which the clandestine and villainous attempts of
> Princes to ruin liberty are pointed out, and the dreadful scenes
> of Despotism disclosed. To which is prefixed an address to the
> Electors of Great Britain, in order to draw timely attention to
> the choice of proper representation.

This fiery document was one of the first traces in Tyneside of the revolutionary ideas that were to sweep across Europe, topple the *Ancien Régime* of France and spark a war that was to last for more than 20 years. The pamphlet was written by one of Newcastle's most unlikely denizens, the French radical intellectual Jean-Paul Marat, one of the driving forces of the French Revolution 15 years later. Marat was in Newcastle working as a veterinary surgeon, having studied medicine at St Andrews University in Scotland.

There's a theory that it was Marat who inspired the intelligentsia of Tyneside to set up a philosophical society which began meeting at a private address in Westgate Road. It was a modest affair, to say the least, with probably no more than 20 members. But one of them was Thomas Spence, a clerk in a merchant's office and a young man with determined views that he was not afraid to air.

One evening at the beginning of March 1755, young Spence stood up to address the Philosophical Society with a paper which startled and dismayed his listeners. It was entitled 'Property in Land Everyone's Right' and argued that private landowning should be abolished, that all land should be owned by the parishes, that every man in the parish should have a vote and that people should pay rent to the parish for the maintenance of roads, bridges, etc. and the upkeep of clergymen, schoolmasters and the poor.

Such ideas – and many far more radical – were common enough in the England of Cromwell's time, but not in the 1770s. Spence's listeners were appalled. So appalled, in fact, that they accused him of using the society as a cover for 'intruding upon the world the erroneous and dangerous levelling principles'. They then booted Spence out and passed a new set of rules banning the discussion of any subject 'which might lead to Arguments, too freely and incautiously calling into question the fundamental principles of religion and good government'.

Not that it stopped Spence. He was a determined radical. After a spell as a schoolmaster, he took himself off to London, where he produced a stream of radical pamphlets and a news-sheet entitled *Pig's Meat or Lessons for the People, alias the Swinish Multitude*. Predictably, perhaps, Spence was in and out of court and was regularly fined and gaoled. He died in London in 1814, one of the heroes of early-nineteenth-century English radicalism.

Thomas Spence was not the only thorn in the flesh of Tyneside's Establishment. One man they took much more seriously was James Murray, the minister at the Presbyterian chapel in High Bridge. Murray was born at Earlston in Berwickshire in 1732 into a Presbyterian family whose memory of the 'killing times' of the 1680s in Scotland, when the Anglican Establishment under Charles II and his brother James tried to ban Presbyterianism, was strong. Like many of his kind, he grew up with a deep distaste for both the aristocracy of Britain and the class-bound hierarchies of Anglicanism.

Murray drifted into England in 1761, first to work as a tutor at Belford, then as assistant minister at the Bondgate Meeting House in Alnwick. When that ended in acrimony, Murray marched out to form his own chapel, followed by most of the congregation.

A few years later, in 1764, Murray was in Newcastle, where the affluent Presbyterians of the town were always on the lookout for new talent. In the 16 or so years James Murray spent ministering to his Tyneside flock, he preached a mixture of religion and radical politics that thoroughly alarmed the great and good of Tyneside. One modern writer has even credited James Murray with more or less inventing modern politics in the north-east of England, which is a large claim and one that's hard to substantiate.

The Reverend Murray's opinions certainly ranged far and wide. He was bitterly opposed to the war against the American colonists and raised petitions to Parliament against it. He despised (albeit politely) both John Wesley's Methodism and the Church of England. He also hated Roman Catholicism and in 1781 penned a couple of particularly stinging pamphlets: *News From The Pope to The Devil* and *Popery Not Christianity*.

Murray was no humourless zealot, however. One of his friends was the artist Thomas Bewick, who described Murray as a 'most cheerful, facetious, sensible and pleasant man – a most agreeable companion'. Which was a view shared by Murray's publisher, William Hone. 'From a cheerful temperament, he was on most topics facetious and playful,' Hone wrote, 'but in defending the rights of civil and religious liberty, either in private conversation, or from the pulpit, he was as grave and stern as Diogenes himself.' It was one of Murray's maxims that 'no man could be a real Christian who was not a warm and zealous friend to civil and religious liberty'.

His most famous work was a collection entitled *Sermons to Asses*. It still makes interesting reading. There's a peculiarly modern resonance about it. Essentially, it's a plea for the ordinary man to get political, to stay political and to use his voice to create a better, fairer Britain. And Murray knew how to coin a phrase. His work is full of staccato sentences that must have stuck in the minds of his listeners. Nowadays, they are known as soundbites. 'Strength without activity debases human nature,' he said in sermon No. 1. 'A nation of slaves is a nation of asses . . . Rest is good but liberty is better.'

As for our rulers:

> The indolence and sloth of a people are a temptation to governors to turn usurpers . . . We lose our liberty by not asserting it properly . . . Members of Parliament are your servants and the servants of their country; it is but reasonable they be made accountable for their conduct.

After an hour or so of listening to Murray, his congregation must have reeled out of the church, their heads buzzing with admonitions and epigrams. Newcastle's fiery cleric died unrepentant in 1782 – the year the rebellious American colonists he admired shrugged off London rule. He was buried in St Andrew's churchyard, one of the many eighteenth-century Tynesiders who deserve to be better remembered than they are.

What is interesting about James Murray and Thomas Spence is that they both represent a strand of radical politics that was to emerge much more strongly – and more dangerously – in the first two decades of the nineteenth century, particularly after the final defeat of Napoleon. This came about partly as a result of idealism of the kind that created the United States and revolutionary France, and partly as a response to the rapid industrialisation of Tyneside and the dismal working and living conditions that went along with it.

James Murray was not the only clergyman to shape the political-philosophical life of eighteenth-century Tyneside. Someone who was quieter but arguably more effective in the long run was the Reverend William Turner, the minister of the Unitarian congregation in Hanover Square. The leading lights of the Hanover Square congregation were middle-class professionals – solicitors, barristers, merchants, publishers, doctors, journalists – the bourgeoisie that became increasingly influential as the eighteenth century wore on.

Of all the Christian denominations, Unitarianism is perhaps the most intellectually challenging. 'A type of Christian thought and religious observance which rejects the doctrines of the Trinity and the Divinity of Christ in favour of the unipersonality of God' is how the *Oxford Dictionary of the Christian Church* describes Unitarianism. For whatever reason, it struck a deep chord among English dissenters (numerous on Tyneside), particularly the Presbyterians. One of Unitarianism's advocates was the great English scientist Joseph Priestley.

So it was fitting that it was the Unitarian minister William Turner who, in 1793, created Newcastle's famous Literary and Philosophical Society (affectionately known as 'the Lit and Phil'). Quite quickly, the Lit and Phil moved into the heart of Tyneside's intellectual life. It hosted lectures on science, technology, philosophy and economics. Late-eighteenth-century Newcastle owed a lot to its Unitarians. And in the early years of the nineteenth century, they were behind many of the town's charitable institutions. They were influential far beyond their numbers.

But it was many years before the Lit and Phil found a permanent home. For years, the intelligentsia of Tyneside met all over Newcastle: the Governor's Hall of the Dispensary; a billiard room in St Nicholas churchyard; the Assembly Rooms in the Groat Market; the concert hall attached to the Turk's Head Inn. It was not until 1822 that they raised enough cash for the building which still stands at the bottom of Westgate Road.

One of the Lit and Phil's early members (he joined in 1799) was an artistic Novocastrian called Thomas Bewick. He was to become one of Tyneside's most important artists. He was a watercolour artist, engraver, naturalist and candid memorialist. Born in 1753, at the age of 14 Bewick was apprenticed to silversmith and engraver Ralph Beilby and proved so adept that he was soon Beilby's partner (although they parted company in 1797). Bewick earned his reputation by rediscovering and refining the old techniques of wood engraving.

They were skills he put to use in the illustrations he engraved for a series of books, among them *Gay's Fables* (1779), *Select Fables* (1784), *The Chillingham Bull* (1789), *A General History of Quadrupeds* (1790), *History of British Birds* (1797 and 1804), *Osterwald's Bible* (1805) and *Fables of Aesop* (1818). He also left a series of unfinished illustrations for a *History of British Fishes*.

One of Bewick's many admirers was the influential critic and aesthete John Ruskin. 'Our own great engraver and moralist' is how Ruskin described Bewick. He relished what he called 'the magnificent artistic power, the flawless virtue, veracity, tenderness – the infinite humour of the man'. From the vantage point of the twenty-first century, Ruskin's judgement seems a bit overheated. Many of Bewick's engravings fall some way short of genius.

But no one was more loyal to Tyneside than Thomas Bewick. He was tempted away to London in the 1770s but found that he just did not like the place. In his *Memoir* he writes that, while he was 'gratified' by everything that London had to offer in the way of the arts and sciences, 'I tired of it and determined to return home – the scenery of Tyneside seemed altogether to form a paradise for me, & I longed to see it again.' Once back on the banks of the Tyne, he never left again.

CUTHBERT COLLINGWOOD

On the shore at Tynemouth, on the north bank of the River Tyne where it opens out into the North Sea, there stands a large and impressive statue on a handsome stone plinth. It's Tyneside's tribute to one of its most famous sons, Rear Admiral Cuthbert Collingwood. The British victory at Trafalgar in October 1805 is usually ascribed to Horatio Nelson, but when Nelson was felled by a French marksman, it was Collingwood – then Nelson's second-in-command – who made sure that the battle was finally won. He also succeeded in keeping the fleet and its prizes together in the teeth of the savage gales that sprang up as the sea fight ended.

Cuthbert Collingwood was born in Newcastle in 1748 and by the age of 12 was at sea. He served on the North America station, won his commission in the American War of Independence and in 1776 was a lieutenant aboard HMS *Hornet*. The young Collingwood became an acquaintance and later a close friend of the up-and-coming Horatio Nelson, a relationship that did him no harm at all.

When the Revolutionary Wars broke out, Collingwood was appointed a flag-captain, took part in the blockade of Toulon and was 'conspicuous' in the British victory at St Vincent. In 1799, he was promoted to rear admiral (his ship being HMS *Triumph*) and organised the blockade of Brest. In 1804, he was promoted again, to vice admiral, and in 1805, his squadron was standing off Cadiz, where it was joined by the fleet led by Horatio Nelson and then pitched into the battle at Trafalgar.

Collingwood's shipmates seem to have found him a distant and sometimes difficult man. 'The Admiral is a very different man from Lord Nelson,' wrote Captain Sir William Hoste, 'but as brave an old boy as ever stood.' For his part, Captain George Elliot admitted Collingwood's bravery and efficiency but found him 'a selfish old bear . . . in body and mind he was iron, and very cold iron'.

Cold iron or not, Collingwood tried to run his ships without resorting to the Royal Navy's tradition of flogging. And he knew how to inspire his men. According to Horatio Nelson's most recent biographer, Edgar Vincent, Collingwood trained his gunners better than any officer in the fleet. 'In this Collingwood was pre-eminent; his crews were trained to fire three broadsides in five minutes and had been known to accomplish three broadsides in three and a half minutes.' Which, Vincent claims in his book *Nelson: Love and Fame*, made the British ships 'far the more efficient killing machines' compared with those of the French or the Spaniards.

Underneath this military zeal was a dedicated family man, much concerned about the welfare of his two daughters, and in his letters he longed for his home and garden in Northumberland. Wherever he sailed, he was never without his little dog, Bounce, who saw some of the fiercest sea battles in nineteenth-century history. Bounce looms large in Collingwood's letters to his friends and family. 'He considers it beneath his dignity to play with commoners' dogs, and truly thinks he does them grace when he condescends to lift up his leg against them. This I think is carrying the insolence of rank too far.'

For his stirring performance at Trafalgar, Collingwood was ennobled to Baron Collingwood and awarded a handsome pension of £2,000 a year. In the five years after Trafalgar, Collingwood's ships dominated the Mediterranean. He died at sea on 7 March 1810 and is buried in St Paul's Cathedral in London, near his friend Horatio Nelson.

The statue of Cuthbert Collingwood in Tynemouth was erected in 1847. The plinth was designed by the Newcastle architect John Dobson, and the huge, 23-ft-high image of the great admiral by the sculptor John Lough. Four cannon from Collingwood's ship *Royal Sovereign* were grouped around the steps in 1848.

While Thomas Bewick was sketching the bird and plant life along the Tyne, the industrial economy of Tyneside was given an enormous boost thanks to the genius of a French chemist called Nicolas Leblanc and the perspicacity of a Newcastle coal owner called William Losh. Once again, coal and salt were at the heart of things.

What happened was this: in 1775, the French Academy of Sciences offered a prize to anyone who could devise a new method of manufacturing alkalis. Leblanc, who was then physician to the Duc d'Orléans, worked out the chemistry for producing soda ash (sodium carbonate) from common salt (sodium chloride). He won the prize, took out a patent in 1791 and, with the backing of d'Orléans, built a soda-ash factory at St-Denis, near Paris.

But after the Duc d'Orléans was guillotined in the Terror, the Committee for Public Safety compelled Nicolas Leblanc to publish his findings and then closed down the St-Denis factory. They then found themselves short of a very useful product and ordered it reopened, instructing Leblanc to resume making the soda that France needed. This he did for a few years before retiring in despair to the country, where he committed suicide.

Meanwhile, William Losh, who happened to be a trained chemist as well as a coal owner, had heard of the Leblanc process and saw its potential for Tyneside. When Britain and France signed a short-lived truce in 1802 (the so-called Peace of Amiens), Losh seized the opportunity, made his way to France, learned all he could about the Leblanc process and returned to Newcastle determined to make it work on Tyneside.

The Leblanc process was simple in principle, although complex in detail. Coarse-grained salt was mixed with the same weight of sulphuric acid and heated by coal in a hemispherical, cast-iron pan to produce what was known as 'salt cake'. The salt cake was then mixed with limestone (or chalk) and coal, and reheated to produce sodium carbonate.

The alkali that emerged from the Leblanc process was invaluable for the manufacture of soap, some types of glass, chlorine and bleaching powder. The downside was that it generated large quantities of carbon dioxide and, particularly, hydrochloric acid, which polluted the countryside for miles around. It was many years before the Government got round to grappling with that particular problem.

William Losh succeeded in transferring Leblanc's ideas to Britain, although it took some time. The result was Tyneside's first alkali factory. It was built on the site of the Walker Colliery (in which Losh had a share) and was fed from a spring of brine-laden water. In the early years of the nineteenth century, other industrialists in the area (and elsewhere) saw the potential and began muscling in on the alkali business. A whole new industry – noisome, hugely polluting, dangerous to health, but enormously profitable – was being born on the banks of the River Tyne.

It was in the nineteenth century that Gateshead was transformed from a small riverside port attached to the north Durham coalfield into one of the powerhouses of the North-east, with industrial muscle that almost (but never quite) rivalled Newcastle's.

But Gateshead had been growing all through the eighteenth century: Ambrose Crawley's ironworks dated back to the late seventeenth century; Isaac Cookson opened an iron and brass foundry on Pipewellgate in 1721; there was a bottle works on South Shore by 1740; and Hawks, Crawshay & Sons got under way in 1748. At the end of the century, a mysterious figure known to the record only as 'the Jew of Oakwellgate' seems to have been manufacturing cyanogen and other chemicals.

The town's population grew in proportion to the number of enterprises that sprang up. According to the census of 1801, there were 8,597 men, women and children living in Gateshead. In the census of 1891, that figure had multiplied by *a factor of ten* to 85,692. Most of Gateshead's new denizens hailed from Northumberland and County Durham but many came from elsewhere in England and thousands more from Ireland and Scotland.

Industrial Gateshead continued to expand through the first half of the nineteenth century. John Winfield opened an iron foundry on Pipewellgate in 1805 and Thomas Waters built another in 1813. In 1827, a factory to make soap and soda was opened by Adam Clapham, and for years it sported the highest chimney in Tyneside (263 ft). In 1840, Charles Attwood's 10-year-old chemical plant was bought by Christian Allhusen and expanded until it was a major operation, occupying 137 acres of South Shore.

THE FIRST MAYOR OF GATESHEAD

Gateshead's first mayor was George Hawks, who held the post three times. He was a wealthy man who had inherited the town's biggest engineering firm, built up by his father and grandfather. A photograph of Hawks shows a dapper, good-looking man with wavy dark hair and a large moustache. He was not well regarded by his contemporaries, who saw him as a foppish socialite with an eye for the ladies. Writing in 1838, one of them described Hawks as being 'fond of associating with dignitaries – infatuated for civic honours – indolent in fulfilling public duties – distrusted by both parties'. Another claimed that 'he has his clothes carefully brushed after contact with the canaille [rabble]'. He lived at Redheugh Hall before abandoning Gateshead for Pigden, near Morpeth, where he died in 1863. There's a rather grand statue of Hawks on Windmill Hill in Gateshead.

Gateshead was well on its way to becoming Tyneside's second city. Industry grew rapidly on the foundations laid down in the eighteenth century. For the first half of the nineteenth century, the backbone of the Gateshead economy was the various collieries which were strung along the Tyne, and the engineering firm of Hawks, Crawshay & Sons. Gateshead was also peppered with new alkali factories churning out a variety of chemicals for the glass, soap, paper-making, tanning and textile industries.

Indeed, Gateshead evolved into one of England's 'alkali towns' of the kind described by J.R. Partington, one-time Professor of Chemistry at the University of London, in his book *The Alkali Industry*:

> The rows of chimneys emitting black smoke from the unscientific combustion of coal, the enormous lead chambers, towers, revolving furnaces, waste heaps with the escaping steam, the noise, and the smell of acids, chlorine and sulphuretted hydrogen, are all familiar.

But it was not until the Municipal Corporations Act of 1835 (which reorganised England's local authorities) that Gateshead became a burgh with its own council. For nearly ten years, the new council met in a solicitors' office and then in temporary accommodation until 1844, when it rented a handsome three-storey house on the west side of the Oakwellgate to serve as a town hall and police headquarters.

It was a time of high hopes. The new town hall and the newly built railway terminus were expected to work wonders for Gateshead's town centre. Robert Stephenson put an end to that in 1849 when he built the High Level Bridge which ran the railway across the Tyne and into the heart of Newcastle.

THE GREAT REFORMER

'The Monument' is how Novocastrians usually refer to the 135-ft-high memorial to Earl Grey which stands at the junction of Grey Street, Blackett Street and Grainger Street in Newcastle. The Roman Doric column was designed by the architect Benjamin Green to accommodate the statue of Grey by E.H. Baily. It was erected in 1838, seven years before Grey died. On the pedestal there's a florid inscription which describes Grey as a 'Champion of Civil and Religious Liberties' and the politician and statesman who 'safely and triumphantly attained . . . the great measure of Parliamentary reform'.

It is Tyneside's tribute to one of its many nineteenth-century notables. Charles Grey, the 2nd Earl Grey, was born at Falloden in Northumberland in 1764, the son of an eminent British soldier. Educated at Eton and Trinity College, Cambridge, he entered Parliament as MP for Northumberland in 1786 and rose through the ranks of back-bench Whigs to become First Lord of the Admiralty, then Foreign Secretary. In 1794, he married Mary Ponsonby, the daughter of a liberal Irish family. A genuinely principled man, he resigned his government post in 1807 when King George III refused to entertain the idea of extending the vote to Roman Catholics.

Grey eventually became Prime Minister of a Whig administration in 1830, and, after a titanic struggle in both houses of Parliament, managed to pass the Reform Act of 1832, which gave more Britons (males only) the right to

> vote. It was a historic achievement, one of the watersheds
> of British political life. In 1835, Grey retired from Parliament
> to the family home in Howick, Northumberland, where he
> died in 1845.

The political temperature of Tyneside – and indeed of Britain – soared in August 1819 after the panicky and ill-disciplined cavalry militias of Manchester charged into a crowd of 60,000 men and women who'd gathered on St Peter's Field to protest against unemployment, low wages and high food prices. Eleven men and women were killed and around 500 injured in what became known as the Peterloo Massacre ('Peterloo' being a conflation of 'St Peter's' and 'Waterloo'). The militiamen got off scot-free. The only people charged after the events were the radical orator Henry Hunt and a few of his followers.

It was a brutal affair that infuriated working people across Britain. And it sparked a series of large protest rallies, one of which was held in October on the Town Moor in Newcastle. A huge event, it attracted people from all over Tyneside and beyond. People came as individuals, in families and as organised groups like the Reform societies, the Political Protestants, women's groups, seamen, keelmen. According to one observer, the march to the Town Moor took more than an hour to cross the Barras Bridge.

Many of the groups carried standards bearing the device of the Roman fasces, representing unity, while others carried various political slogans, such as 'An Hour of glorious Liberty is worth a whole Eternity of Bondage'. On the Town Moor, the hustings were draped with banners declaring 'Truth! Order! Justice!' There were also banners demanding annual parliaments, secret ballots and universal suffrage.

One of the principal speakers was Eneas Mackenzie, who later wrote a history of Newcastle. In a rousing speech, Mackenzie denounced the British government and the men who ran the towns of Tyneside. 'We are groaning under monstrous debt,' he declared. 'Taxes are multiplied to a ruining extent. Our finances are delayed, trade and commerce are languishing. One-fifth of the population is pauperised.'

But the element which worried the authorities most was the men

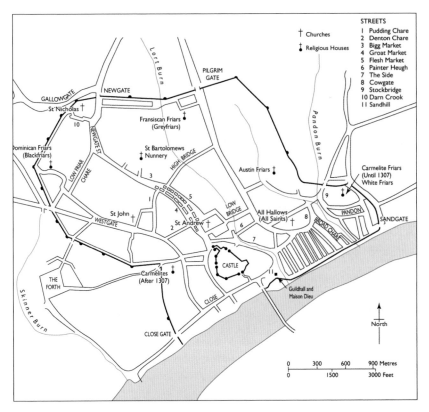

A map of medieval Newcastle.

Newcastle in the seventeenth century. A view from Gateshead showing the
Old Tyne Bridge, swept away in the eighteenth century.

Newcastle in 1745

ABOVE: A view of Newcastle just before the Jacobite rebellion.

JOHN BUDDLE

LEFT: John Buddle (1773–1843). The Tyneside-born pit supervisor and coal owner who is now regarded as one of the fathers of modern mining engineering.

BELOW: Church Pit, Wallsend: typical of the dozens of small collieries that lined both banks of the Tyne and stretched deep into Northumberland and County Durham.

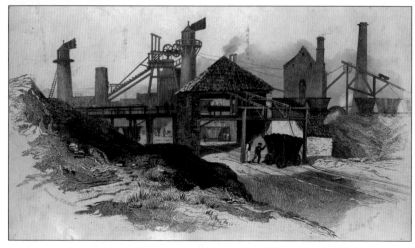

ABOVE: The High Level Bridge, Newcastle. If any one bridge transformed Newcastle, it was this one. Designed by Robert Stephenson and opened in 1849, it allowed the main railway line access to the centre of the city and from there on into Scotland.

BELOW: Industrial Newcastle in the mid-nineteenth century. On the left are Robert Stephenson's High Level Bridge and Robert Mylne's neo-classical Tyne Bridge.

ABOVE: Fish Quay, North Shields. The other face of the Tyne. The fish quay was opened for business in 1886 and has been in use ever since, although the fish landings now are nothing like the quantities that were seen in its heyday.

RIGHT: Lord Armstrong of Cragside (1810–1900). Shipbuilder, arms manufacturer, bridge builder and hydraulic engineer William Armstrong was the greatest of Tyneside's entrepreneurs and, although he died in 1900, the enterprise he created was crucial to Britain in both world wars.

ABOVE: The *Baikal*, one of Tyneside's most extraordinary feats of engineering. This train-ferry-cum-ice-breaker was commissioned in 1896 by the Russians for service on Lake Baikal in eastern Siberia. Shipped to St Petersburg, it was dismantled into thousands of parts which were then sent by rail to distant Siberia.

BELOW: The North Pier in a gale. Sheltering the entrance to the Tyne from heavy seas became a priority in the late nineteenth century. The pier's foundation stone was laid in 1854 but the structure was not completed until 1909 – more than 50 years after work started. The North Sea kept knocking it down.

ABOVE: A crowded beach at South Shields. Taken around 1900, this photograph shows the enthusiasm of Edwardian Tyneside for recreation on the local beaches. A common summer scene around the coast of Britain.

BELOW: The SS *Mauretania*, arguably Tyneside's masterpiece. One of the finest and most successful passenger liners ever built, the *Mauretania* was launched in 1907, worked as a troopship in the First World War and plied the world's seas as a passenger ship until the late 1930s, when it was decommissioned and broken up.

No 171
3.3.28

The Tyne Bridge nearing completion in 1928. Designed by engineers Mott, Hay & Anderson, the structure – which is almost identical to the much larger Sydney Harbour Bridge – has become emblematic of the City of Newcastle.

ABOVE: Carliol House on the corner of Pilgrim Street and Market Street, Newcastle. Designed for the innovative Newcastle upon Tyne Electric Supply Company (NESCo) and opened in 1928, it was one of the most technically advanced office buildings of its day.

BELOW: Colliers loading coal at Dunston Staiths sometime in the late 1930s. The Dunston Staiths on the west side of Gateshead was one of the most important of the many coal-loading points on the Tyne. It is one of the biggest timber-built constructions in Europe and is now a protected structure.

who called themselves 'Crawley's Crew'. They were metalworkers from the Crawley Ironworks at Winlaton who had come equipped to fight off the cavalry militia. They came armed with pikes, hand grenades and 'crows' feet' – small, spiked devices that could be thrown under horses' hooves. But there was to be no repeat of Peterloo. The militias made no move and the great meeting passed off peacefully (although a few days later marines opened fire on a group of protesters in North Shields, killing one man). Among Crawley's Crew that day was a young man of 19 who, many years later, was to galvanise the politics of Tyneside – one Joseph Cowen.

The unrest among pitmen, colliers, keelmen, seamen, engineers and other workers was characteristic of the early nineteenth century. It was watched carefully by the authorities. And it was resisted with skill and occasional ruthlessness by Tyneside's coal owners, ship owners and other employers. There are some fascinating insights into the handling of fractious workers in the journals of one of Tyneside's most able and influential colliery managers and mining engineers, John Buddle.

Between 1799 and 1824, 'combinations' of men (trade unions) were proscribed by law. It was part of the measures passed by the British government during the long wars with revolutionary France. In 1825, the ban was lifted with immediate effect. John Buddle fretted to his journal that 'every class of our workmen is combining, and are one after another compelling us to advance their wages'.

In his defence of the coal owners, Buddle never hesitated to reach for the law. He knew that nine times out of ten it would be on the side of the coal owners. During the Jarrow Colliery strike of 1825, for example, he managed to persuade the local magistrates to lock up 35 pitmen and colliery workers in the local 'House of Correction'.

And the pitmen had a weakness: they and their families lived in houses owned by their bosses. A house was regarded as one of the perks of the pitman's job. A report of 1807 had noticed that 'in almost every colliery on the Tyne pitmen are provided with houses by their employers . . . The occupiers of collieries made a point of situating the houses as near to the concern as possible.'

A man with a tied house is vulnerable. It was a vulnerability that

John Buddle was ready to exploit. During the strike at the Hebburn Colliery in 1826, Buddle sent eviction notices to the strike leaders, giving them two days to quit their homes. A few days later, three of them were marched out of their homes by the parish constable, assisted by six constables from Newcastle. Three days after that, the strike collapsed.

There's an interesting exchange of letters (dated 1830) between Buddle and Lord Durham's agent, who'd written suggesting a 'corps of special constables' to police the collieries, the wagonways, the staiths, the keels and the coal ships. Buddle liked the idea, although he recommended that any such body should be organised secretly.

And he thought there should be no problem recruiting willing hands. 'I have never seen the least difficulty in getting as many "rank and file" for this sort of service as were necessary,' he replied. And he went on to recommend how such a force should be equipped: 'The mounted men ought to have pistols . . . and the foot to have a few muskets at the headquarters of each colliery.'

JOHN BUDDLE

Born in Kyo, County Durham, in 1773, John Buddle was the son of a local schoolmaster whose interest in coal mining led him to become a viewer (a colliery manager) at one of the Bishop of Durham's coal mines. According to Buddle himself, he was 'initiated into the mysteries of pit work when not quite six years old'.

Able, intelligent and ambitious, he rose through the ranks of pitmen and colliery workers to work for just about every major coal owner on Tyneside. According to his entry in the *Oxford Dictionary of National Biography*, it was John Buddle more than anyone in Britain who was 'responsible for converting the old style colliery viewer into the more modern mining engineer'.

Buddle was also a coal owner in his own right, with sizeable investments in the collieries at Benwell, Heaton, Sheriffhill, Backworth and Elswick among others. He also had a 25 per cent share in the Stella Coal Company. He is best remembered for his work with Lord Londonderry, to whom he was very close. Londonderry once described Buddle as a man of 'high intellectual endowments, high character and complete independence'.

Their association began in 1819 when Londonderry hired Buddle to design and build the harbour at Seaham for the export of coal. Buddle went on to become one of the most important and influential coal-industry figures on Tyneside. He was a Unitarian by religion, a reforming Tory by politics and a close friend of the engineer Thomas Sopwith, the geologist William Buckland and the writer Harriet Martineau.

Buddle never married but lived with his sister Ann. He was a careful and austere man who disdained luxury and lived simply in Wallsend House, Wallsend. He died in October 1843, left an estate worth £150,000 and was buried at St James's Church in Benwell.

Even more inclined to strike were the keelmen, who were described by the Mayor of Newcastle in 1746 as being 'too ready to rise and become tumultuous upon the least pretence'. In 1819 and 1822, they became 'tumultuous' yet again when they struck in protest at the direct loading of coal into the ships by 'spouts' and 'drops' erected at the mouth of the Tyne.

The 1822 strike lasted ten weeks, became known as 'the long stop' and was broken by seamen from the Royal Navy manning the keels under armed guard. It was a rare victory over the keelmen, something that John Buddle acknowledged in his journal. He described the breaking of the 1822 keelmen's strike as 'the first battle the coal owners ever gained over that turbulent body'.

There's some irony in the fact that while Tyneside was going through this period of industrial and social turbulence, it saw the start of the building boom that was to transform great swathes of Newcastle into one of Britain's most handsome neoclassical towns. The driving force behind it was a carpenter-turned-builder-turned-property-developer called Richard Grainger. In some ways, Grainger is a very modern figure, an enterpreneur with an eye for a good urban site, the taste to see how it could be developed, and the energy and contacts to put together the permissions and the financing needed to get his scheme built.

RICHARD GRAINGER

Newcastle's greatest property developer was born in 1797 in High Friar's Lane, the son of Thomas Grainger, a quayside porter, and Amelia Burt, seamstress. He was educated at St Andrew's Charity School in Newgate Street and apprenticed to a carpenter at the age of 12. In 1816, at the age of 20, Richard and his brother George set up their own building firm. Richard married Rachel Arundel, the daughter of a well-heeled leather merchant. Richard and Rachel went on to have thirteen children – six sons and seven daughters.

Like many property developers before and since, Richard Grainger became too confident, eventually over-reached himself and almost went bankrupt. But he recovered, and in 1839 he bought the Elswick Hall Estate with an eye to developing it, an ambition he never realised. He died in July 1861 at his home at 5 Clayton Street West and is buried at St James's Church, Benwell. By the time he died, his finances had recovered enough for him to leave £20,000 in his will.

It's hard to overestimate the importance of Richard Grainger to Newcastle. It's fair to say that the best parts of what is now the city centre were built under his direction by talented architects he trusted and commissioned. Most of Grainger's buildings were designed by either John Dobson or Thomas Oliver, two of the most gifted architects working in the north of England.

Grainger's remarkable career began in 1816 when he built a terrace of houses at Higham Place for a local alderman. After that came houses in Carliol Street and New Bridge Street and his first property purchase, houses in Percy Street at the foot of Leazes Lane. His first big development – which he financed with the aid of his wife's money – was the houses and shops in Blackett Street, which were designed jointly by Dobson and Oliver. It was completed in 1824.

One of the most handsome of Grainger's property schemes came next: Eldon Square, named as a tribute to the late John Scott, Lord Chancellor of England, designed by John Dobson and built between 1825 and 1829. This was followed by Leazes Terrace, designed by Thomas Oliver and built between 1829 and 1834. Both these developments were built in sandstone with polished ashlar façades.

One of Grainger's most important contacts was John Clayton, the town clerk of Newcastle. Clayton had the backing of the town council, which was keen on the financial benefits and social kudos that Grainger's high-toned developments would bring to Newcastle. Clayton was briefed to give Grainger and his architects every assistance, financial and otherwise. This Clayton was happy to do. In fact, he put some of his own money into Grainger's schemes, something that would have landed him in jail in the twenty-first century.

In 1834, Grainger put together his most ambitious project to date, a 'mixed' development of houses and shops containing a large covered market (still known as the Grainger Market). Grainger and his associates moved at astonishing speed. The project was approved by the council even before Grainger had completed the purchase of the site. The market, designed by Dobson, was up and running by 1835, and the houses in place and many of them sold by 1840.

In his essay on the architecture of Newcastle in the excellent collection entitled *Newcastle upon Tyne: A Modern History*, Thomas Faulkner compares Grainger's day with modern Britain. He writes:

> Grainger thrived in the hectic, enterpreneurial atmosphere following the Napoleonic Wars, when construction was fuelled by surplus capital and low interest rates. There may be some affinity between this situation and the business-minded

encouragement of market forces characteristic of 'Thatcherism' in the 1980s and even, perhaps, of 'New Labour' today.

In 1845, the Scots journalist and scientific populariser Hugh Miller made his first-ever foray into England. On his way south, he passed through Newcastle and left a vivid picture of an approach from the north. Miller wrote:

> As we drove on we could see the dense smoke of the pit-engines forming a new feature on the prospect; the tall chimneys of Newcastle, that seemed so many soot-black obelisks half lost in the turbid atmosphere, came next in view; and then, just as the evening was falling wet and cheerless, we entered the town, through muddy streets and along ranges of melancholy houses, dropping from all their eaves and darkened by the continuous rain of weeks.

After turning away from 'by far the most splendid temperance coffee house I had ever seen' (although he doesn't name it), Miller found more modest digs, where he spent the rest of the evening arguing religion with assorted Englishmen. This was Miller's first encounter with the English on their home ground, and he was less than impressed by their grasp of theology. But he was hugely impressed by Newcastle's town museum, into which he sallied next day:

> It is superior, both in extent and arrangement of its geologic department, to any of our Scotch collections with which I am acquainted, and its Anglo-Roman antiquities, from the proximity of the place to the wall of Hadrian, are greatly more numerous than in any other museum I ever saw – filling, of themselves, an entire gallery.

He was also delighted that entrance to the museum was free. This he ascribed to the 'liberality of the Newcastle people'.

THE TYNESIDE ALCHEMIST

One of the many Tyneside figures who deserve to be better remembered than they are is Hugh Lee Pattinson, the brilliant, self-taught metallurgist and chemist who some superstitious folk of his day regarded as an alchemist. Pattinson's feat was to devise a method of extracting silver from lead. After patenting the system and selling it abroad, he made himself a tidy fortune, with which he pursued his travels and his studies.

Pattinson was born in 1796 in Alston, Cumberland, the son of a Quaker shopkeeper. In 1821, he moved to Newcastle as clerk to the soap-maker Anthony Clapham. He then returned to Cumberland to become an 'assay master' at one of the local lead mines. In 1829, he noticed that under very high temperatures lead crystallised while the silver it contained remained molten. From that observation, he devised a process for extracting the silver at a rate of roughly 300 ounces per ton of lead. In 1833, he patented the process and a year later founded the Felling Chemical Works to exploit his discovery. By 1850, the Pattinson extraction process was being used in France, Spain and Prussia.

Like many of his kind, Pattinson's interests ranged far and wide. In 1839–40, he visited America and took pictures of Niagara Falls with a daguerrotype camera, and in later years he devoted himself to mathematics, physics and astronomy. At his home at Scotch House, Boldon, in County Durham, he installed a large astronomical telescope. In 1852, Pattinson was made a Fellow of both the Royal Society and the Royal Astronomical Society. He died at his home in November 1858.

The same year that Hugh Miller made his way through Newcastle, a physician called D.R. Reid published his *Report on the State of Newcastle upon Tyne and other Large Towns*. Reid's report was a response to the British government's Health of Towns Commission, which required all sizeable towns in England to examine and report on the health and conditions of their townsfolk. Predictably, perhaps, for an area in the grip of the Industrial Revolution, Tyneside left a great deal to be desired.

Reid's report was critical of just about every aspect of public health, particularly in Newcastle. 'Pandon Dene, on the east side of the town, has now become little better than a public sewer,' was one comment. The water supply was a total disgrace, being contaminated with 'excrementitions [*sic*] and other matters from the common sewers'. Living conditions in the poor parts of the town like All Saints and St John's were damp and squalid inside and no better outside, where 'filth and refuse accumulate in the lanes and vacant corners'.

Worst of all, according to Dr Reid, were conditions inside the common lodging houses which catered for the workers who were flocking to Tyneside from all over Britain and Ireland. These presented 'the most deplorable exhibitions of the want of sanatory [*sic*] regulations to be found in this country, crowded in the extreme, dirty, ill managed, occupied promiscuously by both sexes'. Part of the blame, in Reid's view, lay with the clientele, who were 'tramps, foreign sailors, and Irishmen or Scotchmen seeking casual labour'.

And, as Reid pointed out, the issue was compounded by the fact that the recently formed town council had no idea what the problems were or where they were. There was no up-to-date plan of the town, no maps of the drainage or sewers. Building regulations were virtually non-existent and any that were in place were comprehensively ignored. The result was the urban squalor that was common across industrial Britain. In the middle of the nineteenth century, thousands of people all along Tyneside were huddled in rat-infested, jerry-built slums, some of which were prone to collapse.

At the bottom of Westgate Road in the centre of Newcastle, not far from Central Station, there's an impressive if somewhat over-elaborate group of statues which is dominated by a bronze figure standing on a stone pedestal gazing sternly into the wall of a dismal 1960s office block. At each corner of the pedestal sit four refined-looking men draped in classical garb who are supposed to represent workers paying homage to the great man standing above them (although, as one writer has noted, 'it's obvious they've never done a day's work in their lives').

The statue is Tyneside's memorial to George Stephenson, who is still regarded – wrongly – by many Britons as the only begetter of the steam railway engine and the railway system. The edifice was inaugurated on Thursday, 2 October 1862 in a great ceremony which involved rousing speeches, march-pasts by the town's engineering trades and military music from the band of the 41st Regiment. The statue itself was the work of a young sculptor called John Graham Lough and is a cut-down version of his failed entry for the competition to build a monument to Horatio Nelson in Trafalgar Square.

To many Novocastrians, it has always seemed odd that Stephenson, the so-called 'father of the railways', was placed facing away from the great railway station which opened the year after he died. His bronze persona seems to be peering out past St Nicholas Cathedral towards what used to be the shipyards and collieries of Walker, Wallsend and North Shields. But perhaps that's fitting enough. Stephenson may be remembered as a railway man, but he learned his trade in the collieries of Tyneside.

George Stephenson was born in 1781 near the mining hamlet of Wylam, on the north bank of the Tyne, west of Newcastle. He was the oldest son of Robert Stephenson (known locally as 'Old Bob'), his mother the daughter of a small farmer. Having grown up more or less uneducated, Stephenson scraped a few shillings together herding cows, following plough horses and working as a picker (picking stones from the coals) at the local colliery. He then got a job driving a horse and cart at the Black Collerton colliery, after which he became an assistant fireman to his father at the Dowley colliery. A few years later, at the age of 17, he was employed at the Water Row colliery.

Then, in 1801, Stephenson went back to the Black Collerton colliery as a brakesman, responsible for working the pit's winding gear. An instinctive, hands-on engineer, he did well at the job. A year later, he met and married Frances Henderson, the daughter of a local farmer, and the year after that, their son, Robert, was born. By then, George

Stephenson was working as brakesman at Willington Quay, operating and maintaining the machinery that emptied the ballast from the collier ships returning to the Tyne. His wages were modest, and, to make ends meet, he repaired shoes, clocks and watches.

In 1806, tragedy struck the little family. After giving birth to a baby girl, Frances Stephenson died of tuberculosis, quickly followed by her infant daughter. George handed his son into the care of Old Bob and walked the 120 or so miles to Montrose on the east coast of Scotland to tend a Boulton & Watt steam engine at one of the town's textile mills. He stayed in Scotland for a year, then returned to Tyneside in 1808 to run the engines at the big Killingworth colliery.

Stephenson's opportunity came in 1810 when the big Newcomen engine which drove the pumps in one of the Killingworth pits broke down. The engine seemed beyond repair, and the colliery managers watched helplessly as the pit flooded. Stephenson stepped in, took the engine apart, reassembled it with some adjustments of his own, got it working and saved the pit. The owners, the powerful consortium the Grand Alliance, were so impressed by his performance that they gave him responsibility for all the engines in their collieries and a generous salary of £100 a year.

Like every mining engineer with a conscience and a regard for his own skin, Stephenson was appalled at the way pitmen were being killed and injured by underground explosions of gas. In the summer of 1815, he decided to do something about it: he began working on a safety lamp. In December that year, in front of 100 members of the Lit and Phil, he demonstrated the lamp that became known in the industry as a 'Geordie'. He'd even risked his life by taking it lit into one of the more gas-prone corners of a Killingworth pit. It was Stephenson's bad luck that the renowned Sir Humphry Davy had demonstrated a very similar design a few weeks earlier, on 9 November 1815.

Which, predictably, sparked a long-running scientific row as to which of the two was the creator of the safety lamp. There's no doubt that Davy had a better grasp of the physics and chemistry involved; but there also seems no doubt that the idea had occurred to Stephenson quite independently. But Stephenson was self-taught, tongue-tied and self-effacing, while Sir Humphry was, in the words of Samuel Smiles, 'the scientific prodigy of his day, the pet of the Royal Society, the favourite of princes, the most brilliant of lecturers, and the most popular of philosophers'.

He was also – as Michael Faraday was to testify – a self-centred and notoriously prickly individual. Davy put together a campaign to rubbish Stephenson's design. Sixteen years later, his admirers were still at it. One wrote that it was 'scarcely believable' that such a significant device could have been dreamed up by a mere 'engine-wright of Killingworth, of the name of Stephenson – a person not even possessing a knowledge of the elements of chemistry'. This Tyneside *v.* Thameside tussle was very British, and it was to rumble on for years. It probably bothered the temperamental Sir Humphry Davy more than it did the practical and phlegmatic George Stephenson.

As the Grand Alliance's head engineer, Stephenson was also responsible for the networks of wagonways that shifted coal from the collieries down to the staiths on the Tyne. For hundreds of years, the wagons had moved on railways, drawn by horses – a slow business. But by 1804, a brilliant Cornishman called Richard Trevithick had designed and built the world's first steam-powered locomotive. A year later, his design was copied in Gateshead by the engineer John Whinfield and set to work in the Wylam colliery, owned by Christopher Blackett.

THE PRICE OF COAL

Mining disasters in the North-east coalfield between 1775 and 1850:

1794 at Picktree	30 die
1805 at Oxclose	38 die
1805 at Hebburn	35 die
1812 at Felling	92 die
1813 at Fatfield	32 die
1815 at Newbottle	57 die

1815 at Harraton	38 die
1815 at Heaton	70 die
1817 at West Rainton	27 die
1819 at Sheriff Hill	35 die
1821 at Wallsend	52 die
1823 at Rainton	59 die
1826 at Jarrow	34 die
1833 at Springfield	47 die
1835 at Wallsend	102 die
1841 at Willington	32 die
1844 at Haswell	95 die
1845 at Jarrow	39 die
1849 at Hebburn	31 die

The Wylam colliery project failed (the loco was too heavy for the wooden tracks), but it was obvious that Trevithick's locomotive could move large quantities of coal much faster than the horses could. Various designs sprang up around the British coalfield over the next few years. In 1814, George Stephenson came up with his own, a steam locomotive he called *Blucher* (after the Prussian general of that name) and tried it out on the West Moor colliery. The *Blucher* was far from perfect, but it was better than most of the competition.

And it got better still when Stephenson went into partnership with William Losh, the lawyer-turned-chemist who was in the process of creating Tyneside's alkali industry. Between them, Stephenson and Losh made major improvements to the axles of the locomotives and devised cast-iron, edge-rail track, which they patented together. By the year 1818, the old wagonways at Killingworth had been replaced by the Stephenson-Losh railways, and horses had all but disappeared.

While George Stephenson did not invent either railways or the steam locomotive, he certainly spotted their potential. He saw a technology that could transform Britain. In 1825, he set up the engineering firm of Robert Stephenson & Co. with the help of local businessmen Edward Pease and Thomas Richardson. The firm's first product was *Locomotive No. 1*, an 8-ton steam engine capable of hauling goods and passengers along iron rails at up to 16 miles per hour. In 1829, Stephenson's legendary *Rocket* was entered into the locomotive trials at Rainhill, near Birmingham, and won hands down. Its speed was later increased to an astonishing 29 miles per hour. The railway age was under way. George Stephenson was at the heart of it.

THE *ROCKET*

George Stephenson's *Rocket* must be one of the most famous railway engines on earth. Weighing just under 4½ tons and with a boiler that was 6 ft long and 3½ ft in diameter, it sat on a 4-wheeled bogy. It took 57 minutes for the boiler to reach a working pressure of 50 lb per square inch, and it used up 142 lb of coking coal in the process. Every part of the engine was carefully designed by Stephenson to pull the 12-ton load specified by the organisers of the Rainhill Trials.

Over the 35 miles of the Rainhill track, the speed of the *Rocket* climbed from a little over 13 miles per hour to well over 24 miles per hour. The engine proved to be considerably faster going forward than in reverse, due to an error in the valve settings. On Wednesday, 14 October 1829, after six days of trials, Stephenson's *Rocket* was declared the winner over its four competitors.

In his biography of Stephenson, Samuel Smiles wrote:

> The *Rocket* showed that a new power had been born into the world, full of activity and strength, with boundless capability of work. It was the simple but admirable contrivance of the steam-blast, and its combination with the multitubular boiler, that at once gave locomotion a vigorous life, and secured the triumph of the railway system.

After the Rainhill Trials, the *Rocket* was taken to Chat Moss and used for hauling ballast on the railway line that was being built between Liverpool and Manchester. In

September 1830, the engine ran down and fatally injured William Huskisson, a rising politician and junior minister. What remains of George Stephenson's famous *Rocket* stands in the Science Museum in London, along with other relics from the very earliest days of Britain's railways.

But Stephenson never lost his connection with the coal industry. The same year of his triumph with the *Rocket*, Stephenson married again (to Elizabeth Hindmarsh) and moved to Alton Grange, near Ashby de la Zouch, to help open pits on the Midlands coalfield. By then, he was regarded as one of Britain's finest mining engineers. And when the House of Commons set up a committee in 1835 to look into casualties in the coal industry, George Stephenson was called to give evidence. He gave a chilling description of one lethal firedamp explosion which occurred when he was the brakesman at Killingworth almost 20 years previously. It is quoted at length in Samuel Smiles's biography:

> I had left the mouth of the pit, and gone about fifty or sixty yards away when I heard a tremendous noise, looked round, and saw the discharge come out of the pit like the discharge of a cannon. It continued to blow, I think, for a quarter of an hour, discharging everything that come into the current. Wood came up, stones came up, and trusses of hay that went up into the air like balloons . . . The ground all round the top of the pit was in a trembling state. I went as near as I durst go; everything appeared cracking and rending about me. Part of the brattice [pit partition] which was very strong, was blown away at the bottom of the pits. Very large pumps were lifted from their places so that the engine could not work.

That particular explosion cost ten men their lives (and, in Stephenson's estimate, the colliery owners around £20,000). It was one of many.

As he told the committee, most underground explosions were sparked by pockets of carburetted hydrogen being ignited. That could happen in a number of ways – a spark from a pitman's pickaxe was enough to do it – but usually the gas was ignited by lights carried by men to see their way in the darkness. Various devices were tried to solve the problem, even the phosphorescence from decaying fish skins, but nothing seemed to work. Some pits were considered too heavily laden with gas to be mined. As a result, huge quantities of coal were not being extracted.

THE STAITHS OF THE TYNE

Tyneside folk are inclined to believe that the word 'staith' (or 'staithe') is a Geordie word. It is, of course, the name given to the timber-built piers or quays from which coal was loaded onto the ships. There was a time when coal staiths lined the River Tyne from North and South Shields to Blaydon. But the word is not peculiar to Tyneside. In fact, it's a Teutonic word (both Old English and Norse) for riverbank or landing-place. According to the *Oxford English Dictionary*, it was being used to describe an embankment as late as 1698. Its modern use is nineteenth-century: 'A landing-stage, wharf; esp. a waterside depot for coals brought from the collieries for shipment, furnished with staging and chutes for loading vessels.'

Probably the Tyne's most famous staiths are the coal staiths at Dunston, where the Team flows into the Tyne. Opened in 1893 for the London & North East Railway Co. (LNER), they are reputed to comprise the biggest timber-built structure in Europe. The main structures are made from pitched pine timbers, 13 in. by 13 in. in section and jointed with straps and bolts. Dunston Staiths were built in three stages, in 1890, in 1893 and in 1903. At their peak in 1920, they were used to load around 140,000 tons of coal a week into waiting ships. But as the demand for coal slumped, Dunston Staiths were used less and less, and were finally closed for business in 1980.

The staiths are now part of the Tyne's industrial 'heritage' and are protected by a Grade II listing. Unfortunately, in

November 2003 fire broke out on the staiths (it may have been started maliciously) and a large section was damaged beyond repair.

In the early 1820s, George Stephenson was joined in the business by his son Robert, who had returned from Edinburgh University, where he'd studied natural philosophy and chemistry. There's a tradition that, at first, the two men did not get along. It's certainly true that in 1824 Robert Stephenson left England for Colombia to spend three years working for the Colombian Mining Association digging for gold and silver around Santa Ana on the Magdalena River. He returned to Newcastle in 1827, rejoined his father's works at Forth Banks and, by all accounts, made a crucial contribution to the design of the *Rocket*.

For the next five years, father and son worked together, until, in 1833, Robert Stephenson struck out on his own as a railway and civil engineer. One of his specialities was building bridges, at which his only rivals were Thomas Telford and Isambard Kingdom Brunel. In 1847, he was elected as MP for the Yorkshire town of Whitby. He was an innovative man from an innovative family, but, as is sometimes the case with such men, his politics were high Tory and firmly protectionist. He opposed the building of the Suez Canal on the grounds that it made no commercial sense.

Coal mining, on the other hand, made eminent commercial sense, particularly as it fuelled spin-off industries like salt-making, chemicals and glass-making. By the year 1812, there were more than 30 firms on Tyneside making glass, producing almost 40 per cent of Britain's glass output. With huge numbers of bulky cargoes of coal, salt, chemicals and glass being shipped out of the Tyne, and with more than 600 ships registered to the Port of Newcastle, the harbour facilities were creaking under the strain and had been for some time.

That same year, the engineer John Rennie investigated the problem and reported that unless the River Tyne authorities looked to dredging, quay-building and maintenance, trade on the Tyne might grind to a standstill. Shipping would find other, better-equipped ports. Which was something that shipmasters and seamen had been saying for decades. Rennie's report was an early sign that the people of Tyneside were growing fed up with the way the River Tyne was being run by the politicians and businessmen of Newcastle. It was their fiercely held monopoly on the river that earned them the collective title 'the River Dragon'.

As Newcastle grew, its role as a 'service centre' for the northern parts of Durham and most of Northumberland grew with it. By 1830, Newcastle had no fewer than 28 breweries (most of them very small) and more than 130 pubs (many of them very squalid). In 1828, the Bank of England set up an operation in the town, and 1845 saw the opening of the Newcastle Stock Exchange. Financial crises continued, of course: in 1847 the Newcastle, Shields and Union Bank collapsed.

But more and more of what we now call consumer goods were being shipped up the Tyne. And the business of retailing these goods became more and more important to the economy of the town. In his contribution to *Newcastle upon Tyne: A Modern History*, the historian Oliver Lendrum calculates that by the middle of the nineteenth century, retailing employed around 3,500 men and women in Newcastle. Lendrum writes: 'Although debates surrounding enterpreneurship normally focus on manufacturing industry, the development of Newcastle's retail sector saw revolutionary enterpreneurial developments that easily matched its groundbreaking industrial sector.'

No retailer broke more ground than Emerson Muschamp Bainbridge. Born in Weardale in 1817 and apprenticed at the age of 13 to a Newcastle draper called Robert Kidd, Bainbridge spent two years working in a drapery business in Regent Street, London, before returning to Newcastle in 1838 to set up his own drapery shop in Market Street. Quite quickly, he began selling other lines and before long was running what was arguably the very first department store in Britain, if not in Europe (although that's a claim that would be disputed by Jenners of Edinburgh).

But if any one man defines the sheer energy and industrial genius of nineteenth-century Tyneside, it has to be the lawyer-turned-engineer William George Armstrong, later Lord Armstrong of Cragside. With his huge engineering works at Elswick and his shipyards at Walker, Armstrong left his mark on Tyneside in a way that no other industrialist ever did. By the end of the century, Armstrong's companies were among the biggest warship builders and armaments manufacturers in Europe.

Born in Newcastle in 1810, his father, also William, was a local corn merchant and his mother, Ann, the daughter of a minor coal owner. Armstrong was educated at schools in Newcastle, Whickham and Bishop Auckland before becoming articled to local solicitor Armorer Donkin. In 1835, he married Margaret Ramshaw. He spent a few years studying law in London with William Henry Watson, then rejoined Donkin as a solicitor.

He was no ordinary lawyer. He was interested in technology and all its ramifications, the more advanced the better. Electricity and electrostatics fascinated him, and he corresponded on the subject with the great Michael Faraday. But it was water and its potential that intrigued him most. His mother once quipped, 'William has water on the brain.' In 1844, Armstrong promoted the Whittle-Dean Water Company to build freshwater reservoirs to supply Newcastle with clean drinking water.

In 1846, while he was still working as a solicitor, Armstrong read a scientific paper to the Royal Society in London on 'the electric charge generated by the escape of high-pressure steam' (a phenomenon later known as 'the Armstrong effect'). That same year, he was elected as a Fellow of the Royal Society, a title of which he was hugely proud.

But William Armstrong was no mere theorist. He was a practical, hands-on engineer and innovator. He went on to design a hydraulically operated crane and formed the Newcastle Cranage Company to build and market the device. In 1847, he abandoned his legal career to found W.G. Armstrong & Co., manufacturers of hydraulic equipment, and built a factory on the bank of the Tyne at Elswick, a mile west of Newcastle. Production began in the autumn of that year, with a workforce of 25 men.

As word of Armstrong's hydraulically powered cranes spread, the orders began to trickle in. Within months of starting up, Armstrong was building cranes for the Liverpool docks, the South Hetton colliery and the lead mines at Allenhead in Northumberland. It was the nucleus of a multifaceted industrial empire that was to grow to dominate Tyneside for the latter half of the nineteenth century and into the twentieth.

KINGS OF THE RIVER: HARRY CLASPER

When Harry Clasper and the crew of the *Lord Ravensworth* won the rowing championship of the world on the River Thames on 26 June 1845, it was the culmination of years of hard training and ingenious boat design. Three years previously, Clasper and his team had been humiliated when a crew of Thames oarsmen had made the journey north and, in front of a huge crowd of Tynesiders, whipped the Geordies on their home water. Clasper spent the next three years plotting his revenge by redesigning his boat and training his crew. The strategy paid off when he beat the cockneys hands down on the Thames.

When they returned to Newcastle, the Clasper team met the kind of reception nowadays reserved for footballers who've won a seriously major trophy. Huge crowds turned out to welcome home their heroes. One local bard was inspired to write a piece of doggerel with the rousing chorus of:

> Haud away, Harry!
> Canny lad Harry!
> Harry's the King of the Tymes and the Tyne.

Born at Dunston in 1812, Henry Clasper began his career at the Jarrow pit before joining Brown's boatyard, where he learned the art of boat-building and was able to indulge his enthusiasm for rowing. A fierce competitor, he won race after race, until he felt good enough to challenge the mighty Thames watermen who'd dominated the sport for decades.

> After his great world championship victory on the
> Thames, Clasper spent the rest of his career designing and
> building racing boats and coaching Tyneside teams. When
> he died in 1870, more than 100,000 Tynesiders lined the
> streets to watch his funeral go by. He is buried in St Mary's
> Church, Whickham.

Linking Newcastle to Gateshead had always been an issue with
Tynesiders. For generations, they'd relied on the medieval bridge across
the Tyne which was swept away in 1771 and Robert Mylne's neoclassical, nine-arched exercise that replaced it ten years later. As
Tyneside's population grew in the first half of the nineteenth century
and the railway networks spread across Britain, more and more
influential people began to demand some better way of crossing the
deep gorge between Newcastle and Gateshead. What was needed, they
argued, was a high-level bridge.

In fact, the idea for a high-level bridge between Gateshead and
Newcastle had been around ever since a Newcastle mason called
Edward Hutchinson had proposed one in 1772. In 1826, an engineer,
Captain Samuel Brown RN, came up with another bridge scheme,
which was followed in 1827 by a design by the local engineer William
Chapman. In 1828, Robert Stevenson, the renowned Scottish
lighthouse engineer, came up with a plan to build a new high-level
bridge *on top* of Robert Mylne's eighteenth-century Tyne Bridge.

In 1834, a Mr B.R. Dodd proposed a suspension bridge from Bottle
Bank in Gateshead to Dean Street in Newcastle. Two years later, Dodd
got together with Captain Samuel Brown to promote the scheme more
energetically. By then, ideas were flooding in to the authorities.
Between 1837 and 1845, there were ten ideas for railway crossings of
the Tyne, some of them from serious figures such as John Dobson,
Richard Grainger, John and Benjamin Green, and the great engineer
Isambard Kingdom Brunel. In the end, the job of building the high-
level bridge was given to Robert Stephenson, son of George
Stephenson.

Stephenson's design was masterly. He conceived a 'double-decked' bridge 1,400 ft long, 40 ft wide and 120 ft above the river that would take railway traffic on the upper level, and road traffic and pedestrians on the lower one. The High Level Bridge across the Tyne remains one of the great feats of European engineering. It should be said, however, that Robert Stephenson's design for the bridge was remarkably similar to one published in 1845 by the eccentric William Martin, who liked to call himself the 'Philosophical Conqueror of all Nations'. Predictably, Martin claimed that Stephenson had stolen his design.

The contractors for the great project were all north of England firms. The stone viaducts on the north side were to be built by Wilson and Gibson of Newcastle, and on the south side by Rush and Lawton of York. The bulk of the ironwork was to be produced by Hawks, Crawshay & Sons of Gateshead, with some of it going to Losh, Wilson and Bell of Walker, and John Abbot & Co. of Gateshead.

Work began on the site in October 1845. A year later, the first permanent pile was driven into the riverbed; the first arch was put in place in July 1848, and the last in June 1849. The bridge was tested by a 200-ton train in August that year and was officially opened by Queen Victoria (who was on her way back from Scotland) on 28 September 1849. Her train stopped on the bridge, and, while she did not step out, Her Majesty 'surveyed, with the greatest possible interest, the magnificent scene around and below'. The lower deck was opened for traffic in February 1850. Sadly, perhaps, George Stephenson didn't live to see his son's masterpiece completed. After moving to Tapton House, near Chester, he devoted his declining years to tending his estate and studying horticulture. Ever the innovator, he experimented with different kinds of manure, the best way of fattening chickens and ways of growing straight cucumbers. (It was simple: he enclosed the immature growths in glass cylinders.) He died at Tapton of pleurisy in August 1848.

The cost of Robert Stephenson's bridge across the Tyne Gorge was huge, more than £491,000. But it proved a solid investment for the railway companies. It took their trains right into the heart of the fast-growing town of Newcastle and opened up the railway line into Scotland. Besides, at least some of the bridge's cost was clawed back from tolls on the lower deck: a penny for foot traffic, threepence for a horse and wagon, and tenpence per twenty head of cattle.

Robert Stephenson had planned, or at least hoped, to finish the Newcastle end of his great High Level Bridge with a statue of his father, but by then, the money had run out. The statue of the great railway and mining engineer had to wait.

8

HEAVY INDUSTRY

1850–1900

That most gifted of Tyneside architects John Dobson had his big day on 29 August 1850 when Queen Victoria opened what was his most important commission, the Central Station in Newcastle. Novocastrians trooped out in thousands to gawp at Newcastle's latest tribute to the modern world of steam and iron, and to see the Queen. According to the *Newcastle Daily Chronicle*:

> The platforms on each side commanding a view of the spot where Her Majesty was expected to alight were early crowded with the gentry of the town, the faces of the fair sex decidedly predominating. The approach of the Royal Carriage was announced by a royal salute from the castle guns, immediately after which the train came into sight.

The great event was recorded in an engraving which is certainly no great work of art. It shows the small figures of Victoria and Albert dismounting from the royal train to be greeted by a cluster of Tyneside dignitaries while large crowds look on. From the vantage point of 150 years, the royal train looks primitive, almost toylike, while the sweeping

247

curves of Dobson's wrought-iron and glass engine shed look like they might have been designed yesterday. Newcastle's Central Station is in fact one of the great railway buildings of the mid-nineteenth century.

There's a splendid description of the station in the Northumberland volume of *The Buildings of England*. It's also something of a tribute to the talent of John Dobson:

> Behind the portico, three arches lead to an astonishing train shed, curved to a radius of 243 metres (800 ft) and with its longest platform 407 metres (1,335 ft); roofed in timber and glass on tied, curved, wrought-iron ribs, supported by plain, slender, cast-iron columns 7 metres (23 ft) high. The whole covers an area of 3 acres (1.2 hectares).

Dobson's engine shed was an engineering as well as an architectural innovation:

> This was the first train shed roof to be constructed in this way, a design which came to be much copied in modified form elsewhere. In his presidential address to the Northern Architectural Association in 1859 Dobson explained that he had perceived that curved, wrought-iron sections could easily be made by providing a rolling mill with bevelled rollers and that this innovation made his design a commercial possibility.

And Newcastle's geography being what it is, the railway lines leading into and out of the station had to vault over some formidable gorges by way of viaducts. Here's what *The Buildings of England* has to say about them: 'The railway viaducts from the E[ast] end of the Central Station follow two great curves, one to the High Level Bridge, the other carrying the main line to Edinburgh. Engineering of great beauty.'

JOHN DOBSON

Another Tynesider whose reputation deserves to be revived is John Dobson. He may not have been the greatest architect that nineteenth-century Britain produced, but he was certainly a major talent. In that definitive work of reference, the *Macmillan Encyclopaedia of Architects*, he is described as 'probably the ablest – and certainly the most prolific – early Victorian architect practicing in the North of England'.

Born in 1787 in Chirton, North Shields, the son of an affluent market gardener, he was educated in Newcastle, studied architecture under David Stephenson and then in London, where he became friendly with Robert Smirke, one of the Government's favourite architects. Smirke was so impressed by young Dobson that he tried to persuade him to stay in London where there were big commissions to be won and big money to be made. But Dobson was a loyal Tynesider and returned to Newcastle to build up his practice.

Dobson was a man of prodigious gifts. The *Encyclopaedia* describes him as 'a talented watercolourist, an able engineer, and a meticulous surveyor'. He also played 'a key role in the great rebuilding of Newcastle-Upon-Tyne'. In the course of a long career, Dobson designed more than 50 churches and 100 private houses, from the grand to the modest. Among his better-known buildings are the Morpeth Gaol and Session House; Eldon Square, Newcastle; Seaham Harbour; the Royal Arcade, Newcastle; and Beaufront Castle.

His attention to detail was as legendary as his ability to see a job through with a minimum of fuss. According to his daughter, John Dobson 'never exceeded an estimate and never had a legal dispute with a contractor'. His talent as an engineer was tested to the full when he took on the job of rescuing the tower of St Nicholas Church in Newcastle when it was on the point of collapse. He succeeded.

Dobson died in 1865. The *Encyclopaedia* describes him as one of that 'triumvirate of talents' (the others being

Richard Grainger and John Clayton) who were 'responsible for turning Victorian Newcastle into a rival of Georgian Edinburgh and Regency London'.

There's no doubt that 1850 was a big year for Tyneside. Not only did it see the opening of the new railway station, it saw the passing of the River Tyne Improvement Act. This measure took control of the river away from the old body known as the River Dragon – the conservative, not to say reactionary, merchants of Newcastle – and gave it to a new Tyne Improvement Commission (TIC). It came with a brief to look to the interests of everyone who used the river, not just the town of Newcastle.

If ever a measure was overdue, it was the River Tyne Improvement Act. For generations, shipbuilders, ship owners, sea captains, coal owners, keelmen and the smaller burghs (particularly Gateshead, South Shields and Tynemouth) had been complaining about the dismal way Newcastle had looked after the river. As Maureen Callcott points out in her excellent essay 'The Governance of the Victorian City' in *Newcastle upon Tyne: A Modern History*, the biggest town on the Tyne had made a fortune from the river on which they'd spent as little as possible. Indeed the river was in such a bad way that it had started to lose shipping to the new harbour at Seaham and the greatly improved docks at Sunderland.

> From time immemorial Newcastle had obtained enormous financial benefits from its 'conservatorship' of the River Tyne for the 17 miles of its tidal flow. Indeed the river provided up to half the town's income. During the ten years up to 1833, £137,319 had been raised from river dues while only £5,133 18s was spent on improving the river. Quays were lacking and ships were sometimes beached and looted. The new forces of wealth and business from both sides of the Tyne clamoured for improvement.

Not that Newcastle was removed from the picture altogether. The town was to have six commissioners on the new authority, but they were outnumbered ten to six by two commissioners from Gateshead, three from South Shields, three from Tynemouth and two from the Admiralty. Newcastle was allowed to keep three-eighths of the coal dues (a right which it gave up 12 years later for a lump sum of £130,000).

The wrangling, of course, continued. Maureen Callcott writes:

> Enormous sums of money were needed for the construction of docks, piers, dredging and other necessary improvements, and disputes continued over Newcastle's encroachment on tidal waters by jetties, embankments and other works, which were said to hinder navigation . . . it was late in the century before the work of the Commission was able to proceed without interruption and friction.

But under the chairmanship of Joseph Cowen senior, the TIC argued its way through its difficulties and by the 1860s had worked a serious improvement on the River Tyne. It may not have been the transformation for which many had hoped, but it was a lot better than it had been. In particular, the dredging work had de-silted much of the tidal river, which could now take some of the biggest ships on the high seas. It was largely for the way in which he steered the Tyne Improvement Commission that Joseph Cowen was knighted.

Not far from the junction of Westgate Road and Fenkle Street in the centre of Newcastle, there's a handsome statue by the sculptor John Tweed, which was erected in 1906. It's Tyneside's tribute to the younger Joseph Cowen, the Liberal MP, newspaper proprietor, radical politician, social reformer and supporter of the Irish Home Rule movement who dominated Tyneside politics in the latter half of the nineteenth century. Joseph Cowen was one of Tyneside's most remarkable sons.

Born in 1831, Cowen was educated in Newcastle and then, like many middle-class Novocastrians, at the University of Edinburgh, where he seems to have acquired some of his radical enthusiasms. In fact, it was while he was a student at Edinburgh that Cowen made contact with the Italian revolutionary Giuseppe Mazzini, who later became one of his friends. Cowen never lost his admiration for the cause of Italian nationalism. He returned to Newcastle without completing his studies in Edinburgh and with revolutionary opinions that were so strong that they alarmed his parents, who were no mean radicals themselves.

Cowen worked for a number of years in his father's successful brickworks at Winlaton. Although he proved to be a capable businessman, Cowen never lost his taste for radical politics or his interest in the revolutionary movements that were racking Europe, particularly Italy and Hungary. At the age of 18, the radical Tynesider became a member of the recently formed People's International League and subscribed to revolutionary tracts like the *Red Republican* and the *Democratic Review*.

It says a lot for the tolerance of the British authorities that young Cowen stayed out of jail. One of the best short accounts of his life and career is Joan Hugman's essay 'Print and Preach' (in *Newcastle upon Tyne: A Modern History*). She makes it clear that Cowen was prepared to put his money where his mouth was:

> For Cowen, the war of words was not just a theoretical exercise, for he spent most of the 1850s secretly smuggling weapons and seditious literature on behalf of the Polish Democratic Society, raising money to supply arms for Garibaldi's Sicilian campaign and, it appears, even getting personally involved in a bomb plot to assassinate Napoleon III.

But Cowen's taste for international politics did not eclipse his interest in the needs and concerns of Tyneside. His instincts were genuinely philanthropic and he had the cash to pursue them. In 1847, he set up the Winlaton Sanitary Association (which his father chaired) and the Winlaton Literary and Scientific Institute. His Blaydon Institute was open to all, regardless of class, education, politics or religion. The curriculum was, however, radical. Among the lecturers were the Italian and Hungarian revolutionaries Giuseppe Garibaldi and Lajos Kossuth.

Ten years later, in 1857, Cowen set up the Northern Reform Union to campaign for wider suffrage.

THE PRICE OF COAL
Mining disasters in the North-east coalfield between 1850 and 1900:

1855 at Elemore	28 die
1860 at Burradon	76 die
1862 at Hartley	204 die
1866 at Pelton	24 die
1880 at Seaham	164 die
1882 at Trimdon Grange	74 die
1882 at Tudhoe	35 die
1886 at Elemore	28 die
1896 at Brancepeth	20 die
1899 at Brandon	6 die

Cowen was also an ardent supporter of the new Co-operative Movement, and members of his Blaydon Institute set up the first co-operative in the North-east. With Cowen's zeal behind it, the Co-operative Movement spread rapidly on and around Tyneside. By the 1870s, it was so entrenched that in 1873 the first Co-operative Congress was held in Newcastle and was attended by delegates from more than 70 retail co-ops and allied businesses.

In 1859 Cowen became a newspaper proprietor when he bought over the ailing titles the *Newcastle Daily Chronicle* and the *Newcastle Weekly Chronicle*. His ambition, he declared, was to make the *Chronicle* 'the *Times* of the North', and, to that end, he poured his money and his prodigious energy into the project. These acquisitions, according to Joan Hugman, enabled Cowen 'to be a daily presence in the lives of the population, to drip-feed his ideas about society and democracy in countless ways'. And very successful he was, too. Circulations soared. By the 1870s, Cowen's newspapers were among the most successful outside of London.

Cowen and his papers were staunch supporters of the Irish Home Rule movement. At a time when Fenianism flared into occasional violence, this did not go down well with the authorities. In the wake of the notorious Clerkenwell explosion in 1867, the Irish of Tyneside were viewed with some suspicion. Hundreds of special constables were sworn in (at North Shields) and briefed to keep a close eye on their Irish neighbours and workmates. Cowen's newspapers railed against this heavy-handed coercion, and, in January 1867, the *Daily Chronicle* went so far as to declare that 'The people at all times have the right to revolt against their rulers.'

In 1873, Joseph Cowen was elected Liberal MP for Newcastle, a parliamentary seat his father had held before him. Cowen's relationship with the Liberal Party and the Liberal government was awkward. Gladstone and his colleagues were never comfortable with the outspoken radical from Tyneside. Cowen grew sour as the ideas he espoused ran into the political sand. He began to lose his sense of political direction and in the general election of 1880 he abandoned the Liberal Party and stood as an Independent. He won the seat, but by a narrow margin. He won again in 1885, but then, ageing, ill and disillusioned, he resigned from Parliament. The fiery radical of Tyneside bowed out of public life, and died in 1900.

The poverty and terrible living conditions against which Joseph Cowen and his father had railed for so long took their toll on the people of Tyneside. Like most crowded corners of Britain, the towns and villages of the Tyne were visited periodically by the scourge of cholera. There was an outbreak in the 1830s and a nasty epidemic in 1848. Five years later, in 1853, the disease returned. At least 1,500 people – and possibly more – died in and around Newcastle. The dire warnings contained in Dr Reid's report on Tyneside's sanitary conditions were brought home with a vengeance.

A year after that disaster, another followed when in the early hours of 10 October 1854 at least 53 people died after a fire started in the textile warehouse of Wilson & Sons on the riverfront at Gateshead. The fire quickly spread to Bertram's, one of the nearby warehouses, which was packed with all kinds of combustibles: manganese, brimstone, guano, nitrate of soda, naphtha. The resulting huge explosion tore the buildings apart, hurled lumps of stone and brick across the Tyne as far as Pilgrim Street in Newcastle and left a huge crater 30 ft deep and 50 ft wide in Gateshead.

Along with fragments of building came sparks and blazing embers which set light to buildings on the Newcastle waterfront. The fire spread rapidly among the tightly packed streets and closes. Dozens of businesses and houses – on the Quayside, Sandhill and the Side – were destroyed, and those that survived had their windows and doors blown in. The huge explosion was heard as far south as Hartlepool, as far north as Alnwick and as far west as Hexham. The flames were seen from many parts of Durham and Northumberland.

The crowd that turned out to watch the pyrotechnics, lining the Tyne Bridge and the riverside, got far more than they bargained for. Fifty-three people died in the explosion, most of them killed instantly by the blast and by flying debris. Among the dead were the proprietor of Bertram's warehouse (who was identified by his keys) and Alexander Dobson, the talented son of John Dobson, Newcastle's most gifted architect. The unfortunate Dobson junior was identified by his snuffbox.

Some good came from the calamity, however. The fire had gutted most of the old fever-ridden districts on the Newcastle riverside. When the ashes cooled, the ruins plus a large swathe of the old district were razed to the ground and plans were drawn up for a network of brand-new streets lined with handsome new buildings. By 1866, most of the development was in place: the new Exchange Buildings and Lombard Street, King Street and Queen Street.

KINGS OF THE RIVER: 'HONEST' BOB CHAMBERS

Where Harry Clasper led a team of oarsmen, his protégé Bob Chambers was very much a sculler, a single oarsman. He was probably the finest of that breed that the nineteenth century produced. His successful world championship tussle with Tom White of Bermondsey in 1859 was the kind of sporting encounter that gets talked about with awe for generations. There's an excellent account of Chambers (and the other legendary river athletes) in Peter Dillon's short book *The Tyne Oarsmen*.

Bob Chambers won his world title on 19 April 1859 over a three-mile course on the Tyne between the High Level Bridge and the Scotswood suspension bridge. The two men were racing neck and neck when, not far from Skinnerburn, the two boats collided and Chambers found himself and his boat facing in the wrong direction while White raced on ahead. There were mighty groans from the huge Geordie crowd. The race, to all intents and purposes, was over.

But Bob Chambers was nothing if not determined. He threw himself back into the race with a frenzy and gradually, yard by yard, began to catch up with the Londoner, crossing the finishing line at Scotswood in the lead. It was an extraordinary performance by the Tyneside man. Chambers went on to win the world championship again in 1863, this time against an Australian.

Robert Chambers was born in St Anthony's, Walker, in 1831 and began his career in a local iron foundry before becoming a professional oarsman. Despite the years of training and exercise, his health was never robust and he contracted tuberculosis. He died in June 1868 at the age of 37. His death prompted a verse from the Tyneside vernacular poet Joe Wilson:

Fareweel te the canny Bob Chambers
A man for his honesty famed
Strite-froward, an kind, noble-hearted
Wor champein such qualities claim'd.

The scars of the Great Fire of Newcastle and Gateshead were soon covered up. Life and work went on. By the second half of the nineteenth century, the Tyne was positively bristling with shipyards. Among them were some of the most famous shipbuilders of the nineteenth century: T&W Smith, Wood Skinner, Wigham Richardson, William Cleland & Co., Andrew Leslie & Co. Not all survived, of course, but many did and flourished mightily to create thousands of jobs and a huge reservoir of skills.

One of the most successful was the yard built up by Charles Mitchell, a Scot from Aberdeen who began his working life as an engineering draughtsman before coming south to Newcastle to work in the shipyard of another Scot, John Coutts. Mitchell then spent eight years in London before returning to Tyneside to open his own shipyard at Low Walker in 1852. Over the next 30 years, Mitchell's yard built and launched more than 450 ships. One of Mitchell's most important markets was imperial Russia, and some of his staff were located in St Petersburg to keep track of the work in his shipyard there.

It's interesting to compare the career of Charles Mitchell with that of his erstwhile employer John Coutts. In many ways, Coutts was the more enterprising of the two. Coutts opened his shipyard at Walker in 1842, and was one of the first Tyneside shipbuilders to construct vessels of iron instead of timber. He built fine ships, but he was no businessman. In 1848, he narrowly avoided bankruptcy, took on a partner called William Parkinson to look after the financial side of the business, then ran the business onto the rocks in 1856 after Parkinson died. After failing to make a living as a marine consultant, John Coutts died in poverty in South Shields in 1860. That same year, Coutts's yard was taken over by John Wigham Richardson, who transformed it into one of the most successful shipbuilding operations on the Tyne.

There's an intriguing analysis of the career of John Coutts by Oliver Lendrum in his essay 'An Integrated Elite' in *Newcastle upon Tyne: A Modern History*. He puts Coutts's failure down to a lack of contact with Tyneside's heavy hitters. He writes:

> Despite being an excellent innovator, the first Tyne shipbuilder to use iron, and his progress being hindered by the shipbuilding recession of the 1840s, Coutts was to a certain extent responsible for his own downfall. Unlike most successful

entrepreneurs he did not form partnerships with others who would compensate for his lack of knowledge.

John Coutts, it seems, was altogether too much his own man.

His fellow Aberdonian Charles Mitchell, meanwhile, went from strength to strength. In his biography of Mitchell, *Charles Mitchell 1820–1895*, the historian D.F. McGuire ascribes the Scot's success to his use of 'the talents and abilities of many able men around him'. When Charles Mitchell married Anne Swan of West Farm, Walker, he acquired a network of social and financial contacts that was to stand him in good stead. He also acquired two young brothers-in-law who would become names to be reckoned with in the shipbuilding world – Charles Sheriton Swan and Henry Frederick Swan.

In 1869, Charles Mitchell and his family moved from a (relatively) modest home in Walker near his yard to West Jesmond House, to which he added wings and the grandiose name of Jesmond Towers. The building was originally designed by John Dobson for Sir Thomas Burdon. Mitchell's series of heavy-handed extensions were carried out by Thomas Oliver junior (in 1869) and T.R. Spence (in 1884 and 1895). In the 1880s, Charles Mitchell, by then one of the pillars of the Tyneside establishment, financed the building of St George's Church.

Some of the building work carried out at Jesmond Towers was done to provide Mitchell's artistically inclined son, also Charles, with a studio. Charles Mitchell junior was, in fact, quite an accomplished artist who lived and worked in London, studied in Paris and exhibited his work at the Royal Academy. One of his more successful paintings – *Hypatia* – is currently in the Laing Art Gallery in Newcastle. He returned to Tyneside in 1880, became a director of a clutch of local companies, including Armstrong Whitworth, and worked energetically to promote the arts on Tyneside.

Like many wealthy Victorian businessmen, both Mitchells regarded philanthropy as part of their social obligation. Among the beneficiaries of their largesse were St George's Parish Church, the Walker Hospital, Christ Church in Walker, St George's Cricket Club, the Academy of Arts in Blackett Street and the University of Aberdeen (in Mitchell senior's home town). Charles Mitchell senior died in 1895. His son followed him to the grave eight years later. Both men are buried in St Bartholomew's cemetery in Benton.

The shipbuilding dynasties of late-nineteenth-century Tyneside are fascinating in the way in which they interlock. Two of Charles Mitchell's workers were his wife's brothers, Charles and Henry Swan, both talented and able young men. They worked for the Mitchell interest in Russia, Charles in charge of the Volga Steamboat Company and Henry as manager of Mitchell's yard in St Petersburg. In 1871, Charles Swan returned to Tyneside, became managing director of the Wallsend Slipway Company and in 1874 took over the ailing shipyard of Coulson, Cooke & Co., changing the firm's name to C.S. Swan & Co.

Charles Swan's success was cut short in 1879 when his engineering curiosity got the better of him and he fell into the paddle wheel of a Channel steamer while returning from Russia. He was fatally injured and died at the age of 48. A year later, his widow went into partnership with a Sunderland shipbuilder called George B. Hunter to form the firm of C.S. Swan & Hunter. The company was to become one of the most renowned and successful shipyards in Europe.

Charles Swan's younger brother Henry had a similar – if slightly longer – career path. After an apprenticeship in his uncle's yard and a spell building iron warships for the Tsar of Russia, Henry Swan returned to Tyneside to take over Mitchell's Walker shipyard. An enterprising and far-sighted engineer, Henry Swan upgraded most of the equipment in the Walker yard, which turned out a variety of vessels, from general cargoes to icebreakers. But Henry Swan's speciality was oil-carrying vessels, and by the time of his death in 1908, he'd built half the world's oil tankers. Like the Mitchells, the Swan brothers are buried in St Bartholomew's churchyard in Benton.

KINGS OF THE RIVER: JIMMY RENFORTH

The man who stepped into the shoes of Harry Clasper and Bob Chambers was the powerfully built Jimmy Renforth. Having beaten Londoner Henry Kelley for the world sculling championship in 1868, Renforth took a four-man team of Tyneside oarsmen across to Canada in 1870 to battle it out on the St Lawrence River. The prize was a sizeable £1,000, which the Tynesiders won easily. They returned to Newcastle to huge acclaim.

In 1871, Renforth and another crew (including Henry Kelley) set out to defend their title against a different team of Canadians, this time at Kennebecasis in New Brunswick. As the race got under way, the Tyneside men were drawing ahead when Renforth began to falter and miss his stroke. A few lengths later, he collapsed completely. The race was abandoned. Renforth was carried ashore, where he died from congestion of the lungs. He was 29.

James Renforth was born at Rabbit Banks near Gateshead and worked in local foundries and factories before serving a stint in the British Army in the Caribbean, until his father bought him out. With the support of a local pub owner, Renforth took up competitive rowing and worked his way up the ladder to his world championship. He was buried in Gateshead Cemetery on 10 September 1871 in front of a huge crowd. His grave is now marked with a memorial sculpture of Renforth dying in the arms of his friend and one-time rival Henry Kelley.

The Tyne Improvement Commission may have been a huge improvement on the merchants who ran the Corporation of Newcastle, but it was to be many years before they solved the problems faced by vessels entering and exiting the Tyne between Tynemouth and South Shields. A combination of the Black Midden Rocks, the Herd Sand, North Sea tides and the occasional easterly gale could make sailing into or out of the Tyne a demanding business, even for skilled seamen. For decades, marine experts and engineers had been mulling over the idea of sheltering the river-mouth with two breakwaters, one running out from each bank. In the early 1850s, the new River Tyne commissioners decided to bite the bullet and build the piers.

It was a major engineering project. There were years of dredging to be done to remove sand and reefs before a single stone could be laid. And like many projects on the east coast of northern Britain (such as Thomas Stevenson's aborted breakwater at Wick in Caithness), the work suffered from the easterly gales that seem to have been more common then than they are now. The winter of 1867 was particularly bad. Four of the seven cranes on the North Pier and two of the four cranes on the South Pier were ripped off and swept into the sea.

There was worse to come. The gales of the winter of 1897–8 almost tore the North Pier apart by undermining the foundation courses. Huge chunks of the masonry collapsed into the sea. The damage was so severe that the pier had to be realigned and rebuilt. Work on the North Pier was not completed until 1909 – more than 50 years after it had begun. The shorter South Pier was completed in 1895. It was an expensive business: the South Pier cost £450,000 and the North Pier more than double that, a whopping £1,018,000. But it was money well spent.

THE BLAYDON AND OTHER RACES

Long before Geordie Ridley wrote his resounding anthem 'The Blaydon Races', the horse owners of Tyneside had been pitting their charges against one another. Some historians claim that horse racing goes back to the seventeenth century, when the local gentry (for example the Delavals and the Fenwicks) raced their horses on Killingworth Moor and even erected a makeshift grandstand in front of Benton Church. In the eighteenth century, the racing venue of choice was the Town Moor, and from the early 1750s, an annual Race Week was organised with great success. In fact, the Town Moor races were so successful that in 1800 the sporting gentry of Tyneside dug deep into their pockets and erected a permanent – and quite handsome – grandstand from which the events could be watched in comfort.

The now-legendary Blaydon Races were not instigated

until 1862 (the year before Ridley penned his ditty) but were to be too far west to be much of a success. In 1880, the gents of the Grandstand Committee on the Town Moor decided that the Moor was no longer exclusive enough for their sport and acquired the Brandling estate at High Gosforth. They then converted the grounds into a dedicated racecourse and began charging people for entry. The Gosforth Park Races have been an important item on Britain's sporting calendar ever since.

It's an old saw, but it's true: there's nothing like a war for moving technology forward. In the 1850s, when Britain, France and Turkey were waging war against Russia in the Crimea, the engineering industry of Tyneside took a huge leap forward. It began modestly enough when the War Office commissioned William Armstrong to design underwater mines that could be used to clear the wreckage of Russian ships that were lying on the seabed off Sebastopol by blowing them up. Armstrong came up with a design for a wrought-iron cylinder packed with guncotton. The device was made and tried out but was never used in anger.

In the process, Armstrong and his brilliant colleague James Rendel (who'd seen something of the war in the Crimea for himself) came to the conclusion that the British Army's standard artillery pieces were far too heavy and difficult to deploy. Weighing a whopping three tons apiece, in rough country the guns were difficult to move. And when rain turned unmetalled roads to mud, as it often did, the guns were inclined to sink into the quagmire. Britain's gunners, Armstrong and Rendel decided, deserved better equipment with which to ply their lethal trade around the world.

The two men put their heads together and came up with a design for a lightweight field cannon with a rifled barrel that would fire elongated lead projectiles instead of the traditional iron cannon balls. In December 1854, W.G. Armstrong & Co. presented the War Office with a paper entitled 'The Construction of Wrought-iron Rifled Guns Adapted for Elongated Projectiles'. The response of Her Majesty's

Government was favourable. Armstrong's were given the go-ahead to build their gun. Six months later, the Armstrong gun was wheeled out: a breech-loading weapon that weighed only 500 lb and fired elongated 3-lb lead shot. In trials between 1855 and 1858, Armstrong's new gun was found to be not only more mobile, but also more accurate over two miles than a conventional gun was over one mile.

And while not all the British Army's top brass were impressed by the Armstrong product, enough were for HMG to give the firm the green light. An armaments factory was built by an Armstrong subsidiary, the Elswick Ordnance Co. Managed by James Rendel, the new works was up and running by 1859. It was a state-of-the-art installation but had only one main product – the new Armstrong gun. By 1863, more than 3,000 of the new weapons had been supplied to the artillery units of the British Army.

The gun contract was important for Armstrong's in more ways than one. It brought into the company (in 1860) Captain Andrew Noble, an artillery officer who had been secretary to the Rifled Ordnance Committee of the War Office. Noble's sideways move from the public to the private sector (as common then as it is now) was to prove invaluable. His network of military contacts was worldwide. By the end of the nineteenth century, Armstrong's field pieces were being used by gunners in Italy, Turkey, Russia, Austria, Denmark, Chile, Peru – and by both sides in the American Civil War.

Some historians say it was Andrew Noble rather than Armstrong himself who saw the potential of supplying high-grade weaponry to the world's military. It was certainly a huge market. In the last few decades of the nineteenth century, more and more countries were equipping their forces with the best they could afford. And not just small arms, mortars, field guns and other artillery pieces. The world's navies were growing even faster than the world's armies, which meant a demand for heavily armoured ships driven by powerful marine engines that were, in effect, seagoing platforms for guns large and small. It was a market that no ambitious engineering company could ignore.

And no engineering company was more ambitious than

Armstrong's. In the 1860s, Armstrong's began working closely with the warship builder Charles Mitchell. It was a symbiotic relationship: Mitchell's built the warships at their yard in Low Walker and Armstrong's manufactured the guns at their factory in Elswick. For years, big naval guns made at Elswick were barged down the Tyne to Walker, where they were lifted onto the warships that were being constructed (or onto the deck of the transport on which they were being shipped).

That situation continued until 1876, when Robert Mylne's elegant neoclassical bridge was demolished and replaced by the hydraulically operated Swing Bridge designed and built by Armstrong's. The Swing Bridge over the Tyne was not the only one of its kind built by Armstrong's. Smaller versions were built across Britain, as well as a major railway bridge over the River Ouse at Goole.

THE SWING BRIDGE

It could be argued that the Swing Bridge was the best thing that had happened to Tyneside for a long time. It was certainly a major improvement, and not just for Armstrong's. Decent-sized ships of all kinds could now ply their trade up the Tyne as far west as Blaydon. The lead works, firebrick works and pipe factories on the upper part of the Tyne could be served by cargo steamers. Coal could be loaded from the staiths on the upper Tyne directly onto coal ships instead of being hauled in keels down to the river-mouth. It also enabled Armstrong's to build the Elswick naval shipyard, 11 miles from the mouth of the Tyne.

Designed by John Ure of the TIC and built by Armstrong's, the bridge is just over 467 ft long, of which 282 ft swings (usually in an anti-clockwise direction). The width of the bridge is just under 48 ft. The bridge was designed so that its piers line up with the piers of the High Level Bridge. It was operated by hydraulic machinery designed and made at Armstrong's Elswick factory. It took almost eight years to build at a total cost of £288,000.

This miracle of nineteenth-century engineering was opened without ceremony on 25 June 1876. The first ship through (three weeks later) was the Italian naval transport *Europa* on its way to Armstrong's at Elswick to load a huge 100-ton naval gun, the biggest of its kind in the world. Since then, an estimated 300,000 ships have passed through the Swing Bridge. Traffic reached a peak in 1924 when around 20 vessels a day were going through. The biggest ship to inch its way through the Swing Bridge was a warship, the 32,000-ton HMS *Canada*.

The contribution that the Swing Bridge made to the economy of Tyneside is undeniable. But it did, however, sound the end for the keels which had hauled coal down the River Tyne for centuries. With the advent of the Swing Bridge (and the serious dredging and deepening of the river by the TIC), the keels passed into folk memory.

As the demand for warships grew, in 1882 W.G. Armstrong & Co. formalised their arrangement with the shipbuilder Charles Mitchell & Co. by arranging a merger between the two companies. Two years later, Armstrong's opened their naval yard at Elswick. It was the most westerly of the big Tyneside shipyards. The first warship down the slipway at Elswick was the torpedo cruiser *Panther*, built for the Austro-Hungarian Empire. Fifteen years later, in 1897, the company swallowed the Manchester-based armaments maker Sir Joseph Whitworth, becoming Messrs Armstrong, Whitworth & Co., one of the biggest and most powerful weapons manufacturers in Europe.

But Armstrong's proved no more immune to industrial unrest than any other Tyneside firm. In 1871, the company was hit by a strike of engineering workers when 2,700 men from Elswick joined thousands of their fellow tradesmen in a battle to reduce the working week from 57 hours to 50 hours. As someone who regarded himself as an enlightened employer, William Armstrong took grave affront. He locked the Tyneside men out, imported 'blackleg' workers from the

South, closed down the school he'd built for his workers' children and used it to accommodate the strike-breakers.

As a result, Armstrong's reputation took a serious knock. The local press took a dim view of his activities. From being a benevolent employer, he became one of the *bêtes noires* of Tyneside. The strike lasted four-and-a-half months before it was settled and the men (or at least most of them) went back to work. But it seems to have undermined William Armstrong's enthusiasm for his role as a hands-on businessman. He more or less retreated into the huge and extraordinary gadget-filled house he'd built for himself at Cragside, in the countryside north of Newcastle.

Not that he became any kind of eccentric, super-rich recluse. William Armstrong was no Howard Hughes. In 1879, he presented Armstrong Park to the town of Newcastle, followed a few years later by his estate at Jesmond Dene. In 1883, he was President of the British Association when it met in York and made a speech in which he predicted that the steam engine would eventually be replaced by electric motors and that there was a bright future for both hydroelectricity and solar power. Armstrong enjoyed peering into the future: in 1863, he foresaw Britain adopting a metric system of weights and measures, and forecast that one day Britain would stop producing coal.

In the general election of 1866, he stood (unsuccessfully) as a Liberal Unionist and a year later was elevated to the peerage as Lord Armstrong of Cragside. In 1892, William Armstrong made his last visit to the great engineering works he'd founded at Elswick when he was presented to the King of Siam. A year later, he bought Bamburgh Castle with a view to converting it into a convalescent home dedicated to the memory of his wife. He died at Cragside in December 1900, two days after Christmas. His line died with him and his fortune – £1.5 million plus his estates – was inherited by his nephew William Watson, who died in 1944.

But long before then, the company was in very capable hands. The ordnance side of the business was run – brilliantly, if autocratically – by Andrew Noble, while the naval yard was in the charge of Sir William

White, one-time chief contractor to the Royal Navy. Between them, Noble and White supplied many of the world's navies with warships and guns. The emerging power of Japan was a particularly satisfied customer. So satisfied, in fact, that in 1895 William Armstrong (as titular head of the company) was awarded the Order of the Sacred Treasure of the Rising Sun. Many of the Japanese ships that destroyed the Tsar of Russia's fleet in the war of 1905 were built on the Tyne.

There's an interesting relic of imperial Japan in St John's Cemetery in Elswick. In the middle of the cemetery, there's a tall memorial stone inscribed with a long string of Asiatic writing. It marks the grave of Jushichii Takezo Fukamachi, an officer of the Imperial Japanese Navy. He died in 1885 after a fall aboard the newly built cruiser *Naniwa* while the ship was sitting at Jarrow Slake. The *Naniwa* was preparing to leave the Tyne, where it had been built at the Mitchell/Armstrong yard at Low Walker. The unfortunate Fukamachi was the ship's paymaster.

This huge surge of industrial activity on Tyneside had the effect of sucking in workers and their families from all over the British Isles, particularly from Scotland and Ireland. The population of Tyneside soared. Between the census of 1851 and the census of 1881, Newcastle's population shot up from 87,784 to 149,549. Many working-class families – perhaps even most – were crowded into small, cramped houses and flats with little in the way of amenities and sanitation. Tending to the moral welfare of this large, ever-increasing and often troubled flock was the job of the various denominations of Christianity.

And very varied they were, too. The established Church of England may have been the biggest single denomination on Tyneside, but it was heavily outnumbered by the others. The largest of these dissenting churches were the Presbyterians, the Roman Catholics and the Methodists (of which there were four different varieties). But also in the religious mix (in Newcastle at least) were groups of Congregationalists, Unitarians, Quakers, Baptists, Bible Christians and Jews.

Like those of many other areas of Britain, the churches of mid-

Victorian Tyneside were swept by a wave of evangelicalism. Most of the larger denominations were building new churches, manses, vicarages and rectories, and doing their level best to swell the number of worshippers trooping through their doors on a Sunday. After Roman Catholics were emancipated in 1829, Newcastle's Catholics, most of whom were poor Irish immigrants, raised the money to build the Cathedral of St Mary in Clayton Street. Opened in 1842, St Mary's was designed by that strange Roman Catholic zealot Augustus Welby Pugin, the man responsible for the interior design of the Palace of Westminster.

But although some of the dissenting churches, and particularly those of the Presbyterians and the Roman Catholics, were well attended, none of them had the constitutional and political clout of the Church of England. And nineteenth-century Anglicans took their duties seriously. For centuries, the spiritual needs of Tyneside and Northumberland had been the responsibility of the diocese to the south presided over by the Bishop of Durham. In the 1870s, it was decided that the Bishop of Durham had more than enough to cope with. What was needed was a Diocese of Newcastle, with its own bishop.

Which, 130 or so years on, sounds harmless enough, even benign. But in late-nineteenth-century Britain, religious views were strongly held. The dissenting lobby in Newcastle was strong, and the noisiest part of the local press was in the hands of that radical MP with Unitarian sympathies Joseph Cowen. Cowen did his best to put a stop to this extension of Anglican power. Even after the new diocese was a fait accompli, he dismissed it, claiming that it was only of interest to women, clergymen 'and that small but intelligent section of laymen who took an aesthetic and architectural interest in ecclesiastical matters'.

The Church of England persisted, however, and in August 1878 the House of Commons gave its final approval to the bill to create a new diocese, and the Queen gave it her royal assent a day later. But it was not until July 1882 that Canon Ernest Roland Wilberforce was consecrated the first Bishop of Newcastle at a solemn ceremony in

Durham Cathedral. Bishop Wilberforce did his level best, and for a few years the number of communicants worshipping in his new diocese reached record levels (around 7 per cent of the population). But by the beginning of the twentieth century, attendances were once again in decline.

That decline prompted one contributor to a diocesan conference in 1901 (Commander F.R. Norman RN) to complain that:

> there is no doubt that of late years our British Sunday has to a marked extent lost, and continues to lose, the character by which it was for so long distinguished, and has come to be regarded by a large and increasing number of our population more as a holiday than a holy day.

Which is a lament that still sounds across Britain.

GEORDIE RIDLEY

If Tyneside has an anthem it has to be 'The Blaydon Races', a song that is much loved by the Toon Army, who chant it to great effect on the terraces of St James's Park. Its author was one George Ridley, born in Gateshead in 1835, the son of a rope-maker. At the age of eight, he was sent to work at Oakwellgate Colliery. Two years later he moved to Goose Pit, Felling, where he worked for ten years before taking a job as a wagon-rider with the Gateshead engineering firm Hawks, Crawshay & Sons.

After a near-fatal accident which crushed his leg and made manual work virtually impossible, Geordie Ridley took to writing and performing comic songs, among them 'The Blaydon Races', 'The Stephenson Monument' and 'Blind Willie's Deeth'. He advertised himself as 'George Ridley, Gateshead Poet and Vocalist. The most successful Delineator of the Day of Local, Irish, Comic and Sentimental Songs'.

At the time, Geordie Ridley was less well known than his

> brother John, who was a renowned runner. Geordie Ridley
> died in September 1864, more or less forgotten. He didn't
> even rate an obituary in the *Gateshead Observer* and his
> grave in St Edmund's cemetery is unmarked.

One of Tyneside's most fascinating archives is the one held by the Newcastle Literary and Philosophical Society, the renowned Lit and Phil. The society was at its height in the latter half of the nineteenth century. Most of Tyneside's notables were members, and some served the Lit and Phil as president or vice-president, among them the engineer Robert Stephenson, the industrialist Sir William Armstrong, the barrister James Losh, the mining engineer John Buddle, the retailer John Fenwick, and the chemist and inventor Joseph Wilson Swan.

The Lit and Phil's reputation was big enough to attract lecturers from all over Britain. Some delivered a single lecture, others delivered a series. The range of subjects was extremely wide. In the season of 1868–9, for example, Professor Jevons gave two talks on a subject that no one on Tyneside wanted to hear about: 'The Exhaustion of Coal'. A few years later, the painter and critic Ford Madox Brown was lecturing on 'Art'. The record for 1883–4 is particularly impressive. There was Oscar Wilde on 'The House Beautiful' and 'Impressions of America'. He was followed by Sir William Thomson (later Lord Kelvin) on 'Vortex Atoms'. After that came the Scots author and critic Andrew Lang, who lectured on 'Life in the Heroic Greek Age'.

And it was in the lecture room at the Lit and Phil, one evening in 1878, that the ingenious chemist-turned-electrician Joseph Swan amazed his audience by demonstrating his invention of a glowing carbon filament inside a glass vacuum tube. The modern light bulb had arrived. Historians of science are still arguing about whether it was Joseph Wilson Swan the Tynesider or Thomas Alva Edison the American who first came up with the idea. Some wrangling over patents went on between the two. But Swan was sure enough of his position to start a light-bulb factory at Benwell (he later moved the plant to Enfield, near London). There he went into partnership with

Edison in the Edison & Swan United Electric Light Co., usually known as 'Ediswan'.

The year 1893 was the 100th anniversary of the Lit and Phil. At the beginning of February, a series of anniversary concerts, receptions and special lectures were laid on at the institution's premises in Westgate Road, which had been designed by John Dobson. The secretary of the day, Robert Spence Watson, was delighted with the results. The newly extended premises were looking their best. He described the effect in his book *The History of the Literary and Philosophical Society of Newcastle upon Tyne (1793–1896)*:

> As you lounged beneath tall and graceful palms or wandered in groves of richly-fruited orange trees, and the sweet strains of music stole through the air, it was difficult to believe that you were in 'canny Newcassel' . . . Before leaving the rooms at eleven o' clock on the night of the centenary celebration the writer walked round the galleries gazing on as gay and glittering a scene as any staid and sober old society could possibly afford.

A few hours after Watson's tour of inspection, fire broke out in a corner of the old library and almost devastated the building. The elegant rooms which had given Watson so much pleasure and satisfaction were unrecognisable:

> The floor had partially fallen in, the roof was completely destroyed, the books were burned by fire or drowned with water, and the ceiling of the lecture theatre had fallen in. The destruction was not indeed complete, but the sight was a sorry one.

The Lit and Phil was down but it was far from out. The members rallied round. Funds were raised. And by October 1894, the Lit and Phil was up and running again; but this time the rooms were lit by an electric generator situated in the basement.

NEWCASTLE UNITED F.C.

The black and white 'magpie' strip of Newcastle United is almost (although not quite) as well known around the world as the red and white of Manchester United. Along with Arsenal, Chelsea, Liverpool, Rangers and Celtic, they are one of the dozen or so football clubs that dominate British football. Their fans – the famous 'Toon Army' – are known for their zealous support, and disdain for the weather, hot or cold. And few football stadia loom quite so large over the city centre as St James's Park does in Newcastle. Even if they wanted to, Novocastrians would find it hard to ignore the presence of Newcastle United Football Club.

Like most British football clubs, Newcastle United can trace its beginning back to the latter half of the nineteenth century. It was spawned by the union of two earlier clubs, Newcastle East End (which played near the Heaton railway junction) and Newcastle West End (which played at the bottom of Leazes Park). They were two of the sixty or so clubs that played in Northumberland and Durham in the early 1880s. On 9 December 1892, the two clubs got together to form Newcastle United FC, which took over the lease of the ground at Leazes which was renamed St James's Park. In 1893, the club joined the Second Division of the Football League (along with Arsenal and Liverpool).

At first it was hard going. The merger – as mergers often do – dismayed supporters on both sides. East End fans hated the business of moving out of Byker, while West End fans felt they were being overwhelmed by the more numerous fans from the East End. In those early days, results were poor and crowds were small, and it was not until one Frank Watt (a Scotsman) took over the running of the club that things got better. On Christmas Eve 1898, Newcastle United played their first-ever competitive match against Sunderland, adding another local derby to the long list which is such a feature of British football.

Most football clubs have their glory days, and Newcastle United's were in the early years of the twentieth century. The Tynesiders dominated football in Edwardian England. In the five years between 1904 and 1909 they were three times champions of the Football League and five times FA Cup finalists. Some of the club's finest players came from elsewhere: stars like Andy Aitken, Bob McColl and long-serving goalkeeper Jimmy Lawrence hailed from Scotland; Bill McCracken (the man credited with inventing the offside trap) was an Ulsterman.

Under the gimlet eye of their secretary/coach Frank Watt (who remained with the club for almost four decades), Newcastle United built itself into the best-supported club in England in just over ten years.

The modern world emerged from Tyneside in many different ways. When the Royal Navy held one of its reviews at Spithead in the year 1897, the assembled top brass got something of a shock. Racing across the sea in front of them at a speed they'd never imagined possible was a strange little craft called *Turbinia*. As the astonished admirals watched, the 100-ft-long *Turbinia* hared across the water off the Isle of Wight at more than 37 knots (which is still a very respectable speed more than 100 years on). What the open-mouthed naval officers were seeing was a big step forward in maritime technology – the advent of the steam-turbine marine engine.

That engine was the brainchild of one of the most unlikely engineers ever to set foot in Tyneside, Charles Algernon Parsons, the sixth son of William Parsons, 3rd Earl of Rosse in Ireland. The Anglo-Irish aristocracy are not known for their contributions to industry. We tend to think of them as brilliant military men like Wellington and Montgomery, of course, or literary geniuses like Oscar Wilde and William Butler Yeats. But there were exceptions, and one of them was Charles Parsons, the man who raised the efficiency of electric generators by a factor of ten when he devised the steam turbine.

That such an idea should come out of a boy raised at Birr Castle in Parsonstown, Ireland, comes as a surprise, on the face of it at least. But Parsons came from a family of distinguished scientists. His father, William, was an astronomer who, in 1845, had constructed one of Britain's biggest astronomical telescopes. Charles's eldest brother Laurence, the 4th Earl of Rosse, was also an astronomer. He specialised in studying the Great Nebula of Orion and calculating radiant heat from the moon. Laurence Parsons later became Chancellor of Trinity College, Dublin.

Charles Parsons eventually turned his back on this rarefied aristocratic-scientific background. Educated by private tutors and then at Trinity College, Dublin, he studied at St John's College, Cambridge, where he became an 'eleventh wrangler' in mathematics, one of the best in his year. Then, in a startling break with tradition, he took up a four-year engineering apprenticeship with Armstrong's at Elswick, spent two years with Kitson & Co. of Leeds and in 1884 joined Clarke, Chapman of Gateshead. That same year, he developed an extremely efficient direct drive which evolved into the steam turbine. The patents, however, lay with Clarke, Chapman.

In 1889, Parsons quit the firm to set up C.A. Parsons & Co. at Heaton to produce turbines for the fast-growing power industry. The Forth Banks power station near Newcastle was the first in the world to be driven by turbo generators (two 75 kW sets). Year by year, the Parsons generators grew in power and efficiency, and along with them the firm's reputation for engineering excellence. In 1892, the power station at Cambridge was operating three 100 kW turbo sets.

In 1894, Parsons supplied the Metropolitan Electric Supply Company with a turbine for its power station at Manchester Square in the west end of London. For years, the neighbours had been complaining about noise and vibration from the reciprocating steam engine which drove the generators. They had taken the company to court, and the judge had warned that unless they found a solution to the problem, the power station would be closed down.

Years later, the station manager, Frank Bailey, declared that the Parsons turbines had done the trick. 'After fighting vibration for many years he [Parsons] came to my rescue in 1894. And not only saved my life, but that of the Metropolitan Electric Supply Company.' And, no doubt, the peace, quiet and sanity of the residents of Manchester Square. Two years later, Parsons sold the first steam turbine to the USA. It was bought by the famous engineer George Westinghouse and was the first of a long series of export orders that was to see Parsons turbines operating in most parts of the industrialised world.

But the technology that could drive power stations could also drive ships. In 1894, Parsons set up the Parsons Marine Steam Turbine Company at Wallsend to exploit the maritime potential of steam turbines. In 1899, two years after the experimental *Turbinia* impressed the Admiralty, the Hebburn yard of Hawthorn Leslie launched HMS *Viper*, the first steam-turbine warship. She was a three-funnelled 'torpedo-boat destroyer' powered by engines supplied by the Parsons company. Although she was wrecked in 1901 off the Channel Islands, HMS *Viper* was the prototype of the modern high-speed destroyer. That same year, the world's first turbine-powered passenger liner, the *King Edward*, was launched on the Clyde. Within very few years, steam turbines became marine-engineering orthodoxy.

The enthusiasms of Charles Parsons were numerous and varied. Like his father, he was fascinated by optics. During the First World War, his Heaton works turned out reflectors for searchlights. In 1921, Parsons acquired the firm of Ross Ltd, famous for its quality binoculars and telescopes. In 1922, he acquired the Derby Crown Glass Company, changed its name to the Parsons Optical Glass Company and turned out more than 100 different kinds of high-grade optical glass. In 1925, Parsons took over Sir Howard Grubb & Sons, constructors of astronomical telescopes, and built new works for the firm at Walkergate next to his Heaton works. Through his subsidiaries, Parsons supplied telescopes for astronomical observatories in Greenwich, Edinburgh, Toronto and Praetoria.

In 1883, Parsons married Katherine Bethell, the daughter of a minor

Yorkshire landowner. They had one daughter and one son, who was killed in action on the Western Front in 1918. Their daughter, Rachel, became a naval architect, one of the first women to take up that profession. Charles Parsons died in February 1931 aboard the liner *Duchess of Richmond* in the harbour at Kingston, Jamaica. When he died, he had more than 300 patents to his name. Rachel was murdered at Gosforth Park racecourse in Newcastle in 1956.

The long saga of industrial Tyneside is full of surprises. One of them is that much of Britain's most innovative electrical engineering emerged around the Tyne. Certainly, the industrial background was conducive: coal mining, heavy engineering, shipbuilding. But it was no more conducive than that of, say, the East Midlands or West Central Scotland. The fact that electrical engineering burgeoned so quickly on Tyneside is due largely to a few individuals: Joseph Wilson Swan, Charles Algernon Parsons, John Theodore Merz and his son Charles. The Merz dynasty, in particular, was to play a major role in electrifying Britain. In the process, the Tyneside conurbation became one of Europe's most advanced electric-power centres.

As the name suggests, John Theodore Merz was the son of a German immigrant. He married one Alice Richardson, from a local Quaker family, whose brother John Wigham Richardson was one of Tyneside's shipbuilding tycoons. In 1889, Merz and another brother-in-law, Robert Spence Watson, set up the Newcastle upon Tyne Electric Supply Company (usually known as NESCo) to supply electricity to the booming industries of the north-east of England.

As well as running NESCo, John Merz found time to lecture on philosophy and write *A History of European Thought in the Nineteenth Century*. The Merz home at The Quarries, Benwell, was a centre of local life. John Merz's contribution to the intellectual life of Tyneside was considerable. He was one of the more enthusiastic members of Newcastle's Lit and Phil and, according to the society's records, between 1872 and 1883 he regaled Tyneside with his thoughts on the poet Coleridge, the German Romantic August von Schlegel and the philosophies of Descartes and Leibniz. Merz rounded off his deliberations (in 1883) with a series of six lectures entitled 'An introduction to the study of moral philosophy'.

TOMMY ON THE BRIDGE

In the latter half of the nineteenth century, one of Tyneside's best-known figures was a beggar known to everyone as 'Tommy on the Bridge'. A small, stocky man, the son of a miner, Thomas Ferens was born in 1841 completely blind and partially paralysed. Unable to work, he scraped a living by begging, and his stance was in the centre of the old Tyne Bridge at the blue stone that marked the boundary between Newcastle and Gateshead. It seems that Tommy believed that by standing on the boundary between the towns he could not be arrested by either authority for begging. He begged Monday to Saturday between the hours of 11 am and 4 pm and never on a Sunday or Christmas Day. It's said that, although completely blind, Tommy knew the value of every coin put into his hand and became irate when anyone tried to fob him off with a foreign coin.

When the old Tyne Bridge was demolished, Tommy changed his stance to the new Swing Bridge. He was outraged, however, whenever the bridge was swung over to allow shipping up or down the Tyne. This meant that no pedestrians could cross – hence no money for Tommy. He threatened to sue the authorities for loss of earnings. Tommy on the Bridge was found dead of exposure on 1 January 1907.

While the electricity industry was being born, another was dying. In the face of fierce competition from Germany and the United States, and the advent of the cheaper, cleaner Solvay process, the alkali industry struggled to adapt. The noisome, polluting factories which had proliferated along the Tyne wilted and began to die. Company after company failed. In 1890 what remained was 'rationalised' into the

United Alkali Company. And in 1899, the famous Gateshead engineering firm of Hawks, Crawshay & Sons, the firm which had built Robert Stephenson's High Level Bridge across the Tyne Gorge, closed its gates for the last time. That same year, Newcastle's handsome Theatre Royal was almost destroyed by fire.

The nineteenth century ended on a sour note.

9

WORKSHOP OF
THE WORLD

1900–1918

It's a venerable saying, but it's worth repeating: in the late nineteenth and early twentieth centuries, it was not Queen Victoria and her son King Edward who ruled over Britain, it was Old King Coal. Which is a bit of an exaggeration, but not much. In the first decade of the twentieth century, around a million men were employed in the coal industry. As Roy Church reminds us in *The History of the British Coal Industry 1830–1913*:

> When Britain's first Census of Production was taken in 1907 the coal industry was second to none in the value added to the country's net output, representing approximately 14 per cent of the total. Nearly two thirds of all coal entering world trade was mined in Britain.

Coal, Church writes,

> had come into its own as the overwhelming predominant source of heat, light and power in the expanding world economy as

well as Britain – which was in many respects the centre of that economy. Coal, or its direct derivatives, fuelled the locomotives and steamships which came to dominate transport; smelted the ores which supplied the metals which were ubiquitously used in manufacturing; raised the steam power for the machinery and pumps of modern industry; generated the gas and electricity which, in developed lands, increasingly provided heat, light and power.

It's an argument (paean of praise, really) that was voiced earlier, in Sir John Harold Clapham's *Economic History of Modern Britain*, written in 1932. The author wrote, 'Behind and beneath the technical development of all the industries lay the coal and the technique of the collier and the mining engineer.' In other words, coal was vital to nineteenth and twentieth-century Britain in the way that canals, water mills and other forms of water power were to late-eighteenth-century Britain. If it was water and water power that kick-started the Industrial Revolution, it was coal that sustained it.

THE PRICE OF COAL

Mining disasters in the North-east coalfield between 1900 and 1918:

1906 at Wingate	24 die
1908 at Washington Glebe	14 die
1909 at West Stanley	168 die

The coal output figures are remarkable. In the year 1850, the British coal industry produced 62.5 million tons of coal. Twenty years after that, in 1870, output had almost doubled to 115.5 million tons. Another two decades on and it had reached more than 181 million tons. And by 1913, the year before the outbreak of the First World War, more than 287 million tons of coal was hacked and gouged from Britain's coalfields. Only the Americans came close to matching Britain's coal output.

FIRE-CLAY

Where there is coal, there is often fire-clay, that valuable mineral that is usually low in iron and lime, and resistant to heat. It was a seam of high-quality fire-clay west of Newcastle that persuaded the twin brothers Moses and Samuel Adams to abandon the town of York in 1902 and take over the fire-clay works of W.C. Gibson at Scotswood. From there, the Adams brothers (who were Quakers) launched the 'Adamsez' range of sanitary ware that became world famous. The Adamsez factory in Scotswood survived into the 1970s.

As the biggest single source of that coal was Northumberland and Durham, the strategic and economic importance of Tyneside can hardly be exaggerated. Only London was more important to Britain's economic welfare. As the nineteenth century had proved, cheap and plentiful coal had a way of spawning industries. By the beginning of the twentieth century, the factories of Tyneside were turning out (among much else) chemicals, glass, railway engines, armaments, mining equipment, machine tools and maritime equipment. Meanwhile, the shipyards that lined the Tyne from Scotswood down to South Shields produced vessels of just about every type and size for customers across the planet.

There's a graphic and rather stirring description of late-Victorian/Edwardian Tyneside by the writer David Bean in his highly readable book *Tyneside: A Biography*, published in 1971. He writes:

> Now the whole river began to boom. Coal-based, this prosperity took in iron and later steel, shipbuilding, chemicals, light and heavy engineering. This was the era of invention, and the Tyne was at the forefront. From her banks came the first railways, the first electric lamp, the first big guns, the first Dreadnoughts, the first life boats, the most daring bridges . . . Now on both banks Tyneside filled with windmills and pits and factories. The gaps between, and the long sweeps up the

hillsides behind, were crammed with terrace rows of brick to house the thousands of workers who were streaming in from all over the kingdom to get richer than all but a few of them ever really did. The salmon twitched in liquid poison and gave up the ghost.

David Bean's version of Tyneside's history is well worth reading for his vivid turn of phrase. He has this to say about Gateshead: 'It has always been Newcastle's poorer neighbour, or rather the mousy, industrious spouse of the good-looking rake over the river. As Southwark is to the City of London, Salford to Manchester, so Gateshead is to Newcastle.'

And the last decades of the nineteenth century and the first of the twentieth proved difficult for the mousy, industrious spouse. Having lost its industrial anchor in 1899 with the collapse of the famous engineering firm of Hawks, Crawshay & Sons, in 1909 the town lost another important manufacturer when John Abbot & Co. closed its doors. Which left as Gateshead's biggest employer the locomotive works of the North Eastern Railway Company (the NER) at Greenesfield, on a site perched on the northern edge of the town overlooking the Tyne Gorge.

Greene's Field had been a railway site since the 1840s, when it served, to all intents and purposes, as Newcastle's main railway station. Because there was no railway bridge across the Tyne, Greenesfield (as it came to be called) was the terminus for trains from the South. The advent of the High Level Bridge (in 1849) and Newcastle's Central Station (in 1850) changed all that, and in 1854 Greenesfield became the site of the NER's main locomotive works.

By 1909, the Greenesfield loco works employed more than 3,300 workers, many of them highly skilled men. It was by far Gateshead's biggest single employer, and one of the best-paying. But Britain's twentieth-century railway system was hungry for bigger, heavier and faster locomotives, which the cramped Greenesfield site could not provide. So, in 1910, the NER moved the business of building the new locomotives to Darlington in Yorkshire, keeping the Greenesfield works as a loco repair shop, which is how it functioned for the next 22 years, until it was run down and then finally closed in 1932.

There was some modest consolation for Gateshead in the years before the First World War when a well-heeled Newcastle lawyer called Aynsley Davidson Shipley died leaving a huge collection of paintings to the City of Newcastle, along with £30,000 to build a gallery in which to house them. As Newcastle had opened the Laing Art Gallery a few years previously and were definitely not impressed by Mr Shipley's paintings, they declined the offer. The collection and the money were then offered to Gateshead, which, after some hesitation, took up the bequest.

The result was the Shipley Art Gallery, one of Gateshead's architectural showpieces. Built between 1914 and 1917 to a design by Newcastle architect Arthur Stockwell, the building is both handsome and workmanlike. It's described by Simon Taylor and David Lovie in their publication *Gateshead: Architecture in a Changing English Urban Landscape* as 'an elegant building in an Edwardian baroque style . . . Its controversial beginnings aside, the gallery remains an elegant and attractive building that graces its location and has proved itself, in many ways, to be an asset to the town.'

In fact, Gateshead has a very decent collection of public buildings, most of them built in the second half of the nineteenth century. Some have been lost, but some are still standing, among them the handsome 1830s mansion on Nelson Street that once housed the town's dispensary and John Johnstone's Town Hall. Also still intact is the rambling, brick-built Gateshead Borough Lunatic Asylum, which was designed by G.T. Hine and opened in 1910 to house 400–500 of the town's mentally ill. Eventually known as St Mary's Hospital, it has been described as a 'splendid example of an early 20th century municipal lunatic asylum'.

The economy of Gateshead may have been flagging, but that did not stop the town expanding to the south and west. The inner suburbs of Bensham and Shipcote were rapidly covered with housing, largely to rehouse the folk who were being cleared out of the old town-centre slums. For decades, the middle classes had been building nicely designed terraces on the greenery of Bensham. That changed at the turn of the century when a combination of population pressure and money-hungry builders and landlords covered Bensham in working-class housing. Most of the housing was two or three-storey flats, usually in reddish brick, some of it quite spacious and most of it very soundly built.

They were far from being slums. Indeed, Taylor and Lovie (whose book is published by English Heritage) describe these Tyneside flats as:

> a success in their time, significantly reducing overcrowding and improving sanitary conditions as well as fostering a sense of community that is still valued by their inhabitants today. With the corner shops, corner pubs, places of worship and of recreation, they give Bensham a very distinct character.

The physical connections between Gateshead and Newcastle had always been problematical. The gorge of the Tyne is a serious piece of geography and one that is not spanned easily or cheaply. In 1871, a new toll bridge across the Tyne was opened at Redheugh to the west of Gateshead. Designed by the engineer Thomas Bouch, it was a slender, relatively lightweight and reasonably inexpensive steel structure which, after a few years, began to make money for the bridge company. But by the 1890s, the Redheugh Bridge was showing signs of being the worse for wear, and it was decided to erect a new bridge on the same site (even though the approach roads left a lot to be desired).

The job was given to the Glasgow engineer Sir William Arrol, whose reputation was high after the success of his railway bridge across the Firth of Forth. Arrol's tender of £72,411 was accepted, as was his estimate of two years to finish the job. As is the way of these things, the project took more time and more money (£5,000 more) than the original estimate. Arrol's bridge was opened for traffic at the end of August 1901. In 1906, the engineers noticed that the bridge was beginning to move laterally on the Gateshead side. The movement was stopped by the speedy erection of timber trestle. The Redheugh Bridge continued to spin money for its proprietors until it was taken over by the local authorities of Gateshead and Newcastle in 1937.

As the economy of Gateshead proved, the early-twentieth-century boom on Tyneside was patchy. But the economy got another shot in the arm: cheap electricity. Charles Hesterman Merz was born in 1874 the son of the pioneering John Merz. After an education at Beetham School in York and Armstrong College in Newcastle, young Merz became an engineering apprentice at the Pandon Dene power station. After a year at Pandon Dene, and encouraged by his father, he joined Robey Engineering in Lincoln and then the City of London Electric Supply Company at their Bankside power station.

During a spell working at Cork in Ireland, Charles Merz met a young Scotsman of his own age called William McLellan. A graduate of Liverpool University, McLellan had worked at the Siemens Brothers factory at Charlton in south London. The two electro-enthusiasts hit it off and in 1902 set themselves up as Merz & McLellan, consultant electrical engineers. Thanks to Charles's uncle John Richardson, their first job was to design the power supply for the Tyneside shipyards. They also designed the Neptune Bank power station at Wallsend, the first in the UK to generate power at 5,500 V and which was opened with a flourish by the great Lord Kelvin.

The Neptune Bank power station was eventually bought by NESCo. The Merz-designed power station was so far ahead of its time that the trade magazine *The Electrician* saw in it 'the beginning of the era of electric power utilisation all over the kingdom'. Within a few years, Neptune Bank boosted its capacity by installing two 1,500-kW generators driven by steam turbines manufactured by Parsons. There's a theory that it was the success of the steam turbines at Neptune Bank that prompted Cunard to order the system for their liner *Mauretania*, being built on the Tyne.

Success breeds success. In 1904, NESCo built an even more advanced power station at Carville on the bank of the Tyne, which supplied most of the local collieries and provided the power for the electrification of the NER's line between Newcastle and Tynemouth. Carville also supplied power to Gateshead (via the High Level Bridge) and to Hebburn (via a 1,000-ft-long cable tunnel under the bed of the Tyne). Carville proved to be an even bigger success than Neptune Bank.

With two such power stations under its belt, Merz & McLellan quickly established itself as one of Europe's top electrical consultancies. They worked for NESCo and most of the other British and American generating companies. Having electrified the railway line between Newcastle and Tynemouth, they acquired a taste for electric traction which they deployed to great effect on railways in Australia, Argentina, South Africa, India and the USA. Their fees were usually 5 per cent of the cost of the project.

In 1911, Merz & McLellan were called to Chicago by that city's English-born electricity supremo Samuel Insull to advise on the best way of pushing out the electric frontier. It was on the advice of Merz & McLellan that Insull commissioned Parsons steam turbines for Chicago's Fisk Street power station, which were installed in 1913. The equipment proved so efficient that the American workforce dubbed the Tyneside-built generating set 'Old Reliability'. In 1923, Parsons installed an even larger generating set for the city's Crawford Avenue power station.

Merz & McLellan is another of those Tyneside enterprises which was ahead of its time. In their study *Power Station Design* (published in 1904), they indicated the direction which Britain and all the industrialised countries had to take. They wrote:

> large power schemes will probably eventually consist of a network of transmission cables, sub station and distribution cables, supplying all the power requirements of a neighbourhood, the latter being located where electricity is to be obtained cheaply from either coal or waste products.

Which is exactly what happened – more than 20 years later.

The Merz dynasty was crucial to the industry of Tyneside. The supply of cheap electricity from the efficient NESCo power stations was a major boost to the economy of the area. In 1899, the price of electricity worked out at more than fourpence a unit. Six years later, in 1905, NESCo was charging its industrial customers a shade over one penny a unit. In the decade before the First World War, the use of electricity in Tyneside increased by a factor of 30, which far outstripped growth anywhere else in the UK.

As that shrewd and lively historian Sydney Middlebrook wrote in *Newcastle upon Tyne* (1968), electric power flowed into every corner of Tyneside:

> Shipyards and engineering shops installed electric cranes, winches, pumps and other machinery; collieries began to use electrically driven coal-cutters and conveyors; electric lighting of mines and works became general; and a few firms, including the Newcastle Alloy Co., even adopted the electric furnace.

Nor did the men who ran the region miss the electric trick. With Tyneside's towns and cities sprawling in all directions, the demand was growing for safe, comfortable and reasonably priced public transport. Old-fashioned horse-drawn tramcars would just not do the business. Middlebrook writes:

> In 1901 the electric tram was introduced in Newcastle by the Corporation, and in 1904 the North Eastern Railway Co. opened the first electric railway in Britain outside London. The line was the circular suburban route for passenger traffic between Newcastle and the coast.

Boosted by cheap coal and cheap electricity, the first two decades of the twentieth century were a boom time for the shipyards of the Tyne. The Tyne turned out an astonishing proportion of the world's shipping. In 1902, Wigham Richardson's yard at Walker (which merged with Swan & Hunter in 1903) launched the cable-laying ship *Colonia*, the first of 24 such sophisticated vessels. The nearby Armstrong Whitworth yard at Low Walker specialised in icebreakers for the Russians and the

Canadians, and oil tankers for the world. In fact, Tyneside led the world in the production of tankers until the year 1913.

One of Armstrong Whitworth's most dazzling feats of engineering was the ship known as the *Baikal*. This was an order by the Russian authorities for a large, icebreaking train ferry to plough up and down the 400-mile-long inland sea known as Lake Baikal in the depths of eastern Siberia, not far from the border with Mongolia. The ship was duly designed and built on the Tyne, then taken apart and shipped to St Petersburg. From there, it was transported by rail in thousands of pieces across Russia and Siberia to the shores of Lake Baikal, where it was reassembled, piece by piece, under the expert eyes of a team of Geordies from the Low Walker yard. It was a heroic piece of British engineering.

Old photographs of the *Baikal* in action show an extraordinary vessel. She seems to be all hull and hardly any superstructure, with a bow that's almost as blunt and rounded as the stern. Two rows of ports – square rather than round – run the length of the hull. But the ship's most distinguishing feature are the four funnels arranged in two pairs side by side, rather than in a line. Doors on the stern section swung open to allow railway carriages and trucks to be loaded into the hold. If ever a shipbuilding story deserved to be better known, it's the tale of the *Baikal*.

Armstrong Whitworth's naval yard at Walker – which began work in 1912 – was equally accomplished, turning out warships for the Japanese and the Norwegians as well as the Royal Navy. Among them the battleship *Malaya* and the cruisers *Invincible*, *Canada*, *Agincourt*, *Superb* and *Birmingham*, plus nine submarines. One of the yard's ships was the ill-fated *Hampshire*, which was lost off the Orkneys in 1916 while carrying Field Marshal Horatio Kitchener on a mission to Russia. The yard's last warship was the aircraft carrier HMS *Eagle*, which was launched on the Tyne in 1924.

THE TYNE'S MASTERPIECE

Of all the ships launched on the Tyne, none was so renowned as the RMS *Mauretania*. Built for Cunard by

Swan Hunter & Wigham Richardson at their Wallsend yard, it was funded by the British government, along with its sister ship, the Clyde-built RMS *Lusitania*. His Majesty's Government was tired of seeing German liners like the *Kaiser Wilhelm der Grosse* outpacing British ships on the transatlantic passenger run. So Cunard were handed £2 million of public money to build two fast liners, along with a promise of $150,000 a year for their upkeep. In return for the cash, the company had to pledge that the ships could be used by the Government in time of war.

The *Mauretania* was launched on the Tyne in September 1906, two years after the keel was laid. It was just under 800 ft long and 88 ft wide, weighed almost 32,000 tons and was the first liner to be powered by a steam turbine which drove four screw propellers. The Tyneside-built marine engines were the creation of that genius from the Anglo-Irish gentry Charles Parsons. Built to accommodate 2,165 passengers and a crew of 812, the *Mauretania* was named after an African province of the Roman Empire.

After a dazzlingly successful series of sea trials (during which it reached a speed of 26.75 knots), the *Mauretania* left Liverpool on its maiden voyage on 16 November 1907 with Captain John Pritchard in command. It made the journey to New York in 5 days, 18 hours and 17 minutes, at an average speed of just over 21 knots. In September 1909, it took the record from its sister ship *Lusitania* with an average speed of 26.25 knots between the US coast and Cherbourg. The record was to stand for 20 years. There's general agreement among historians that the *Mauretania* was one of the finest passenger liners ever built.

During the First World War, it was converted for use as a troopship, then as a hospital ship bringing injured soldiers back from Gallipoli and then back into a troopship, ferrying US and Canadian forces across the Atlantic. It returned to civilian duties in 1919, and, after a fire in 1921, its coal-burning engines were replaced with oil burners. When it was retired from transatlantic service in the 1930s, it worked for a short time as a cruise liner. The *Mauretania* was taken out of service in 1935 and broken up in 1936 at Rosyth on the Firth of Forth.

Its ill-starred sister ship *Lusitania* was sunk by a German U-boat in May 1915, killing 1,198 passengers and crew, many of them Americans. The outrage caused by the attack cranked up American hostility to Germany and helped bring the USA into the war on the Allied side two years later.

Armstrong Whitworth were distinctly less successful when it came to building motor cars. On the face of it, diversifying into car-making was a good idea. By the turn of the century, it was plain that the internal-combustion engine had a big future, and there was serious money to be made in building motor cars. The company tested the water in 1902 by manufacturing a small van that ran on paraffin. Then, in 1904, Armstrong Whitworth paid the London car-maker Wilson, Pilcher & Co. for the rights to produce their vehicles at Elswick. That foray into the car industry was not a success. The advertising slogan 'Built like a battleship' did not play well with the car-buying public.

Another Tyneside industry that failed to flourish in the early years of the twentieth century was the alkali industry. The four companies which survived of the twenty-four there had once been were all trading under the banner of the United Alkali Company. The industry was down, but not quite out. It was still a presence on the banks of the Tyne. In 1906, the Castner Kellner Alkali Company transferred its production of sodium from Runcorn in Cheshire up to Wallsend to take advantage of Tyneside's cheap electricity. The 1911 census recorded more than 1,000 chemical industry workers in Gateshead alone.

By the beginning of the twentieth century, the railway system that ran into Tyneside was hard pressed. As factories and shipyards all over northern Britain boomed, more and more trains ran into Tyneside, some of them terminating in Gateshead and Newcastle, more of them on their way north to Scotland. Which meant that Robert Stephenson's High Level Bridge, that masterpiece completed in 1849 and which had served Tyneside well for more than 50 years, was now a serious 'choke point'. The High Level's three railway lines carried about 800 trains a day, regional trains into the towns of County Durham as well as the main north–south traffic.

For years, the directors of the NER fretted over how to overcome the problem. One suggestion was to widen the High Level to double the number of railway tracks to six. Another was to build a new railway bridge to cross the Tyne between Dunston Staiths and Elswick to join up with the Newcastle-to-Carlisle line. In the end, the directors decided to bite the bullet and build a new high-level bridge across the Tyne Gorge which would carry the main north–south line right into Newcastle Central Station in the heart of the city.

Once the decision was taken, the NER moved. Parliamentary powers were obtained in 1899 and the design work was handed to Charles Harrison, the NER's chief engineer in the North. The contract to build the bridge was let in March 1902 to the Cleveland Bridge & Engineering Company of Darlington. In July that year, Harrison laid the foundation stone. His design was simple: four huge stone piers of Norwegian granite standing on steel caissons each weighing more than 667 tons which were sunk deep into the bed of the Tyne then filled with concrete. The steel deck carrying the railway lines spanned between the stone piers. The result was, in the words of one historian, 'a highly efficient, although extremely heavy, railway bridge'. It cost £500,000 to build.

Five years later, the bridge was more or less complete. As was the custom of the time, the project was named after the reigning monarch, who was Queen Victoria's son Edward VII. On 10 July 1906, the new King Edward VII Bridge was declared open by the man himself – before it was quite ready for traffic. The structure was not declared safe by the Board of Trade until 27 September 1906, when two sets of locomotives crossed the bridge at the same time at eight miles per hour. On 1 October, the last great railway bridge built in Britain was opened for traffic. It has remained open for the last 100 years.

There's an interesting reflection on the King Edward VII Bridge by F.W.D. Manders in his *History of Gateshead*. He writes:

> This was the last bridge on Tyneside to be built by huge gangs of migrant labourers, many of them worked a short time only on the site before moving on. Men were dismissed for breaking pick-shafts or barrow-handles and were easily replaced. The master of the Gateshead Workhouse found that men were tramping from Manchester and Liverpool to work on the bridge.

THE TYNE FERRIES

Bridges were not the only way over the Tyne. Ever since medieval times (and probably before), ferrymen had been plying their trade back and forward across the river. That ancient tradition continued well into the twentieth century. Between 1904 and 1911, four new ferries began shuttling people between North and South Shields.

Three of them carried foot passengers only: the *George Armstrong* (1904); the *Thomas Richardson* (1906); and the *U.A. Ritson* (1906). One vehicle ferry was put into service on the same route, the *South Shields* (1911). It operated until 1968.

The day after King Edward inaugurated the railway bridge which had been named after him, he declared open the new hospital which had been named after his mother. This was the Royal Victoria Infirmary; designed by W. L. Newcombe and Percy Adams and built on a 10-acre site carved out of the grounds of the Castle Leazes, it is something of an architectural oddity. It's been described as an essay in red-brick baroque.

The fund which was used to build the new hospital was opened to mark Queen Victoria's diamond jubilee in 1897. It raised the necessary £200,000 in a few years. There's a vaguely art nouveau statue by the sculptor George Frampton standing in front of the hospital's main entrance. It's of a slim, rather svelte young monarch, an image a long way from the dumpy little Queen with whom Britain had become familiar.

As Tyneside's economy boomed, so did the population, particularly of Newcastle. More and more people – skilled and unskilled – flooded into the city in pursuit of work and prosperity. They came from all over the north of England, southern Scotland and Ireland. According to the census of 1891, the population of Newcastle was 186,345. Ten years later, it had shot up to 215,328. Newcastle became one of the fastest-growing cities in Britain.

From the old city centre, people spilled west into Elswick and Westgate, east into Byker and Heaton, north into Jesmond, Fenham and Gosforth. In 1904, the previously independent burghs of Benwell, Fenham and Walker were incorporated into the City of Newcastle, a municipal arrangement that did not meet with everyone's approval. This fresh crop of Novocastrians was reflected in the 1911 census returns – 266,671, almost *ten times* what it had been 100 years previously.

THE TYNESIDE SCOTS

Traditionally, the people of Tyneside had good reason to be wary of the Scots. For centuries, cross-border warfare and raiding was endemic all along the frontier between Scotland and England. As late as 1745, Newcastle had to close its gates and man the town walls against a Jacobite army composed mainly of Scots. It says a lot for Tynesiders that by the end of the eighteenth century they were accepting – even welcoming – Scots into Tyneside society. Most of these immigrants from north of the Tweed were ordinary working folk whose lives went unrecorded. But some of them made important contributions to the life and work of Tyneside. Among them:

William Cleland Shipbuilder and ship-repairer who began his career as a manager of Palmer's yard at Howdon. His yard at Willington Quay claimed to have the best slipway on the Tyne.

John Coutts Pioneering shipbuilder and the first on the Tyne to build iron ships, both steam and sail. In the 1850s, his business collapsed, and he later died in poverty.

John Burghersh Forbes Crimean War veteran and survivor of the charge of the Light Brigade at Balaclava. He later ran a famous riding school in Newcastle.

Alex Gardner Captain of Newcastle United before the First World War. He was one of six Scots in the team which won Newcastle's first league championship.

Alexander Laing Wine merchant, hotelier and art-lover. Founder of the Laing Art Gallery in Newcastle.

Andrew Leslie Shipbuilder and philanthropist. Leslie's yard at Hebburn built more than 50 ships before merging with the engineering firm R&W Hawthorn to become Hawthorn Leslie. Leslie funded the building of St Andrew's Church and social centre in Hebburn.

Eneas Mackenzie Social reformer, printer and publisher.

William McLellan Electrical engineer and co-founder with Charles Merz of the famous Tyneside engineering consultancy Merz & McLellan.

Henry Milvain Shipowner and one of the River Tyne commissioners.

Charles Mitchell Shipbuilder whose Low Walker yard launched 450 ships in 30 years. He financed the building of St George's Church.

James Murray Presbyterian clergyman, reformer and radical pamphleteer.

Andrew Noble Artillery officer, ballistics expert, engineer and industrialist. He was right-hand man and successor to William Armstrong.

John Hunter Rutherford Evangelist, physician, reformer and influential educationalist. The Rutherford Memorial

College (now part of Northumbria University) was named for him.

William Bell Scott Artist and master of the School of Design in Newcastle.

Of course, living standards among Tynesiders varied from those of fabulously wealthy industrialists like William Armstrong and Sir Charles Palmer to desperately poor Irish and Scots immigrants crowded into Tyneside's most fetid slums. For many people, surviving from day to day was a fairly desperate business. A report dated 1904 suggests that many families spent two-thirds of their income on food and drink, leaving very little for rent, heat and clothing.

And the quality of that food was not good. As in the rest of industrial Britain, the diet of the working-class Tynesider consisted mainly of stodge enlivened with jam, treacle and syrup. Fruit and vegetables were almost unknown and milk was often contaminated. On Saturday nights, the butcher stalls in the Grainger Market sold off cheaply what was left of their stocks of meat, the ensuing scramble for meat, according to the authorities, 'occasionally causing disorder'.

But that was not the whole picture. Tyneside's middle class was large and growing. Newcastle had become – as it still is – the shopping centre for a large hinterland. The 1901 directory lists 600 grocers' shops, including the London & Newcastle Tea Company, Home and Colonial, Lipton's and the Newcastle upon Tyne Co-operative Society (which had 13 stores). There were also 300 butchers' shops supplied by no fewer than 124 slaughterhouses, the quality of which varied enormously.

As the population of Tyneside swelled, so did the demand for amusement. Gosforth Park racecourse continued to boom right up to the First World War, when it was taken over by the army, under whose stewardship the grandstand was almost burned down. Huge crowds flowed into St James's Park to watch Newcastle United, who had a truly golden period in the first decade of the twentieth century. The Northumberland Golf Club was formed in 1898, followed by the Gosforth Golf Club in 1906. Boxing was popular, particularly after

Jack Palmer from Benwell became British heavyweight champion between 1903 and 1906. In 1909, a boxing stadium was opened at St James's Hall.

And while the game of cricket never defined Tynesiders in the way that it did Yorkshiremen and Lancastrians, the game was popular, particularly among the gentry and middle classes. The Gosforth Cricket Club began in 1864, and by the time it changed its name to the South Northumberland Cricket Club, it was being supported by more than 200 members. There were other – less exalted – clubs, too: the Mechanics, the Claremont, the Newcastle. Some had their own grounds, others played on the Town Moor. In their essay 'Sport on Tyneside' in *Newcastle upon Tyne: A Modern History*, writers Richard Holt and Ray Physick point out that:

> A survey of match results in the Newcastle press in 1900 revealed 143 clubs in the Northumberland cricket league of which around a dozen came from Newcastle itself, including Walker, Heaton, Newcastle Victoria, Gosforth Percy, Blaydon, Newcastle St. Phillip's, Westgate, Jesmond, Rutherford College and, of course, South Northumberland.

Drink, however, continued to plague industrial Tyneside, as it plagued other parts of urban Britain. According to Brian Bennison in his essay 'Drink in Newcastle' (also in *Newcastle upon Tyne: A Modern History*), at the end of the nineteenth century, the city hosted no fewer than 691 licensed premises, which was 1 for every 43 dwellings and for every 307 people. It was one of the highest concentrations of boozers in Britain, and the results were predictable.

Bennison writes: 'Late 19th century drunkenness proceedings [i.e. legal proceedings] expressed in terms of the number per 10,000 persons averaged 62 across England but stood at 207 for Newcastle.' It's worth pointing out, however, that not all these drunks were Novocastrians. Around 40 per cent of these proceedings were against travellers from all over Britain and, of course, other Tynesiders.

But it was a bad situation. And when the magistrates of Newcastle were given the power in 1904 to shut down pubs on the grounds of 'redundancy' (i.e. proliferation) or for being 'badly adapted' (i.e. a shambles), they took the opportunity to close down 16 pubs in 1905, 21 in 1906 and 17 in 1907. Which worked in favour of the big brewing companies, who had the cash to give their pubs the makeover they needed. Gradually, the most noxious of the drinking dens faded, although they never disappeared altogether.

THE LAST HANGED MAN

The last man hanged in His Majesty's Prison Newcastle met his end at 9.15 on Wednesday, 26 November 1919. He was 28-year-old Ambrose Quinn, and he'd been tried and sentenced to death for the murder of his wife Elizabeth Ann at Hawes Street, Newcastle. As was the custom by then, he was buried in a numbered grave inside the prison walls.

Ambrose Quinn was the last of eight men to be hanged at Newcastle prison in the twentieth century. The others were: John Miller and his nephew John Robert Miller (1901); Henry Perkins (1905); John Alexander Dickman (1910); John Vickers Amos (1913); William James Cavanagh (1917); and Ernest Bernard Scott (1919).

On 31 March 1925, five years and four months after the execution of Ambrose Quinn, H.M. Prison Newcastle was closed down and the prisoners moved to H.M. Prison Durham. Thereafter, Durham took over the grim business of putting to death the convicted murderers of Tyneside and the north-east of England.

The temperance movement did its best to curb Tyneside's alcoholic enthusiasms, without too much success. In fact, the temperance movement proved to be no great threat to the profits of the brewers and the grog-shop owners. The only real threat they faced was from the network of working men's clubs which grew up around Tyneside in the late nineteenth century, some of which still flourish under different names. By 1914, there were more than 50 such clubs in Newcastle alone.

Among them were the Elswick Collieries' Workingmen's Social Club; the National Union of Gasworkers & General Labourers' Club; the Tramway & Vehicle Workers' Social Club; and the Elswick Conservative Workingmen's Club. They had middle-class counterparts in the Elswick Shipyard Officials' Dining Club, the Walker Shipyard Messroom and the Post Office Dining Club. According to Brian Bennison, the St. Dominic's Catholic Recreative Club was blessed by Pope Leo XIII in 1902.

Ironically, perhaps, it is to Tyneside's drinking classes that Newcastle owes its finest art gallery, the Laing. It was paid for by Alexander Laing, an Edinburgh-born beer salesman who'd descended on Newcastle in 1849 to peddle the wares of a Scottish brewer and stayed on to make big money as a wine merchant, bottler and hotelier. A man of some taste and discrimination, Laing was an enthusiastic collector of Pre-Raphaelite paintings, most of which are now housed in the gallery he funded, which was opened by Lord Ridley in October 1904.

Yet another art-loving drink salesman was A.H. Higginbottom, who is described in 'Drink in Newcastle' by Brian Bennison as a 'wine and spirit merchant, cocoa-room proprietor, licensed victualler and pioneer of "snack lunches for your busy city man"'. Higginbottom, it seems, was a serious connoisseur of Japanese and other oriental art and donated almost his entire collection to the Laing.

Life got even better for Tyneside's culturati in 1901 when John and Benjamin Green's splendid Theatre Royal reopened for business. Opened in 1837, the theatre had been badly damaged by fire in 1899 (during a performance of *Macbeth*). But in the same year that the Theatre Royal reopened, a blaze totally gutted the interior of the Central Exchange, part of the renowned Grainger development. The interior was rebuilt to form the tile-clad Central Arcade, now an upmarket shopping precinct. In 1906, the Newcastle branch of the International Labour Party (ILP) pepped up the intellectual atmosphere of Tyneside by publishing the *Northern Democrat*.

Getting about Tyneside became easier as the nineteenth century became the twentieth. There had been horse-drawn tramways in Newcastle and its suburbs for some time, but in 1901 the tramway system was bought by the Newcastle Corporation – 'municipalised' – and electrified. Miles of new track were laid for the 100 much heavier, electric-powered tramcars, which had their own power station at Manors off the City Road. There were tram depots at Byker, Haymarket, Gosforth and Wingrove. By 1903, there were no fewer than 163 cars in service.

Over the next decade or so, the tram network spread across Newcastle and its suburbs. By 1906, it had reached Scotswood Bridge. A year later, it was Fenham. By 1912, it had gone as far as Sandyford. The year after that, it was the turn of Jesmond and Heaton. That same year, tramcars were trundling out to Newburn. By the outbreak of the First World War in 1914, Newcastle had 200 tramcars running around the city and its suburbs, one of the most comprehensive tramway systems in Britain.

It was the spread of the electric tramway that galvanised the North Eastern Railway Company into electrifying their own local services to Tynemouth and Whitley Bay in 1904. In 1917, a new Central Station-to-coast-to-Central Station loop was opened. That same year, the line along the south bank of the Tyne to South Shields was electrified. In effect, the towns of Gateshead, Hebburn, Jarrow and South Shields were becoming suburbs of Newcastle. That suburbanising effect has continued with every bridge and tunnel that's been built and every road that's been improved.

Given the overwhelmingly industrial nature of Tyneside, it's perhaps surprising how slow Geordies were to take to trade unionism. Tyneside radicalism found its home inside the Liberal Party, and anyone who criticised or barracked Liberal Party candidates could expect a hard time. One Liberal MP (for North Durham) was that brilliant but hard-nosed shipbuilder Sir Charles Mark Palmer, whose loyalists liked to pelt with eggs anyone who criticised him. Even that legendary man of the left, Arthur Henderson, was elected to the Newcastle council in 1892 as a Liberal 'in the labour interest'.

But the political left in Tyneside was struggling to find a voice. In 1893, the ILP was formed and soon found supporters on the Tyne. In 1900, the Labour Representation Committee (LRC) came into the political world, and within a year it had a branch in Newcastle. In 1904, Alexander Wilkie, a member of the LRC's national executive, was elected to the Newcastle Council. Two years later, the LRC changed its name to the Labour Party, and by 1914 Newcastle had seven Labour Party councillors, six of them working men and one of them a merchant.

At the same time, Tyneside's women were making their presence felt. In her intriguing essay 'A Woman's Place' in *Newcastle upon Tyne: A Modern History*, Maureen Callcott traces the rise of female suffrage in the north-east of England. In the year 1900, Mrs Mona Taylor of Chipchase Castle formed the Newcastle and District Women's Suffrage Society and tramped around Tyneside addressing meetings in factories and workplaces, and in the streets.

She soon found influential supporters. Among them were schoolmistress Florence Harrison Bell; Lisbeth Simm, the wife of an ILP organiser; and two female doctors who shared a Tyneside practice, Ethel Williams and Ethel Bentham. Bentham went on to become a Labour MP. The group met every Monday evening in the genteel surroundings of the Drawing Room Café in Fenwick's department store.

In 1908, the group split between the Women's Social and Political Union (the WSPU, headed by Emmeline Pankhurst) and the National Union of Women's Suffrage Societies (the NUWSS, led by Millicent Fawcett). That same year, more than 3,000 women flocked to a rally on the Town Moor before marching down – banners flying – to Central Station to greet two women who'd just been released from a spell in prison for the cause of women's suffrage.

As Callcott points out, the local leadership was distinctly middle to upper class. WSPU activists included Lady Parsons, the Irish-born wife of Sir Charles Parsons, and Lady Blake, wife of Sir Francis Blake. The tone of the organisation can be judged from one of their missives, which asked, 'Will ladies with large kitchens sometimes arrange a meeting for servants and their friends?' Such middle-class support had its advantages: between 1908 and 1913, the WSPU on Tyneside were able to pay for a full-time organiser.

Not all the ladies of the suffrage movement were as genteel as the leadership. There were some very determined activists among them, women who were prepared to do damage and risk going to jail. At various times, these women poured corrosive liquid into letter boxes, cut telephone wires, smashed windows at the Globe Theatre in Gosforth, burnt down the pavilion in Heaton Park and broke the windows at one of the offices of the Northumberland Education Committee. They also set off 'incendiary devices' at various places around Tyneside, including Barras Bridge Post Office, Gosforth Golf Club and Kenton railway station.

The women certainly had cause for complaint. The idea of women having a political voice and wielding any kind of political power was being resisted at every level. Concessions were grudging and hard to come by. Although various municipal measures enfranchised women, progress was slow. By the end of the nineteenth century, women were eligible for appointment to parish councils, council committees and school boards, and as Guardians of the Poor, but such appointees were few and far between. From 1907, women were eligible to stand in municipal elections but, pre-1919, only one female candidate – Ethel Bentham – stood for election in Newcastle, and she was defeated.

EMILY WILDING DAVISON

One of the most renowned martyrs of the women's suffrage movement was, of course, Emily Davison, the 41-year-old political activist who threw herself under the King's horse Anmer during the Epsom Derby on 4 June 1913. She died under the horse's hooves. The jockey was injured but the horse was unharmed. The whole incident was captured on a now-famous piece of black-and-white film.

A few days later, Davison's coffin was taken through London draped in the colours of the suffrage movement on an open carriage drawn by four black horses. It was followed by more than 2,000 uniformed suffragettes. The streets from Victoria to King's Cross stations were lined with female mourners.

Although born in London, Emily Davison was the product of a Northumberland family. Intelligent, well educated, a graduate of Oxford and London universities and a schoolteacher by profession, in 1906 she joined the Women's Social and Political Union and became one of its most strident activists. Before her fatal encounter with Anmer, she'd served several prison sentences for stone-throwing, setting fire to pillar boxes and bombing Lloyd George's country house.

After the grand suffragette procession in London, her body was shipped back to Northumberland, where it lies in the family plot at Morpeth. She was buried under a purple cloth inscribed by her mother 'Welcome the Northumbrian hunger striker'.

On Wednesday, 5 August 1914, one Gateshead diarist made a striking entry in his journal:

> The streets are alive today with Territorials. The Drill Hall in Burt Terrace was the scene of great activity this morning, and about 2.30 pm the men who had reported (they numbered, I am told, about a thousand) marched off to entrain . . . It is too sad and solemn for words.

Sad and solemn indeed. War had come to Tyneside. Before it was over, out of the 18,000 or so Gateshead men who served in His Majesty's forces more than 1,700 would be killed. The Gateshead battalion of the Durham Light Infantry alone would see 786 men killed in action or dead from their wounds. Much the same 'sad and solemn' story can be found in the battalion histories of the Northumberland Fusiliers.

Like many of the great regiments of the British Army, both the Royal Northumberland Fusiliers (RNF) and the Durham Light Infantry (DLI) raised an extraordinary number of battalions – 38 in the case of the RNF and 30 in the case of the DLI. Some became reserve battalions which never left Britain. Others were training or garrison battalions. A few were raised then quickly absorbed into other units. The 38th RNF, for example, were formed in June 1918 and were part of the 22nd RNF within two weeks. But these were the exceptions. Most of the men who served with the two Tyneside regiments found themselves in the squalor and horror of the trenches.

The young men of Tyneside flocked to the colours when war broke out in 1914. Many of them enlisted in 'pals' battalions' of men from the same industry or even from the same company. The 17th RNF, for example, was mostly made up of men from the North Eastern Railway Company. The 16th RNF was formed from volunteers from the Newcastle Chamber of Commerce. The 19th DLI was one of the army's famous 'bantam' battalions, made up of men whose lack of height never impaired their fighting prowess. The Germans were reputed to be extremely fearful of the bantams.

There was also an interesting 'ethnic' dimension to the RNF. Both the large Scots and Irish communities on Tyneside felt duty-bound to make their own contributions to the war effort. Between September and November 1914 – with the encouragement and financial assistance of the Newcastle Establishment – they raised four battalions of the Tyneside Scottish and four battalions of the Tyneside Irish. Officially, the Scots were the 20th, 21st, 22nd and 23rd RNF, while the Irish were the 24th, 25th, 26th and 27th RNF. Later in the war, both groups added reserve battalions to their number.

Both the Tyneside Scottish and the Tyneside Irish took a terrible mauling on the Somme in the summer of 1916. There exists a moving account of one advance by the 2nd Tyneside Scottish across one of the Somme battlefields. It was penned by Private Tom Easton:

> Then we got orders to advance. My Colonel had gone sick and Major Heniker was in charge. He got killed by a shell even before we started. Major Neven was second in command – a big, noble-looking fellow. He got killed too. They all got killed. All the officers. I couldn't do anything but pray for my mother to protect us.

When Brigadier General Trevor Ternan, the commander of the Tyneside Scottish Brigade, came to address his unit after the battles, he was shocked to the core. In her gripping book *Somme*, the historian Lyn Macdonald writes:

> A day or so before he had addressed the officers of his Brigade en masse in the village schoolroom. Now there was more than enough room for them all in his office at Brigade Headquarters. Eighty officers had gone into action with the four Battalions of the Tyneside Scottish Brigade. Ten now remained. In the Tyneside Irish it was the same sorry tale.

Despite the slaughter on the Western Front, men from all over the north-east of England continued to flock to the recruiting stations. And the great industrial economy of Tyneside shifted up a gear. The wartime demand for coal, coke, steel, iron, ships and engineering products breathed fresh life into a sector that was flagging. Coal mining in particular was given a huge boost by wartime demand, as Barry Supple explains in *The History of the British Coal Industry 1913–1946*:

> Coal accounted for virtually all Europe's fuel supplies, and Britain's mining industry was crucial for the effectiveness of the navy, the war potential of the allies, the home transport system, the morale of the civilian population, the output of the munitions industries, and the supply of TNT and a wide range of strategic products . . . By the early months of 1915 Germany's exports had dried up; France had lost half her mines and was effectively dependant on British coal; neutral nations were desperate for supplies; and even the domestic economy had begun to experience shortages.

The problem was not so much a shortage of coal as a shortage of transport. The Admiralty had commandeered about 80 per cent of the Tyne's ships, and the ones that remained were under constant threat from German submarines and surface raiders. This meant that coal had to be transported by rail, which, in turn, created huge pressure on the railway system. Vast amounts of coal (and other raw materials) sat in railway sidings for days waiting for their turn on the main lines. It was not unknown for a consignment of coal to take three weeks to reach London from the north of England and then for the wagons to take another three weeks to return.

But it was during that war that Tyneside's shipbuilders and engineering firms came into their own. They achieved levels of productivity that had never been seen before and were never to be seen again. Armstrong Whitworth, in particular, emerged as one of the great powerhouses of Britain's wartime industry. The Tyneside engineering giant was one of a small group of companies that Prime Minister Lloyd George regarded as particularly efficient, reliable and trustworthy. (The others were the Coventry Ordnance Works, William Beardmore & Co. of Glasgow and Vickers of Sheffield.)

Despite having to 'dilute' their workforce with women and unskilled men, Armstrong Whitworth's wartime output was enormous. By 1918, the company had produced 13,000 guns, 12,000 gun carriages, 47 warships, 230 armed merchant ships, 102 tanks, 14.5 million shells, 18.5 million fuses and 21 million cartridge cases. Armstrong Whitworth went into the First World War with around 25,000 employees; by the end of it, more than 60,000 men and women were trooping through the gates of the firm's factories and shipyards.

HMS *INVINCIBLE*

One of the finest warships built by Armstrong Whitworth was the heavy battlecruiser *Invincible*. Launched on the Tyne in 1908, the *Invincible* was 17,250 tons of finely crafted steel driven by state-of-the-art turbine engines and capable of speeds of more than 28 knots. Armed with 8 12-in. guns and 16 4-in. guns (also made by Armstrong Whitworth), it was one of the fastest and most formidable ships in the Royal Navy. When the First World War broke out, HMS *Invincible* became the flagship of Rear Admiral

H.L.A. Hood, commander of the Third Battlecruiser Squadron. Its sister ships, *Inflexible* and *Indomitable*, made up the rest of the squadron.

It was in that role that *Invincible* was pitched into the great naval battle off Jutland on 31 May 1916, when the British Grand Fleet took on the powerful (and, it has to be said, more up to date) German navy. Late in the afternoon, Hood's squadron hurled itself headlong at Admiral von Hipper's First Scouting Group of five heavy cruisers, forcing two of the German ships out of the line. But at a terrible cost. In making its attack, the British squadron came within range of the German battleship *König*, and a salvo from the battleship's guns more or less blew HMS *Invincible* apart.

The Tyne-built cruiser went down within minutes, taking with her 59 officers and 961 ratings, including Rear Admiral Hood and his flag-captain A.L. Cay. Casualties from the *Invincible* came from the length and breadth of Britain, from Cornwall to Caithness. Only six of the cruiser's crew survived – two officers and four ratings. The *Invincible* was the last battlecruiser sunk that terrible day, which saw 21 British and German ships sent to the bottom of the North Sea along with 9,823 men.

It was not only warships, munitions and Russian icebreakers that Armstrong Whitworth produced during the First World War. It's often forgotten that the firm also built aircraft for the newly fledged Royal Flying Corps. Between 1914 and 1918, the Tyneside company produced more than 1,000 aircraft. They ranged from the successful Armstrong Whitworth FK3 and FK8 reconnaissance biplanes to the distinctly odd four-winged FK10 (of which very few were made). The company's aviation arm also produced a range of airships (the R33, R34 and R38), mostly for anti-submarine work.

Armstrong Whitworth also manufactured aeroplanes designed by the Royal Aircraft Factory. They were the BE2 series, light biplanes which functioned as fighters, artillery observers, reconnaissance scouts and light bombers. Most of them were powered by a 90 hp engine. It was a BE2 fighter that scored the very first British victory of the air war when it forced down a German aircraft on 25 August 1914. Armstrong Whitworth continued to build aeroplanes long after the First World War was over.

JOHN MEADE FALKNER

When Sir Andrew Noble, the chairman of Armstrong Whitworth, died in 1915 at the height of the First World War, he was succeeded by the extraordinary persona of John Meade Falkner. A giant of a man – he was 6 ft 9 in. tall – Falkner was a brilliant businessman and one of the country's most subtle and skilled international arms traders. He was also a devout and scholarly Anglican, a poet and a novelist, author of the famous children's adventure story *Moonfleet*, which is regarded by many as superior to anything written by Robert Louis Stevenson.

The son of a Wiltshire clergyman, Falkner was born in 1858. While at Oxford, he met Sir Andrew Noble's son John and moved to Newcastle to become the boy's tutor. Falkner so impressed Sir Andrew Noble that in 1888 he gave the one-time tutor the job of company secretary to the firm Armstrong Mitchell (later Armstrong Whitworth). In 1901, Falkner became a director of the huge engineering empire.

But the business of helping to run one of Europe's biggest and most powerful enterprises never stopped Falkner writing. His *Pocket Guide to Oxfordshire* (1894) was followed by his novels *The Lost Stradivarius* (1895), *Moonfleet* (1896) and *The Nebuly Coat* (1903). He is believed to have written a fourth novel but lost the manuscript on the railway journey between his home in Durham and Newcastle. He also wrote poetry and collected rare books and manuscripts.

Falkner stepped down as chairman of Armstrong Whitworth in 1920 and then retired from the board in

1926. After his retirement, he became Honorary Reader in Paleography at Durham University and Honorary Librarian to the Dean and Chapter of Durham Cathedral. He died in July 1932 and is buried in a tomb he shares with his brother at Burford in Oxfordshire.

Falkner's great story *Moonfleet* has never been out of print, and the recently formed John Meade Falkner Society is planning to publish a collection of his poems.

Not that Armstrong Whitworth had a monopoly on wartime production on the Tyne. Most of the big shipyards and engineering firms boomed during the war. The Low Walker yard of Swan Hunter & Wigham Richardson, for example, had a shell shop in which hundreds of women worked putting together high-explosive devices for the use of His Majesty's forces. At the end of the war, the women were thanked for their efforts with a lavish party, and gold bracelets and brooches all round – and then sacked to make way for the men returning from the forces. For their part, the Parsons works at Heaton produced thousands of reflectors for the military's searchlights.

The war did not stop Armstrong Whitworth building ships for foreign customers, although such orders sometimes led to awkward diplomatic tangles. For example, in 1913 the firm's Elswick yard built the battleship *Almirante Latorre* for the Chilean government. But in September 1914, to the dismay of the Chileans, the ship was taken over by the Royal Navy, completed and renamed HMS *Canada*. The Chileans were repaid the money they'd spent (with interest) but were indignant at being deprived of a warship they needed to defend their territory against their likely enemies (Argentina and Peru).

YEVGENI ZAMYATIN

Traditionally, one of Tyneside's most loyal customers was the Tsar of Russia. As late as 1917 – the year that the Tsar and his family were shot to death by the Bolsheviks – Armstrong Whitworth was building two icebreakers for the Russians. They were the *Sviatogor* (Holy Mountain) and the *Saint*

Alexander Nevski. Their construction was supervised by a young Russian engineer called Yevgeny Zamyatin. Zamyatin was also a talented novelist and playwright and, like a good writer, made use of the two years he spent living in the Newcastle suburb of Jesmond – which he saw as a community of repressed, petty-bourgeois conformists.

In his novella *Islanders* he writes:

> The Sunday gentlemen were produced at one of the Jesmond factories and on Sunday mornings, thousands of them would appear on the streets with the Sunday edition of St Enoch's parish newspaper. Sporting identical canes and identical top-hats, the Sunday gentlemen strolled in dignified fashion along the street and greeted their doubles.

After he returned to Russia in 1917 (along with the Russian icebreakers), Zamyatin completed his dystopian fiction *We*, the first book to be banned by Lenin's censors. It portrays a regimented, well-drilled society presided over by a Benefactor in which intellectual freedom and social spontaneity are remorselessly crushed. People have numbers instead of names (there's been some speculation that those numbers were taken from the specifications of the Tyneside icebreakers).

Zamyatin's powerful fable is usually regarded as the original of the twentieth-century anti-utopian novel and the inspiration for Aldous Huxley's *Brave New World* and George Orwell's *Nineteen Eighty-Four*. Certainly Orwell had read Zamyatin's work (in French) and the similarities between the two books are striking.

Although a controversial and outspoken figure (who was known in Moscow as 'the Englishman'), Zamyatin managed to survive Stalin's version of the Soviet Union and in 1931, thanks to the pleading of Maxim Gorky, he was allowed to emigrate to Paris, where he died in 1937. His seminal fable

> *We*, with its many subtle references to industrial Tyneside, was not published in Moscow until 1988, shortly before the Soviet system went into meltdown.

Zamyatin was not the only world-class littérateur who passed through Tyneside during the First World War. Rudyard Kipling (who lost his son in the war) was in Newcastle in 1915, as was Ivor Gurney, who spent time in the Newcastle General Hospital being treated for the inhalation of gas before being shunted out to New Hartley Camp, another of whose inhabitants was J.R.R. Tolkien, creator of *The Lord of the Rings*. In 1915, the novelist, playwright and essayist J.B. Priestley was also billeted on Tyneside.

Priestley seems to have taken rather a dim view of Tyneside and Tynesiders. He particularly disliked their dialect. He wrote later, in his book *English Journey*:

> To my ear it still sounds a most barbarous, monotonous and irritating twang. Every short phrase rises in exactly the same way, almost to a scream – taw taw, ta ta, tee tee, ti ti. The constant 'Ay-ee, mon' or 'Ay, ee, yer –' of the men's talk and the never ending 'Hinnying' of the women seem to me equally objectionable.

Throughout the war, the industries of Tyneside remained relatively free of the industrial disputes and disruption that plagued other parts of the British economy. The workers of Clydeside in particular were inclined to down tools when they saw an affront to their wages and conditions. There was an engineering strike on Tyneside in 1917, but it was short-lived and ineffective. One of the chroniclers of the rise of trade unionism in Britain came to the conclusion that 'Tyneside was the most important gap in the development of the shop stewards' movement.'

Given the strategic importance of the industries of Tyneside to the British war effort, it's perhaps surprising that the Germans did not do more to disrupt them. The Tyne was well within the range of the

Kaiser's long-range Zeppelin airships, which regularly menaced the south of England. One exception, however, was a Zeppelin raid on the night of 15 June 1915 which killed 12 men working the night shift at Palmer's shipyard in Jarrow. One of the workmen killed was only 18 years old. There were other, less damaging Zeppelin raids along the Tyne in 1916.

During the First World War, the electrical engineer Charles Merz was chairman of an obscure government committee which was to prove hugely influential. This was the Electric Power Subcommittee of the Coal Conservation Committee. It was Merz's subcommittee that produced the plan that created the national grid, as laid out in the Electricity (Supply) Act of 1926. Merz's calm, clear, forceful evidence before a series of parliamentary committees is often cited as the reason why the Act was passed.

The 1926 Act was probably the most important piece of electric-power legislation the British parliament ever passed. It rationalised the dozens of companies that were jostling for customers. It reduced the number of power stations to those that were big enough to operate efficiently and profitably. It set up the Central Electricity Board of eight commissioners, with the duty of establishing a sensible national grid of transmission and distribution lines to take electricity into every part of Britain (except Scotland, which made its own, very different, arrangements). By 1928, the national grid that so many engineers had long talked about was under way. By 1935, it was complete.

In 1913, Charles Merz had married Stella de Sater of Dublin. Their marriage was a happy one, and they had one son and one daughter. But it ended in tragedy. In October 1940, Charles Merz, his children and two of his servants were killed when their house in Kensington in London was struck by a bomb. It was a cruel irony. Charles Merz, descendant of German immigrants, was killed by a German bomb. Stella Merz survived.

The First World War ended with Tyneside celebrating along with the rest of Britain and the British Empire. There's a fascinating account of the festivities in David Bean's *Tyneside*:

Children's impromptu bands roamed the streets with tin-can drums, mouth organs, kazoos, combs and paper, and anything that would make a noise. The Percy Street youngsters made two effigies, one of the Kaiser and one of the Crown Prince, and swung them from street gibbets. Round the Kaiser's neck was a placard: 'Kaiser Bill, he's got to go to Hell.' And round the Crown Prince's: 'Little Willy will follow his father, silly.'

After the straitened and usually dismal war years, such juvenile exuberance was understandable. But the omens for the long term were not good. As David Bean writes,

> The main trouble was the very thing that had made Tyneside so powerful in the latter half of the nineteenth century – reliance upon a small number of heavy industries. Tyneside had all its eggs in too small a number of baskets – coal, shipbuilding and heavy engineering.

Finding other baskets was proving very difficult. The firm of Atkinson & Philipson of Pilgrim Street in Newcastle began by building horse-drawn carts, landaus and phaetons, then switched to making railway carriages for the new railway industry. When the motor car made its appearance at the turn of the century, the firm switched again and began making handmade, custom-built motor cars for affluent Tynesiders. But in 1919, Atkinson & Philipson folded, 'extinguished', in the words of one historian, 'by the competition of the mass-produced car'.

10

WAR TO WAR

1918–1945

One of the most vivid accounts of a British miner's working life between the wars is contained in a book entitled *These Poor Hands*, written by one B.L. Coombes and published in 1939. In it, he describes his first day underground:

> My legs became cramped, my arms ached, and the back of my hands had the skin burned off by pressing my knee against them to force the shovel under the coal. The dust compelled me to cough and sneeze, while it collected inside my eyes and made them burn and feel sore. My skin was smarting because of the dust and flying bits of coal. The end of that eight hours was very soon my fondest wish.

He goes on:

> How glad I was to drag my aching body towards that circle of daylight! I had sore knees and was wet from the waist down. The back of my right hand was raw and my back felt the same. My eyes were half closed because of the dust and my head was

aching where I had hit it against the top, but I had been eight
hours in a strange world.

It's an account that any pitman in Britain would have recognised. As it
happens, Coombes was writing about the time he spent underground
in South Wales, but the same conditions – and worse – were
experienced by the men working under Northumberland and County
Durham. In *The History of the British Coal Industry 1913-1946*, Barry
Supple presents an extraordinary array of statistics which demonstrate
just how dangerous the coal industry was for the men working below
the surface:

> In the mid 1920s it was calculated for every 100 men working
> for 20 years, the probabilities were that two would be killed,
> nine would suffer a major fracture or a serious injury, 16 would
> incur a serious disease and each would incur an accident
> involving an absence from work for more than seven days, at
> least once every eight years.

In other words, no pitman could expect to work for any length of time
underground and emerge unscathed. The very least he could expect
was two spells off work for injury.

And for most pitmen and colliery workers, conditions at home were
wretched. In 1919, Sir John Sankey was asked by the Government to
look into the conditions in which Britain's mineworkers and their
families were living. Sankey was appalled by what he found.
Conditions were, he wrote, 'a reproach to our civilisation. No judicial
language is sufficiently strong or sufficiently severe to apply to their
condemnation.' The only thing that could be said in favour of the
houses in which miners and their families lived was that, in Tyneside
and Durham at least, they were rent-free.

One way or another, it is hardly surprising that coal miners were
among the most militant workers in Britain. They'd spent generations
clawing half-decent wages and working conditions from hard-nosed
coal owners. They did their very best to hang on to what they'd won

and to build on it if they could. Most coal miners lived in pit towns and villages (some of them very isolated) where it was possible to maintain solidarity and a united purpose. In the first half of the twentieth century, mineworkers comprised around 6 per cent of the industrial workforce but accounted for 42 per cent of the strikes.

But in the 1920s, the power of the mineworkers was on the wane. In the wake of the First World War, the demand for coal went into decline. In the first few years after the war, business was brisk as industry in Britain (and elsewhere in Europe) rebuilt itself. But after 1921, recession began to bite. And as Northumberland and Durham comprised the biggest coalfield in Britain, the effect on Tyneside was serious. Writing in 1925, Sir Ernest Gowers – who'd taken a good hard look at the coal industry – declared that ever since the early 1920s a major recession had 'been lying in wait for the coal-mining industry'.

When that recession did pounce, it pounced with unexpected savagery. The extent of it can be seen in the wages paid to the pitmen of Tyneside and Durham. In 1921 – the last of the good years – they were being paid nineteen shillings for one shift underground. By 1926, that rate had plummeted to nine shillings and sixpence, half of what they were being paid in 1921. Miners and their families were not to see nineteen shillings per shift again until the year 1944, more than twenty years later. Even then, it had been eroded by inflation.

The coal owners responded to the recession by declaring that the only way that the industry could be saved was to cut the wages of miners and extend the number of hours they worked underground from seven hours to eight. The miners and their leaders – Herbert Smith and Arthur Cook – were outraged. The bosses' demand was a flagrant breach of the deal on wages and conditions that had been hammered out in 1924. Smith and Cook refused to talk to the coal owners, negotiations were handed over to the Trades Union Congress (TUC) and events descended into the disastrous General Strike of 1926.

While the General Strike lasted only nine days (from 3 to 12 May), the mineworkers either stayed away from work or were locked out for most of 1926. The well-informed *Colliery Guardian* of 7 May 1926 described the strike as a 'bitter conflict of irreconcilable opinion which, it would seem, can only be ended by sheer exhaustion'. The coal industry's historian Barry Supple writes, 'The strike/lockout of 1926 – a wound that would never heal – led to another defeat for the miners, another reduction in wages, and an increase in the length of the working day.'

As the months dragged on in bitterness and occasional low-level violence, the miners' strike began to crumble. By the end of August 1926, some 70,000 men had returned to work. By the end of September, they'd been joined by another 140,000. A month later, yet another 230,000 had gone through the colliery gates. By the end of November, the remaining 400,000 mineworkers had gone back to work. The long miners' strike of 1926 was over.

The miners had returned to an industry that was facing even harder times than before the strike. 'The competition from Germany and Poland which moved to fill the gap left by the effective cessation of British exports was not subsequently driven back,' Barry Supple writes. 'Markets were lost, never to be completely regained.' As for the miners themselves, they had 'returned to work on the basis of district agreements, at increased hours, and with the likelihood of lower pay'.

Nowhere did that lower pay prevail more bitterly than in the Northeast. The miners of Northumberland and Durham, along with their fellow workers in South Wales, were the worst-paid pitmen in Britain. For many families, wages had been hammered down below the official level of subsistence. In the late 1920s and into the 1930s, report after report talks about families having to make do on white bread, margarine and jam, tea and potatoes, with the occasional rasher of bacon. In one of its reports, *The Times* of London came up with the memorable description (which still applies) that most people 'were neither hungry nor healthy'.

That fact was reflected in the sharp rise in the number of children born with rickets. Often it was the women who suffered most, as wives and mothers sacrificed their own interests for those of their families. Many observers noted cases of 'langour' and 'anaemia' among the women of the mining communities. They were malnourished, run down, fatigued and particularly vulnerable to illness.

When Edward, the Prince of Wales, made a three-day visit to the North-east coalfield in January 1929, he found himself steered by his officials into the house of an old colliery worker whose wife had just died. There's a cringe-making account of the incident by Arthur Lambert, then Lord Mayor of Newcastle, in his book *Northumbria's Spacious Year – 1929*:

> But the Prince never hesitated, right into the chamber of death he stopped and grasped the hand of the stricken daughter who received him. A few minutes talk of manly, sympathetic character did much to lighten that burden of sorrow, and the old husband who met us a little later was a proud man indeed to have had such an august caller.

But even the relentlessly optimistic Arthur Lambert had to concede that a fleeting glimpse of the Prince of Wales was not about to cure the industrial malaise of Tyneside. A government report dated 1934 on conditions in 'certain depressed areas' (one of which was Tyneside) paints a dismal picture.

> Prolonged unemployment is destroying the confidence and self respect of a large part of the population, their fitness to work is being steadily lost, and the anxiety of living always upon a bare minimum without any margin of resources or any hope of improvement is slowly sapping their nervous strength and their powers of resistance.

There's no denying that for many Tynesiders – and not just miners – the 1920s and 1930s were a very hard time. Unemployment was high, poverty was rife, benefits were meagre, the much-loathed means test was harsh and, for many, housing was wretched. It's a dismal picture, but it's not the whole picture. For many folk on Tyneside, things were getting better. Slowly, perhaps, but distinctly. In *The Banks of Tyne: A*

Historical Survey, Norman McCord claims that 'The inter-war depression and unemployment burned so deeply into the North East's consciousness that it is not always remembered that the years 1918 to 1939 saw the greatest improvement in social conditions which the region had ever experienced.'

Certainly the river was busy enough in the inter-war years, as Ken Groundwater points out in his book *Newcastle and the River Tyne*. The coal-loading staiths that lined the Tyne had never worked harder, the barges that removed the pulverised fly ash from Tyneside's power stations never stopped working, the giant flour mill at Gateshead needed constant attention, and, in the 1930s, there were regular sailings from the Tyne to Antwerp, Bordeaux, La Coruña and even Istanbul.

Tyneside's timber trade was enormous. According to Groundwater, the collieries of Northumberland and Durham consumed timber pit-props at the rate of 10,000 a day, which meant that huge stores of timber were scattered along the banks of the Tyne, particularly at Tyne Dock. Timbers were sometimes tied into 200-plank 'rafts', dropped into the river and floated down to Jarrow Slake, which he describes as the 'biggest wet-seasoning pond' outside of Scandinavia. 'At high tides and full the ponds resembled a gently undulating wooden platform,' Groundwater writes of Jarrow Slake. 'Local children used to run and skip across the timbers up to the distant edge of the river – unafraid of the dangers.'

THE BROON DOG

If there's one product that defines Tyneside, it has to be the dark-brown beer which the world knows as Newcastle Brown Ale. Launched onto the market in 1927 just as the Depression was getting serious, the famous logo has hardly changed since then. In fact, the five-pointed blue star against an orange-and-white background has been spreading across the planet as the brewers – Scottish & Newcastle – entice more and more people into drinking the brew. The five points of the star are said to represent the five founding breweries of Newcastle.

Known locally as 'Broon' or 'The Dog', or sometimes as 'The Broon Dog', the beer had huge success in the north of England long before it crossed the border into Scotland or made its way south to London and the Home Counties. It is so rooted in its home city that the European Union granted it Protected Geographical Indication status (along with, for example, Parma ham or Champagne wine).

But a problem has emerged. Scottish & Newcastle have decided to switch production from Newcastle across the Tyne to the Dunston Federation Brewery in Gateshead, County Durham. Which means that the beer's EU status will have to be revoked because it will no longer be brewed in Newcastle. None of which is likely to bother the Broon Dog's millions of fans across the world.

One way out of the recession of the 1920s and 1930s for a young man was to join the British Army, which is what many enterprising young Tynesiders did. Although the local regiments, the Durham Light Infantry and the Royal Northumberland Fusiliers, had been reduced to two battalions each after the war, they were well up to strength. The inter-war history of the RNF is an interesting commentary on the global reach (overreach might be a better word) of the British Empire. Both at home and abroad, wherever there was a trouble spot involving British interests, the Tynesiders seem to have been there.

The 1st Battalion of the RNF, for example, was dispatched to London to stand by in case the coal strike of 1921 turned nasty, then to Ireland, where events had turned nasty, followed by a spell as occupation troops in Germany, then back to Northern Ireland, followed by a posting to Glasgow for the General Strike of 1926 'as a precautionary measure against lawlessness', in the words of the regiment's historian, Brigadier C.N. Barclay. After a few years in Northern Ireland and York, it was east to Egypt and in 1936 to Palestine 'in order to assist in winding up the Arab rebellion'.

For their part, the 2nd Battalion RNF were assigned to that 1920s trouble spot Mesopotamia, now known as Iraq. In 1921, they sailed from Basra to Bombay, then in 1926 they were on the North-west Frontier – the border between Afghanistan and India – where 'an almost continuous state of war existed'. In 1931, they were in Shanghai in China, where 'on St George's Day the colours were trooped in front of a crowd of 1,500 spectators including representatives of American, Russian and Japanese units'. Then it was back to York, followed by a posting to Palestine (where Jews and Arabs were then, as now, at one another's throats), then back to Britain, to Bordon Camp in Hampshire.

THE HOPPINGS

In the summer of 1924, the popular fair known as the Hoppings returned to the Town Moor, Newcastle. It had been banished for more than a decade following a dispute between the Freemen (who ran the Town Moor) and the showmen who ran the stalls and sideshows. The row flared in 1912 after a combination of heavy rain and the showmen's vehicles churned the Town Moor into a quagmire. Between 1914 and 1922, the Hoppings was replaced by a small fair held in Jesmond Vale.

Instigated in 1882 by the temperance movement as a modest, alcohol-free, gambling-free event designed to wean Tynesiders away from the demons of drink and gaming, the Hoppings had long lost its original function and had grown into one of the biggest travelling funfairs in Europe.

Like much else, the Hoppings fell victim to the Second World War, then re-emerged in 1947 and has been going ever since. Staged for a week every June, it now consumes 40 acres of the Town Moor and is opened with a municipal flourish by the Lord Mayor of Newcastle. In the past few years, there has been a 'Hoppings School' for the children of the travelling families who run the rides, stalls and sideshows.

If any of the bridges spanning the Tyne can be called iconic, it has to be the Tyne Bridge of the 1920s. With its great steel arch, from which the road deck is suspended, and its abutments of pale Cornish granite, it has come to define the River Tyne in the way that Tower Bridge defines the River Thames. It's a worthy successor to the old medieval bridge that was washed away in 1771 and the neoclassical bridge by Robert Mylne that replaced it. Like Tower Bridge in London, it's the star of a million postcards. It says 'Newcastle and Tyneside' louder than any other structure on the river.

There's a 75-year-old legend that the Tyne Bridge was the model for the very similar, but very much bigger, Sydney Harbour Bridge. It's an idea that probably gained some currency because the bridge at Newcastle was done and dusted three years before the one at Sydney Harbour. But it's a mistake. The contracts for both bridges were let on the same year, 1924, the one for Sydney in March and the one for the Tyne in December. Site work began in Sydney in January 1925 but did not start on the Tyne until August that year. The Tyne Bridge was completed first because it was, quite simply, a much smaller and much less ambitious project.

But ambitious enough, in all conscience. Spanning the deep gorge of the Tyne between two urban centres was (and still is) a major undertaking. It's one that had been talked about in the latter half of the nineteenth century, when the towns of Newcastle and Gateshead began to resent the fact that the North Eastern Railway's High Level Bridge had a monopoly on tolls. The idea for a new high-level road bridge across the Tyne cropped up in 1864, in 1883, in 1892, in 1907 and again in the early 1920s.

By then, the need had become pressing. As Frank Manders and Richard Potts point out in their splendid and informative book *Crossing the Tyne*, Robert Stephenson's double-decked masterpiece of 1849 was being stretched to its limit: 'The High Level Bridge had just been strengthened to carry tram tracks and was increasingly congested; the Swing Bridge was frequently open for river traffic; and road traffic was increasing dramatically in volume.' Something had to be done before the cross-river road traffic ground to a halt.

At the end of September 1922, a group of engineers from both sides of the Tyne called the North and South Tyneside Joint Town Planning Committee stepped in with a suggestion for three river crossings, all of which were eventually built. They were for a new road bridge to the west of Newcastle at Scotswood, a tunnel under the Tyne between North and South Shields, and a high-level bridge downriver to the east of the existing High Level Bridge. A year and a half later, the plan for a new high-level bridge was carried unanimously by the Newcastle and Gateshead councils, and the necessary Act of Parliament (the Newcastle upon Tyne and Gateshead Corporations (Bridge) Act) was given His Majesty's assent on 7 August 1924.

By December 1924, the authorities had received five tenders to build Tyneside's latest and greatest bridge: Dorman Long for £571,225; Cleveland Bridge and Engineering Company for £604,421; Sir William Arrol & Co. for £606,454; Armstrong Whitworth for £743,229; and the Motherwell Bridge Company for £743,938. All the engineering companies bid on a design by the consultants Mott, Hay & Anderson. There was some discontent on Tyneside when the job was given to the lowest bidder (Dorman Long of Middlesbrough) over Tyneside's own engineering superstars, Armstrong Whitworth.

Work began on the bridge in the summer of 1925 at both sides of the river, with men digging deep into the river-bed, reaching bedrock at around 82 ft. On the Gateshead side, old buildings (many of them in a terrible state of repair) were cleared from Bottle Bank and Church Street. 'This part of Gateshead was the location of many cheap lodging houses,' Manders and Potts point out. 'No record seems to have been kept of where the displaced people were moved to.'

The great arch of the bridge, with its span of 531 ft, was finally 'closed' on 25 February 1928, to a show of municipal celebration. The road deck was 84 ft above the river, the clearance demanded by the river authorities. The granite-clad towers at either side of the river have no structural function other than to conceal the bridge's hinges and abutments. They were designed to act as warehouses, but no floors were installed and they were never used for that purpose. But the towers on the north bank did contain lifts to transport passengers and goods from the road deck down to the Quayside.

None of which came cheap. The total cost of the new Tyne Bridge was just over £1.2 million, 60 per cent of which was provided by the Government as a way of making some inroads into the post-war unemployment problem. In its day, it was the largest single-span bridge in Britain and a serious engineering achievement. The new Tyne Bridge was opened with great ceremony by King George V on 10 October 1928.

The construction of the new Tyne Bridge between Newcastle and Gateshead did not go down well further down the river. To the folk of Tynemouth, North Shields, Jarrow and South Shields, it seemed that Newcastle and Gateshead were getting more than their fair share of river crossings. The towns of the lower Tyne were home to about 200,000 people, but there was no bridge for miles. Anyone wanting to cross the river in the lower reaches had to make use of the various passenger or vehicle ferries, none of which ran 24 hours a day and all of which were susceptible to bad weather and routine breakdowns.

With industry and road traffic growing fast, the problem was becoming serious. The authorities of Tynemouth and South Shields had been discussing the idea of a bridge across the lower Tyne off and on since the end of the nineteenth century, discussions that usually set the Tyne Improvement Commission worrying about obstructions to shipping. A tentative plan for a new bridge was put forward in 1901, approved by a House of Lords committee, but then dumped by a House of Commons committee, probably due to strenuous anti-bridge lobbying by the TIC.

After it became clear that His Majesty's government was funding most of the new Tyne Bridge at Newcastle, the idea of a bridge over the lower Tyne emerged once again. In 1926, a certain Councillor E.F. Jackson proposed a bridge modelled on the Forth Rail Bridge and with a clearance of 250 ft above the sea, which was calculated to keep the TIC happy. The cost was estimated at around £1 million.

Three years later, Councillor Jackson's scheme was trumped by a similar, but much more ambitious, scheme designed by the borough engineer of South Shields, J. Paton Watson. In Watson's scheme, the vehicle traffic would have got onto the bridge via ramps at either side of the river, which would spiral upwards from the street below. The project was costed at around £2 million but would almost certainly have cost much more had it ever been built.

Other schemes followed. A South Shields haulage contractor came up with yet another Forth-Bridge-style cantilever structure, between West Percy Street in North Shields and Mile End Road in South Shields. Then a radical double-swinging cantilever was proposed (again modelled on the Forth Bridge) which was high enough to let most maritime traffic slip under the cantilever but would swing open to let the biggest ships through. Another project, as part of the 'North East Arterial Highway', looks like an exact replica of the new Tyne Bridge between Newcastle and Gateshead.

But all these ambitious schemes came to nothing. The local authorities had appointed Mott, Hay & Anderson to advise, and the firm's advice was that any bridge was bound to be a lot more expensive than a tunnel. And the government let it be known that it would stump up for no more than 60 per cent of the cost, leaving large sums to be found by the cash-strapped councils of Tynemouth and South Shields. It was a bridge too far. In 1931, all the projects were shelved – where they've remained ever since.

DOWN UNDER

Bridges, of course, are only one way of getting across a stretch of water. Tunnelling is another, and in the first three decades of the twentieth century, there were a number of plans to tunnel under the Tyne, usually between North and South Shields.

One of the earliest schemes, floated in 1902, was for a tunnel to carry an electric railway, which would disappear underground at Bedford Street in North Shields and resurface at Mile End Road in South Shields. The trains were to run every 6 minutes for 24 hours a day, and passengers would reach them by lifts at either end. Although the necessary legislation was passed and given royal assent in 1902, the project ran into the sand just before the First World War.

The idea of a Tyne tunnel was revived in 1922 by one Chalmers Kearney, an Australian engineer with strong Geordie connections. Kearney designed an interesting monorail system, running in a tunnel 15 ft in diameter. He calculated that his trains could run every 5 minutes and could carry around 5 million passengers a year. The council at South Shields were keen on Kearney's project, but Tynemouth was lukewarm and the TIC were hostile. By 1929, the whole idea had run out of steam and Chalmers Kearney abandoned Tyneside for his native Australia.

Mr Kearney was nothing if not persistent, however. Back he came in 1934 with an even more ambitious plan to carve out a tunnel which would carry both trains and road traffic. By then, however, the respected engineers Mott, Hay & Anderson had come up with plans for a major road tunnel linking North and South Shields, which knocked Kearney's plan on the head. The Mott, Hay & Anderson plan was for a combined vehicle/pedestrian tunnel running between New Quay in North Shields and Waterloo Vale in South Shields. The whole project was costed at £1.3 million, although the TIC would have to be compensated for the loss of revenue from their ferry services.

It was a realistic enough scheme and would have solved many of lower Tyneside's traffic problems. But when a deputation from Tyneside met the Transport minister, Leslie Hore-Belisha, in February 1936 to argue for the tunnel, they were told that their case was not nearly strong enough and that they should concentrate on improving the existing ferry services.

The same year – 1928 – that the new Tyne bridge opened, Tyneside's biggest employer, Armstrong Whitworth, was forced to join forces with Vickers of Sheffield and become Vickers Armstrong. Naturally, the firm put a positive gloss on the merger, but most historians claim it was the result of a series of bad post-war moves by the Tyneside giant: a disastrous diversification into the building of railway locomotives and an even more disastrous development on the other side of the Atlantic in Newfoundland.

But elsewhere in the economy, things were better. Tyneside's electrical supply industry was in good health. Despite the recession in the coalfield and the shipyards, NESCo was acquiring more and more customers and was steadily adding electricity substations and transformers to its network. Reyrolles of Hebburn, who specialised in heavy electrical equipment and switching gear, had a healthy order book all the way through the 1920s and 1930s.

And in 1928, Newcastle saw the opening of what has been described as 'one of the best inter-war buildings in Northumberland'. That was NESCo's new headquarters building, which stands on the corner of Market Street and Pilgrim Street. A joint design effort by the firms of Burnet, Tait & Lorne (of London) and L.J. Couves & Partners (of Newcastle), the building is a remarkable piece of 1920s urban architecture, which was, in many ways, years ahead of its time.

According to the Northumberland volume of *The Buildings of England*:

> It is a magnificent Portland-stone-clad building of classical proportions and with the barest of classical decorative motifs. The long front to Market Street is broken by an entrance flanked by massive columns of dark limestone, the rounded corner to Northumberland Street by a low dome.

But there was more to Carliol House than the face it presented to the street. Its structure was reinforced steel clad with Portland stone (instead of Newcastle's usual sandstone). The building's heating and ventilation systems were state of the art, and it was probably the first in Britain to incorporate a vacuum-cleaning system whereby the cleaners plugged directly into ducts built into the wall, through which dust and dirt were removed. The lifts at Carliol House travelled at a nifty 430 ft a minute and were reputed to be the fastest in Britain.

And while the interior design may not have matched the excellence of the technology, it was handsome enough. The designers were more than generous with marble, mahogany and brass finishes, even if the admixture of art deco, stripped-down classicism and Egyptian struck an odd note. Carliol House also incorporated a 70-seat lecture theatre and cinema in which the Tyneside public were regaled with information on the wonders of electricity (as generated by NESCo).

Another building in a very similar vein is the department store in Newgate Street built for the Newcastle upon Tyne Co-operative Society in 1931–2. Designed by the London Co-operative Society's chief architect, one L.G. Ekins (who used to work for the Newcastle Co-op), the building has been described as a 'stylish, rather "Art Deco"' exercise, typical of the period.

Both Carliol House and the Co-op building suggest that the recession was not all-consuming. There were a surprising number of decent new buildings put up around Tyneside in the 1920s and 1930s. Some of the best were designed by that gifted local architect Robert Burns Dick, who acquired a reputation for public buildings like police stations, magistrates' courts and fire stations. Dick also rebuilt Kirkley Hall, north of Ponteland, after it had been almost burned down in 1928. Robert Dick's grandest design – dated 1934, for a new civic centre to be built on the south-east corner of the Town Moor – was never realised.

There were other bright spots in Tyneside's economic gloom. On 5 May 1929, the Prince of Wales was back in Newcastle to open the North East Coast Exhibition, a grand trade-cum-industrial jamboree, which was staged on the south-east corner of the Town Moor, the same site on which the Royal Jubilee Exhibition had been staged in 1887. As was the convention in that post-war decade, the Prince did the honours dressed in full military khakis (of the Welsh Guards) complete with Sam Browne belt, riding breeches, high boots, ceremonial sword and a chestful of medal ribbons.

In his opening speech, from a platform under a gaily striped awning, the Prince of Wales summed up what the event was all about:

> The aim of the exhibition is to revitalise existing industries, to discover what should be adapted and if necessary improved . . . it's hoped that this great enterprise may serve in no small measure, to discover the weak spots: and by encouraging the establishment of new works and new methods, providing further channels of labour in an area that has more than its share of hard times.

The man behind the exhibition was the energetic Sir Arthur Lambert, then the (Conservative) Lord Mayor of Newcastle. Lambert's intention, or at least hope, was that the exhibition would lift the spirits of Tynesiders, provide a showcase for Tyneside's wares and put some fresh heart into the economy. In *Northumbria's Spacious Year – 1929*, he waxes lyrical about the exhibition. In his preface, he writes:

> The year of Our Lord 1929 is likely to stand out as a landmark in the history of the ancient city of Newcastle, which lies upon the north bank of Old Father Tyne, some nine miles from its mouth by road, though a little further by river.

Plainly, Sir Arthur was no writer. But he was a Novocastrian of substance, a director of companies and the holder of a Military Cross from his stint with the Royal Northumberland Fusiliers in the First World War. By and large, the exhibition he championed was a success. Laid out and designed by the Sunderland architect Stanley Milburn, the show comprised a Palace of Engineering, a Palace of Industry, a Palace of the Arts, a Festival Hall (with 1,400 seats) and a stadium built to take 20,000 people.

With the exception of the Palace of the Arts, the pavilions were steel-framed structures standing on brick-and-concrete foundations. They were clad in sheets of compressed asbestos – something unthinkable in the twenty-first century. The whole site was put together by local contractor Henry Kelly Ltd for £114,000, and the progress of the work was supervised by his daughter, who made sure it ran remarkably smoothly.

Most of the notable Tyneside firms played their part, among them Vickers Armstrong, Parsons, NESCo, the Co-op and the Newcastle & Gateshead Gas Company, along with smaller fry like Brady & Martin, Rington's Tea, Angus Watson & Co. and George Davidson & Co. (who boasted the Lord Mayor as one of their directors). Special products were cooked up for the exhibition, including an 'exhibition ale' and an 'exhibition Xmas pudding' which was demonstrated to the press by the Lady Mayoress, Ethel Lambert.

Over the next eight months, the people of Tyneside were entertained by orchestral concerts, brass-band competitions, military marching bands, cycle races, gymnastic displays, a Highland games, sheepdog trials, wrestling competitions, events staged by Boy Scouts, Girl Guides and the Boys' Brigade, not to mention ten separate fireworks displays. There was a boating lake and an amusement park with an 80-ft-high and mile-long 'Himalayan Railway'.

Before it closed at the end of October, more than four million people trooped in and out of the pavilions. Among them were an assortment of gentry and minor royals, with a few star turns such as the Sultan of Zanzibar and King Alfonso of Spain. Ever the royalist, Sir Arthur Lambert described the Spanish king as 'Brainy, courteous, shrewd, a good sportsman, a debonair cavalier; how does it arrive that his country is not united behind him as we would expect?'

The exhibition came to a well-attended close on 26 October 1929, with Newcastle's irrepressible Lord Mayor conducting the local orchestra himself through a rendition of Handel's 'Hallelujah Chorus', followed by 'Abide With Me' and 'Auld Lang Syne'. For his closing speech, he chose a golfing metaphor that teetered towards the absurd. 'Let us press forward with renewed hope and courage,' he told the large crowd. 'Our industries were badly bunkered, but the Exhibition niblick has placed them safely on the green and each one must help to hole the putt.'

TYNESIDE ON THE PITCH: HUGHIE GALLAGHER

In their fascinating account of sport on Tyneside, the historians Richard Holt and Ray Physick argue that Newcastle United had 'the best all-round attacking player in Britain and arguably in the world' in the little Scotsman Hughie Gallagher. Gallagher's scoring record was formidable. In his 174 appearances for Newcastle United, he scored no fewer than 143 goals. He was also a member of the so-called 'Wembley Wizards', the Scottish team that trounced England 5–1 on their home turf in 1928.

Holt and Physick describe Gallagher as 'standing only five feet five . . . sturdy, two footed, good in the air and as hard as nails'. He was also, they point out, 'a hard and difficult man, a drinker and a brawler'. Before he joined Newcastle FC, Gallagher played for the Scottish clubs Queen of the South and Airdrie. In his 19 games for Scotland, he scored 24 times – a ratio that has never been bettered.

After being sold by Newcastle (much against his will) in 1930, Gallagher went on to play for Chelsea, Derby County, Notts County, Grimsby and finally Gateshead. It was a long, slow decline. In the end, Gallagher was an unhappy man. He ended his own life in 1957 by throwing himself under a train, shortly before he was due to appear in court charged with child neglect.

The North East Coast Exhibition was a good idea and a modest success. It does seem to have given the local economy a bit of a boost; but it was never going to be enough to save Tyneside from hard times. In 1933, the town of Jarrow was sent reeling when its biggest employer, the shipyard founded by the legendary Charles Mark Palmer, closed its doors for the last time. The economic blizzards of the late 1920s and early 1930s proved too strong for the debt-laden yard. The yard's last ship was HMS *Duchess*, a destroyer built for the Royal Navy which was launched in 1932. When Palmer's workforce was laid off, the town's unemployed numbered 7,000, or more than 70 per cent of the entire workforce.

Palmer's yard at Jarrow was sold to National Shipbuilders' Security Ltd, an organisation which had been set up to 'rationalise' the industry by buying up and closing down failing shipyards. On the other hand, the Palmer yard at Hebburn – which had one of the largest dry docks in Britain – was snapped up by Vickers Armstrong as a ship-repair facility. Which was very little consolation to the people of Jarrow.

TYNESIDE'S SHIPBUILDING CASUALTY LIST

Palmer's of Jarrow was not the only Tyneside shipyard to disappear during the 1920s and 1930s. Quite a number of shipbuilding and ship-repair businesses gave up the ghost or were taken over during those two decades. Some of the firms that closed had histories that reached a long way back into the nineteenth century. The year 1928 seems to have been a particularly bad one for Tyneside.

1921	the Newcastle Shipbuilding Co., Hebburn
1924	Hepple, Low Walker
1926	J.P. Rennoldson & Sons, Lawe, South Shields
1928	J&D Morris, Pelaw Main, Hebburn
1928	the Tyne Iron Shipbuilding Co., Willington Quay
1928	Wood Skinner & Co., Bill Quay
1930	Charles Rennoldson, Lawe, South Shields
1931	Renwick & Dalgliesh, Hebburn
1933	J.T. Eltringham, South Shields and Willington Quay

The writer J.B. Priestley – who was never an admirer of Tyneside – made his way back to Jarrow while researching his book *English Journey*, published in 1934. He was appalled by what he found. He wrote: 'A stranger from a distant civilisation, observing the condition of the place and its people, would have arrived at once at the conclusion that Jarrow had deeply offended some celestial empire of the island and was now being punished.'

A harsh sentiment, but one that was shared by many Jarrovians. The devastation wrought on Jarrow by the hard times of the 1930s was appalling. The misery ran wide and deep. It took Jarrow some time to recover from the blow. One man who was not prepared to suffer in silence was Councillor Paddy Scullion, who got to his feet in the council chamber and in a telling phrase declared that 'only when a wheelbarrow started squeaking did anyone do anything about oiling it'.

The 'squeaking' began on Sunday, 4 October 1936, when 200 of Jarrow's unemployed set out to march the 280 miles to London. Their aim was to take their protest to the heart of the British government. They took with them an oak casket containing an 11,000-signature petition from the townsfolk of Jarrow. The sum of £800 had been raised to support the men on their trek. Some of it was spent on leather and nails to mend boots worn out by the walking. Another £1 per head was reserved for the train fare back from London. The Jarrow Crusade was the banner under which they marched, and as they made their way down the country, they became a cause célèbre.

There was huge sympathy for the Tyneside marchers. All the way down England, they were welcomed, fed and accommodated, often by local councils run by Conservatives. The good-natured dignity of the Jarrow men impressed many people who were their political enemies. There's a sad irony that, thanks to good feeding en route and days of outdoor exercise, most of the Jarrow marchers arrived in London fitter and healthier than they'd ever been.

His Majesty's Government, however, was not at home when the Jarrow crusaders called on Downing Street. On 11 November 1936, the Tory prime minister Stanley Baldwin declared that it would have been 'cowardice' on his part to receive the Jarrow marchers, listen to their plea or accept their petition. 'This is the way in which civil strife begins,' he declared, 'and civil strife may not end until it is civil war.'

THE PRICE OF COAL

Mining disasters in the North-east coalfield between 1918 and 1945:

1942 at Murton	13 die

Of course, Jarrow did not suffer alone. The whole of Tyneside was badly affected as orders for new ships or ship repairs failed to appear. According to Fraser and Emsley in their book *Tyneside* (published in 1973):

> In January 1933 it was estimated that 82.5 per cent of the northern shipbuilding and ship repair employees were out of work, against a national average of 63.5 per cent . . . Men were glad to be hired as ship breakers or factory dismantlers.

The slump hit the shipping lines too. As world trade declined, so did the demand for merchant ships and the men who crewed them. Master mariners were just as likely to be laid off as able seamen, engineers and deck hands. That excellent oral history *South Shields Voices* (by John and Joyce Carlson) contains a vivid passage by one Jean Shanahan, the daughter of a Tyneside skipper:

> During the slump the master mariners were working in the Marine Park Gardens because they hadn't any other work. My mother used to say that sea captains were now ten a penny in Woolworth but you could go to the Marine Park and pick one up for nothing.

There was one 1930s development that was small beer at the time but which, many years later, became a linchpin of the economy of the north-east of England. It was Tyneside's first serious airport, which sprang up in July 1935 at Woolsington, about seven miles north-west of Newcastle city centre. It was a modest affair consisting of a grass landing strip, a clubhouse, a small hangar, an ambulance station and a fuel store and pump.

But that's all that was needed for North Eastern Airways to begin scheduled flights to Croydon, south of London, and to Perth in Scotland. The company's aircraft were as modest as the airport – a twin-engined de Havilland DH89 Dragon Rapide biplane (a 1930s classic) and a twin-engined Airspeed AS6 Envoy monoplane. When the Second World War erupted, the Woolsington airfield was taken over by the military. It was returned to civilian use in the late 1940s.

The decline of traditional industries like shipbuilding, shipping, coal mining and heavy engineering on areas like Tyneside had wrong-footed the British government. All through the 1930s, successive administrations thrashed about for remedies. One was the Special Areas (Development and Improvement) Act of 1934, which set aside millions to be injected into sickly local economies in the hope of bringing them back to health. The plan – or at least hope – was that the kinds of light industries which were flourishing in the South would take root in the North.

On Tyneside, the strategy gave birth to the North Eastern Trading Estates Ltd (NETE), which in turn spawned the Team Valley Trading Estate (TVTE) to the south and west of Gateshead. As projects go, the TVTE was nothing if not ambitious. The plan was to employ something like 15,000 people within 15 years, all working in clean, efficient, modern factory units, producing the kinds of goods that the modern world wanted. Work began on the TVTE in 1936, and it was declared open by King George VI three years later.

It's still there, of course, a sprawl of low, workaday industrial buildings of varying quality and vintage. None of them is great architecture, perhaps, but there's a sympathetic and interesting testament to the TVTE by Simon Taylor and David Lovie in *Gateshead: Architecture in a Changing English Urban Landscape*:

> It is easy to forget the significance of the TVTE. Its architecture is modest, its layout more suburban than heroic, but the contrast with what had gone before and the boldness of the experiment – it was intended to bring social stability and a new economic base to the area – should not be overlooked.

The writers go on:

> Nearly two miles long, it was the size of a small town, with what was then one of the widest roads in the country, Kingsway (which included the canalised River Team running in the

middle of the southern half), as its spine. The estate was attractively landscaped; football pitches were laid out on vacant parts; and it was hoped that its park-like appearance would engender leisure use. At the centre NETE built for itself an extensive, crescent-shaped headquarters, with detached blocks containing a bank and a post office.

More to the point were the factories. They came in three sizes, the biggest being just over 14,000 sq. ft, with a standard size of 8,000 sq. ft and a so-called 'nursery' unit of around 1,500 sq. ft. These small units were available for a token weekly rent of £1 and were aimed at 'start-up' ventures, which, if they flourished, would move into bigger units, employing more people as they grew. The TVTE got off to a good start. Industrialists liked the spanking new factories, the landscaped surroundings and, above all, the low (i.e. subsidised) rents. By the end of 1939, more than 100 firms had moved into the TVTE, employing something like 5,000 people.

And, according to Taylor and Lovie, 'Many of the first factories built at TVTE were tenanted, with the encouragement of the Government, by central and east European refugees escaping from oppression on the Continent.' One such enterprise was Loblite, which made small-scale equipment and accessories for the electricity supply industry. It was set up on the TVTE in 1939 by the German-Jewish brothers Fritz and Robert Loebl, refugees from Hitler's regime.

By then, of course, another war with Germany was a distinct possibility. Neville Chamberlain may have returned from Munich in 1938 waving his piece of paper and declaring 'peace in our time', but the country was distinctly uneasy and began to steel itself for war. Events in Gateshead were typical of preparations that were going on the length and breadth of Britain. The 9th Durham Light Infantry (the Gateshead battalion) was at full strength, and in July 1938 an Air Raid Precaution (ARP) headquarters was set up in South Dene Towers in Saltwell Park.

Air-raid shelters began to spring up all over the town, and a large underground shelter was constructed beneath Bensham Terrace.

People feared for the safety of their offspring, so 80 per cent of Gateshead's children were registered for evacuation if and when war came. More than 3,000 people volunteered to be ARP wardens, another 350 were either full-time or part-time firemen and 1,500 men signed up for the Local Defence Volunteers (later the Home Guard). Mayfield, in Low Fell, was taken over to house Czech refugees.

When war eventually came, the town of Gateshead, like the rest of Tyneside, got off relatively lightly. There was nothing like the devastation that German bombers wreaked on London, Coventry, South Wales or even Clydeside. It's estimated that only five Gateshead folk were killed in the air raids, probably because most bombs fell on Saltwell Park. In *A History of Gateshead*, F.W.D. Manders speculates that 'More damage may have been caused by the reverberations of the anti-aircraft guns at Lobley Hill than by enemy action.'

There was more bombing on South Shields and Tynemouth, probably due to the Germans trying to block the mouth of the river to stop shipping. For two and a half years, from April 1941 to October 1943, the communities at the mouth of the Tyne had to put up with the occasional air raid. Bombs fell on South Shields railway station, the Queen's Theatre, the Market, the houses on Lisle Road, Harton House Road, the Brinkburn playing fields, King George Road, Centenary Avenue, Stevenson Street and Westoe.

'My Uncle Charlie's cousin was killed by a bomb up King George Road,' writes Joyce Carlton in *South Shields Voices*. 'The family had moved from London to escape the blitz.' John Tinmouth has a gruesome anecdote: 'One bomb even came down on Harton Cemetery and exploded among the graves. There was bits of bodies lying everywhere amongst the houses, and they got the lads from the pits to pick up the bits.'

And, of course, the Italian community on Tyneside fell under a cloud when Mussolini joined Hitler in the war against Britain. The Minchella family owned a café and ice-cream parlour in South Shields, and, despite having served in the British Army during the First World War, the paterfamilias, Joe Minchella, was rounded up. Says his grandson Michael Minchella:

They took all of the Italians in South Shields down to the North Pier. They were there for one night then Joe was sent to Bishop Auckland. Strangely he was allowed back to Shields at the weekend. They didn't seem to be so hard on the Italians in South Shields as they were in other places.

THE TRAITOR OF TYNESIDE

Tyneside has produced many men and women of which to be proud. But there are exceptions, and one of them is George Johnson Armstrong, the Newcastle man who was one of the few Britons to be hanged for treason during the Second World War. Armstrong was a merchant seaman – an engineer – who found himself in New York in the autumn of 1940 and being chatted up in a Manhattan bar by a glamorous woman, who happened to be a German agent. She was anxious to find out details of the convoys then running much-needed supplies across the Atlantic to Britain.

Armstrong was later picked up by US Immigration officers in Boston and sent to a detention camp, where he mixed with German detainees. That Armstrong ever supplied the Germans with any damaging information seems unlikely. He was in no position to know very much. But he made the mistake of writing to the German consul in Boston, one Hubert Scholz, offering information which he was sure would be 'greatly appreciated' by the German authorities. The letter was intercepted by the FBI and passed to British agents, and Armstrong was shipped back to Britain to stand trial.

He was charged under the Treachery Act of 1940 of having 'intent to help the enemy' and was tried at the Old Bailey, found guilty and sentenced to death. His appeal against his sentence was dismissed on 23 June 1941 and he was hanged at Wandsworth Prison on 10 July 1941.

Presiding over Tyneside's war was Sir Arthur Lambert, one-time Lord Mayor of Newcastle. A well-connected local businessman and a veteran of the trenches in the First World War, Lambert was appointed regional commissioner for Number 1 Region, Northern Area. Under him were two deputy regional commissioners, J.J. Lawson, the local MP, and Colonel C.J. Pickering. Also on Tyneside's 'high command' was Admiral Maxwell, the flag-officer for Tyneside.

Sir Arthur seems to have pitched into the job with his usual energy. His role as regional commissioner was to coordinate the emergency services, including the new ones that had sprung up since the outbreak of war. Some were military, some civilian: the police, the Home Guard, the fire services, the ARP wardens, the ambulance service, the hospitals, the various women's voluntary services. Tyneside was divided into no fewer than 18 districts, each responsible for putting together a defence plan that would stop – or at least delay – any German invaders who came onto their patch.

It's not widely known (or has been largely forgotten) that the British government put in place plans to deny German invaders British factories and workshops – by sabotaging them. It was Arthur Lambert's responsibility to work out how best to do this on Tyneside. Factory owners and industrialists were called in to the regional commissioner's headquarters to discuss how best to disable machinery, by removing vital pieces of equipment or simply destroying it. These must have been strange and disturbing conversations for men who'd spent their lives struggling to build up their factories and companies.

Lambert was also tasked with preparing plans to resist the invaders. It was a job he took seriously. If and when the day came when German landing craft sailed into the Tyne or German paratroops floated down in the surrounding countryside, they would have found roadblocks on every road, road signs dismantled, tractors and ploughs littering the fields (to deter gliders), bridges blown, electricity lines cut, railway lines severed, locomotives tucked away in remote and unusable sidings and the cross-Tyne ferry boats scuppered. There were plans to block the Albert Edward Dock, immobilise the floating crane and lay torpedo-launching tubes on either side of the Tyne to wreck incoming ships. The TIC's tugboats had been briefed to ram any flying boats or seaplanes that tried to set down in the Tyne.

In the event, of course, the invasion never came. Sir Arthur's elaborate defence planning was never converted into action. In fact, the City of Newcastle had a relatively quiet war, given its strategic importance. The city did suffer some bombing, and one raid in September 1941 killed more than 50 people and made another 1,000 homeless. But it was nothing compared to, say, the havoc the Luftwaffe wreaked on Hull 100 or so miles down the coast. Before the war ended, the Yorkshire port had suffered 70 air raids which killed 1,200 men, women and children, and damaged the majority of the city's housing stock.

A few historians have puzzled over why the Luftwaffe paid so little attention to Tyneside. One of their number is David Bean, who wrote:

> An interesting suggestion is that Hitler left the Tyne more or less alone because he wanted to use it as an extension of his own industrial empire after invasion. William Joyce, 'Lord Haw Haw', the fascist broadcaster, gave a clue once when he announced that Knott's Flats, the rather fine but monolithic-looking block of pre-war flats overlooking the estuary at Tynemouth, would make a rather splendid administrative headquarters for the Nazi occupation.

Elsewhere, of course, Tynesiders were in the thick of the war: the Royal Navy, the merchant marine, the Royal Air Force, the Royal Marines, the British Army. The professional and territorial battalions of Tyneside's famous regiments – the Durham Light Infantry and the Royal Northumberland Fusiliers – seem to have been involved in every major campaign of the Second World War, from the Home Front to the war against Japan in the Far East.

Five of the six battalions of the RNF who were with the British Expeditionary Force in France were evacuated from Dunkirk and returned to Britain to regroup and retrain before returning to the fray.

But one battalion – the 7th RNF – had been attached to the 51st Highland Division which fought a heroic rearguard action before 'going into the bag' at St-Valery in France.

Some elements of the 1st RNF had been in Egypt and in June 1940 were part of the stunningly successful British campaign in the desert against Mussolini's forces. Things got more serious for the British when Rommel's Afrika Korps made an appearance, and it was for his conduct in the battles against the German tanks and infantry around Tobruk that Captain James Jackman of the 1st RNF won the regiment's first Victoria Cross of the war. Jackman's exploits are described in *The History of the Royal Northumberland Fusiliers in the Second World War* by Brigadier C.N. Barclay: 'Captain Jackman drove round the positions in his vehicle coordinating the defence and encouraging his men,' Barclay writes. 'For a considerable time he bore a charmed life.' But on 25 November 1941, the charm wore off, and Jackman was killed by a German mortar round. In the furious engagement, the machine-gunners of Z Company of the 1st RNF won twelve medals, including a VC and two Military Crosses. 'The award of so many decorations to the personnel of one sub unit for operations lasting only a few days must be almost unique,' is the opinion of Brigadier Barclay.

Another Fusilier won a Victoria Cross a few years later. He was Major Robert Henry Cain, who was attached to the 2nd South Staffordshire Regiment. Cain won his VC at Arnhem in September 1944 when he single-handedly destroyed a German Tiger tank and drove off three others with a hand-held anti-tank weapon.

Later in the war, the 1st RNF and the 2nd RNF joined the Allied drive up Italy to force the first German surrender on the Western Front. The 2nd RNF were then transported (in cattle wagons) all the way back down Italy to Taranto and shipped out to Greece, where the German retreat had left a power vacuum which had sparked a left–right civil war. The Tynesiders found themselves holding the ring while Greek communists and royalists fought with one another.

The 9th RNF, however, had a dreadful war. After Dunkirk and the long spell of retraining late in 1941, they were shipped across the Atlantic to Newfoundland, then down to Cape Town, across the Indian Ocean to Bombay and from there to Singapore. It was a 14-week trip during which, according to Brigadier Barclay, the battalion got 'somewhat soft'. They sailed into Singapore just as the Japanese were sweeping down the peninsula and were part of the British force that surrendered on 15 February 1942. 'For the 9th Battalion of the Royal Northumberland Fusiliers the capitulation was indeed a tragic climax to their twenty months hard training after Dunkirk,' wrote Brigadier Barclay in the regimental history.

HMS *PUSHMEPULLU*

This strange vessel is testament to a very different kind of Geordie shipping enterprise. The *PushmePullu* was the nickname given to an 18-ft-long rowing boat which a small party of the 9th RNF under Major B.J. Leech commandeered to escape from the Japanese at Singapore. Leech and his Fusiliers were among the very few Britons to get out from under the clutches of the Emperor of Japan's soldiers on a day that Churchill called the 'greatest defeat' that the British Empire ever suffered.

Having commandeered the leaky boat, somehow the Fusiliers managed to rig a mast and a sail, and with part of a broken oar acting as a rudder, they sailed and rowed their unlikely craft 80 miles west across the Straits of Malacca, under constant threat from Japanese aircraft. They landed at Sumatra, then part of the Dutch East Indies and which had also just been invaded by the Japanese.

At first, Major Leech and his men steeled themselves for another (hopeless) fight against the Japanese, but they were taken off Sumatra by a British destroyer in the nick of time, just hours before the Japanese arrived. The escape of the men of the 9th RNF and their vessel *PushmePullu* is one of the Second World War's many forgotten stories.

The 800 or so men of the 9th RNF spent the next three years working as slave labourers on the notorious Burma Railway. Although 151 of them died as prisoners of war, the Tynesiders held together under terrible conditions in a way that some other units did not. That was recognised by the Inspector General of the Army in Burma, who wrote at the end of the war that 'Nothing, simply nothing, broke their spirit, and they even won the admiration of the Jap.'

Brigadier Barclay's account of the RNF in the Second World War makes stirring reading, there's no doubt about that. It's all the more effective for being written in a low-key, fact-driven way. Tyneside has good reason to be proud of its great regiments. But at the back of the book, there is a long roll-call of the men from all RNF battalions who were killed between 1939 and 1945. And that makes sombre and depressing reading.

As the war progressed, the coalfields of Northumberland and Durham saw a return of the problem that had plagued them in the First World War – lack of transport. German submarines, surface raiders and aircraft were making life difficult and dangerous for coastal shipping. Sea transport was increasingly hard to come by. As a result, more and more southbound coal was being loaded onto railway wagons, which overburdened the railway system and created long delays. Combined with a severe winter in 1940, this led to a shortage of coal and a government decision to give priority to vital industries.

The coal-supply problem was exacerbated by thousands of young colliery workers joining the armed forces or being conscripted. In June 1940, there were 767,500 men working in the coal industry; a year later, the number had dropped to 690,000. As a result, coal output slumped from 231,000 tons per week in 1939 to 203,500 tons in 1942. This vital industry seemed to be slowly collapsing in on itself.

The state of the coal industry certainly bothered the Government. In March 1942, Hugh Dalton, the president of the Board of Trade and the man responsible for keeping the country's industry going, stood up in the House of Commons and crystallised the problem: 'Unless we get the coal, we cannot get the arms. Unless we get the arms, we cannot win the war.'

There were Tyneside delegates among the miners and coal owners who were called to a mass meeting in Westminster Hall at the end of October 1942. Ministers were nervous about the situation, so the press was excluded from the meeting to prevent scaremongering reports. The main speaker was Winston Churchill himself. The Prime Minister told the miners and the coal owners:

> We must carry our work to its final conclusion. We shall not fail. And then some day, when children ask, 'What did you do to win this inheritance for us?' one will say, 'I was a fighter pilot,' another will say, 'I was in the submarine service,' another, 'I marched with the eighth army,' a fourth will say, 'None of you could have lived without the convoys and the Merchant Seamen.' And you, in your turn, will say with equal pride and with equal right, 'We cut the coal!'

Stirring stuff, certainly, and classic Churchillian rhetoric. But the evidence is that it didn't do much good. Morale in the coal industry continued to slither downhill. In September 1943, almost a year after Churchill's pep talk, the Durham Coal Owners' Association reported that 'war weariness' among colliery workers was to blame for the rising level of absenteeism, sickness and 'a complete breakdown of discipline'.

In the archives of the Foreign Office, there's an interesting report by a team of American mining experts who looked at the British coal-mining industry in 1944. They were shocked by what they found:

> Industry wide morale is low. We believe that there does not exist in the minds of the coal owners, management, labour leaders and the individual miners an adequate willingness to subordinate all considerations to the Military necessity of increasing production.

One way or another, the coal industry was a mess. No one seemed to have any idea how it could be repaired. A fundamental change of some kind was clearly necessary. On 1 January 1945, the Miners' Federation of Great Britain changed its name to the National Union of Mineworkers – the NUM.

11

MANAGING DECLINE

1945–2000

The end of the Second World War saw the beginning of the long change in the industrial landscape of Tyneside. It was slow, it was painful and it was sometimes heartbreaking; but it was inevitable. Quite simply, the rest of the world was not prepared to allow Britain's industrial centres – Birmingham and the Midlands, West Central Scotland, South Wales, Teeside, Tyneside – to continue to operate as the planet's workshops. The days when Britain could rely on supplying much of the world's coal and most of the world's ships were gone, whether the people of Britain realised it or not.

It was a hard truth to confront. The challenges it posed were not apparent. On the face of it, Britain's shipyards were well placed. The shipyards of Germany and Japan lay in ruins, the Americans were not much interested in selling abroad, the Soviet Union and its satellites formed an inward-looking world of their own and the idea that countries like Korea or China might rival Britain as shipbuilders was risible. When it came to building ships post-war, it seemed that Britannia still ruled the waves. As late as 1948, the UK took more than 50 per cent of the world's shipping orders.

But these post-war days were a false dawn for Tyneside and the rest of Britain's shipbuilding centres. Bad times were on the way. The situation is neatly described by Lewis Johnman and Hugh Murphy in their book *British Shipbuilding and the State since 1918*:

> The 1950s would, however, become something of a 'devil's decade' in terms of the shipbuilding industry. It would bask in the easy conditions of the late 1940s and early 1950s, but when the cosy world of cost-plus building and a sellers' market gave way to serious competition with fixed prices and a buyers' market, British shipbuilding began to fall apart.

In fact, the world was changing in ways that were hard for Britain's shipbuilders to keep up with. 'New trade routes, new trades, new construction methods, the decline of liner traffic and the rise of the airliner,' write Johnman and Murphy, 'all hammered traditional British approaches to the market.'

And that hunger for new technologies which had once marked the Tyne's shipbuilders had fled. In 1947, N.M. Hunter, the chairman of Swan Hunter & Wigham Richardson, declared there was nothing to be learned from the American mass-production techniques that had been developed during the war:

> I think there is a great danger of the spectacular building of a very simple type of comparatively small cargo ships of one design . . . creating the impression that the methods used were now so far ahead of any in this country that they should be slavishly copied.

The kind of conservatism voiced by Hunter – the boss of Tyneside's biggest shipbuilder – did not bode well for the future. That mindset manifested itself in a number of ways. According to Johnman and Murphy, our shipbuilders were slow to adopt diesel marine engines, slow to find new and more efficient ways of building oil tankers and particularly slow to introduce the welding techniques that were being used to great effect in Sweden and in the reviving shipyards of

Germany and Japan. There seemed to be a consensus among British shipbuilders that welding would never replace riveting (which was a bit like contending that the tank would never replace the cavalry horse).

The result was inevitable. As the 1950s wore on, Britain slipped steadily down the world's shipbuilding league. In 1956, Japan toppled Britain as the world's number-one shipbuilder (in terms of tonnage, at least), with other countries coming up fast. As the historian Natasha Vall points out in her essay 'The Emergence of the Post-Industrial Economy in Newcastle 1914–2000' in *Newcastle upon Tyne: A Modern History*, in the early 1960s British shipbuilding output fell 19 per cent, 'whereas Swedish output saw a 78 per cent increase, and Japan a staggering 210 per cent'. She goes on:

> Faced with the rise in international competition, Swan Hunter's earlier position of strength (most of Tyneside's tonnage was launched from the company's Neptune yard during the war) appeared to be on the wane. By the early 1960s, the Neptune yard was only able to offset foreign rivals for the order of a bulk cargo vessel for Ghana with the help of a substantial government loan.

In the late 1940s, the nationalisation of Britain's 'strategic' industries was near the top of the Labour government's agenda, and one of those industries was electricity supply. Which meant that NESCo, Tyneside's renowned supplier of electricity, was duly taken into public hands in 1948, along with a clutch of smaller fry. At which point NESCo and the others became the North Eastern Electricity Board (NEEB), under whose banner they traded for the next 40 years.

The NEEB became one of Tyneside's major employers. One of its achievements during the 1950s and 1960s was to complete (more or less) the electrification of the rural areas of Northumberland and Durham. At its peak in 1965, the NEEB employed more than 9,000 men and women as engineers, administrators, maintenance people, clerical workers and sales folk. That figure shrank as the industry's technologies became more and more efficient. By the late 1980s, the workforce had dropped to around 5,000.

And anyone who thought that nationalising the huge coal industry would work miracles was to be disappointed. When vesting day came on Wednesday, 1 January 1947, every colliery in the land sprouted a noticeboard declaring that: 'This colliery is now owned and managed by the National Coal Board on behalf of the people.' But, in fact, very little changed, as the Welsh MP Gwilym Lloyd George had warned in a House of Commons debate a year previously. Nationalisation would not have the transforming effect that most hoped and some feared:

> On the date when the State takes over the mines, what will the effect on him be? He will go to the same pit and get the same lamp from the same man; he will go into the same cage, will probably be lowered by the same man, and when he gets to the bottom he will, if he is in certain parts of the country, see the same expression on the face of the pony. He will see the same manager, the same deputy, the old roadway, the same coalface, and, on Friday, he will probably be paid by the same man.

Within months of its creation, the new National Coal Board (NCB) was facing a crisis. 'The mines had been transferred to public ownership on 1 January 1947 and on 23 February the country's power generation and transmission systems virtually collapsed under the impact of the severest winter in living memory,' is how Andrew Taylor puts it in *The NUM and British Politics: Volume 1: 1944–1968*.

The winter of 1946–7 was one of the harshest of the twentieth century. Deep falls of snow the length and breadth of Britain disrupted road and rail traffic, brought down power lines, shut down companies and brought misery to millions of people already hard pressed by the post-war shortages and rationing. The British government were in no mood to concede the NUM's 'charter of demands' or give in to the Union's clamour for compulsory NUM membership.

Deputy Prime Minister Herbert Morrison told an NUM special conference that:

We have got to have a new mentality, a new soul in industry. We are in the midst of transition, if not a peaceful revolution, and if men are going to vote Socialist and want Socialist things, they must act Socialistically in their daily life.

THE PRICE OF COAL
Mining disasters in the North-east coalfield between 1945 and 2005:

1947 at Louisa	21 die
1951 at Easington	81 die

But the coal industry survived and, for a time at least, flourished under its new owners. Coal was still the most important of all fuels, for railways, power stations, most factories and almost all households. And as Britain's industries struggled to rebuild after five years of ruinous warfare, the demand for coal was high. High enough to keep most of the collieries in Northumberland and Durham producing large quantities of coal and the area's colliery workers in (relatively) well-paid employment and subsidised housing.

Digging out the coal was only part of the process. It had to be transported down to the wooden staiths on the Tyne, then graded and loaded onto the ships. There's a fascinating glimpse of this side of the industry in John and Joyce Carlton's *South Shields Voices*. They quote Bill Henderson, who worked on the coal shutes at the staiths in South Shields. He gave this account of his work:

Coal from Harton, Whitburn and Bolden came down to the old dry cleaner at Westoe where it was segregated by compressed air and vibrators. The cleaner was six floors tall, about ninety feet high. The coal was streamed onto a conveyor then run up to the top. The first thing that happened was it was run over a guide tray with a magnet above it to take the metal out. Then the coal dropped down to the next floor where it was segregated into the big and small chunks, then on the floor below the heavier stone was shaken out. By the end of the process the coal was running as smooth as water. It was beautiful.

TYNESIDE ON THE PITCH: JACKIE MILBURN

If there's one sporting hero to whom every Tynesider defers, it's Jackie Milburn, universally known throughout Tyneside as 'Wor Jackie'. As Richard Holt and Ray Physick point out in their essay on Tyneside's sporting ways, Milburn came from a footballing family. His great-grandfather had played for Northumberland in 1888, four of his cousins were professional footballers and another cousin – named Cissie – was the mother of Jack and Bobby Charlton. Milburn was born in 1924, the son of a miner from Ashington.

Milburn's career with Newcastle United began in 1943 and ended when he retired from the game in 1957. In the course of it, he made 492 appearances and scored 238 goals. He scored the two goals by which Newcastle beat Blackpool in the 1951 FA Cup final and was in the team that beat Arsenal in the Cup final of 1952. In the 1955 Cup final, he scored the fastest goal then recorded at Wembley – a header from a corner within the game's opening minute.

Holt and Physick sum him up:

> modest to a fault, friendly and decent, a family man who married and settled back in Newcastle after a few years away, Jackie Milburn's fame seemed to grow rather than to fade with the passage of time as poor teams and hooligans dragged the club's reputation down.

In 1980, Milburn was made Freeman of the City of Newcastle along with Cardinal Basil Hume. When Wor Jackie died in 1988, the streets of Newcastle were lined with people to see his funeral procession pass.

The Carltons also teased out some fascinating stories about the business of working on the river for the TIC – the Tyne Improvement Commission, known to its workers as 'Take It Canny'. Retired diver Ernie Keedy gave a grim account of his job.

> When you went down you used to see things lost overboard – fouled propellors, anchors and even bodies occasionally. Through working in it I could never romanticise about the river ... One day when at the Mill Dam, I dropped a bucket into the river to get some water to clean the decks, when I pulled it back up there was a dead baby inside. There used to be a lot of stillbirths just dumped in the river.

Bill Salkend, one of the TIC's tug men, was someone else with a grim story:

> When we were towing *The Leader* with the new diesel tugs *Impetus* and *Maximus* the skipper did not know how much weight to put on the hawser. Well, it snapped and killed the lad on the deck. He was only eighteen.

And Jim Thompson recalled the hazards of working on the high crane: 'Getting up top to make repairs was never a problem, but once you were there it was always cold, even in the summer. You didn't wipe your nose, the wind blew it away.'

ORWELL'S WIFE

One native of South Shields was Eileen Maud O'Shaughnessy, better known to the literary world as Eileen Blair, the first wife of the man who wrote under the name of George Orwell and whose real name was Eric Blair. Born in 1905, the daughter of a customs officer, Eileen was a bright girl. She was educated at Sunderland High School and then Oxford University, after which she became a radio producer with the BBC. She met Orwell in 1936 when he was dispatched by the Left Book Club to write about unemployment in the north of England.

When the Second World War broke out, both the Blairs worked for the BBC, Eileen as the producer of the food programme *Kitchen Front* and Orwell as a war correspondent for the BBC's India service. In March 1945, Eileen Blair died of a sudden heart attack at a private clinic in Jesmond, Newcastle, after a routine operation. She's buried in St Andrew's Cemetery in Jesmond under a simple headstone describing her as the wife of Eric Arthur Blair. After Eileen's death, Orwell credited her with contributing to both *Animal Farm* and his dystopian masterpiece *Nineteen Eighty-Four*.

Tynemouth, North Shields, South Shields and Jarrow had long resented the fact that while the city of Newcastle positively bristled with river crossings, they had to make do with small and inadequate ferries. There was a powerful feeling that unless cross-Tyne links were established, the economies of the lower Tyne would continue to fall behind the towns upriver. An assortment of bridge schemes were mooted in the 1930s but none of them came to anything, mainly due to the concerns of the TIC that a downriver bridge would impede shipping.

The TIC, however, had no objections to the idea of a tunnel under the river; but in the late 1930s the various small local authorities (Tynemouth, South Shields, Gateshead, Jarrow and Hebburn) could never agree where exactly any tunnel should be sited. In the end, it was left to the British government to decide. In 1946, Parliament gave the go-ahead for two separate tunnels under the Tyne, one for pedestrians and cyclists, the other for road traffic. The site chosen was between Howdon on the north bank and Jarrow on the south.

Despite the economic problems of post-war Britain, work began on the pedestrian and cyclists' tunnel in November 1947. Tunnelling was completed in March 1950 and the new crossing was declared open by Transport minister Albert Barnes on 24 July 1951. It was an impressive piece of engineering. More than 900 ft long and around 12 ft in diameter, the pedestrian tunnel was reached via escalators which were at the time the longest in the world. There were also lifts at either end for the elderly and disabled. The tunnels were accessed from Ferry Street in Jarrow and Church Street in Howdon. In the 1950s, around 12,000 to 14,000 people used the tunnels every day, most of them shipyard workers. By the late 1990s, that had slumped to 7,000 people a week.

The road tunnel, on the other hand, was a long time coming. It was a much bigger and more costly project. Although the scheme had been agreed in principle, the Government fretted about the price and the engineering complications, and did not give the final go-ahead until March 1958. It took another year to finalise the line of the road tunnel and to pass the necessary legislation, which was given royal assent in July 1960. Work began in October 1961 and was not completed until 19 October 1967, when it was opened with some ceremony by the Queen.

Designed by engineers Mott, Hay & Anderson and constructed by Edmund Nuttall, Sons & Co., the road tunnel is almost 32 ft in diameter and more than 5,500 ft (almost a mile) long, of which only 600 ft runs under the river. The total cost of the project, including the approach roads, the cost of borrowing and the price of buying and demolishing properties on either side of the Tyne, was around £22 million. It was an immediate success, so much so that within weeks there were complaints that cars were having to queue up to get onto the new road under the river.

Since then, of course, road traffic has grown exponentially. At the last count (in 2005), there were more than 30 million vehicles on Britain's roads, one for every two people. The pressure on the vehicle tunnel under the Tyne is now immense. There are plans afoot for a second vehicle tunnel, to run alongside the 1960s version and to carry the traffic going south, while the existing tunnel would handle northbound vehicles.

Impressions of old heavy-industry areas like Tyneside are dominated by the plight of coal-mining, shipbuilding and engineering. They're the high-profile businesses whose crises (and occasional triumphs) make the headlines. But their media dominance usually obscures the fact that while they are ailing, other industries are doing well, sometimes very well. It's a rule to which Tyneside was no exception. In the post-war years, while the traditional industries were in decline, new enterprises began to spring up and many old-established firms flourished and grew. The jobs they created may have been mostly for women but they were none the less welcome.

One of the first of the post-war newcomers was Imperial Tobacco, which opened a Wills cigarette-making factory at Heaton in 1950. Although it was designed and built in the late 1940s, the Wills factory is a splendid example of 1930s design, by the company's own architect Cecil Hockin. A few years later, the famous York-based firm of Rowntree Mackintosh set up a factory on the Fawdon Industrial Estate, employing almost 900 people making confectionery. In a few years' time, they were joined at Fawdon by Winthrop Laboratories, which opened up an operation to produce liver salts and toothpaste.

At the same time, home-grown enterprises like Ross's Pickles, the saddlers Thomas Owen, the British Electrical and Manufacturing Company (Bemco), the printers Ward Philipson, timber merchants F.H. Thompson & Sons and the shipping line Stephenson Clarke all flourished and grew in the post-war years, along with a plethora of other Tyneside firms. And retailing – which had grown hugely in importance in the 1930s, particularly after the advent of C&A Modes and Marks & Spencer in 1932 – reasserted itself in the post-war economy of Tyneside.

But the arrival of big-time retailing spelled the end of independence for one of Britain's oldest department stores, Bainbridge's of Newcastle. The Bainbridge family had done well from the business. Well enough, in fact, for George Bainbridge to buy the Glenfinnan estate on the shores of Loch Shiel in the Scottish Highlands, where he and his guests enjoyed some of the best deer-stalking north of the border. But by the late 1940s and early 1950s, pressure from the big firms was unrelenting, and in August 1952 Bainbridge's was sold to the John Lewis Partnership.

Some London-based clothing manufacturers made their way to Tyneside during the war, mainly to take advantage of the surplus of female labour in the region. By the time the war was over, the industry employed more than 10,000 people. One local firm which flourished hugely in the post-war years was Jackson the Tailor, run by Lionel Jacobson. In 1953 Jackson's of Newcastle merged with Burton's of Leeds and Lionel Jacobson became chairman of the group. He presided over a business with 600 high-street shops throughout Britain, employing around 6,000 people. Another 20,000 men and women worked in the group's clothing factories.

MISTER LENNIE

Lionel Jacobson was one of the most successful Tyneside businessmen of the twentieth century. Born in Newcastle in 1906 to a family of Russian Jews who had fled the Tsarist pogroms and started the firm they called Jackson the Tailor, he was educated in Newcastle and then at Oxford University, where he took a degree in law. After a short – and reputedly unhappy – period as a barrister in London, he returned to Newcastle to join the family business, into which he threw his formidable talent and energy.

Known to his employees as 'Mister Lennie', he was renowned as a friendly and accessible employer whose door was always open. Jacobson is reputed to have coined the phrase, 'If you offer peanuts, you can't expect to get anything but monkeys. And who wants monkeys to run a business?' A generous donor to many charities, he contributed to the coronary unit at Newcastle's General Hospital and left £120,000 to Newcastle University to found and finance a chair of clinical pharmacology.

Mister Lennie died in February 1978 at the age of 72. He's buried in the Jewish section of the Byker and Heaton Cemetery in Newcastle.

Banking, insurance and finance have never loomed large on Tyneside in the way that they do in, say, Edinburgh or Manchester. The region's building societies – the Newcastle upon Tyne Permanent, the Northern Counties and the Rock – were modest affairs which grew slowly. Traditionally, Tynesiders rented houses rather than bought them, which meant there was little demand for mortgages. This drove the Rock Building Society down to London in the early 1950s, where it flourished. The region's financial sector was dealt another blow in 1965, when the Newcastle Stock Exchange was merged with others to form the Northern Stock Exchange. This arrangement lasted only a few years until all the provincial stock exchanges were subsumed into the London-based Stock Exchange.

Tyneside saw the advent of its own commercial television station at 5 p.m. on 15 January 1959, when Tyne Tees Television began broadcasting to viewers in the North-east. The inauguration was a distinctly upmarket affair. The opening ceremony was performed by the Duke of Northumberland, with Prime Minister Harold Macmillan in attendance. After a tour of the new studios (on the City Road in Newcastle), the viewers were treated to an hour's light entertainment called *The Big Show*, hosted by Jimmy James (in place of Dickie Henderson, who'd been felled by a cold).

It was all very upbeat, but in fact the North-east was fairly slow on the television uptake. The big London companies had been on the air since 1955, and Roy Thomson's Scottish Television began beaming its programmes to the nation at the end of August 1957, a good two years before Tyne Tees got its act together.

In the 1960s, a problem emerged when the new high-powered transmitter built by Tyne Tees at Bilsdale began beaming programmes deep into the territory of Yorkshire Television. That particular problem was solved, with the blessing of the Independent Television Authority, when both companies became subsidiaries of Trident Television Ltd. The arrangement lasted until 1992, when Yorkshire Television took over Tyne Tees. Five years later, in 1997, both companies were swallowed up by the Granada Media Group, which is now part of the giant broadcaster Independent Television.

TYNESIDE ON DISC: THE ANIMALS

One of the best of the rock-and-roll groups to emerge in the early 1960s was the Tyneside band known as The Animals. Formed in 1962 by its lead singer, Newcastle-born Eric Burdon, the original band comprised Alan Price (from Fatfield), Chas Chandler (from Heaton), John Steel (from Gateshead) and Hilton Valentine (from North Shields). The Animals fell out with one another in 1966, then reformed under the leadership of Eric Burdon in 1983. Bass player Chas Chandler (real name Bryan Chandler) died in 1996 after a long illness.

Between 1964 and 1966, The Animals had a string of hit singles, the most famous of which is 'House of the Rising Sun', which reached number one in the British charts. Among the band's other singles which made the top ten were 'I'm Crying' (1964), 'Don't Let Me Be Misunderstood' (1965), 'Bring It on Home to Me' (1965) and 'We Gotta Get Out of this Place' (1965).

In the 1960s, the coal industry was in crisis again. As had been predicted by its opponents, nationalisation had not proved the panacea for which the left had hoped. Essentially, there were just too many pits chasing too few customers. Many of them had to go. In 1965, Fred Lee, then the Minister of Power and the man responsible for the coal industry, announced that 150 pits were to close, 95 of them due to 'exhaustion' and 55 for 'economic reasons'. To those Labour MPs representing the British coalfields, Lee's announcement was a stab in the back.

Tom Swan, an NUM-sponsored MP, told the House of Commons:

> When I pulled the string which raised the [NCB] flag at my pithead on 1 January 1947 I was the proudest man alive. Not only because we had achieved nationalisation but because *Socialism* had achieved nationalisation. I never thought that I would find a Minister of Power on the Socialist benches

357

introducing a bill of this character. He has completed the work which the saboteurs opposite [Conservative MPs] have been trying to carry on for 13 years.

Swan's sense of betrayal was shared by all the Labour MPs from Northumberland and Durham. But the harsh fact was that the world's economy was learning to do without coal. The mineral which had made Tyneside into one of the world's great workshops was no longer at the very top of everyone's shopping list. Power stations, engineering plants, shipyards and domestic users were finding other fuels. Gas, oil and even nuclear power were muscling into the market that was once dominated by coal. With the decline in demand for coal went a decline in demand for pitmen and other colliery workers.

TYNESIDE ON SCREEN: *GET CARTER*

It was Michael Caine, that archetypal cockney, who starred in one of the most famous modern films set on Tyneside. But there's no doubt that his co-star was the gritty, sometimes stark, urban landscape of early 1970s Newcastle. Directed by Mike Hodges, and also featuring Britt Ekland and Ian Hendry (with a minor role for the playwright John Osborne), it was released in 1971. *Get Carter* was a box-office success at the time and has since become something of a cult movie.

Described as a 'classic revenge tragedy', the story of a London-based gangster returning to his northern home town to find out who killed his brother, *Get Carter* was a bleak and savage fable, a long way from the traditional British crime movie. Ironically, the book on which it is based – *Jack's Return Home* by the late Ted Lewis – is set not in Newcastle but in a fictional version of the small industrial town of Barton-on-Humber where Lewis (Manchester-born) was raised. The idea of locating the film in Newcastle came from Hodges.

As the film's producer Michael Klinger told one film magazine:

> Newcastle is in an incredible state of transition at present, changing from the old to the new. Buildings are being demolished and new ones are going up all over the place and we took advantage of the resulting, often highly dramatic, locales when shooting the film.

In June 1962, the folk of Tyneside decided to celebrate the 100th anniversary of the famous Blaydon Races. The festivities reached a peak on Saturday, 9 June, when something like half a million people pitched in with street parties, fireworks, dances and all-day drinking, specially licensed for the occasion. To mark the event, a local bard (of the distinctly amateur variety) penned a ditty:

> Old Scotswood Road must live again
> To carry further still its fame.
> We're soon to have a celebration –
> Let Tyneside rise in jubilation.

> From Cruddas Park to Rye Hill
> We are determined, have the will
> That horrid slums we shall erase
> With surgeon's knife and then replace.

The author of that jaunty piece of doggerel was T. Dan Smith, then leader of the Labour group on Newcastle City Council. Two years later, in 1964, one of Smith's public-relations companies was hired by the Labour Party to help them win the general election which brought to an end 13 years of Conservative rule and ushered in Harold Wilson's version of Socialism. Labour's majority was small, and the party's grip on power was tenuous, but they did well in the north-east of England. Part of that success may (may) have been due to the efforts of the energetic and politically adroit T. Dan Smith. In 1964, and for most of the 1960s, Smith was riding high.

But T. Dan Smith was to bring down on Tyneside the kind of publicity that no region wants. Fewer than 10 years after helping

Wilson to power, Smith was at the centre of one of the most notorious corruption trials in modern British history. The ripples from the collapse of Smith's wayward career damaged the careers of a few local politicians and at least one national figure. The names of T. Dan Smith and his corrupt architect pal John Poulson were to become bywords for local-authority malfeasance. The rise and fall of T. Dan Smith – a hugely talented and energetic man – was one of Tyneside's tragedies.

The son of a miner and a charwoman, Thomas Daniel Smith was born in May 1915 at No. 62 Holly Avenue, Wallsend. After a fairly elementary schooling, Smith trained as a house painter and in 1939 married a typist called Ada Simpson. He then started his own painting company, which became known for cutting corners (he acquired the nickname of 'One-Coat Smith'). But he was energetic, resourceful and enterprising at a time when money was scarce. By 1957, the miner's son from Wallsend owned no fewer than seven companies and was fast acquiring a taste for the good things in life.

Interestingly, Smith held none of the political views normal to the small businessman. He was a man of the left, and the strident left at that. During the Second World War he was a conscientious objector and helped organise the wartime strikes that erupted across Tyneside from time to time. He drifted from the ILP to the Revolutionary Communist Party to the Labour Party, under whose banner he was elected to Newcastle City Council (as councillor for the district of Walker).

Smith took to municipal politics like a duck to water. In 1952, he was chairman of the Newcastle branch of the Labour Party; in 1953, he was chairman of the Housing Committee; in 1958, Labour leader; in 1960, chairman of the powerful Northern Economic Planning Council. In 1962, he was named Planner of the Year by the magazine *Architectural Review*. By the middle of the 1960s, T. Dan Smith dominated Tyneside politics in a way that hadn't been seen since the days of the nineteenth-century Cowens, father and son.

It has to be said that T. Dan Smith was a man with a vision. He was the political driving force behind Newcastle's Development Plan of

1963, which envisioned the city being criss-crossed by a network of motorways from which pedestrians were strictly segregated. Other components of the scheme included the regeneration of the Quayside, a comprehensively redeveloped Eldon Square dominated by a glitzy hotel, offices around the All Saints Church and a so-called 'cultural plaza' based around a new Central Library to be linked to the Laing Art Gallery. All of which was to be designed by top architects – or at least Smith's idea of top architects.

In *Newcastle upon Tyne: A Modern History*, the historian Thomas Faulkner writes:

> Smith and his associates – principally his Chief Planning Officer Wilfred Burns – were seeking what they saw as a clean, new, international image which, they believed, would dispel unfavourable industrial myths and attract new business. To publicise his schemes Smith used exhibitions of plans and models and the services of a sympathetic press in a manner pioneered by Grainger more than a century before. Both men dreamed of glorifying their native city. Smith, in his desire for what he called the 'Brasilia of the North', employed big-name architects to build it . . . and even dreamed of employing Le Corbusier.

But where Richard Grainger used his own (and his wife's) money to realise his dreams, Smith's were financed by the British taxpayer and the Newcastle ratepayer. And where Grainger restricted himself to schemes that had a chance of making money, Smith was a mid-twentieth-century idealist. In the opinion of Thomas Faulkner, he was 'propelled by the kind of progressive ideology which underpinned the policies of comprehensive urban development fashionable at the time. He was an enthusiastic promoter of tower blocks and other Utopian housing schemes.'

But this domineering politician never neglected his own personal and business interests. His politics and business affairs dovetailed into one another. Like many other businessmen/politicians, he did well from the post-war public-spending boom. So well, in fact, that by 1960 there were mutterings that one of Smith's companies had won more than 60 per cent of Newcastle Council's repainting contracts.

The rot set in in earnest when T. Dan Smith got together with the Yorkshire businessman and architect John Poulson, whose Pontefract practice was one of the largest in the UK. Poulson's entry in the new *Oxford Dictionary of National Biography* (*ODNB*) describes him as a man who 'believed that everyone had their price and he had the knack of knowing what it would be and how it could benefit his practice'.

Between 1962 and 1969, Poulson's practice paid Smith's public-relations companies £156,000 in fees, a huge sum in the 1960s. Ostensibly, this was for public-relations work, but, according to the *ODNB*, it was 'in reality for bribing councillors and officials in various parts of the country to steer contracts into the right hands'. The 'right hands' were, of course, John Poulson's.

Some intriguing documents saw the light of day during the various legal proceedings. In 1967, for example, one of Smith's companies handled the public relations for the new town of Peterlee. Smith wrote to his benefactor, 'I am 100 per cent loyal . . . I am currently working on almost £8 million worth of architect work for you and I certainly intend that you shall have this work.' Dissatisfied with the slow progress of the Peterlee gravy train, Poulson wrote to Smith in 1969, 'What about the brief for the Arts and Sports Complex at Peterlee, and what about some housing? I thought we were going to get it?'

Ironically, it was when Poulson's financial affairs began to unravel in the early 1970s that Smith came a cropper. The corrupt relationship between the two emerged at Poulson's bankruptcy hearings. Eventually, Smith was arrested in October 1973 and charged with corrupt practices in his dealings with John Poulson. He pleaded guilty to six of the charges and was sentenced to six years in jail, although he served only three. After he was released, Smith worked for the Howard League for Penal Reform, was readmitted to the Labour Party in 1987 and died of a heart attack in the Freeman Hospital in Newcastle in July 1993. He was 78 years old.

T. Dan Smith's obituary notice in the *Newcastle Journal* (published on 28 July 1993) described him as:

> An abrasive and often ruthless Town Hall politician, who had an intimidating physical presence and a booming voice which didn't brook argument. He could rule a committee room with a rod of iron. He could strike the fear of God into City Hall officials.

In 1965, Smith told a newspaper that 'the democratic voice is no way to get the sort of changes we need in the North'.

The same dismal can of worms brought down another powerful Tyneside politician. He was Andy Cunningham, one-time regional officer for the General and Municipal Workers' Union and councillor on the Felling Urban District Council. He was also, at various times, chairman of the Northern Area of the Labour Party, Newcastle Airport Authority, Northumberland River Authority, Durham Police Authority, Tyneside Passenger Transport Authority and Durham County Council. After being introduced to Poulson by T. Dan Smith in 1963, Cunningham was soon on Poulson's sub rosa payroll.

And the benefits were generous. Between 1963 and 1971, Cunningham and his wife, Freda, enjoyed no fewer than nine family holidays at Poulson's expense, while Freda was employed as an 'interior design advisor' to the Poulson companies for a very useful £1,500 a year. When the law caught up with them, it was decided not to prosecute Freda, but Andy Cunningham was tried and sentenced to five years in jail (one of which was knocked off on appeal). After his trial, Cunningham was quoted as saying, 'All this sort of business goes on. So if I am corrupt, half the country is corrupt.'

It should be said that Poulson's web of corruption extended far beyond Tyneside. The influential men who became enmeshed included George Pottinger, a senior Scottish Office civil servant; Graham Tunbridge, estates surveyor for British Rail; Alfred Merrit, a Ministry of Health civil servant; William Sales, chairman of the Yorkshire division of the National Coal Board; Sydney Hepworth, then Mayor of

Southport; Edward Newby, one-time Lord Mayor of Bradford; Roy Hadwin, one-time Lord Mayor of Newcastle; and former Tory cabinet minister Reginald Maudling.

For his part, John Poulson was sentenced to seven years in jail in March 1974. He was released on parole in May 1977 and died in the General Infirmary in Pontefract in January 1993, six months before T. Dan Smith. Of the two, Poulson was the more cynical and sinister. His entry in the *ODNB* says of him: 'He made a lasting impression on the face of British towns, particularly in the North, where old civic centres were destroyed in the name of urban improvement but often, in fact, to line the pockets of Poulson and his associates.' Poulson's obituary in *The Independent* was even more scathing: 'John Poulson was an ambitious, ruthless and friendless man whose object in life was to get as much money and work as he could by bribery and corruption.'

The reign of T. Dan Smith over Newcastle left a number of high-profile buildings, none of which are great adornments to the city. Among the more conspicuous are the Newcastle Civic Centre, designed by the City Architect George Kenyon (completed in 1969 but begun in the 1950s); the building known as Swan House, designed by Robert Matthew (completed 1969); and the Central Library, designed by Basil Spence (completed 1970). These buildings are described by the magisterial *Buildings of England* as 'brutally assertive, to say the least'. One part of T. Dan Smith's dream that was never realised was the upmarket hotel in Eldon Square, which was to be designed by the renowned Danish architect Arne Jacobsen (a much better designer than either Basil Spence or Robert Matthew).

TYNESIDE ON SCREEN: *THE LIKELY LADS*

When Terry Collier (played by James Bolam) and Bob Ferris (played by Rodney Bewes) first appeared on the small screen as *The Likely Lads* in 1964, they raised the profile of Tyneside enormously. The interplay between the roguish, feckless but engaging Terry and the serious, striving Bob made for a great comedy that had the British public entranced for three series and twenty episodes. Written by

Dick Clement and Ian La Frenais and transmitted by the BBC, *The Likely Lads* was screened between 1964 and 1966 and ended with Terry marching off to join the army.

The odd couple reappeared in 1973 in *Whatever Happened to the Likely Lads* (also written by Clement and La Frenais), in which Terry arrives back from the army to find that his old mucker Bob is about to marry one Thelma Chambers (played by Brigit Forsyth). The second series is all about the problems that Terry causes to Bob and Thelma's marriage. The second time round for Terry and Bob ran for 27 episodes between 1973 and 1974.

The series' theme tune – 'What Happened to You' – was written by Ian La Frenais and Mike Hugg, one-time member of the band Manfred Mann. Hugg had a modest success with the number when he released it as a single by the group, calling themselves The Highly Likely.

The Eldon Square Shopping Centre – which was largely the creation of T. Dan Smith – was a bold project, to say the least. In its day, it was the biggest city-centre shopping precinct in Britain, and it reinforced Newcastle's position as the north-east of England's prime shopping venue (a position that was later challenged by the advent of the huge MetroCentre in Gateshead). And while it involved the destruction of much valuable classical architecture (most of it by John Dobson), in its own way the Eldon Square Shopping Centre was an ambitious piece of planning.

Opened with a flourish in 1976, the Eldon Square development was a key part of the council's Central Area Plan and has thrived – more or less – ever since it opened. It now comprises 961,000 sq. ft of retail space, room for 140 shops, including such 'anchor' businesses as John Lewis, Fenwick's, Boots and Argos. There are, its owners claim, a million shoppers within half an hour's drive, and in the year 2004 the centre's 'footfall' (i.e. people who set foot in the place) was more than 25 million.

Thirty years on, Eldon Square is typical of the retail emporia that are now a feature of British cities. With its mixture of multinational, national and local enterprises and a food court that accommodates familiar food-chain names such as McDonald's, Pizza Hut and Starbucks (plus the wonderfully named Bagel of the North), the centre sucks in shoppers from all over Northumberland and Durham, particularly at weekends.

Eldon Square's operators, Capital Shopping Centres (CSC, a subsidiary of Liberty International), say they are about to spend £150 million remodelling part of the Eldon Square centre to add another 318,000 sq. ft of retail space and a new bus station at the north end of the mall. In 2005, the ownership of the centre split three ways: 45 per cent to CSC, 40 per cent to Newcastle City and 15 per cent to the Shell Pension Fund.

TYNESIDE ON DISC: UPSTARTS AND SPROUTS

Tyneside's renowned contribution to the punk culture of the late 1970s was a band who called themselves Angelic Upstarts. The brainchild of a singer called Mensi (real name Thomas Mensforth), the band were up and running in South Shields in 1977. Backing Mensi were Ronnie Wooden (bass), Mond (guitar) and Decca (drums). Pop history books record that the band broke up in 1986 then reformed in 1988. Their most successful single was 'Teenage Warning', which made it to number 29 in the British singles charts.

Better known were Prefab Sprout, a Newcastle-based band formed by Paddy McAloon (from Consett), together with his brother Martin, Wendy Smith (from Durham) and Mick Salmon. Between 1984 and 1997, Prefab Sprout had 16 singles in the British top 100. The most successful of them was 'The King of Rock and Roll' (1988), which made it to number seven and stayed in the charts for ten weeks.

Eldon Square's only real rival is the Gateshead MetroCentre, also partly owned and operated by CSC. Opened in 1986 on an old industrial site west of Dunston, the MetroCentre is strategically placed, bounded to the south by the A1 trunk road and to the north by the local railway line which, of course, has a stop for the MetroCentre. The operators claim there are three million shoppers within an hour's drive of the centre, which has more than 9,000 free car-parking spaces to accommodate them.

The MetroCentre's 'anchor' businesses are Marks & Spencer, House of Fraser and Debenhams. The other 300 or so shops are a huge mixture of national and international brands, seasoned by some local businesses. They consume a whopping 1.78 million sq. ft of retail space. With its food courts, multi-screen cinemas, leisure centre and theme park, the Gateshead MetroCentre is one of the biggest of its kind in Europe. Interestingly, 10 per cent of this temple of Mammon is owned by the Church of England Commissioners. The other 90 per cent belongs to CSC.

Another corner of the Tyneside economy which shone brightly all the way through the 1960s and 1970s was Newcastle Airport. From its modest beginnings in 1935, the little airport at Woolsington had grown quietly but steadily until, by the early 1960s, it was plain that it had become an institution of real economic importance not just to Tyneside but to the whole North-east. In April 1963, control of the airport passed to an inter-municipal body called the North East Regional Airport Committee, whose job was to make the business of flying as accessible (and profitable) as possible.

The rest of Europe began taking Newcastle Airport seriously in 1965, when the operators opened a new runway, 2,332 metres long, which proved long enough to take the jumbo jets which appeared in the 1970s. In 1978, it was officially described as a Category B regional airport and given the go-ahead to extend the passenger terminal. By then, most Tynesiders were enamoured of their foreign holidays, and traffic through the airport climbed steadily. By 1984, Newcastle Airport was handling just under 1.25 million passengers a year. By 1991, that figure had increased to 1.67 million.

TYNESIDE ON THE TRACK: BRENDAN FOSTER

There's no doubt that Tyneside's star athlete of the last half-century was Brendan Foster. Having won medals at Olympic, Commonwealth and European games, and set two world records, Foster went on to found Tyneside's famous Great North Run, as well as becoming an accomplished television commentator and a high-flying corporate executive.

Born in 1948, Brendan Foster attended St Joseph's Grammar School in Hebburn then went on to do a B.Sc. at Sussex University, followed by a teaching degree at Carnegie College in Leeds. He then returned to Tyneside to work as a teacher at his old school.

As an athlete, Foster climbed to prominence in the 1970s. At the European Games he won bronze in the 1,500 metres (1971) and gold in the 5,000 metres (1974). At the various Commonwealth Games between 1970 and 1978 he won: a bronze medal in the 1,500 metres (1970); a silver medal in the 5,000 metres (1974); bronze in the 5,000 metres; and gold in the 10,000 metres (1978). He added to his medal hoard by winning a bronze in the 10,000 metres at the 1976 Olympic Games, the only track-and-field medal Britain won. Foster held the world record for the two miles (in 1973) and for the 3,000 metres (in 1974).

Between 1974 and 1981, Foster was sports and recreation manager for Gateshead Metropolitan Borough Council. In 1980, he instigated the Great North Run, now second only to the London Marathon in the number of participants it attracts. Brendan Foster was the BBC's Sports Personality of the Year in 1974 and was awarded an MBE in 1976. His career as a television commentator began in 1981 and runs alongside his job as a sports-event executive.

In July 1968, the old Tyne Improvement Commission was dissolved and replaced by the Port of Tyne Authority. It was a new lease of life. Over the next few decades, the Port of Tyne saw a number of new developments, among them a new, heavy-duty roll-on/roll-off (RoRo) berth at the Albert Edward Dock to handle electrical equipment from the Parsons works; a Danish RoRo service from the new International Ferry Terminal; the lease of the yard at Howdon to an offshore fabrication company to build equipment for the North Sea oil and gas fields; the infilling of Jarrow Slake to build a new deepwater berth and coal terminal; and a new container terminal behind Riverside Quay.

TYNESIDE ON THE PITCH: JACK AND BOBBY CHARLTON

No two brothers have made a weightier contribution to English (and Irish) football than Jack and Bobby Charlton – as players, managers and ambassadors for their game. The sons of Robert and Elizabeth Charlton were both born on Tyneside, Jack in 1935 and Bobby in 1937. Their paths began to diverge when it came to secondary school: Jack went to Hirst Park School in Ashington and Bobby to Bedlington Grammar. They began their footballing careers within two years of one another.

Jack joined Leeds United in 1952 and played for the club for more than 20 years, until 1973. He was capped for England 35 times between 1965 and 1970, and was a member of the England team that won the World Cup in 1966. When his career as a player ended, he took to management: Middlesbrough (1973–77); Sheffield Wednesday (1977–83); Newcastle United (1984–85). In 1986, Jack Charlton took on the job of managing the Republic of Ireland. The lanky Tynesider proved the most successful manager the Irish team has ever had.

His younger brother, Bobby, joined Manchester United in 1954 and played in the club's famous red shirt until 1973. In 751 games, he scored 245 goals. Between 1957 and 1973, he was capped for England no fewer than 106 times and, like his brother, played in the England team that defeated West Germany 4–2 in the final of the World Cup

---

in 1966. After Bobby Charlton stopped playing in 1973, he became manager of Preston North End for a short period between 1973 and 1975. He was knighted in 1994. Like Pelé of Brazil and Maradona of Argentina, the Tyneside-born Bobby Charlton was one of those players whose name was known to football enthusiasts around the world.

In his engaging and nicely written *Biography* of Tyneside, David Bean argued that, so far as officialdom was concerned, there was no such place as Tyneside. There were only 18 local authorities of varying sizes governing 'just under one million, mainly proletarian, largely hard-working, and usually pessimistic souls called Tynesiders or Geordies'. Which, he said, was ridiculous. 'The barriers are all arbitrary bar the Tyne itself, and all created by the accidents of history, mainly Victorian and industrial.'

He was only half joking. The idea that Tyneside was a municipal shambles was not new. Politicians and local-authority bureaucrats (including Richard Crossman and T. Dan Smith) had been arguing for years that serious tidying-up was necessary. What was needed, they said, was an overarching authority which could ensure that the whole region was properly coordinated, sensibly planned and adequately provided for. It came with the reorganisation of local government in 1974, which created a two-tier system of county (or regional) councils on top of rural and metropolitan district councils.

On Tyneside, the new deal manifested itself in the Tyne and Wear County Council, which made its debut in 1974 and lasted until 1986. As the strategic authority responsible for coming up with big-time, long-term solutions for roads, transport, water and the rest of Tyneside's infrastructure, Tyne and Wear almost immediately ran into hostility from the Metropolitan District of Newcastle City. The politicians and their officials wrangled for years; then, just when the two-tier system was settling down, Margaret Thatcher's Tory Party swept to power in 1979 and set about changing the rules. The various 'structure plans' which had been worked out by the County Councils were more or less ignored in favour of business-friendly 'enterprise zones', which carried with them all kinds of subsidies and tax breaks. It was in such enterprise zones that the Gateshead MetroCentre and the various business parks were built or extended. They had the effect of sucking businesses and shoppers away from the centre of Newcastle, which was something the city could ill afford.

All the evidence is that the centre of Newcastle has done well from the activities of the property developers. Elsewhere on Tyneside, the benefits are not so obvious.

In 1986, the Tory government blew the whistle on Tyne and Wear County Council, gave some of its powers to the unelected Tyne and Wear Development Corporation and brought back a revised version of the old-time (and smaller-time) local authorities. Tyneside is now regulated by four so-called Metropolitan Borough Councils: Newcastle, Gateshead, North Tyneside (which includes Wallsend and Tynemouth) and South Tyneside (South Shields, Hebburn and Jarrow). Given that the towns on both sides of the river now pretty well run into one another, that represents a fair-sized conurbation of around 800,000 people.

THE TYNESIDE LITERATI

The twentieth century saw Tyneside produce a prodigious crop of literary talent. Novelists, poets, dramatists, screenwriters, journalists, publishers – they all made their mark on the British scene. Some have been sadly overlooked or forgotten; others still sell their work by the shedload. Among the finest literati of Tyneside are:

Basil Bunting (1900–85) Born in Scotswood, and a journalist to trade, Bunting has been described as Britain's first modernist poet. He was a friend and associate of inter-war poets like Ezra Pound and T.S. Eliot, and his long, autobiographical work *Briggflats* has been compared to Eliot's *The Waste Land*.

Sid Chaplin (1916–86) Influential as both a poet and a novelist, Chaplin began his working life as a baker, then became an apprentice blacksmith at the Dean and Chapter colliery in County Durham. His collection of stories *The Leaping Lad* was a major success and led to the publication of his Newcastle-based novels *The Day of the Sardine* and *The Watcher and the Watched*. His papers are held by the University of Newcastle.

Jack Common (1903-68) One of Britain's best working-class novelists, his books *The Freedom of the Streets*, *Kiddar's Luck* and *The Ampersand* are all set in his home town of Newcastle. One of Common's admirers was George Orwell, who regarded the Tyneside writer as the most genuine 'proletarian' voice in Britain. Common's papers and manuscripts (some unpublished) are held by the University of Newcastle.

Catherine Cookson (1906–98) Born at Tyne Dock in South Shields the illegitimate child of a drunken mother, she became one of Britain's most successful popular novelists. She was enormously productive and her 90 or so books have been translated into more than 20 languages. Most of Cookson's intelligent and well-written historical romances are set on or around Tyneside, and they sell in huge quantities across the world. In the late 1980s, Cookson's books made up one third of *all* the fiction borrowed from British libraries. She was made a Dame in 1993, five years before she died at the age of 92 at her home near Newcastle.

Alan Plater (1935–) Born in Jarrow but raised in Hull, he studied architecture, which he abandoned to become one of Britain's most successful stage and television writers. His book of short stories *The Thin Seam* became the basis for the successful stage play *Close the Coalhouse Door, Boys*, which he wrote with fellow Geordies Sid Chaplin and Alex

Glasgow. It was later adapted for television. Plater had a major success with one of his latest stage pieces, *Blonde Bombshells of 1943*.

At the same time as the Labour government of Harold Wilson set about reshaping Britain's local authorities, it was reshaping Britain's shipbuilding industry. That changed radically in the late 1970s with the Aircraft and Shipping Industries Act 1977, which nationalised every shipyard in Britain. The idea had been around since Harold Wilson's comeback in 1974 and had generated one of the fiercest parliamentary debates of the 1970s. Three times, the House of Lords rejected the Bill, until the Government was forced to threaten their Lordships with the Parliament Act. When the Bill became an Act, what was left of Tyneside's shipyards became public property.

But Her Majesty's Government and its corporate creation, British Shipbuilders Ltd, were no more effective at winning shipbuilding orders than their private-enterprise predecessors. Swan Hunter and the rump of the once-great Tyneside shipbuilding industry continued to struggle against ferocious worldwide competition. By the 1970s, the South Koreans and the Taiwanese were in the market, along with the Japanese and the revived shipbuilding industries of France, Italy and Germany.

And international events had a way of impinging on Tyneside. In February 1977, the Shah of Iran's brother and his wife launched the *Kharg*, a supply ship built by Swan Hunter for the Imperial Iranian Navy. But while the ship was going through her lengthy sea trials off the coast of Britain, the Shah of Iran was toppled by the Ayatollah Khomeini, and in 1980 Iranian zealots stormed the American Embassy to take the staff hostage – at which point Prime Minister Margaret Thatcher ordered that the *Kharg* had to stay on the Tyne until the American hostages were released. Thatcher's order effectively stranded the 150-strong Iranian crew at the ship's berth in Walker. Some of them applied for political asylum, while others stuck by the ship.

The export order for the *Kharg* was not issued until September

1984, more than seven years after she'd been launched. 'By that time,' says one Tynesider, 'the poor bloody Iranians on board were speaking with Geordie accents. God knows what they made of their English when they got back home.'

Like all industrial enterprises, shipbuilding companies have a way of evolving. Mergers, takeovers, nationalisation and assorted crises all have their effects. The great Tyneside yard universally known as Swan Hunter began life in 1874 as C.S. Swan & Co., four years later it became C.S. Swan & Hunter then in 1903 it was Swan Hunter & Wigham Richardson. That corporate identity lasted until 1968, when it changed to Swan Hunter & Tyne Shipbuilders Mid-Tyne but then, after almost a decade as part and parcel of the nationalised British Shipbuilders Ltd, it reverted to being Swan Hunter in 1986.

What was left of British shipbuilding was re-privatised when Margaret Thatcher's government passed the British Shipbuilders Act 1983. After a series of lengthy negotiations in 1986, Tyneside's biggest shipyard, Swan Hunter, was sold to Swan Hunter (Tyneside) Ltd, then owned by four shipbuilding executives, Roger Vaughan, Peter Vaughan, Ken Chapman and Alex Marsh. The price they paid for the once-great company – £5 million.

Under its new owners, Swan Hunter struggled to create the kind of lean, efficient operation that seemed to be flourishing elsewhere in the world. Which, of course, meant laying off workers. Six months after the new owners took over, the redundancies began. After every order sailed out of the Tyne, men and women would be laid off. In 1986, Swan Hunter was employing more than 4,500 people. By 1993, the figure had slumped to 1,800, about a third of what it was at privatisation. In May that year, Swan Hunter (Tyneside) Ltd stunned the North-east by collapsing into receivership.

Immediately, Tyneside fought back. A campaign (neatly labelled SOS – 'Save Our Swan') was launched to keep the enterprise alive. It was backed by, among others, local MPs Stephen Byers and Nick Brown, the industrialist Sir John Hall, the rock stars Sting and Mark Knopfler, the novelist Catherine Cookson, the actors Jimmy Nail and David Jenkins, and the controversial Bishop of Durham. The situation was summed up by journalist-turned-rock star Mark Knopfler: 'Lose the shipyard, you lose the skills, you lose the community. Keep the shipyard open.'

The Bishop of Durham was outraged. 'Management and workers have sweated blood to produce a well-trained workforce using excellent technology,' he declared. 'To write this off is to send out a message that it does not matter how hard you work, you can have the plug pulled.' Sting was quoted as saying, 'Coming from Wallsend, I know how profoundly the closure of Swan Hunter will affect the community. Six thousand jobs are at stake here.'

In the end, Swan Hunter was bought by a company of hard-headed Dutchmen from THC Fabricators of Holland. Under its chairman Jaap Kroese, Swan Hunter has diversified into converting and repairing drill ships and processing vessels, as well as 'conventional' shipping. Over the past ten years or so, the company have had their ups and downs but have landed orders for two of the Royal Navy's 16,000-ton alternative landing ship logistic vessels (ALSLs), to be known as *Largs Bay* and *Lyme Bay*. Kroese and his team have also won a share of the new (and hugely expensive) aircraft carrier to be built for the Royal Navy over the next 10 years.

TYNESIDE ON SCREEN: *AUF WIEDERSEHEN, PET*

Another hit television comedy show, this time featuring a crew of Tyneside workers seeking their fortunes in the international building industry, *Auf Wiedersehen, Pet* reintroduced the British public to the Geordie humour they'd come to relish via *The Likely Lads*. The cast list for *Auf Wiedersehen, Pet* is nothing if not starry: Kevin Whately (as Neville), Tim Healy (as Dennis), Timothy Spall (as Barry), Jimmy Nail (as Oz), Garry Holton (as Wayne), Pat Roach (as Bomber) and Christopher Fairbank (as Moxey), with original scripts by Dick Clement and Ian La Frenais (who dreamed up *The Likely Lads*).

The first two series, screened between 1983 and 1986, featured our seven heroes trying to make their way in the

---

German building boom and sharing a Nissen hut in
Düsseldorf. In the third and fourth series, screened between
2002 and 2004, the amiable seven (with a replacement for
Gary Holton) find themselves working for Tyneside gangster
Ally Fraser (played by Bill Patterson) and then trying to
restore the ambassador's residence in Havana, Cuba.
Unable to film in Cuba itself, the producers had to make do
with the Dominican Republic.

In 1989 it was all change for the electricity supply industry when it was
re-privatised at the behest of the Tory government. The North Eastern
Electricity Board (the nationalised version of the legendary NESCo)
changed its name to Northern Electric and in December 1990 was
floated on the Stock Exchange, where its shares could be bought by
anyone with deep enough pockets. Which, of course, is what happened
at the end of 1996 when Northern Electric plc was swallowed up by
CalEnergy of the USA and became part of that company's worldwide
empire. With the nationalisation and then the privatisation of what
was once one of the world's most advanced electrical supply companies
(NESCo) yet another centre of decision-making had drained away
from Tyneside.

But the change of ownership did not stop there. In 1988, CalEnergy
was sold to MidAmerican Energy Holdings of Des Moines, Iowa,
which now supplies electricity to the north-east of England through a
company called Northern Electric Distribution Ltd (NEDL), a
subsidiary of a subsidiary entitled CE Electric UK.

Nor is that the end of the corporate chain. MidAmerican Energy
Holdings is owned by the fabulously wealthy investment company
Berkshire Hathaway of Omaha. And Berkshire Hathaway's biggest
shareholder is the legendary Warren E. Buffet, reputed to be the
second-richest man in the world (after Bill Gates of Microsoft). So
every time someone in Tynemouth or Gateshead switches on a light,
he or she makes that elderly American billionaire just a little bit richer.

TYNESIDE ON THE PITCH: GAZZA

Paul Gascoigne – known to football aficionados everywhere as Gazza – is not everyone's idea of a sporting hero. An explosive mixture of footballing genius and wayward spirit, Gascoigne's roller-coaster career has been the subject of endless tabloid stories ever since he erupted onto the British footballing scene in the 1980s. Long past the peak of his career, Gazza and his lifestyle still fascinate the British media.

Born in Gateshead in 1967, Gascoigne crossed the Tyne to play for Newcastle United in 1984 and stayed with them until 1988. In 107 appearances for the Magpies, he scored 25 goals. That was followed by four seasons with the London club Tottenham Hotspur, then Gazza was off to Italy to work his magic for SS Lazio. After Lazio, it was back to Britain and a contract with Glasgow Rangers, followed by a stint with Middlesbrough between 1998 and 2000.

The first two years of the new millennium saw Gazza playing for Everton, then with Burnley, after which he did a season with the Chinese club Gansu Tianma, for whom he managed only four goals. In 2004, Gascoigne returned to Britain and signed up as player–coach for the lowly Lincolnshire club Boston United. Tyneside's footballing genius is reputed to be finding it very hard to retire from the game.

One way or another, the 1980s and 1990s were a difficult time for many Tynesiders. The slow but inexorable decline of the old heavy industries was making itself felt on both sides of the Tyne, from Blaydon down to Tynemouth. It created swathes of long-term unemployment, poverty and feelings of hopelessness in many corners of Tyneside. Vandalism, low-level crime, alcoholism, drug-taking, litter and graffiti spread like scars across the faces of what were once tight-knit and relatively prosperous working-class areas.

The New Labour government of Tony Blair recognised the

problem. In December 1997, Tony Blair launched his government's Social Exclusion Unit. Social exclusion, he said, was:

> more harmful to the individual, more corrosive for society as a whole . . . than material poverty. The problems of social exclusion – of failure at school, joblessness, crime – are woven together when you get down to the level of the individual's daily life, or the life of a housing estate.

He might have been talking about the district of Walker, to the east of Newcastle. Walker is typical of a traditional, working-class area blighted by industrial decay. In 1999, two academics from the Centre for Research on European Urban Environments (CREUE) made a study of how the economic downturn had impacted (as they say) upon Walker. Entitled 'Walker, Newcastle upon Tyne: A Neighbourhood in Transition', its language is dry and academic, but the message is chilling.

'All indicators show that the neighbourhood is suffering from severe social problems,' the authors write. 'It suffers from population loss, poor education and health, high rates of housing vacancy, high crime rates, high unemployment and inadequate services.' They go on to make the point that with the collapse of shipbuilding and engineering, 'the economic base of the neighbourhood has eroded to be replaced by state subsidy'.

They note the socially corrosive effects of what they describe as 'the loss of connection with the world of work' and declare that:

> With the decline of employment opportunities in Walker a major dilemma for its residents is whether to leave the neighbourhood in search of work . . . Those who remain show a relatively low degree of mobility, where lack of resources keeps them confined, almost trapped.

Most poignant, perhaps, are the remarks of some Walker folk themselves. 'It is a wrong place for certain people to be honest,' said one. 'The rougher you are, the more you can steal etc., the more you are accepted.' Another resident averred that 'Drugs round here is a way of life.' Yet another claimed that 'Most of the kids around here steal cars, they steal property, they don't give a damn.'

Local youngsters running wild were seen as a major irritant. 'There's nobody there to look after the park so you get all sorts in,' claimed one woman. 'You get all the kids sitting and drinking cider and stuff when the little ones are playing, swearing their heads off and stuff like that.'

It all makes dismal reading. And it prompted the authors to the sad conclusion that 'Walker has long been known as a respectable working-class area, an image that is now changing into one of social decline and crime. The local people suffer from this stigmatisation.'

Since then, of course, things have been improving. Newcastle has had a decent share of public and lottery money. The city's East End Partnership has worked hard to breathe new life into areas like Walker, Byker and Heaton. Small service industries, shops, retail developments and so on have been springing up, although it will be a long time before they replace the shipyards and engineering shops of the twentieth century. If, that is, they ever do.

Most of the council housing built on Tyneside in the 1960s and 1970s was typical of the undistinguished stuff that was rushed up all across Britain. Newcastle, Wallsend, Gateshead, Tynemouth and South Shields saw the usual uninspiring and often bland mixture of terraces, three or four-storey 'walk-ups' and tower blocks of varying success. But there is an exception; it is on the Byker estate and it won worldwide plaudits (and many awards) for its architect, Ralph Erskine, who was commissioned by Newcastle City Council in 1969.

The heart of the estate, and the best part of Erskine's design, is the so-called Byker Wall, a five-storey complex of 620 flats and maisonettes, the backs of which face north and are turned to the traffic. Most of the rooms on the north side are bathrooms and kitchens. The houses on the south-facing front of the wall have balconies to catch whatever sun Tyneside has to offer. Houses on the ground floor – which are reserved for families with children – have small front gardens.

The Northumberland volume of *The Buildings of England* waxes lyrical about the Byker estate and the Byker Wall in particular:

> The steeply sloped old people's home rides high over all at the w[est] end of the wall with views of the whole river. Variety of scale and form, texture and colour are the visible signs of the architect's high regard for the human part of the equation which makes good housing. The whole undertaking was carried out in consultation with the people of the area.

Ralph Erskine practised in Scandinavia for many years, so it's not surprising that there is a distinct flavour of Scandinavia about his designs for Byker. But Newcastle is not Scandinavia, and in recent years the Byker Wall has had its problems. This was acknowledged in a council report in 2001 which declared that while 'Byker is a pioneering social housing development of European importance and influence . . . in recent years a number of problems have developed that threaten the quality of life on the estate and may undermine its long-term sustainability.'

But every part of urban Britain has its problems. The towns of Tyneside have done a better job of reinventing themselves than most of those parts of Britain that were once dominated by nineteenth-century heavy industries. But then, Tyneside had a lot going for it. Outside of London itself, it's hard to think of another part of England which has such a vibrant regional identity, such a powerful regional culture, and which is so steeped in British (and European) history. Converting that history into the kinds of attractions that spin money and function as educational centres is something at which the Geordies have proved very adept. Tyneside is now recognised as one of Britain's cultural hot spots.

TYNESIDE ON DISC: JIMMY NAIL

Following his television success with *Auf Wiedersehen, Pet*, the actor Jimmy Nail went on to become a presence in the charts. One of the few actors who has managed to make a success of both acting and singing, Nail (real name James Michael Aloysius Bradford) had a succession of chart successes in the 1980s and '90s. He also starred in the television series *Spender* and *Crocodile Shoes* and appeared in the feature films *Evita* and *Still Crazy*.

Jimmy Nail's first release was 'Love Don't Live Here Anymore' (1985), which made number three and won a silver disc. Five years later, he had an even bigger success with 'Ain't No Doubt' which stayed at number one for three weeks and won a gold disc. Two years later, his song 'Crocodile Shoes' made it to number four, but sold enough copies to win Nail yet another gold disc.

Outside of London and Edinburgh, it's hard to think of another British city that runs to quite so many well-stocked art galleries, museums and exhibition spaces, and concert halls than Newcastle. In no particular order they are: the Hancock Museum (antiquities and natural history); the Laing Art Gallery (a fine collection of eighteenth- and nineteenth-century painting and sculpture); Bessie Surtees' House (a rare example of domestic Jacobean architecture); the Discovery Museum (which explores the history of Tyneside and houses the amazing *Turbinia*); the Life Science Centre (a combination of education and working laboratories); the Newcastle Arts Centre (the liveliest gallery/theatre centre in the North-east); and the Military Vehicle Museum (in the only building that remains of the 1929 North East Coast Exhibition).

The city has also taken to embellishing its streets with some intriguing modern sculptures. In Wesley Square, there are 100 carvings on a sandstone wall by Neil Talbot. On the Sandgate, a bronze statue of a mythical river god blows at a bronze siren, both sculptures by Andre Wallace. At the top of the Sandgate Steps, another of Wallace's sculptures celebrates the life and work of the Tyne's famous keelmen. On the Quayside, a 25-ft-high *Blacksmith's Needle*, designed by Alan Dawson, was erected by the British Association of Blacksmith Artists. It has to be said that not all Novocastrians are enthusiastic about these street artefacts. 'Bloody expensive litter' is the opinion of at least one denizen of Newcastle.

But if any one artefact represents Tyneside, it has to be Antony Gormley's now world-famous sculpture *Angel of the North*, which stands at the head of the Team Valley to the south of Gateshead. Built from weather-resistant steel (which is oxidising to rich golden-brown), the *Angel* stands 65 ft high, with outspread wings that are 175 ft wide. Since it was erected, the *Angel of the North* has become part of the landscape. Tynesiders claim that it is seen by more than 90,000 people every day who drive along the A1, and by passengers on the main railway line between London and Edinburgh.

THE GEORDIE DIALECT

It often seems to Scots that their dialect has spread down to the Tyne. This is the exact reverse of the truth. The linguistic imperialism was from south to north, from the Tyne into Scotland. The many dialect words that Geordies and Scots share – for example, 'gang' for 'go', 'doon' for 'down', 'hame' for 'home', 'dub' for 'puddle', 'deid' for 'dead', 'burn' for 'stream', 'clash' for 'talk', 'fash' for 'bother', 'bairn' for 'child', 'toon' for 'town' and so on – are a common heritage. They come down from the language of the Angles, the Teutonic folk from what is now Denmark and North Germany who settled around Tyneside in the fifth century. There is a theory that the Angles were invited by the Romanised Britons to help defend against marauding Picts and Scots.

By the seventh century, the Angles had formed the powerful kingdom of Northumbria, which reached into Scotland as far north as the Firth of Forth. When the Angles tried to extend their empire to the north, they were halted with great slaughter by the Picts and pushed back across the Forth, where they remained. But the language now called Scots (once known as 'Inglis') and which is used to such powerful effect by Scots poets like Robert Burns is an

> eighteenth-century version of the language spoken by
> settlers from Tyneside. The Geordie empire is bigger than
> most Geordies realise.

The town of Gateshead was once famously described as a narrow lane which led to Newcastle. Not any more. Sterling work over the past decade by the organisation known as Gateshead Quays (whose 14 members include such heavy hitters as English Partnerships, the Millennium Commission, Newcastle City Council, the North East Chamber of Commerce and the Port of Tyne) has transformed the Baltic Quay, a run-down stretch of Tyneside, into one of the liveliest concentrations of the arts in England.

The old St Mary's Church, which lies just under the south end of the Tyne Bridge, has been converted into Gateshead's visitor centre. Bottle Bank, once notorious as a riverside slum, is now a clutch of upmarket restaurants, clubs and bars, lying close to a glossy Hilton hotel. The Baltic Flour Mills (designed in the 1940s by Hull architects Gelder and Kitchen, and opened in 1950) has been converted into a handsomely equipped, multi-storey art gallery/library/auditorium with a glass-and-steel rooftop restaurant that offers splendid views over the river to Newcastle.

Even more striking is The Sage Gateshead. Named after Sage Software, who provided some of the funding, and designed by Foster and Partners (the firm of Sir Norman Foster, the *éminence grise* of British architects), this stainless-steel-and-glass-clad complex of concert halls, rehearsal rooms and public spaces was built at a cost of £70 million and opened in December 2004. The Sage is now home to the Northern Sinfonia and the folk and dance organisation Folkworks. The building houses two concert halls (one seating 1,650, the other seating 400) and, like the Baltic art gallery, its glass-fronted public concourse and foyers make the most of the view across the Tyne.

The Sage is one of those buildings that critics love to hate. The well-informed 'Piloti' in *Private Eye* was particularly scathing about Foster's contribution to the Tyneside landscape. He wrote:

The character of the Tyne gorge used to be of majestic bridges leaping across the river – heroic engineering and landscape combining to create a dramatic picture in which even public buildings were subservient. But now this big, bulbous steel sheath looms over everything . . . its crude, tinselly form screams for attention and diminishes even the great high level bridges . . . As architecture the Sage Gateshead is childish; in urban, townscape terms it is offensive.

WHAT THEY SAID ABOUT THE SAGE

Early in 2005, BBC Tyne's website invited opinions of The Sage and suggestions for a nickname. Replies poured in, most, but not all, hostile. And it's interesting that, among the BBC's correspondents, the musicians who had performed in the building declared that the acoustics were wonderful, maybe even the best in Britain. Here are a few of the comments, descriptions and nicknames: '"Slug" is the only description that comes to mind' (Dennis Watson); 'A beautiful building, inside and out' (Lindsay D.); 'A true atrocity' (Steve); 'Like a friendly hippo just emerged from the water, relaxing in the sunshine' (Joan); 'Beautiful, shiny and curvy' (Judith Ramsay); 'Given it looks like a bulging pair of stockings, "the Saggy Bum" seems appropriate' (Steve); '"the Platinum Peanut"' (Pat); 'Another magnificent icon for the North-east' (Greg Walker); '"the Grub"' (Steve Kelly); '"the Chrysalis"' (Nick Simpson); '"the Hunchback of the Toon"' (Sean Congo).

For his part, Dave Williams referred back to another piece of architectural criticism: 'It kinda reverses Prince Charles's architectural comment – it being a loved building . . . on a carbuncle of a town.'

Linking The Sage and Baltic to the Newcastle Quayside is the Tyne's newest crossing, the footpath and cycleway known as the Gateshead Millennium Bridge. An extraordinary piece of engineering 413 ft long and 26 ft wide that rotates to allow ships to pass under, the bridge was built at a cost of £22 million to a design by the architects Wilkinson Eyre and the engineers Gifford and Partners. The bridge was constructed by the Gateshead-based company Harbour & General between May 1999 and September 2001.

Trumpeted as 'the world's first rotating bridge', with a sophisticated, inbuilt lighting system, there's no doubt that the Millennium Bridge is a striking addition to the riverscape of the Tyne. It has already acquired a nickname – 'the Blinking Bridge', because of the way it opens and shuts like a human eye. Decorative or not, a bridge is a bridge and the Tyne is still a working river. The Millennium Bridge is opened and closed to suit the shipping traffic and not the convenience of the art-loving public.

THE POST-WAR BRIDGES

The Gateshead Millennium Bridge is not the only Tyne crossing to be built in the second half of the twentieth century. Images of Tyneside may be dominated by the iconic forms of the 1928 Tyne Bridge and the 1849 High Level Bridge, but more bridges have been built across the Tyne in the last 40 years than in any previous period. With the exception of the Gateshead Millennium Bridge, they are not as dramatic as their stone-and-iron predecessors; but they do the business. They move the traffic, vehicles, trains, cyclists and pedestrians from one side of the river to the other. In chronological order, the modern bridges are: the Scotswood road bridge, 1964–7; the Metro rail bridge, 1976–81; the Redheugh road bridge, 1980–83; the Newburn road bridge, 1990; and the Gateshead Millennium Bridge, 1999–2001.

In its enthusiasm for riverside developments, the town of Gateshead has not neglected its other municipal assets. Saltwell Park, for example, which lies more or less in the heart of the town and which was opened to the public in 1876, has had more than ten million pounds' worth of lottery funding and council cash lavished on it. The money was spent in an effort to recreate the kind of green space in which the Victorians loved to parade. It was money well spent. Saltwell Park is home to no fewer than 11 listed buildings and monuments, including a remarkable Victorian Gothic mansion known as Saltwell Towers.

Of course, Newcastle and Gateshead do not have a monopoly on Tyneside's museums and visitor attractions. Almost every town on the river has got in on the heritage/history act. There are places of genuine interest all the way down the river. From west to east: George Stephenson's cottage at Wylam; Bede's World at Jarrow, which gives an insight into the life of the Angles, the Teutonic folk who gave their name to England; the South Shields Museum and Art Gallery explores local history; the Stephenson Railway Museum at North Shields has locomotives that pre-date Stephenson's *Rocket* and is a terminus for the North Tyneside Steam Railway; and the Blue Reef Aquarium at Tynemouth is one of the best of its kind in Britain.

Away from Tyneside itself, some 30 or so miles into Northumberland, stands Cragside, the huge house built by the Tyneside engineering tycoon William Armstrong. Set in more than 14,000 wooded acres (much of it planted by Armstrong), it is described in *The Buildings of England* as 'the most dramatic Victorian mansion in the North of England'. Designed by the architect Norman Shaw and built in three stages between 1870 and 1885, Cragside and its gardens are now in the care of the National Trust and are open to the public. The Trust claims that Cragside is the 'first house in the world to be lit by electricity'. The claim may be dubious, but the house and its contents offer a fascinating insight into what vast wealth could buy in the late nineteenth century.

Just as interesting is Cragside's collection of ancillary buildings. Like others of his kind (Thomas Alva Edison, for instance), William Armstrong was an inveterate tinkerer and inventor. He never lost his interest in the potential of water power. The tumbledown Ram House below the dam housed the hydroelectric gear that supplied electricity to the main house. Other structures that played their part in the running of Cragside are Debdon Sawmill, Burnfoot Power House,

Tumbleton Stables and Cragside Park House. The iron bridge that spans Debdon Burn was built at Armstrong's Elswick works. Like most of the National Trust's more important properties, Cragside comes complete with shop and restaurant.

And Tyneside has the extraordinary good fortune to inherit a chunk of what is now a World Heritage Site – the great wall built in the second century AD by the Emperor Hadrian. After centuries of neglect, Tyneside is making the most of this priceless asset. The site known as Segedunum at Wallsend combines the excavated remains of one of the wall's most important forts with reconstructions of living quarters and baths, plus models of how the Roman military system on the wall worked. There is also a 100-ft-high viewing tower which offers an outlook over the excavated fort, and a computer-generated display which chronicles changes at Wallsend from Roman times to the twenty-first century.

On the other side of the Tyne at South Shields is the Arbeia Roman Fort and Museum, the remains of a fort and supply base that was used to support the garrisons on the wall. The museum at Arbeia contains Roman weapons, armour, tools, cooking utensils and jewellery, as well as a gallery on the Roman way of death and burial. The reconstructions are carefully done and some are built on the original foundations. There are reconstructions of the fort's gateway, the commander's quarters and a barracks block, complete with equipment, utensils and furniture. Taken together, they offer a glimpse of how life was lived by Tyneside's Roman occupiers almost 2,000 years ago.

12

MILLENNIUM AND AFTER

2000–2005

For Tyneside, the new millennium got off to an ironic start. In December 2002, the Port of Tyne Authority dismantled all its coal-loading equipment and sold it to the Port of Lyttelton in New Zealand. It was a genuinely historic moment. The great coal-exporting trade on which Tyneside's industries had been built was now at an end. The ingenious hardware through which millions of tons of hard-won Northumberland and Durham coal had poured onto the world's ships was itself shipped off to the other side of the world.

Then, two years later, something odd happened. The coal trade was resumed – but in reverse. In 2004, the Port of Tyne began *importing* coal. For the first time in 2,000 years, coals really were being taken to Newcastle. A few months later, it was announced that Allerton Colliery, the last working mine in Northumberland, was to close and more than 300 men were to be laid off. No more coal was to be dug from the north bank of the Tyne. The world had turned upside down.

Not that Tyneside paid much attention. Tyneside at the start of the twenty-first century was not what it was. Newcastle had rebranded itself as Britain's party city and was awash with cafés, bars, restaurants, clubs, art galleries, concert halls, museums and all the treats and trappings of urban middle-class life. On the Tyne itself, expensive yachts and pleasure cruisers had taken the place of many of the cargo ships and the colliers. There are now flourishing upmarket marinas at the old King Edward VII dock at North Shields, at St Peter's Basin within a mile of Newcastle city centre, and upriver at Derwenthaugh, near Blaydon.

The idea of the North Sea (or the German Ocean, as it was once called) being used as a playground would have seemed fantastical to the eighteenth and nineteenth-century seamen who ploughed across it in all weathers to supply Europe with coal and the north of England with timber. But that's what has transpired, and not only on the inshore waters. In July 2005, the River Tyne played host to 100 or so sailing ships from more than 20 countries. These beautiful vessels were taking part in the Tall Ships' Race from Waterford in Ireland down to Cherbourg in France, round the east coast of Britain to Newcastle, then across the North Sea to Fredrikstad, near Oslo.

The race has been described as 'the biggest free visitor attraction in the United Kingdom', and the 2005 race was the third time that the ships have put into the Tyne (the previous occasions were in 1986 and 1993). Tyneside is an ideal stopover for the race. It compares well to, say, the Port of Leith in Edinburgh, where the ships docked in the early 1990s and were rather lost against the wide sweep of the Firth of Forth. But in the narrow confines of the River Tyne, the great forest of masts and sails looks splendid.

TYNESIDE ON SCREEN: ANT AND DEC

Tyneside's latest on-screen heroes are the brash and breezy duo known to their fans as Ant and Dec, and to their families as Anthony McPartlin and Declan Donnelly. Born in 1975 within a few months of one another, both hail from the working-class West End of Newcastle. The pair made their national television debut in 1990 in the series *Byker Grove* as the characters PJ and Duncan. They quit the show in 1993 to chase musical stardom and had serious success with their albums *Psyche* and *Top Katz*.

In 1996, Ant and Dec returned to tellyland and made a series of popular light-entertainment shows, among them *SM:TV Live*, *Ant and Dec's Saturday Night Takeaway*, *Friends Like These*, *Ant and Dec Unzipped* and the hugely successful *Pop Idol*. Early in 2005, the pair endeared themselves to fellow Geordies with a 'tribute' remake of that Tyneside classic *The Likely Lads*. In an episode entitled 'No Hiding Place', Bob and Terry do their best to avoid hearing the result of an England football match.

Tyneside has always been one of Britain's sporting hot spots and still is. Every year, the Great North Run attracts thousands of serious and not-so-serious athletes to a half-marathon that starts in the centre of Newcastle, makes its way through Gateshead, Hebburn and Jarrow, and ends in South Shields. The Gateshead International Stadium is one of the best and most hard-working athletics stadiums in Britain. It's also home to the Gateshead Senators, the North-east's best-known and most successful American football team. The Senators have an interesting history. The team began as the short-lived Newcastle Browns, changed its name to the Newcastle Senators, then in 1988 moved across the Tyne to Gateshead, becoming the Gateshead Senators in the process.

Across the Tyne, the stadium at Kingston Park is home to Tyneside's professional rugby union team, the Newcastle Falcons. In 2004, more than 50 busloads of Tynesiders made the journey down to Twickenham to see the Falcons beat Sale Sharks in the final of the Powergen Cup. The Falcons also have a history of name changes. They began (in 1877) as the Gosforth Football Club, became the Northumberland Rugby Football Club, then became Gosforth again, a name they kept for many decades before becoming Newcastle Gosforth in 1990. In 1996 – after rugby union players were allowed to turn professional – the club changed its name to the Newcastle Falcons and its home colours to black and white.

For most of their history the rugby club played at their North Road ground, which they sold in 1989 (to a housing developer, for £1.7

million). They then purchased what used to be the *Newcastle Chronicle and Journal* sports ground at Kingston Park, which they set about upgrading and developing. At the end of 1995, Sir John Hall, one of the North-east's biggest businessmen and then chairman of Newcastle United, bought 76 per cent of the rugby club and brought in Rob Andrew as director of rugby. In 1999, Sir John Hall sold his shareholding to the club's current chairman, Dave Thompson.

TYNESIDE ON THE PITCH: ALAN SHEARER

If any one player has dominated Tyneside football since the turn of the twenty-first century, it is Alan Shearer. He may not have the wayward footballing genius of, say, Paul Gascoigne or Hughie Gallagher, but he has proven himself to be combative, steady and opportunistic, with an excellent tactical and strategic grasp of the game. In short, ideal material for a captain – in which role he's served both Newcastle United FC and England.

Born in Newcastle in 1970, Shearer was a pupil at Gosforth High School before joining Southampton FC in 1988. After four years at Southampton, he transferred to Blackburn Rovers FC for whom he played between 1992 and 1996. That same year saw him back in his home town as captain of Newcastle United, and also captaining England. In the 63 games Shearer has played for England, he has scored 20 goals. In 2001, he was awarded the OBE for his services to football. In 2005, he was reported as saying that the 2005–06 season will be his last as a player.

The Newcastle Falcons and the Gateshead Senators have done well for the North-east's sporting reputation, but they'll never have the same grip on Tyneside's imagination as Newcastle United Football Club. Anybody with even a passing interest in football knows of the Magpies and their long line of footballing legends, from Hughie Gallagher and Jackie Milburn to Malcolm Macdonald and Kevin Keegan to Paul Gascoigne and Alan Shearer. The Magpies are one of a handful of

British football clubs which have a worldwide presence almost regardless of how well they are performing.

But if Sir John Hall (as chairman) and Kevin Keegan (as manager) hadn't taken a grip of the club in 1992, it might have toppled into Third Division obscurity. With Hall's financial backing, the club redeveloped St James's Park into one of the finest stadiums in Britain, while Keegan brought in a string of world-class players. In 1993, Newcastle were back in the Premiership among the big boys – where they have stayed. There are few home games for which not every one of the 55,000 seats in St James's Park is filled.

SIR JOHN HALL

'An off-field dynamo' is how one football pundit described the Tyneside businessman Sir John Hall, who at one time was chairman and virtual owner of both Newcastle United Football Club and Newcastle Falcons Rugby Football Club. He is also the man credited with rescuing the financial and sporting fortunes of both historic institutions. The biggest stand at St James's Park (at the Leazes End) is named the Sir John Hall Stand and seats 10,156 spectators.

Born in 1933 and educated at Bedlington Grammar School, he trained as a chartered surveyor and quickly became one of the North-east's most successful property developers. His firm Cameron Hall Developments (which he chaired between 1973 and 1993) was behind the MetroCentre in Gateshead, one of the biggest shopping malls in Europe.

Although best known for his involvement with Tyneside's football and rugby clubs, Hall is also renowned as a shrewd and canny businessman. Between 1996 and 1998, he was one of the governors of the Bank of England and a commissioner of the Millennium Fund. A proud regional patriot, Hall was a leading light in the (failed) campaign for an elected assembly for the north-east of England.

So far, so spectacular. But it all raises the question: can this glittering new Tyneside of art galleries, concert halls, heritage sites and sporting stadiums be sustained? Are the economic underpinnings in place? Can the economy of the area grow sufficiently to fund – and keep on funding – the kind of society which the planners and politicians are working to build along the River Tyne? Or does Tyneside's recently erected panoply of institutions dedicated to the arts, culture, sport, heritage and all the rest of it merely provide a shiny cover for an economy that is in relentless decline?

Certainly there are enough concerns about Tyneside's industrial base to keep the area's promoters busy. There are now a clutch of organisations (private and public sector) seeking to breathe new life into the Tyneside economy. The most powerful of them is probably One NorthEast, one of the Regional Development Agencies set up by the British government in 1999 to 'create and sustain jobs, prosperity and a higher quality of life', in the words of its publicity. One NorthEast is behind what they say is 'the UK's largest reclamation project', the new riverside industrial estate at Newburn, west of Newcastle. One NorthEast say that 21,000 sq. ft of offices and factory units are already occupied (a sizeable chunk of them by its own headquarters).

Less well known is Northern Defence Industries (NDI), a non-profit umbrella organisation briefed to win defence-industry contracts for the North-east. According to its publicity, NDI 'promotes the engineering, fabrication, manufacturing and supply-chain strengths of our members to the global defence and aerospace market'. The NDI's various special-interest groups meet every few months to swap ideas and information. Members include big-time players like BAE Systems, Lockheed Martin, Raytheon, Boeing and Alvis Vickers, with academic input from the universities of Newcastle, Durham and Sheffield.

Meanwhile, Newcastle's airport continues to flourish. According to the Civil Aviation Authority, Newcastle is the fastest-growing of all Britain's major regional airports. The advent of the low-cost airline easyJet in 2002 made a huge difference to traffic at Newcastle. It's now forecast that something like 5.5 million passengers will pass through Newcastle airport in 2005, an increase of 13 per cent on 2004. If that trend continues, by 2016 the airport will be handling almost 10 million people a year, making it one of the busiest in Britain. The airport is now known as Newcastle International Airport.

Airport spokesman Chris Sanders is on record as saying:

> Not only are we seeing new customers using the airport, we are also noticing a growing trend for holidaymakers taking several shorter trips each year. Popular destinations include Budapest, Cologne, Nice, Milan, Munich and Barcelona, as well as new resorts such as Egypt's Sharm el Sheikh, which is almost fully booked throughout the season.

Of course, growth has to be paid for. New passenger terminals, air-traffic-control systems, extensive car parking and so on are expensive items. Money is not easy to find. In May 2001, the municipal owners of Newcastle International sold 49 per cent of the operation to the owners of Copenhagen Airport. This is generally regarded as a shrewd move. At a stroke, it puts more cash in the airport's development kitty and strengthens Tyneside's already strong links with Scandinavia and its well-heeled populations.

There's no doubt that Tyneside is more affluent than it used to be. Tynesiders have shared – more or less – the affluence that has spread across Britain. But things can change. There are some signs that industry-boosters like One NorthEast and NDI will have their work cut out. The first few years of the twenty-first century have not been too kind to industrial Tyneside. For example, the firm of McNulty Offshore, which specialises in work for the world's offshore oil and gas industry, went into administration in April 2005. McNulty had been working on a 3,900-ton accommodation module for the French company Technip, due to be delivered to ExxonMobil. When the North Shields company fell out with Technip over payment, it was edged into administration 'due to cash constraints'.

Steve Keyworth (who bought McNulty Offshore back from

Technip in 2002) said later: 'It looks as though we have lost the [ExxonMobil] contract now. It will go to a foreign yard. We have given up hope for it unless we can get some outside help.' A spokesman for the GMB union described the company's plight as 'the worst possible news for our members working on the river'.

Most of what remains of the Tyne's great shipbuilding industry now resides with the Dutch-owned firm of Swan Hunter and their yard at Wallsend. And while the yard did well to win the Ministry of Defence contract for two 16,000-ton, £240-million supply-ships-cum-landing-crafts and a slice of Britain's proposed new aircraft carrier, there is likely to be a two-year gap between finishing one contract and starting the other. Which left the company with the problem of how to plug that gap, between 2006 and 2008.

Swan Hunter and One NorthEast put their heads together and came up with a solution. To keep the yard open and the men working, they suggested to the Ministry of Defence that for an extra £50 million the yard would convert one of the four Royal Fleet Auxiliary (RFA) ships now under construction into an up-to-the-minute hospital ship to replace the ageing RFA *Argus*. At the time of writing, Swan's chairman Jaap Kroese said that Swan's were awaiting a decision by the MoD: 'However, we know that a new hospital vessel has been on the cards for some time.'

Just as Swan Hunter is a shadow of its previous incarnation, so, on the face of it, is the River Tyne. The days when the river swarmed with ships of every description – colliers, keels, coasters, timber-ships, fly-ash barges, warships – have long gone. Nowadays, the upper reaches of the river see little traffic. Newcastle still sees some shipping, but the busiest part of the port is a long way downriver from the city. It's where the Tyne takes a sharp bend to the north between Jarrow and East Howdon. And it's here – within roughly one and a half square miles – that most of the Tyne's business takes place.

And there's still a lot of it. On the north bank: quays and berths for the tankers and coasters that service the site run by Velvet Liquids; Whitehill Point, where thousands of Volkswagen cars are imported every year and where the Tyne's annual intake of twenty or so cruise liners are berthed; the two roll-on/roll-off terminals at which the Tyne-to-Europe ferries berth; and behind the ferry terminals, acres of car- and coach-parking space. A mile or two down the north bank, the fish quay at North Shields is still used by local fishing boats. The quay is owned by the port authority but operated by a separate company.

On the south bank: the Tyne Car Terminal, a 100-acre site used by Nissan to export the vehicles it manufactures at its plant in Washington, County Durham; a container terminal run by Tyne Logistics Company; the Riverside Quay, now a complex of new and upgraded transit sheds, engineering workshops and a bulk-cargo loading plant with a gantry crane on a lengthened rail track; and Tyne Dock, which handles general cargoes (export and import) of scrap metal, forest products, aggregates and coal.

Unlike most ports in the UK, the Tyne managed to avoid privatisation in the 1980s and '90s. In fact, it fought very hard to remain one of Britain's publicly owned trust ports. That status was saved by the advent of the Labour government in 1997, which stopped the privatisation process in its tracks. The Port of Tyne Authority is now run by a board of executive and non-executive members, the chairman and deputy chairman of which are appointed by the Secretary of State for Transport. In recent years, the authority has spent more than £80 million (all self-generated) upgrading the port.

TYNESIDE ON DISC: STING

If Tyneside has produced one world-class show-business figure in recent years, it has to be the singer who calls himself Sting. Born Gordon Sumner in Wallsend in 1951, Sting worked as a schoolteacher and played in local jazz bands for years before he joined the Police, the group with whom he made his reputation. After the Police went their separate ways in 1985, Sting made a huge success as a solo artist. He also acted in a number of movies of varying quality: *Radio Man*, *Quadrophenia*, *Plenty*. In 1993, Sting was made a CBE in the Queen's birthday honours list.

Interestingly, while Sting has produced any number of

superb singles, only three of them have made it into the British top ten. They were: 'All for Love' (made with Bryan Adams and Rod Stewart), which made number two in Britain in 1994 but number one in the USA; 'When We Dance', which reached number nine later in 1994; and 'Rise and Fall' (made with Craig David) which climbed to number two in 2003.

Some of Sting's songs are now widely regarded as modern classics, particularly 'Englishman in New York' (a tribute to the late, outrageous Quentin Crisp, released in 1988), 'Moon over Bourbon Street' (1986) and the haunting 'Fields of Gold' (1993), which did wonders for the posthumous career of the American singer Eva Cassidy.

One huge project which would give Tyneside a serious boost is, at the time of writing, awaiting the go-ahead from Her Majesty's Government, or, to be more specific, the department run by John Prescott. It's the New Tyne Crossing (NTC), a second tunnel to run alongside the existing Tyne vehicle tunnel between East Howdon and Jarrow. The new tunnel would handle the southbound traffic, leaving the older tunnel with the northbound vehicles, thus making the A19 dual carriageway all the way from its junction with the A1 down to North Yorkshire. It's an idea that's been talked about for years and has the backing of the local authorities and the Tyne and Wear Passenger Transport Authority (PTA).

'The A19 is a very important road in the north-east of England because it links the conurbations of Tyneside, Wearside and Teeside,' is how the PTA argue the strategic case. 'At the moment, the existing vehicle tunnel is a bottleneck and suffers serious congestion at peak times. This has a knock-on effect on other crossings of the Tyne as motorists find ways of avoiding the congestion at the Tyne Tunnel.'

Certainly, the existing tunnel is overloaded. Designed in the 1960s to carry 25,000 vehicles a day, it now carries 34,000 and, unless the new tunnel is built, it will be carrying 43,000 by the year 2021. But if the traffic is split between two tunnels, they could handle a whopping 76,000 vehicles a day, and probably even more.

The design as it stands is for a crossing just to the east of the existing vehicle tunnel. Including the approach roads, it would be 2.6 km long with a two-lane carriageway approximately 7.3 m wide, on which traffic would be limited to speeds of 40 mph. The cost is estimated at £180 million, to be paid for by a consortium of private-sector companies who would get their money back from charging tolls. The work would create 3,000 jobs. Opponents of the project say the £180-million estimate is wildly optimistic and that jobs would be temporary.

The NTC was subjected to a lengthy public inquiry (held in Jarrow) in the summer of 2003, which gave the plan a thumbs up. But the work cannot proceed until it gets the green light from John Prescott. The new tunnel's backers are at a loss to understand why this is taking so long. The objectors are finding some encouragement in the delay. In the summer of 2005, Tyneside was still waiting to hear whether it would get its badly needed new road tunnel under the river.

In the year 2000, Newcastle City Council published its notion of how the city – and by extension much of Tyneside – would develop up to the year 2020. The document is called 'Going for Growth' and makes it plain that going for growth will not be easy. Indeed it will be very difficult. The population of Newcastle has been declining steadily as more and more people take to the countryside and the outlying suburbs. Five years ago, there were around 276,000 men, women and children living within the city boundaries. If the flight from the city continues, that figure will drop to 259,000 by 2020.

So the problem confronting the politicians and the planners is how to keep people – especially the better-heeled people – within Tyneside's boundaries. The answers are easy to state but hard to deliver: decent jobs, better housing, safer streets, better transport, better health services and, perhaps above all, better schools. There's nothing like a local school with a bad reputation to send the middle classes scattering, either into leafier catchment areas or into the private education system. Failing hospitals have a similar, if less dramatic, effect.

Newcastle/Gateshead will always be Tyneside's focal point. That's inevitable. They are the region's political, economic and cultural engines. Over the past two decades, both have gone a long way to heal the scars left by dead and dying industries. New hotels, shiny new riverside flats, the shops, bars and clubs of the Newcastle Quayside, the Millennium Bridge, the Baltic arts centre, The Sage concert hall – they're all testament to the huge quantities of private and public money that have been poured into Tyneside.

The workforce has changed too. The traditional heavy-industry labour force has all but disappeared. More and more Tyneside folk are working at white-collar jobs in the professions, central and local government, the broadcasting companies, the quangos, hospitals, schools, universities and colleges. Taken together, they far outnumber the men and women still plying their trades in the manufacturing industries.

This new Tyneside is calculated to make the area a better place in which to live and work, and to reverse the population decline of the late twentieth century. Whether the strategy works or not remains to be seen. It may not. Better roads, for example, are inclined to work against cities. They allow more and more people to commute from further and further away. Improving the surrounding road infrastructure is one way of draining a city of many of its most affluent citizens. The law of unintended consequences applies as much to planning as it does to everything else.

But the evidence is that it is working. Tyneside has changed and is continuing to change. In the summer of 2005, the *Lonely Planet* travel-book series – which is one of the bibles of the peripatetic young – waxed almost lyrical about twenty-first-century Newcastle and surroundings. 'Miraculous powers of regeneration' was the judgement of the authors on the Tyneside conurbation. It seems that Britain's party city is one of the places to be.

TYNESIDE ON SCREEN: *55 DEGREES NORTH*

Traditionally, television has treated Tyneside as a source of comedies such as *The Likely Lads* and *Auf Wiedersehen, Pet*. But in July 2004, the BBC came up with a new take on Tyneside – a cop series with a geographically correct title, *55*

Degrees North. Politically correct, too, given that the hero was a charismatic black detective who'd abandoned the Metropolitan Police after blowing the whistle on some of his corrupt colleagues before heading for Newcastle.

Not that everything on Tyneside is sweetness and light. DS Nicky Cole (Don Gilet) is given a hard time by his new boss DI Dennis Carter (Christian Rodska) and an even harder time by the love interest, feisty prosecutor Claire Maxwell (Dervla Kirwan). And some of his Tyneside colleagues are none too happy to see their thunder being stolen by a chirpy Londoner, and a black one at that. As the BBC press release said at the time, 'Nicky quickly discovers that being a good cop doesn't always win you friends.'

Written by Timothy Prager (who also wrote *Two Thousand Acres of Sky*), it was produced by Zenith North for BBC Scotland and not for BBC Tyne. The second series was screened in the summer of 2005.

It's generally agreed that no part of England has a stronger sense of itself than the North-east. For centuries, it has been self-sufficient, enterprising, hard working and a long way from London. If any part of England wanted and deserved its own directly elected assembly, it should have been the North-east. That's what Deputy Prime Minister John Prescott argued when he pushed through his scheme for English regional assemblies in an attempt to provide some balance against the new parliament in Scotland and the new assemblies in Wales and Northern Ireland.

The scheme had its enthusiasts. Two separate organisations sprang up and began to push hard for an assembly. They were the Campaign for a North East Assembly and the North East Constitutional Convention. But in Britain, it seems that for every political action there is an equal and opposite reaction. And that reaction took shape in two separate 'No' campaigns – North East No (headed by businessman Neil Herron) and North East Says No (fronted by businessman John Elliot).

On the face of it, the 'Yes' campaign should have won hands down. It had the backing of Her Majesty's Government, the trade unions, the Labour Party, the Liberal Democrats, most of the local authorities and well-known North-east figures like Ray Mallon, the recently elected mayor of Middlesbrough, and Sir John Hall, chairman of Newcastle United FC. In the weeks before the referendum, big-time politicians stalked the North-east urging folk to vote yes. Among them were Tony Blair, John Prescott, Nick Raynsford, Alan Milburn and Gordon Brown.

Against this barrage of political heavyweights, the 'No' campaigners produced their own spiky and often quite witty propaganda. With a slogan of 'Politicians Talk, We Pay', the campaigners denounced the assembly idea as part of 'a culture of high salaries, expenses and spin'. Unveiling a 15-ft-high inflatable white elephant, 'No' spokesman Graham Robb pointed to it as a metaphor for the proposed assembly. He announced, 'It's unwieldy, cumbersome, serves no useful purpose at all and is full of hot air.'

It was left to Chancellor of the Exchequer Gordon Brown (an ardent supporter of the Scottish Parliament) to make the weightiest case for an assembly. In a speech at Newcastle, he claimed that without regional government a properly balanced economy was virtually impossible 'where we have unemployment, emigration and unused resources in one part of the country and congestion and overcrowding and huge inflationary pressures in the other'.

But Brown might just as well have been talking to himself. When the votes were counted in October 2004, the Government was left with egg on its face. The people of the North-east announced in no uncertain terms that they didn't want a directly elected assembly. Only 48 per cent of the electorate bothered to vote, and of those who did 78 per cent voted against the idea, leaving only 22 per cent in favour. The 'Yes' vote was a small minority of a minority. On 8 November, a plainly discomfited John Prescott told the House of Commons that 'I will not, therefore, be bringing forward orders for referendums in either the North West or Yorkshire and the Humber.'

Proud as they were to be Tynesiders or Teesiders, it seems that the folk of the north-east of England could see no point in another layer of politicians arguing over what should and should not be done. Local patriotism, the vote said, was not the same as nationalism. Tyneside was not Scotland or Wales or Northern Ireland. It was part and parcel of England. A long way from London, perhaps, and in the process of changing into something new; but still English to the very bone.

And with that great English talent for working change while remaining the same. There's no doubt that George Stephenson, William Armstrong, John Merz and all the other industrial giants of nineteenth-century Tyneside would gape in astonishment at the glittering new concert halls, art galleries, restaurants, museums and pleasure-boat marinas that now string the banks of the Tyne. They'd certainly wonder what happened to the shipyards and the engineering shops, the coal mines and the loading staiths, the keels and the colliers, the power stations and the fly-ash barges.

But they'd recognise the great buildings that still remain, they'd be familiar with the faces in the streets of Newcastle, Gateshead, Wallsend and Jarrow, and the Geordie dialect would sound the same as it always did. They'd know that the resourceful, adaptable, hard-working folk who'd made Tyneside into one of the workshops of the world were still there, still intact. And were still bellowing out 'The Blaydon Races' at St James's Park on a Saturday in that challenging, heartfelt way that the rest of Britain has come to know so well.

BIBLIOGRAPHY

Airey, Angela and John, *The Bainbridges of Newcastle: A Family History* (A&J Airey, 1979)

Barclay, C.N., *The History of the Royal Northumberland Fusiliers in the Second World War* (William Clunes & Sons, for the Regimental History Committee of the Royal Northumberland Fusiliers, 1952)

Barrow, G.W.S., *Feudal Britain* (Oliver and Boyd, 1956)

Barrow, G.W.S., *The Kingdom of the Scots* (Edward Arnold, 1973)

Bates, Cadwallader J., *History of Northumberland* (Sandhill Press, [1895] 1966)

Bean, David, *Tyneside: A Biography* (Macmillan, 1971)

Beckensall, Stan, *Northumberland Place-Names* (Butler, 1992)

Beckensall, Stan, *Life and Death in the Prehistoric North* (Butler, 1994)

Bede, *The Ecclesiastical History of the English People*, trans. Leo Sherley-Price (Penguin, 1955)

Bedoyere, Guy de la, *Gods with Thunderbolts* (Tempus, 2002)

Betts, Graham, *Complete UK Hit Singles 1952–2005* (Collins, 2005)

Bindoff, S.T., *Tudor England* (Harmondsworth, 1950)

Bowman, Alan K., *Life and Letters on the Roman Frontier* (British Museum Press, 1994)

Breeze, David and Dobson, Brian, *Hadrian's Wall* (Allen Lane, 1976)

Brown, Michelle, *Painted Labyrinth* (British Library, 2003)

Cadogan, Peter, *Early Radical Newcastle* (Sagittarius Press, 1975)

Campbell, James (ed.), *Anglo-Saxons* (Penguin Books, 1982)

Carlton, I.C., *A Short History of Gateshead* (Gateshead Corporation, 1974)

Carlton, John and Joyce, *South Shields Voices* (The Chalford Publishing Company, 1997)

Church, Roy, with Hall, Alan and Kanefsky, John, *The History of the British Coal Industry Volume III 1830–1913* (Clarendon Press, 1986)

Colls, Robert and Lancaster, Bill (eds), *Newcastle upon Tyne: A Modern History* (Phillimore & Co., 2001)

Coombes, Bert Lewis, *These Poor Hands: The Biography of a Miner working in South Wales* (University of Wales Press, [1939] 2002)

Cunliffe, Barry (ed.), *The Penguin Atlas of British and Irish History* (Penguin Books, 2001)

Dark, Ken, *Britain and the End of the Roman Empire* (Tempus, 2002)

Davies, Norman, *Europe: A History* (Oxford University Press, 1996)

Davies, Norman, *The Isles* (Macmillan, 1999)

Davis, Ralph, *The Rise of the English Shipping Industry in the 17th and 18th Centuries* (National Maritime Museum, 1962)

Decharne, Max, *Hardboiled Hollywood: The Origins of the Great Crime Films* (No Exit Press, 2003)

Dillon, Peter, *The Tyne Oarsmen: Harry Clasper, Robert Chambers, James Renforth* (Keepdate Publishing Ltd, 1993)

Doig, Alan, *Corruption and Misconduct in Contemporary British Politics* (Penguin Books, 1984)

Ellis, J., 'The Decline and Fall of the Tyneside Salt Industry 1660–1790: a Re-examination', in *Economic History Review*, Vol. 33, 1980

Embleton, R. and Graham, Frank, *The Outpost Forts of Hadrian's Wall* (Frank Graham Publishers, 1983)

Farmer, D.H. and Webb, J.F., *The Age of Bede* (Penguin Books, 1998)

Ferguson, George, *Signs and Symbols in Christian Art* (Oxford University Press, 1966)

Fields, Nic, *Hadrian's Wall AD 122–410* (Osprey, 2003)

Flinn, Michael W., *The History of the British Coal Industry Volume II 1700–1830* (Oxford University Press, 1982)

Flowers, Anna and Histon, Vanessa (eds), *Water Under the Bridges: Newcastle's Twentieth Century* (Tyne Bridge Publishing, 1999)

Foster, Joan, *Newcastle upon Tyne: A Pictorial History* (Phillimore & Co., 1995)

French, Ron and Smith, Ken, *Lost Shipyards of the Tyne* (Tyne Bridge Publishing, 2004)

Frere, Sheppard, *Britannia: A History of Roman Britain* (Routledge & Kegan Paul, 1977)

Goff, Jacques Le, *The Birth of Europe* (Blackwell, 2004)

Graham, Frank, *A Dictionary of Roman Military Terms* (Frank Graham Publishers, 1989)

Graham, Frank, *Holy Island* (Butler, 1987)

Graham, Frank, *Newcastle: 900 Years* (Frank Graham Publishers, 1980)

Green, David G., *Power and Party in an English City. An Account of Single-Party Rule* (George Allen and Unwin, 1981)

Green, Miranda, *The Gods of the Celts* (Sutton, 1986)

Groundwater, Ken, *Newcastle and the River Tyne* (Silver Link Publishing, 1998)

Guthrie, J., *The River Tyne: Its History and Resources* (River Tyne Commission, 1880)

Hepple, Leslie W., *A History of Northumberland* (Phillimore & Co., 1976)

Horsley, P.M., *Eighteenth Century Newcastle* (Oriel Press, 1971)

Hunter-Blair, Peter, *Northumbria in the Days of Bede* (Gollancz, 1976)

Hutton, Ronald, *The Pagan Religions of the British Isles* (Blackwell, 1991)

Hutton, William, *The First Man to Walk Hadrian's Wall* (Frank Graham Publishers, [1802] 1990)

Johnman, Lewis and Murphy, Hugh, *British Shipbuilding and the State since 1918: A Political Economy of Decline* (University of Exeter Press, 2002)

Johnson, Stephen, *Hadrian's Wall* (English Heritage, 1986)

Lambert, Sir Arthur W., *Northumbria's Spacious Year – 1929* (Andrew Reid & Co Ltd., 1930)

Leslie, Jack and John, *Down Our Streets: Newcastle's Street Names Explored* (Tyne Bridge Publishing, 2003)

Madanipour, Ali and Bevan, Mark, 'Walker, Newcastle upon Tyne: A Neighbourhood in Transition' (Centre for Research on European Urban Environments, 1999)

Manders, F.W.D., *A History of Gateshead* (Gateshead Corporation, 1973)

Manders, Frank and Potts, Richard, *Crossing the Tyne* (Tyne Bridge Publishing, 2001)

Marsden, John, *The Fury of the Northmen* (Kyle Cathie, 1993)

Mason, David J.P., *Roman Britain and the Roman Navy* (Tempus, 2003)

McCall, Andrew, *The Medieval Underworld* (Hamish Hamilton, 1979)

McCord, Norman (ed.), *Essays in Tyneside Labour History* (Newcastle Polytechnic, 1972)

McCord, Norman, *The Banks of Tyne: A Historical Survey* (Newcastle-upon-Tyne, n. d.)

McCrum, Robert, MacNeil, Robert and Cran, William, *The Story of English* (Faber, 1986)

McGowan, Christopher, *The Rainhill Trials* (Little, Brown, 2004)

McGuire, D.F., *Charles Mitchell 1820–1895: Victorian Shipbuilder* (Newcastle upon Tyne City Libraries and Arts, 1988)

Middlebrook, Sydney, *Newcastle upon Tyne: Its Growth and Achievement* (S.R. Publishers Ltd, 1968)

Morgan, Alan, *Beyond the Grave: Exploring Newcastle's Burial Grounds* (Tyne Bridge Publishing, 2004)

Morrison, P.J.T., Campbell, W.A. and Roberts, H.L. (eds), *Milestones in 150 Years of the Chemical Industry* (Royal Society of Chemistry, 1991)

Partington, J.R., *The Alkali Industry* (Bailliere, Tindall & Cox, 1925)

Pevsner, Nikolaus et al., *The Buildings of England: County Durham* (1953)

Pevsner, Nikolaus et al., *The Buildings of England: Northumberland* (Yale University Press, 2004)

Power, Eileen, *The Wool Trade in English Medieval History* (Methuen, 1941)

BIBLIOGRAPHY

Redfern, Barry, *The Shadow of the Gallows: Crime and Punishment on Tyneside in the Eighteenth Century* (Tyne Bridge Publishing, 2003)

Renfrew, Jane, *Food and Cooking in Roman Britain* (English Heritage, 1980)

Rose, Alexander, *The Kings in the North: The House of Percy in British History* (Phoenix, 2003)

Simkins, Michael, *The Legions of the North* (Osprey, 1979)

Simpson, David, *The Millennium History of the North East* (Business Education Publishers, 1999)

Simpson, David, *Northern Roots* (Business Education Publishers, 2002) Smiles, Samuel, *The Life of George Stephenson* (John Murray, 1881)

Smith, Mark and Holland, Phil, *Memories of Newcastle upon Tyne* (True North Books, 2002)

Supple, Barry, *The History of the British Coal Industry Volume IV 1913–1946* (Clarendon Press, 1987)

Taylor, Andrew, *The NUM and British Politics Volume I 1944–1968* (Ashgate, 2003)

Taylor, Simon and Lovie, David B., *Gateshead: Architecture in a Changing English Urban Landscape* (English Heritage, 2004)

Waddington, Clive and Passmore, Dave, *Ancient Northumberland* (Country Store, 2004)

Waddington, Clive, *Land of Legend* (Country Store, 1997)

Ward, Benedicta, *The Venerable Bede* (Geoffrey Chapman, 1990)

Ward-Perkins, J.B., *Roman Imperial Architecture* (Penguin, 1970)

Warren, K., *Chemical Foundations: The Alkali Industry in Britain to 1926* (Oxford, 1980)

Watson, Robert Spence, *The History of the Literary and Philosophical Society of Newcastle Upon Tyne (1793–1896)* (Walter Scott Ltd, 1897)

Wilkes, Lyall, *Tyneside Portraits* (Frank Graham Publishers, 1971)

Wilkes, L. and Dodds, G., *Tyneside Classical: The Newcastle of Grainger, Dobson and Clayton* (John Murray, 1964)

Yates, Frances A., *Theatre of the World* (Routledge & Kegan Paul, 1969)

INDEX

408

INDEX

INDEX

413

INDEX